The U.S.-Canada Security Relationship

STUDIES IN GLOBAL SECURITY
Alan Ned Sabrosky, Series Editor

Security in Northeast Asia: Approaching the Pacific Century, edited by Stephen P. Gibert

Alliances in U.S. Foreign Policy: Issues in the Quest for Collective Defense, edited by Alan Ned Sabrosky

The U.S.-Canada Security Relationship: The Politics, Strategy, and Technology of Defense, edited by David G. Haglund and Joel J. Sokolsky

Defense and Détente: U.S. and West German Perspectives on Defense Policy, Joseph I. Coffey and Klaus von Schubert (forthcoming)

The U.S.-Canada Security Relationship

The Politics, Strategy, and Technology of Defense

EDITED BY
David G. Haglund
and Joel J. Sokolsky

Westview Press
BOULDER, SAN FRANCISCO, & LONDON

Studies in Global Security

Table 3.1 and Figure 7.1 reproduced by permission.

Published in 1989 in the United States of America by Westview Press, Inc., 5500 Central Avenue, Boulder, Colorado 80301, and in the United Kingdom by Westview Press, Inc., 13 Brunswick Centre, London WC1N 1AF, England

Library of Congress Cataloging-in-Publication Data
The U.S.-Canada security relationship: the politics, strategy, and
  technology of defense / edited by David G. Haglund and Joel J.
  Sokolsky.
    p. cm.—(Studies in global security)
  Includes index.
  ISBN 0-8133-7685-8
  1. Canada—Military relations—United States. 2. United States—
Military relations—Canada. I. Haglund, David G. II. Sokolsky,
Joel J., 1953–   . III. Title: US-Canada security relationship.
IV. Title: United States–Canada security relationship. V. Series.
UA600.U18   1989
355′.03307—dc19   88-29025
                                                                              CIP

Printed and bound in the United States of America

The paper used in this publication meets the requirements of the American National
Standard for Permanence of Paper for Printed Library Materials Z39.48-1984.

10   9   8   7   6   5   4   3   2

Contents

Tables and Figures

Acknowledgments

In 1938, during the midst of the Sudetenland crisis, which threatened another European and perhaps global war, President Franklin Roosevelt delivered an address at Queen's University, in Kingston, Ontario, that explicitly recognized the American security interest in the defense of Canada. Canada's own security interest in the defense of the United States was acknowledged a few days later by Prime Minister William Lyon Mackenzie King. Thus began what has developed into America's longest-standing alliance.

In June 1988, the Queen's Centre for International Relations sponsored a conference on Canada-U.S. security to mark the fiftieth anniversary of the Roosevelt address. The chapters in this book originated as papers for that conference. In holding its annual conferences on security issues, the Centre depends upon the generous support of several institutions and individuals, whom we would like to take this opportunity to thank. Foremost is the Canadian Department of National Defence, whose Military and Strategic Studies Program has been an invaluable contributor to the work of the Centre for more than a decade. A Public Programmes grant from the Canadian Institute for International Peace and Security helped make possible the publication of this volume. The work of the Centre is enriched by the presence of several Visiting Defence Fellows, senior officers in the Canadian, German, and U.S. armed forces. Finally, all the papers benefited from the expert commentary of discussants at the conference, drawn from a variety of academic and government positions. Taking part were Oran Young, the keynote speaker, and discussants Paul Buteux, David Cox, Ernie Gilman, René Gutknecht, Peter Haydon, Dan Hayward, David Huddleston, Jim Moore, Kim Nossal, Ron Purver, Tariq Rauf, and Ernie Regehr.

Indispensable, as always, have been the competent and consistent efforts of the Centre's technical staff. In the organization of the conference, and preparation of the manuscripts, Mary Kerr and Kay Ladouceur continued to demonstrate their usual high level of excellence. Marilyn Banting's editorial skills never flagged, despite the heavy demands put on her by the editors. Darrel Reid did yeoman work in laser typesetting this book. Warmly we thank them all.

David G. Haglund
Joel J. Sokolsky

Introduction

David G. Haglund
and
Joel J. Sokolsky

I

The fall 1988 Canadian election campaign attracted unprecedented attention in the United States because of its single overriding issue, the Canada-U.S. Free Trade Agreement (FTA). The solid parliamentary majority achieved by Prime Minister Brian Mulroney's Progressive Conservative party removed all doubts about its eventual implementation, which was accomplished by year's end.

Not so certain, however, of full implementation in a second Mulroney government is the program outlined in the June 1987 White Paper on defense.[1] During the election, defense issues were eclipsed by the vigorous, often emotional and occasionally even paranoiac, debate over Canada-U.S. free trade, which some in this country argued would result in the erosion — perhaps disappearance — of Canadian sovereignty. The release of the White Paper had also generated considerable controversy within Canada prior to the election campaign. During the campaign, it is true, defense was overshadowed by the FTA; however, it is expected that as the Conservatives confront the decisions arising out of the White Paper, particularly with regard to capital spending, the defense debate will heat up again.

American audiences are unlikely to take notice of this debate. But they should. Canada, as do other members of the Western Alliance, confronts an array of strategic, political, and technological challenges in the conduct of its defense policy. How it meets these challenges will have profound implications for the future of bilateral military relations with the United States, and indeed for American security interests.

Fifty years ago Franklin Roosevelt gave the first explicit commitment that the United States would not "stand idly by" in the event that Canadian physical security was threatened by a third party. Responding, Canadian Prime Minister

William Lyon Mackenzie King said that as a good and friendly neighbor Canada had a responsibility to see that it did not become an avenue of attack against the United States. Since the exchange of these pledges, much has happened to alter, perhaps forever, the fundamental nature of the security challenges facing each of these two North American countries. Most importantly, the United States abandoned its long-standing policy of attempting to isolate itself from the major security and political focus of the international system, Europe.[2] One concomitant result of its entry into global security politics has been that the United States extended to its other allies a security guarantee not unlike, in some respects, that which it had earlier given to Canada and which in many ways overshadowed both the prior American pledge and the Canadian response.

In recent years, much has been written on the future of the North Atlantic Treaty Organization (NATO) and the American role in the defense of Europe.[3] A consensus seems to be emerging that while the Alliance will survive with substantial U.S. forces remaining in Europe, NATO will be based upon a new transatlantic bargain — one that sees the European members assuming more responsibility for their own conventional defense and playing an increasingly important role in the management of allied affairs. There are, of course, no certainties here. There is nothing monolithic about NATO's European "pillar" and profound disagreements persist on how best to assure security and stability.[4] Nevertheless, with the European Community moving toward greater economic integration, with a new era of détente and arms control already begun, and with pressures building within the United States for change, it seems likely that steps will be taken to provide for an enhanced European role within the Alliance.

Discussions of the future of NATO in the U.S. or in Europe invariably omit mention of Canada. Although in part due to selective cognition (most non-Canadian analysts of allied affairs simply forget that there are *two* North American members of the Alliance), the omission is largely a measure of the extent to which Canada's place within NATO has long been trouble-free. To be sure, the Alliance would like Ottawa to spend more than the current 2 percent of Gross Domestic Product (GDP) on defense. Yet whether Canada does so or not, it is hardly considered crucial to NATO's future. As long as some Canadian air and armored units remain in Germany and the bulk of the small Canadian Navy is earmarked for SACLANT (Supreme Allied Commander, Atlantic), and assuming that Canada's diplomats continue to work for allied unity, both Washington and Brussels are satisfied.

From the perspective of United States security interests, Canada has usually been a "good ally," indeed. Since the early 1950s it has postured its armed forces to mesh with NATO's strategic and political requirements, even if this meant having fewer forces to undertake North American and national-defense roles. Within NATO councils, Ottawa has lent its support to every major policy initiative, often helping to shape the kinds of consensus decisions that have kept the transatlantic bargain viable, and the allies allied.[5] Because Canada's role in the Alliance has been so uneventfully positive, it is easy to overlook the importance the country has attached to NATO, as well as the potential relevance of the current debate about United States-European relations for the future of Canada's own defense policy.

Canada was not only one of NATO's original twelve members; it also took an active role in the very establishment of the Alliance. With the early and obvious failure of the United Nations to provide a system of collective security, Canada saw a western defensive compact, in which the United States would play a major role, as the best means to prevent war and assure a degree of international stability. By bringing together the British and the Americans, along with the rebuilding European democracies, into a multilateral arrangement, Ottawa also sought to avoid a strictly bilateral security relationship, one that would have it bonded tightly with the United States; for such a two-pillar approach has always been anathema to Canada's conception of NATO as a truly multilateral Alliance.[6] Ottawa has long believed that its influence within allied councils, which have been structured to give every member a distinct voice, would be diminished if the Europeans assumed that North America spoke with one (American) voice. Canada has always coveted its "seat at the table." The maintenance of air and ground forces in Germany for more than thirty years has been based upon the belief that this contribution is the *sine qua non* of its Alliance commitment; without it, Canada's voice in allied councils and its influence therein, it has been feared, would be negligible. Under the 1987 White Paper proposals, Canada plans to enhance its air and ground forces in Germany, not so much because the defense of Western Europe "contributes to the defence of Canada" but because these forces ensure "that we will have a say in how key security issues are decided."[7]

Ottawa's concern is that in a reformulated transatlantic bargain it will have less say in how these "key security issues" relating to European defense get decided, because its influence, never substantial, will decline even further relative to the major European members. Canada will be considered part of NATO's North American voice, but there will be little Canadian "tone."[8] All of this may be compounded by Europe's move toward further economic integration, espoused in the 1992 project, and by Canada's own decision to seek shelter from American protectionism via the Free Trade Agreement.

Other considerations, not readily apparent at the time of the White Paper, will come into play as well. The Intermediate-Range Nuclear Forces (INF) Treaty marked an important step in nuclear arms control, yet it raises new questions about the conventional balance and allied burden sharing. Under familiar pressure from Washington, NATO has turned to considering a Conventional Defense Improvements Initiative (CDI); as well, it continues to examine the modernization of shorter-range nuclear forces. Canada's decision to enhance its German-based forces is in line with these possible responses to the INF Treaty. The very success of the INF process and the latest Soviet announcements of unilateral conventional force reductions, made by General Secretary Gorbachev during his visit to New York in December 1988,[9] render it likely that both the modernization of shorter-range nuclear weapons and significant increases in conventional force improvements will be delayed, and that the Europeans will attempt to enhance their security through more arms-control negotiations. All of this will necessarily affect European-American relations and, as a consequence, Canadian defense policy regarding NATO. Thus while Canada will doubtless remain a member of the Alliance, its involvement in European security affairs will be subject to reevaluation over the next few years, in the same way that America's own European involvement will be increasingly scrutinized in Washington and elsewhere.

In fact, it could be argued that despite its pledge to enhance ground and air units in Germany, the 1987 White Paper has already signaled a new Canadian approach to collective defense. For some time, the major deficiency in Canadian defense policy has been the gap between the capabilities and commitments of the Canadian Forces (CF). With a force level of roughly 86,000, the unified CF is tasked with contributing to the air and sea defense of North America in cooperation with U.S. forces, maintaining and reinforcing air and ground units in Europe, asserting Canadian sovereignty, and supplying personnel for a variety of peacekeeping roles throughout the world. Moreover, all of this is to be done with an annual budget of about nine billion U.S. dollars, or 2.1 percent of GDP. The equipment to support these roles is, the White Paper acknowledged, "in an advanced state of obsolescence or is already obsolete." Nor can numbers compensate. Canada has fewer than twenty surface ships, sixteen of which are more than twenty-five years old, three aging conventional submarines, only eighteen maritime patrol aircraft, fewer than 120 main battle tanks (only seventy-seven in Europe), and little airlift capacity. To be sure, the air posture has been improved with 138 CF-18 fighters, but these must be divided between North American and European commitments. Thus, as the White Paper also admitted: "Even if the Canadian Forces were fully manned and had modern, state-of-the-art equipment, to fulfill existing defence commitments would be a daunting challenge."[10]

To help close the commitment/capability gap, the Conservative government announced in the White Paper that Canada would be terminating its commitment to send two air squadrons and a brigade group to Norway in the event of a crisis or war in Europe. These forces will now be earmarked for reinforcement of those permanently stationed in Germany. Since the Canadian troops were the only external allied units specifically designated for Norway, the Alliance has been compelled to look for replacements.

The core of the effort to close the commitment/capability gap is the modernization of the Canadian Navy. Promising to give the country a "three-ocean navy," the White Paper proposes six more anti-submarine warfare (ASW) frigates, to be added to the six already under construction; new ASW helicopters for the frigates; six more long-range patrol aircraft; minesweepers; a fixed acoustical system in the Arctic; and, above all, ten to twelve nuclear-propelled attack submarines (SSNs).

This ambitious naval rebuilding program would strengthen Canada's ability to contribute to NATO security in the Atlantic. Its major result, however, would be to improve dramatically the Navy's contribution to North American defense and national-sovereignty protection by providing the wherewithal to operate in all three of Canada's ocean approaches, especially the Pacific and the Arctic, where virtually no capabilities currently exist. The need to improve maritime defenses is based upon the expectation that the strategic importance of North American waters will increase in the coming years as the Soviets deploy more advanced SSNs with sea-launched cruise missiles (SLCMs). Ottawa also expects both superpowers to become more active in the Arctic region.

The White Paper's naval program is also consistent with efforts underway since 1985 to improve the NORAD (North American Aerospace Defense Command) air-defense system. Included in the Reagan Administration's strategic-modernization program have been the modernization of NORAD's radars and a provision to deploy interceptor aircraft to more Forward Operating Locations (FOLs) in the Canadian North. While most of the radar modernizations will occur in the United States, a new North Warning System (NWS) will replace the Distant Early Warning (DEW) line in the Arctic. Most NWS facilities will be owned and operated by Canada, which will also attempt to supply more interceptors for the FOLs. This upgrading of NORAD's capabilities is premised upon the expectation that a Soviet bomber threat will continue to exist and that in fact it will increase with the advent of more advanced Soviet air-launched cruise missiles (ALCMs).[11]

From the Canadian perspective, it is not just the continued Soviet threat to North America that necessitates greater attention to continental security, but also the new emphasis of the United States upon strategic defense, symbolized by the Strategic Defense Initiative (SDI). Here again, as with discussions about the future of NATO, the Canadian component has often been lost. Yet NORAD can properly be viewed as the original strategic-defense organization, one whose functioning has involved close Canada-United States cooperation. Hence any effort by Washington to expand current aerospace activities into ballistic missile defense (BMD) — of whatever kind — will automatically have an impact upon Canada. Even if Canada were not itself involved in BMD, there would be implications for air defense that would necessarily touch directly upon Canadian interests. In particular, the prospect of space-based air surveillance, currently being examined by the U.S. Air Force's Air Defense Initiative (ADI), raises questions about the future importance of Canadian territory and the participation of the CF in the air defense of the United States.

There is a direct and profound link between the White Paper's assessment that changing strategies and technologies will make the naval and air defense of North America more important and Canada's concerns about the protection of its own sovereignty. As do other countries, Canada uses its armed forces to assert its claims and to back up the civil power in such instances as violations of fishing agreements, where there is essentially a non-military sovereignty challenge; but Canada has also viewed its contributions to North American defense as a means of reducing its reliance on U.S. forces. Under various informal and formal arrangements, American forces do operate in waters and airspace for which Canada is responsible, largely because of a lack of adequate Canadian capabilities. One of the major goals of the White Paper proposals is to close the commitment/capability gap so as to reduce the need for this help. Thus with regard to maritime defense, particularly in the Arctic, the Minister of National Defence has stated that while the Government "was prepared to discuss cooperation," it would "not allow Canada's sovereignty to be compromised. We will be a partner with our allies and not a dependent."[12] In a similar vein, Canada will explore the efficacy of space-based radar on its own or in cooperation with the United States, or both, because failure "to meet this challenge would mean forfeiting the responsibility for surveillance of Canadian airspace to the United States."[13]

By approaching defense needs in this fashion, the Conservative government evidently hopes to draw wider support from the Canadian public. The most recent public opinion polls do show that Canadians, like many Europeans (and, for that matter, Americans), no longer perceive a real and immediate Soviet threat either to themselves or Western Europe. Overall, the "confidence" of Canadians in the ability of both superpowers to deal with world problems and in their desire to bring about arms control remains quite low; still, the same polls show Canadians' continued commitment to the Alliance, and to conventional defense even if this means increases in defense spending. However, the protection of Canadian territory and sovereignty is viewed as "the best reason for any possible increase in Canadian forces." Significantly, more than three-quarters of those surveyed in 1988 offered this rationale "rather than the promotion of Western defence or increased influence in NATO."[14]

If this support for more defense spending on North American roles translates into a greater Canadian capability to monitor the country's air and sea approaches, then it can be argued that the United States would benefit, regardless of the patent national-sovereignty objectives perceived by the public. Any improvement in Canada's maritime and air-defense forces could free up American forces for their multitude of other global commitments, even as the strategic defense of the continent increases in importance and technological complexity. In light of expected strains on the U.S. defense budget, a Canada that regards itself as less of a dependent and more of a partner should be welcomed in Washington — and this all the more so if American-European relations are tending toward a more equal sharing of the collective-defense burden.

At the same time, Washington must recognize that the Canadian public's concern with sovereignty may make it difficult for the re-elected Conservative government to move in the direction it wishes on defense. While the recent election gave Brian Mulroney a Parliamentary majority, enabling him to implement the Free Trade Agreement, that agreement in a sense "lost" the battle for public opinion, as the Conservatives took only 43 percent of the popular vote, with the staunchly anti-FTA Liberals and New Democrats combined commanding a clear majority. More importantly, both opposition parties, especially the Liberals, who doubled their Parliamentary representation, aroused visceral, and often angry to the extent of xenophobic, anti-American sentiment.

It is not unprecedented in recent years for the same type of emotional appeal to be linked to the protection of sovereignty. For instance, strong anti-American sentiments have been expressed with regard to the continued refusal of the United States to recognize the Northwest Passage as internal Canadian waters.[15] The transit of a U.S. Coast Guard icebreaker through the passage in 1985 touched off a storm of protest in Canada. Since then, the United States has agreed to seek Canadian permission for such transits, and one actually took place in the midst of the election campaign without any repeat of the earlier publicity. Nevertheless, both the FTA debate and the Northwest Passage dispute indicate that public opinion in Canada may well set new, more narrow, limits with regard to the scope of bilateral defense cooperation if Canadian sovereignty, and indeed independence, is perceived to be in jeopardy.

The Mulroney government must also take into account the continuing, perhaps growing, public demand for social services — a demand that, not surprisingly, is accompanied by opposition to new taxes.[16] Finally, while support for defense improvements is now relatively high, it could diminish as the prospects for real conventional arms reductions improve. In sum, the Conservatives could find their mandate for implementation of the White Paper dissolving. This could mean that just as strategic, political, and technological trends seem to be focusing renewed American attention on the security of Canada, the latter might need or wish to reconsider its interest in assuring the United States that it would tend to its own, and by extension, American security interests.

II

Each chapter in this volume touches upon the themes we have introduced above. Of those themes, few can have greater relevance to either U.S. and Canadian security interests, taken individually, or the bilateral military relationship, than the future defense prospects of Western Europe. It is upon those prospects that our first two chapters, respectively by Hans-Jochen Annuss and Bruce Harris, concentrate.

Annuss proceeds on the clear assumption that the INF Treaty will vastly complicate NATO's strategy of flexible response. He argues that a strategy designed to prevent war, of any kind, must not be radically changed simply because one class of weapons is taken away, largely for political reasons. Nevertheless, in military-strategic terms the dismantling of the INF missiles does restrict allied escalation options, leaving the structure of NATO's weaponry, in Annuss' view, imbalanced.

All of this has obvious implications for North America. Adverting to what has become known as the "two-pillar" thesis, Annuss warns of a situation in which Canada, squeezed out in the new transatlantic bargain that appears to be taking shape, might withdraw from the allied military commands, if not the Alliance itself. Stressing, however, that the Western Allies are primarily threatened by the strength of the Warsaw Pact forces in Europe, Annuss concludes that the improvement of defense capabilities in this region must remain the primary goal of NATO, notwithstanding the arguably growing importance of North American defense. Modernized nuclear weapons must continue to play an important role in assuming the workability of flexible response; conventional defense, by itself, is not enough.

Bruce Harris' chapter, "Trends in Alliance Conventional Defense Initiatives," provides ample illustration of the prospects and problems associated with a relative de-nuclearization of European defense arrangements. The recent program to enhance the third leg of the NATO triad, the Conventional Defense Improvement Initiatives, sometimes abbreviated as CDI, is the latest in a series of such initiatives dating back to the beginnings of the Alliance. Improving NATO's conventional posture has never been easy, for it has never been cheap; indeed one very important source of the Alliance's nuclear proclivities has been the budgetary one. Harris stresses that the current CDI must be examined with reference to the present strategic and political environment. In his view, flexible response remains valid, but it will demand continual conventional force modernization on the part of the allies. However, if the Alliance is to stay together, with the retention of sizable American forces in Europe, a new transatlantic security arrangement may have to be negotiated, one in which more responsibility gets vested in the European pillar.

Harris thinks the current CDI can help both to sustain the credibility of flexible response and to provide a basis for greater equality among member states, thereby supporting evolutionary change within the Alliance. This evolution will not only affect the Europeans and Americans; for as Canada has announced its intention to undertake a consolidation and improvement of its air and ground forces in Germany, CDI could also be highly relevant to it. Harris concludes that the CDI and complementary national efforts at conventional force improvements represent a "window of opportunity" that could nevertheless be closed.

The situation in Europe remains what it has been for the entire postwar period in Canada, namely a central element in the country's larger defense debate. John Young's chapter three analyzes this debate, and observes that whatever disquiet there may be with the country's Alliance commitments tends to surface as tensions between the superpowers rise, and subside when relations improve between Washington and Moscow. For Young, then, much of Canada's defense debate is driven by external variables; nowhere is this more apparent than in respect of the alignment/neutrality dichotomy that sometimes captures the attention of Canadian defense intellectuals and media.

Young argues that relations of power (i.e., the "structure" of the international system) condition the way in which pressure groups' and even parliamentary and governmental definitions of the threat have been articulated. He develops his argument by drawing on the Canadian pro-neutralist literature, public opinion survey data, government source materials, and political party policy statements. Placing current Canadian neutrality thinking in the context of the "widening-Atlantic" thesis, Young emphasizes that Canada has an important stake in the continuation of détente, which he argues contributes signally to the preservation of the country's Alliance commitments

Douglas Bland's chapter, "Canadian Neutrality: Its Military Consequences," adopts as a point of departure the possibility of a future Canadian government taking Canada out of NATO and NORAD. Although not favoring such an orientation (quite the contrary) Bland does concede that a substantial minority of Canadians, as well as the country's third-largest party at the federal level, the New Democrats, desire a withdrawal from the Atlantic Alliance, as well as from the North American Aerospace Defence Command. The basis of their advocacy is the premise that neutrality would not only enhance the prospects of peace (on the assumption that a causal link can be established between alliances and war) but would also enable Canada to spend much less on defense than it now does.

Typically, however, such entreaties to dismantle collective defense have tended to skirt over the practical consequences that would attend their implementation. In this chapter, Bland assumes that Canada, even if it became a neutral state, would still have certain security obligations under international law — obligations that, ironically, might require greater military expenditures on its part. He sets out to elaborate those obligations — in particular those to the United States — and to discuss their practical military consequences in terms of force structure, capital costs, and deployments. He concludes that whatever else the neutrality option might imply for Canada, it will not mean a less-costly defense establishment.

If neutralism has been the expressed security preference of a significant minority of Canadians, it has in large measure been a result of disquiet — on a variety of grounds — with the dilemmas of nuclear deterrence. One of the most vocal segments of society to express itself in this regard has been organized religion, whose views on contemporary defense Roger Epp surveys in his chapter, "No East or West: Canadian Churches and Collective Defense in the 1980s." In Canada, as elsewhere, the major churches recently have taken a more active, critical approach to foreign and defense policy, but their positions have been shaped by a distinctly Canadian context. While they have rejected nuclear deterrence "without reservation," they have given more attention, for example, to the extent of Canadian cooperation with American weapons programs and to membership in a nuclear alliance.

Epp's chapter examines the churches' critique and its sources. The critique includes a case against nuclear weapons, modified by a concern for bilateral disarmament and a crucial distinction between "mutual deterrence" and war-fighting weapons and doctrines; the demonstration of Canadian complicity; and, the urging of a "non-provocative" defense posture, which demands greater control of Canadian territory so as to enhance strategic stability. Such a position finds parallels in the "mentor-state" internationalism ascribed to the Trudeau government, wherein national initiatives are taken ostensibly on behalf of the global community. While Epp criticizes the churches on several points, he argues that they should be situated within the voluntaristic tradition in Canadian foreign policy and understood as "connected critics" who often adopt government declarations as criteria.

One of his more intriguing contentions is that the Canadian churches, while committed to nuclear disarmament in theory, have in practice shown "a somewhat surprising preference for mutual assured destruction as the posture from which to move toward nuclear disarmament." To be sure, this preference is rooted in a comparative context, one that finds the churches vehement in their denunciation of a perceived shift toward war-fighting strategies. Nevertheless, the preference does, to Epp, raise interesting questions from the perspective of just-war theory, among which are "the moral status of targeting civilian populations and of threatening, for the sake of the deterrence relationship, to do what could not in conscience be carried out."

Given the myriad of common interests in the security domain shared by Canada and the United States, it is often easy for observers (especially those in the latter country) to overlook points of disagreement between Ottawa and Washington on defense matters. Such points, however, do exist, and there is no reason to suppose that they will become less numerous over time. Withal, the bilateral defense relationship has been marked by greater harmony during the past few decades than is usually the case in international security arrangements between allies. It is sometimes assumed that the reason such relative accord has been attained (and maintained) is that there exists a well-developed coordinating structure that effectively monitors and manages the bilateral defense regime. Some analysts identify the binational Permanent Joint Board on Defense (PJBD) as being at the core of this structure. This institution is the subject of Christopher Conliffe's chapter.

The oldest of the Canada-U.S. defense organizations, the PJBD has proved to be surprisingly enduring yet, as Conliffe argues, its effectiveness has been of variable quality. Indeed, it is his judgment that "the PJBD has been effective for only six of its forty-eight years." The Board has evolved in six reasonably discreet phases. The first one, during the war years (1940-1945), saw the PJBD move from an initial three-year period of high activity and relevance to inactivity in the subsequent two years. There followed the years of uncertainty (1945-1950), succeeded by the third phase (1950-1953), in which the PJBD had its "last fling" in terms of effectiveness. During the next three phases, and up to the present, the Board has hardly been the focal point of bilateral defense cooperation; to be blunt, it has been in "limbo" since 1963.

Key to the PJBD's utility (or lack thereof), Conliffe argues, has been the use made of it by its "patrons," whether the President and Prime Minister or the Chiefs of the armed forces. When they elected to achieve their aims by other means, "the PJBD was reduced to house-keeping or make-work activity." Even though he takes a critical view of the PJBD's actual accomplishments, Conliffe concludes that since Canada's military alliances are so integral to its defense policy, the very existence of the PJBD is more important for symbolic reasons than for any practical or concrete achievements.

More than any formal agencies, it is person-to-person or service-to-service rapport — often achieved on an ad hoc basis — and the persistence of a web of common interests that have facilitated the relatively frictionless (with some notable exceptions) workings of the bilateral defense regime. This is not to say that Ottawa and Washington, when they do cooperate on defense matters, do so for identical reasons. A good case in point is the most recent air-defense modernization effort the two countries have launched. As John Anderson shows in his chapter, "Canada and the Modernization of North American Air Defense," Ottawa's approach to the 1985 Canada-U.S. agreement on air-defense modernization was inspired by a rather different objective from Washington's. Anderson, who was directly involved in various stages of planning and discussion of this project, traces its origins from the first appearance, in the United States, of a conceptual plan for modernization during the late 1960s.

He shows that, from the Canadian point of view, the impetus toward modernization derived more from the felt need to replace obsolete surveillance and warning systems than it did from any new departure in strategic thinking. He further demonstrates the extent to which specific Canadian interests were incorporated into the final design of the modernization program.

It is upon the question of whether and to what degree Canadian interests can get incorporated in the next generation of air-defense improvements that Charles Tutwiler's chapter is focused. Tutwiler analyzes the continuing relevance of continental air-defense systems in the late 1980s, and argues, the current mood of superpower détente notwithstanding, that recent changes in weapons technology, especially in the realm of the "air-breathing threat," have been forcing a relative re-emphasis upon North American air defense. One important component of this reassessment has been the U.S. Air Defense Initiative (ADI), which seeks to develop the technology necessary to counter Soviet capabilities in low-observable bomber and cruise-missile systems that are anticipated for the 1990s.

In the 1987 Defence White Paper, reference was made to Ottawa's desire to participate in ADI-related projects. Although some academics have assumed that such participation would, at minimum, require an American invitation to take part in the program, Tutwiler indicates that there already is Canadian involvement in ADI — involvement that includes both the Canadian Forces (through representation, *inter alia*, on the NORAD staff) as well as the private sector — and that there is likely to be further such involvement, at least in the short term. Probing both the sovereignty-protection and security interests that Canada can be said to have in ADI, Tutwiler concludes by suggesting that longer-term collaboration in this project could be greatly affected by shifting political tides in Canada, and by the perception of those political changes in the United States.

Many of the issues that Tutwiler regards as potential constraints upon closer bilateral cooperation in ADI have, of course, already been glimpsed in the recent Canadian debate over participation in the U.S. Strategic Defense Initiative. Boris Castel addresses that debate in his chapter, "Ballistic Missile Defense, Arms Control, and the Implications for Canada."

In the six years since it was unveiled in President Ronald Reagan's celebrated speech of March 1983, the U.S. Strategic Defense Initiative has occasioned a great deal of discussion, both in the United States and elsewhere. Although a variety of questions have been posed concerning SDI, the two most important matters raised by analysts have been the program's feasibility and its desirability. Castel directs his inquiry toward both these concerns, with the view to assessing their likely implications for Canada. Although the full-blown, and oft-caricatured, strategic-defense system known as "star wars" is unlikely, there is a reasonable prospect that a more modest ballistic-missile-defense capability could be developed by both the United States and, it should be noted, the Soviet Union.

Customarily, commentators in Canada have adopted a wary attitude toward ballistic-missile defense, usually on the assumption that it must by definition prove destabilizing to the overall strategic balance between the superpowers. Castel challenges this position, and argues that limited BMD, if accompanied by meaningful arms-control measures, might not only be stabilizing, it might also provide a context for Canadian initiatives undertaken to enhance — within the context of the BMD/arms-control symbiosis — global and therefore

Canadian security. Specifically, he argues that Canada might make a major contribution in the area of arms-control verification.

Aerospace strategic-defense initiatives have not been the only subjects of controversy lately in the bilateral defense relationship; over the past year, the North American maritime (or, more specifically, underwater) domain has become a topic of some moment to defense planners and analysts in Canada and, to a lesser extent, the United States. The importance of the maritime dimension of bilateral defense has been highlighted by the Mulroney government's announcement, made in the White Paper, that Canada would be acquiring a fleet of nuclear-propelled attack submarines. No other aspect of recent Canadian defense planning has attracted as much attention as has the proposal to acquire SSNs. Among the concerns raised by critics of the submarines, in Canada and elsewhere, have been questions about their cost-effectiveness, their implications for nuclear nonproliferation, their bearing upon global arms-control initiatives, and their potential impact on Canadian Alliance commitments. Given the importance of the SSN decision, we have dedicated our final three chapters of this volume to an exploration of the major questions it has raised.

The first of these chapters is written by S. Mathwin Davis, and constitutes a technical introduction to (and critique of) the SSN program. This is not the first time, Davis states, that the Canadian Navy has looked into acquiring SSNs. In the past, however, their acquisition has been rejected on the grounds that they were too expensive and unnecessary. In the early 1980s, however, sovereignty emerged as a major defense-policy consideration, particularly with regard to the Arctic. Thus simultaneously with the on-going study of conventional submarine (SSK) options, the Department of National Defence (DND) initiated a Nuclear Submarine Option Study at the behest of the Minister during the preparation of the White Paper. By March 1987 it was evident that the Navy would proceed with the SSNs, and this of course was confirmed in the June White Paper. If SSNs eventually do get funded, Canada will select between the British *Trafalgar* and the French *Rubis/Améthyste* classes.

Davis, who was personally involved in previous SSN studies, believes that while these boats have certain clear advantages over SSKs, the proposed Canadian contribution obtained at an expense that would appear to constrain or unbalance the overall defense budget, seems to be of doubtful significance in relation to the overall East-West balance of power. Nor are these the best weapons for NATO or for sovereignty protection. What is more, he deems it unwise for Canada to commit itself to a twenty-seven year program that he argues cannot possibly be sustained, given political realities. Davis concludes that, as an alternative, Canada should acquire SSKs, in batches of six at a time. Technological developments such as Air Independent Propulsion may give SSKs some of the advantages now associated with nuclear submarines.

In his chapter, David Haglund probes an issue that has taken an interesting bilateral twist of late, namely the potential implications (if any) of the Canadian SSN program for nuclear nonproliferation. Interestingly, one of the most unanticipated objections to the SSN acquisition has turned out to be the argument that it would have adverse implications for the global nonproliferation regime. This would be so, critics of the SSN program maintain, because of the "precedential" implications of Canada's becoming the first state to avail itself of a clause in the Nonproliferation Treaty (NPT) allowing for the "non-proscribed" military use of nuclear materials. Haglund analyzes this argument, and finds that logically one implication of the SSN program *might* be such a weakening. There are, however, two other logically tenable assumptions: that the Canadian program might, ironically, strengthen the nonproliferation regime (as the government maintains); or that it might have no impact on the regime, as it appears that other states (e.g., Brazil, Argentina, India) have been developing their own SSN programs irrespective of any Canadian actions.

In addition to his analysis of the precedential issue, Haglund explores a second major connection between nonproliferation and the Canadian SSN program. This inheres in the complicating impact that American nonproliferation mechanisms (in the event two bilateral agreements — one with the U.K., the other with Canada — dating back to the late 1950s) could have on the Canadian boat-acquisition process. This nonproliferation question, he argues, could well be a major factor in Ottawa's eventual choice between the British *Trafalgar*-class SSN and the French *Améthyste* update of the *Rubis*-class boat.

Joel Sokolsky concludes with an analysis of the strategy and politics of the SSN proposal, and argues that the acquisition of a fleet of ten to twelve SSNs would not change the fundamental anti-submarine warfare emphasis of the Canadian Navy or its missions in NATO and in North American defense. Given likely trends in American and Soviet naval strategy and posture, the SSNs, he finds, make strategic sense for Canada and for its allies. They will also further Canadian national-sovereignty interests by affording Canada a better capability to operate in all three of its oceans. However, Canada's allies would have preferred more surface ships and more resources for European defense; thus the SSN program, however, could continue to raise questions about Canada's future in NATO.

Sokolsky observes that while the SSNs, and for that matter the White Paper itself, might indicate a higher priority for North American and national roles, NATO political interests will actually be better served in the long run. The SSN program, however, does not enjoy strong parliamentary or public support despite the consensus within Canada in favor of higher defense spending, especially for more naval forces. There are several reasons for this, chief among them the negative, not to say sinister, connotation of the word "nuclear." In light of domestic and allied opposition, the waves made by the SSN proposal, ironically, could sink the Navy it was intended to save.

Notes

[1]Canada, Department of National Defence, *Challenge and Commitment: A Defence Policy for Canada* (Ottawa: Minister of Supply and Services, 1987), 61. (Hereafter cited as White Paper.)

[2]For the origins and rationale of the policy of isolation, see David G. Haglund, *Latin America and the Transformation of U.S. Strategic Thought, 1936-1940* (Albuquerque: University of New Mexico Press, 1984), chap. 1.

[3]See, for example, *NATO in the 1990s*, Special Report of the North Atlantic Assembly, 18 May 1988; Stanley R. Sloan, *NATO's Future: Toward a New Transatlantic Bargain* (Washington, D.C.: National Defense University Press, 1985); Eliot A. Cohen, "The Long-term Crisis of the Alliance," *Foreign Affairs* 61 (Winter 1982/83): 325-43; Henry A. Kissinger, "A Plan to Reshape NATO," *Atlantic Community Quarterly* 22 (Spring 1984); Melvyn Krauss, *How NATO Weakens the West* (New York: Simon and Schuster, 1986); Andrew J. Pierre, ed., *A Widening Atlantic? Domestic Change & Foreign Policy* (New York: Council on Foreign Relations, 1986); and David P. Calleo, *Beyond American Hegemony: The Future of the Western Alliance* (New York: Basic Books, 1987).

[4]See, for an analysis of this "pillar," Josef Joffe, *The Limited Partnership: Europe, the United States, and the Burdens of Alliance* (Cambridge, MA.: Ballinger, 1987).

[5]For background on Canada's defense policy and its participation in NATO, see Danford W. Middlemiss and Joel J. Sokolsky, *Canadian Defence: Decisions and Determinants* (Toronto: Harcourt Brace Jovanovich, 1989).

[6]See Douglas L. Bland and John D. Young, "Trends in Canadian Security Policy and Commitments," *Armed Forces & Society* 15 (Fall 1988): 113-30.

[7]White Paper, 6.

[8]On Canada's view of its role in NATO and current trends, see John W. Holmes, "The Dumbbell Won't Do," *Foreign Policy* 50 (Spring 1983): 3-22; and Gerald Wright, "Canada and the Reform of NATO," in John Holmes et. al., *No Other Way: Canada and International Collective Security Institutions* (Toronto: University of Toronto, Centre for International Studies, 1986).

[9]See, for the initial effect upon NATO of the Gorbachev proposals, Peter Adams, "West Readies Reaction to Soviet Troop Cuts," *Defense News*, 12 December 1988, 1.

[10]White Paper, 43.

[11]For the impact of Soviet ALCM capability on North American air defense, see David G. Haglund, "Les Missiles de Croisière Soviétiques Aéroportés et la Géopolitique de la Défense Aérienne de l'Amérique du Nord: Une Nouvelle Perspective du Nord Canadien," *Etudes Internationales* 19 (June 1988): 245-72.

[12]Perrin Beatty, Minister of National Defence, "Address upon the Tabling of the Defence White Paper in the House of Commons," 5 June 1987.

[13]White Paper, 59.

[14]These comments are based on the 1988 survey conducted by the Canadian Institute for International Peace and Security. See Don Munton, "Canadians and their Defence," *Peace & Security* 3 (Winter 1988/89): 2-4.

[15]A good source for the Northwest Passage controversy is Franklyn Griffiths, ed., *Politics of the Northwest Passage* (Kingston and Montreal: McGill-Queen's University Press, 1987).

[16]See Ross Howard, "PM Faces Calls for Deficit Cuts, Social Spending," *Globe and Mail* (Toronto), 2 January 1989, A1.

PART ONE

Canada, the United States,
and
Collective Defense

1

The Future of Transatlantic Defense: Canada, the U.S. and NATO in the Post-INF Period

Hans-Jochen Annuss

INTRODUCTION

On 8 December 1987 President Reagan and General Secretary Gorbachev signed an agreement in Washington spelling out the terms for the global destruction and dismantling of Soviet intermediate-range SS-4, SS-5, SS-12/22, SS-23, SS-20 and SSC-X-4 ballistic missiles along with American intermediate-range Pershing I, Pershing II, and Ground-Launched Cruise Missile (GLCM) systems. The Pershing IA missiles of the German Air Force have been excluded from this agreement, widely known in abbreviated form as the INF Treaty.

On 11 December 1987 the Federal Republic of Germany and the other European countries in which INF forces have been stationed signed with the United States the Multilateral Basing Country Agreement in Brussels. In so doing, the basing countries established the legal framework to enable the United States to meet its obligations under the INF Treaty, in particular the inspection protocol with the Soviet Union (which includes the provisions providing for Soviet inspection teams in the basing countries). In addition to this Multilateral Basing Country Agreement, there is also provision for the bilateral exchange of standardized notes between each of the Western basing countries and the Soviet Union expressing the willingness of the particular basing country to permit Soviet inspections on its soil as stipulated.[1]

In the public debate over the INF Treaty and its celebrated "double zero option," neither proponents nor opponents of the accord have devoted much attention to strategic arguments. Many backers have given the impression of wanting disarmament at any cost, while some opponents felt that the double zero option did not go far enough. The latter pointed out, quite rightly, that the proposal would have the effect of concentrating the nuclear missile threat in Europe on the two Germanys. Few seemed interested in the fact that while arms-control agreements can and do diminish a given threat, they also involve relinquishing one's own capabilities and options. Nor has there been much recognition that the capabilities at issue here are the very ones that make deterrence possible: i.e.,capabilities intimately linked to NATO's declared aim of preventing war — any kind of war.[2] This goes relatively unnoticed, given the public popularity of the goal of nuclear arms control and disarmament, now so prominent in Western public opinion. The public mood today, so recently fixated upon the perils of the nuclear age, now seems to reflect the conviction that the abolition of nuclear weapons will also abolish the prospect of war.

When it comes to arms-control offers, the Soviet Union is dealing from a position of almost unlimited resources; for NATO, on the other hand, agreeing to balanced disarmament measures is a more difficult matter. Some will express skepticism about such a line of argumentation, and reply that after all, NATO will still have an additional 4,000 nuclear warheads once the INF systems are dismantled. Although the reply is numerically correct, it avoids the real question of whether these remaining weapons are suitable for meeting the requirements of the deterrence strategy of flexible response. In this context, the accent must be on the word "flexible."

Beginning with a description and evaluation of the flexible response strategy and the NATO two-track decision of 1979, I attempt in this chapter to outline what I take to be the military consequences of the INF agreement. In so doing, I address the question of whether the treaty is prejudicial to the presently existing military strategy, and if so, in what way. I then examine ways in which the Alliance can respond to the agreement, paying attention to what has been an often-overlooked consideration, namely the potential commitments of both the U.S. and Canada to NATO.

THE STRATEGY OF FLEXIBLE RESPONSE AND THE ROLE OF NUCLEAR WEAPONS

The prime goal of NATO's security policy is the creation of a just and lasting peace in Europe with appropriate security guarantees.[3] Geared to this are the two major objectives of the Alliance, providing a secure defense capability while at the same time attempting to reduce tensions in Europe. Military security and a policy of détente, far from being contradictions, complement one another. In this context, however, the issue of military parity is of crucial importance. This does not refer to numerical equality in personnel and weapons, but to equality of response capabilities or options in both the political and strategic military spheres.

Of pivotal importance in evaluating the security threat facing the West is the military power of the Warsaw Treaty Organization (WTO); associated with this evaluation must be an inquiry into both the military doctrine and strategy of the Soviet Union and its allies. The military power of the Warsaw Pact is the product of large-scale, operationally ready armed forces that are well-equipped, well-trained, and heavily deployed in the Warsaw Pact countries. This power reflects a strategic doctrine of offense in which special emphasis is given to superiority in strength and surprise.

This is not to state that the Warsaw Pact necessarily has offensive political intentions. Military power can, perhaps, be gauged by the use of facts and figures, but by their very nature political motives do not lend themselves to evaluation of this sort. Moreover, they may change rapidly. The key point is that military power is available to carry out offensive intentions. Therefore the offensive military capacity of the Warsaw Pact must govern the defensive efforts of NATO and this irrespective of the political intentions of any particular Soviet leadership.

The spectrum of possible forms of aggressive action that the Warsaw Pact could take against NATO ranges from subversive operations and attacks confined to certain areas and limited to certain types of weapons, and extends all the way to large-scale aggression conducted with conventional and nuclear weapons.

NATO's military strategic concept, set out in NATO document MC 14/3 of 16 January 1968 and since known as "Flexible Response," defines the alliance's military-strategic aim as the maintenance of peace and the protection of NATO territory. To achieve these ends, the strategy calls for credible deterrence, and in the event that this should fail, for effective defense designed to end hostilities quickly under politically acceptable conditions.[4]

NATO's strategy of deterrence is based on the following:

— unmistakable determination on NATO's part (resolve) to act in concert (collective action) and to defend the territory of the NATO countries against all forms of aggression (solidarity);
— the visible ability of the alliance to respond effectively and in an appropriate manner regardless of the level of aggression (defensive capacity); and
— flexibility of potential courses of action which precludes the aggressor from determining in advance how NATO will respond and which in any case threatens him with an unacceptably high risk.

In addition to being based on resolve to defend oneself, deterrence is based on the sum of all NATO's military capabilities. In this context, nuclear capability is of special importance. Under the present political and military conditions, only the threat of the use of nuclear weapons can make it clear to the

Warsaw Pact that the latter simply cannot achieve its aims in any reasonable cost-benefit reckoning.

NATO's strategy is one designed to prevent any war. However, anyone proposing to use force for deterrence must, in order to assure credibility, be able to demonstrate their operational readiness and their capability in defensive operations. This is the only way of convincing an adversary that an attack is not worthwhile. Although it might sound paradoxical (and perhaps oxymoronic), it is a crucial element of NATO's military strategy that the Alliance must demonstrate its resolve to defend itself, if need be with nuclear weapons, to prevent war of any kind.[5]

The present military strategy of the Alliance embodies three types of responses to any kind of aggression: Direct Defense, Deliberate Escalation, and General Nuclear Response. These types of reactions are, depending upon the situation, practical either consecutively or simultaneously. The type, scope, and point of time of each form of response must be incalculable for the attacker and is defined by the type of aggression, as well as by the goal of terminating the war as quickly as possible.

This strategy can succeed only if NATO is willing and able to provide the requisite conventional and nuclear weapons and if such willingness and ability to rise in collective defense is beyond the sphere of doubt of any potential aggressor. For this reason NATO has had to maintain conventional forces, short- and intermediate-range nuclear weapons, and strategic nuclear weapons. As an interlinked combination tailored for deterrence and defense they must form an inseparable complex, the so-called NATO Triad.

The three elements of this NATO Triad are designed to provide a complete spectrum of options for response and escalation, thus assuring effective deterrence. They are to complement one another and none can take the place of the other. To offer an effective deterrence, the elements must be proportionately balanced and each must function credibly and reliably. This notion must be emphasized because it is the key element of NATO's doctrine of deterrence. All of the elements of the NATO Triad, as well as their individual components, must be linked with one another through an organized structure and coordinated operational planning. This way they form a single solid unit.[6]

This combination gives NATO the opportunity to take measures to increase or possibly restore deterrence, and if need be, to escalate appropriately, in line with the political objective. The aggressor, meanwhile, has no way of knowing when or with what resources the Alliance will respond to a continuation of the attack. This makes it impossible for the aggressor to assess his risk.

Here, short- and intermediate-range nuclear weapons have a particular importance. They form the link between the conventional forces and the nuclear intercontinental ballistic missiles of NATO. Their purpose is to prevent the Warsaw Pact from using similar weapons in support of quick-thrust operations to seize territory. They are also intended to be used within the context of Direct

Defense to retaliate in kind in the event of first use by the Warsaw Pact or to deliberately escalate a conflict to force a quick end to hostilities.

Were these short- and intermediate-range nuclear weapons to cease being available, NATO's options for military and political action would be severely restricted. An aggressor would again find it possible to calculate the risks of a conventional attack. As a consequence, the Alliance could quickly find itself facing the alternative of capitulating or activating its intercontinental ballistic missiles.[7]

Nuclear weapons have been an integral part of NATO's strategy since the early 1950s. Their role within the strategy has on numerous occasions been adapted to suit changing conditions and circumstances. Undoubtedly, the biggest change was the switch from the strategy of Massive Retaliation to the present one of Flexible Response. The prime question at issue in this changeover was how to alter the strategy and design the equipment systems to keep the threat of using nuclear weapons credible; for the credibility of this threat is the crucial item in assuring that the potential opponent continues to choose political settlement over war as a means of resolving conflict.

The strategy of Flexible Response was designed to address the security interests of Europeans as well as those of the United States.[8] This statement is not a platitude. Rather, it faces the fact that the North Atlantic Alliance must deal with an enormous geostrategic problem. Europe is separated from its major Alliance power by some 6,000 kilometers of the ocean that has given the Alliance its name. In addition, there are the great distances within the United States and Canada, something not usually considered. Europe is in the position of having to assert itself against the major power of the East, which dominates the Eurasian land mass and which has pushed its control in Europe right up to the internal German border dividing not only Germany, but all of Europe. By itself, Europe cannot assure its independence against this nuclear superpower, which at the same time operates the most powerful conventional forces in the world. Hence, the fundamental strategic problem of the Alliance has always been to bridge the Atlantic Ocean and to design strategy and mechanisms that will cut down the geographic distance to the United States in such a manner as to make it impossible to separate the security of Europe from that of the U.S.

By contrast, the geographical area of the Warsaw Pact is a self-contained unit. To the west, it narrows like a funnel, with the result that if the forces of the Warsaw Pact ever mounted an attack, they would of necessity be concentrated into a spearhead. The Pact can operate on internal lines over short distances, and therefore can assemble concentrations of forces quickly and with surprise. It is also capable of moving its reserves over short distances through a physical area that it alone controls.

Because of this geographical problem, Europe and North America have different interests as far as the consequences of a conflict are concerned. For the Federal Republic of Germany, for example, the chief interest is to stop an attack as quickly as possible, using the means that will imperil the very existence of the attacking superpower if it continues its hostilities. Of course, this final threat of general nuclear response would also imperil the very existence of the United States. For its part, the United States will have a quite different objective in mind, one that seeks to keep the conflict confined to Europe if possible before risking destruction of the North American homeland from intercontinental ballistic missiles.

These two different and understandable positions can be resolved by the strategy of flexible response as long as sufficiently credible response options are available between conventional defense and general nuclear response to show the aggressor at any early stage that he is running a risk that is and must remain untenable for him. It cannot be in the interest of either North America or Europe to become involved in waging a protracted conflict if deterrence fails. A conflict must be terminated quickly and the integrity of NATO territory quickly restored. To do this, the strategy must have the necessary resources to provide credibility as a function of deterrence.

THE NATO TWO-TRACK DECISION OF 1979

As I have mentioned, NATO's strategy is predicated upon equilibrium between forces and options. For almost twenty years it has formed the basis for the political and security-policy actions of the Alliance. The high expectations placed on the policy of détente, particularly in the seventies, aroused hopes that could not be fulfilled. This was the period in which there occurred the rapid build-up of the Soviet fleet, the enormous increase in conventional arms, and the development of an intermediate-range arsenal for which at the time NATO had no equivalent.[9]

Following extensive consultations within the Alliance, during which Germany in particular made its influence felt, NATO reached the unanimous decision on 12 December 1979 to modernize its intermediate-range nuclear missile arsenal capable of longer ranges. Combined with this decision was an offer to negotiate with the Soviet Union.

What was the status of the military arsenals of the two sides? In 1979, there was approximate parity between the superpowers in the field of strategic nuclear weapons, and this is still the case today. On the conventional side, the Warsaw Pact has always had superiority over NATO in Central Europe. In the area of intermediate-range nuclear weapons (range in excess of 1000 km), the Soviet Union likewise had an advantage and was tending to widen this gap both in quality and quantity. To that point NATO had nothing equivalent to put into the field.[10]

The result was an upset of the balance between the two Alliances — a balance whose preservation has been vital for peace. The Soviet Union was in a position to assume that with its beefed-up intermediate-range arsenal it had at its disposal a threatening political tool and the military means to get around the American nuclear shield for Europe. Because of this situation and in light of the approximate parity in intercontinental ballistic missiles, the potential for adverse developments could not be dismissed. The Soviet Union could have seen its objective of reduced security for Western Europe made more attainable and could have attempted to bring political pressure to bear on the region. In the most extreme case, the USSR could have attempted to open hostilities on a regional basis, even to the point of unleashing intermediate-range nuclear weapons able to reach quite distant targets.

NATO countered this danger of strategic-military imbalance with its two-track decision of December 1979 in which it acted to replace 108 American Pershing IAs in West Germany with 108 Pershing IIs and to station 464 new cruise missiles in Great Britain, the Netherlands, Belgium, the Federal Republic of Germany, and Italy. In settlement of the total of 572 new systems the same number of older nuclear warheads would be withdrawn from Europe.

In a second part of the decision, an offer was made to the Soviet Union to negotiate on intermediate-range missiles with the aim of agreeing on as low a level as possible. In fact, NATO's offer even included a proposal to drop plans to upgrade weapons systems if the Soviets would agree to dismantle their intermediate-range nuclear missiles. This proposal by the West (known as the "zero option") was presented for negotiation at Geneva with even further modifications. Also, as part of the two-track decision, NATO opted to reduce its nuclear arsenal in Europe by a thousand warheads.[11]

In October 1983, the Alliance confirmed at a meeting of the Nuclear Planning Group at Montebello, Canada, that the reduction by a thousand nuclear warheads had been accomplished. It further decided to remove an additional 1400 warheads from Europe by 1988, putting the total arsenal at its lowest level in twenty years.

The effective reduction of the nuclear arsenal by a total of 2400 warheads established a new framework within which the modernization of the intermediate-range missiles would be taking place. The latter, seen in this light, did not represent the addition of new warheads to Europe, since they were to form part of the new total inventory.[12]

The reasons for such unilateral prior concessions have to be assessed almost exclusively as political in nature; nevertheless the unilateral measures were consistent with the strategy of Flexible Response. For in the event that deterrence fails, it is NATO's objective to end the conflict with the application of the lowest possible level of military force and to restore the integrity and security of the Alliance. Given this, NATO can have no interest in conducting an unlimited nuclear war in Europe. The use of nuclear weapons is seen instead as a means of inducing the aggressor to re-evaluate his own risk and his assessment of NATO's resolve to defend itself, and hence to halt his attack. In this context then the role of nuclear weapons is primarily political, as many analysts have observed.[13]

NATO's need, thus, is for a broad spectrum of options. It must have weapons capable of posing a major threat to concentrations of forces on the battlefield to prevent a strategic breakthrough and hence a *fait accompli*. This is the task of the short-range nuclear forces. However, the use of these "battlefield weapons" cannot be the intentional and clear political signal of a crucial qualitative change in hostilities designed to end the conflict. The use of "battlefield weapons" as an operational emergency brake must therefore be combined with similar use of weapons over a broader geographical area to achieve the goal of controlled escalation.

The Alliance must also have weapons capable of posing a major threat to the second echelons of the fronts in the strategic concentration areas of the Warsaw Pact. This task is performed by the shorter-range intermediate nuclear force inventory.

Finally, NATO must have in Europe longer-range intermediate nuclear force systems capable of being used against targets on Soviet soil. These are of vital importance to the political objective of preventing war and terminating hostilities. They prevent the Soviet Union, the political executive authority behind an attack in Europe, from concluding that it could wage war in Europe without suffering damage to its own territory. Therefore they keep the Soviet risk calculable.[14]

A MILITARY STRATEGIC EVALUATION OF THE AGREEMENT

For many years, every government of the Federal Republic of Germany has viewed the concentration of the nuclear forces of the Alliance on the battlefield as incompatible with German security interests. After years of deliberation in the Alliance, the General Guidelines on the Use of Nuclear Weapons for the Defence of NATO were adopted by the Nuclear Planning Group in the fall of 1986. The West German government was able to have a significant effect on what the guidelines said, being successful in having included the so-called "shift of emphasis," meaning a shift of the main focus of nuclear options from the battlefield to the so-called extended geographical area, which includes vital regions of the Soviet Union.[15]

These German efforts were significantly influenced by the issue of how credible the threatened use of these weapons really was. Just as in the era of strategic nuclear parity it was no longer reasonable for the United States to plan the use of strategic systems from the outset in a conventional war in Europe, it is likewise unacceptable for the Federal Republic of Germany to permit the threat of nuclear strikes primarily against targets on German soil. In this respect, NATO's intermediate-range nuclear weapons are those systems most likely to meet its approval for use by the Alliance.

The double-zero option raises the question of what resources the Alliance has for alternatives as part of Deliberate Escalation in the extended geographical area. The systems NATO still has in Europe, besides the 400 SLBM-Poseidon warheads, are exclusively nuclear weapons delivered either by aircraft or artillery.[16] Their number (about 4000) is affected by many factors, one of which is the short range of tube artillery. To prevent concentration of Warsaw Pact forces on the battlefield along every possible frontal sector, artillery weapons have to be evenly distributed geographically. This alone means a relatively high number of these weapons would be required.

The nuclear-capable aircraft presently in Europe are above all needed for conventional defense.[17] To task them alone with nuclear operations in the extended geographical area would mean stripping important resources from the conventional capability. In any event, the powerful Soviet air- defense system could be expected to take a heavy toll of them. Furthermore, they are spread out over only a few air bases in Europe. The deliberate destruction of these air bases in the initial phase of a conflict could quickly leave the Alliance facing the choice of using battlefield weapons or strategic systems for limited escalation options. This would not only break open the deterrent interlinked system; it would also confine the threat of Deliberate Escalation to German territory.

The number of nuclear weapons remaining in Europe is undoubtedly substantial. However, those that are left are "bogus" weapons, or, to put it more accurately, the structure of their deployment has become imbalanced. The first zero option has removed the most effective weapons against targets on Soviet soil; the second removes the most effective system against the second echelons of the fronts and other key targets such as airports.[18] The result of this is that a heavier burden has been placed on the conventional forces ranged in defensive positions along the internal German border. Furthermore, recourse to nuclear weapons would arguably have to be taken more quickly. Both of these developments have ramifications, military as well as political.

It is only superficially correct to say that the second-zero option offer is a unilateral concession by Gorbachev, for in its upgrading program, the Alliance consciously refrained from replacing the American Pershing IA because its task was to be partially taken over by the Pershing II. The prospect of reactivating at some future date its shorter-range intermediate nuclear missiles (since it is foregoing longer-range intermediate nuclear forces, in compliance with the INF Treaty) has not been renounced by the USSR. But NATO's opportunity of proceeding with shorter-range intermediate nuclear weapons has effectively been blocked, as has the option of strengthening its conventional defense capability with modern shorter-range intermediate ballistic missiles.

While the dismantling of the Pershings and the land-based cruise missiles does not take away NATO's ability to move to Deliberate Escalation, it nonetheless restricts flexibility within this type of response. It restricts the very options for Deliberate Escalation that are capable of keeping the risk over the head of the Soviet Union from European soil and beneath the threshold of the strategic nuclear potential of the United States. Admittedly, there is still the option of reaching the territory of the Soviet Union with aircraft based in Europe (F-111s), and with SLBMs.[19] However, because of the heavy air defenses of the Warsaw Pact, the ability of these aircraft to penetrate the area is limited. As for the SLBMs, their lack of accuracy constrains their applicability.[20]

The conventional superiority of the Warsaw Pact and the overwhelming predominance of Soviet missiles of less than 500 km range (particularly about 580 SCUD systems) assume greater significance and have a special impact on German interests, particularly since these missiles can reach targets mainly in the Federal Republic of Germany. It is true that the significant threat posed to NATO Europe by the SS-20s and SS-4s is dispensed with. This is the military gain. However, the Soviet Union and the Warsaw Pact retain their conventional superiority. Combined with its similar superiority in nuclear weapons of less than 500 km in range, this conventional edge does endow the WTO with the capacity for far-ranging offensive, surprise, and preemptive strikes. At the same time, the Soviet Union may now deem the risk to its own territory to be lower than previously anticipated.

Nor is that all. The Warsaw Pact can also deploy against Europe an extensive land-, sea-, and air-based nuclear potential that includes strategic systems. Hence, whereas the double-zero option weakens NATO's capabilities in the fields of escalation and deterrence, there are no such restrictions on the operational and strategic options of the Warsaw Pact. This is because although the Soviet Union did do away with its intermediate-range nuclear weapons systems, it kept intact its options toward Europe by switching to such weapons systems as the variable-range SS-24 and SS-25.[21] In this context, special note must be made of the SS-24, with its variable range from 3000 to 9000 km and capability of moving on the tracks of the Soviet rail system. Each missile is capable of carrying ten MIRVed warheads; thus some eighty SS-24s could take the place of the roughly 800 LRINF warheads within range of western Europe that are scheduled for removal by the INF Treaty. In addition, one must note the mobile SS-25 which is mounted on a wheeled platform and carries a single warhead.[22] (Even should there be a 50-percent reduction in the number of each superpower's ICBMs, the Soviet Union would still be able to target Western Europe with as many as 1,000 warheads as a component of its global strategic missile potential.)[23]

Despite the disadvantages in military-strategic terms that I have cited, the INF Treaty also conveyed benefits which were of prime importance in the decision of the European NATO countries to go along with the agreement. For one thing, the INF Treaty represents a very important political accomplishment for the Alliance. It confirms that NATO was wise in its two-track decision of 1979 and in its systematic deployment (despite considerable resistance) of Pershing IIs and cruise missiles. Moreover, the INF agreement sends a clear signal on arms-control policy. For the first time not only are upper limits established, but weapons systems are dismantled as well. For the first time the Soviet Union is undertaking asymmetrical reductions; and for the first time, the Soviet Union recognizes a far-reaching verification system, to which its policy of secrecy has to date been diametrically opposed.[24] This could lead to progress in other forums where arms-control policy is negotiated.

A COMPREHENSIVE CONCEPT FOR SECURITY, ARMS CONTROL, AND DISARMAMENT?

The INF agreement has raised very difficult but not insurmountable problems for the strategy of Flexible Response. It has revealed the weakness of the current arms-control policies.[25] Strategy and arms-control policies are complementary elements of western security, neither can be an end in itself. Each must complete the other, if security is to be maintained and improved.[26]

The major task of the Alliance is to impose conceptual order upon western arms-control policy, orienting it to the overall picture of threat and strategy.[27] In its 11-12 June 1987 meeting in Reykjavik, the NATO Council charged the Permanent Representatives of the member-countries with the development of a comprehensive blueprint for arms-control policy that took into account the interests of the strategy.[28] This blueprint was to be developed in concert with the appropriate military agencies and authorities. It remains to be seen, however, if the Alliance will or can learn any obvious lessons, particularly in view of pressure from the public for quick continuation of steps toward disarmament.

In Section 7 of the communiqué the following are cited as elements of a comprehensive blueprint in conjunction with the INF treaty:

— 50 percent reduction in strategic nuclear offensive weapons by the Soviet Union and the United States;
— the world-wide elimination of chemical weapons;
— the establishment of a stable and secure level for conventional armed forces by eliminating imbalances in the whole of Europe; and

— in conjunction with the establishment of a conventional balance and global elimination of chemical weapons, clear and verifiable reductions in nuclear missile systems of short range to the same upper limits.

This listing of elements does not suggest any chronological preference. However, it is laid down as mandatory that land-based short range missiles be dealt with in planned correlation to conventional forces. It also bears remembering that under recommendations of the Harmel report, which is still current, consideration must be given to the future role of nuclear weapons in deterrence and to their effects on arms control. This applies especially to nuclear systems having ranges of less than 500 km.

The conceptual linking of the conventional side with short-range nuclear systems is of exceptional importance. A number of the Alliance's members do not want any active arms-control negotiations in the area of short-range nuclear missile systems and talk of a "fire wall."[29] Thus, existing conventional imbalances are to be eliminated before there are any further reductions in nuclear weapons in Europe. Given this and considering specific German interests, it is necessary to explore what is meant by the term "in conjunction with."[30] Basically, this expression implies a need for clarification of the relationship between conventional ratio of forces and nuclear weapons through extensive investigations within NATO.

In order to address this need, the following questions have to be answered: how must the conventional ratio of forces between NATO and the Warsaw Pact be organized to make reductions of nuclear forces in the range area from 0-500 km possible?, and what method of investigation is appropriate to determine a stability-oriented evolution of the conventional ratio of forces?

Through concrete investigations, opportunities will arise for approaching and perhaps resolving the still very divergent national viewpoints on setting goals and priorities. Even now, NATO is in agreement on countering the Warsaw Pact concept of equal reductions, which assumes overall parity of forces despite admitted areas of Warsaw Pact superiority, with the Western concept of common ceilings.[31]

Arms-control policy only contributes significantly to security when it is successful in eliminating military superiority. Europe's specific security problem is the overwhelming conventional and chemical superiority of the Warsaw Pact. In future, this must be the focus of arms-control policy. Here, the interdependence of conventional and nuclear forces as part of the existing Alliance strategy must be kept in mind. The layer-by-layer dismantling of individual weapons categories "from the top down" according to range breaks apart NATO's interlinked arrangement of deterrent systems; moreover, it creates new grey areas. This can be illustrated most strikingly by the missile systems remaining in Europe: of these, the Warsaw Pact will have some 1,350, mainly targeted on West Germany, compared with only eighty-eight for NATO.[32]

The attempt at damage control with the so-called "fire wall" is unsuitable for resolution of the problems at hand. It is true, it could be interpreted as an attempt to put an end to the process of negotiations in stages operative to date and to guard against a step-by-step denuclearization of Europe and hence the transformation of Western Europe into a theater for conventional forces. The inventory of nuclear weapons below 500 km must not be allowed to be a sacred cow. Nor can the Alliance foresake its future ability to also strike at targets far to the rear with nuclear weapons as a means of deterrence. The "fire wall" must not be allowed to run horizontally; it has to run vertically, which means that the present spectra of ranges necessary for the ability to escalate a conflict must be retained if an attempt is to be made to further reduce the overall number of nuclear weapons. In the German view, then, the emphasis of future reductions must be on short-range weapons systems.

The vast majority of the delivery systems remaining under the terms of the double zero option are bivalent. In the case of the Warsaw Pact they are even trivalent.[33] It will be necessary to differentiate future nuclear arms control in Europe from conventional arms control, while at the same time recognizing that the two are linked and interdependent. A drastic reduction in delivery systems would have serious consequences for the conventional defense capabilities of the Alliance. Furthermore, reducing delivery systems alone would not be an appropriate means of cutting the nuclear capability of the two sides. Quite obviously tube artillery and aircraft can be reloaded. Even if the number of aircraft each side possesses were halved, it would not reduce any arms unless the number of nuclear bombs were also cut.

There are two clear areas in which further disarmament would be possible and desirable, without negative impact on deterrent or defensive capability. These are the global elimination of all chemical weapons and the reduction of the strategic arsenals of the superpowers by 50 percent. The degree to which further nuclear arms reductions in Europe will be possible hinges to a crucial degree on the willingness of the Soviet Union to eliminate military superiority in the conventional area.

In the wake of the INF Treaty, the issue of conventional parity has become even more pressing. The Supreme Allied Commander Europe, General John R. Galvin, has expressed the concern "that the military balance, particularly in the conventional area, will so erode that the West will find itself vulnerable to Soviet intimidation and coercion."[34] For reasons of military and political logic, conventional disarmament is the priority item for Europe and in particular for Germany. The goal is increased stability by reducing the Warsaw Pact's invasion capability while at the same time maintaining conventional defense capability. The objective cannot be achieved solely by establishing parity in manpower and weapons, although the elimination of numerical superiority in the major weapons systems is an important first step.

If there were to be dramatic progress in the conventional field, it would be easier to contemplate a further reduction in short-range nuclear weapons without endangering Western security. For it must not be forgotten that one of the important roles of tactical nuclear weapons in Europe involves (and has always involved) neutralizing the conventional superiority of the Warsaw Pact.[35] It is not correct in this regard to say that the Federal Republic of Germany is in a unique and isolated position.[36] Leaving aside SS-24, SS-25, *Backfire* bombers, etc., short-range nuclear weapons up to 500 km in range pose a threat not only to German soil but also to the forces of the NATO allies stationed in Germany. Furthermore, if deployed where they would be for an attack, these weapons are also capable of striking Germany's western neighbors. The fact that allied troops are stationed in Germany demonstrates the willingness of the NATO allies to share in the risk involved and to form a cooperative defense effort.[37] The challenge for the Alliance in coming years will be to preserve and strengthen this community of risk.

Action is also needed to maintain capability for conventional defense and deterrence, primarily based on appropriate nuclear forces. The publicly stated resolve of the Alliance and each of its member countries to maintain undiminished conventional defense capability simultaneously lends support to the negotiating position of NATO in conventional arms control.[38] It follows from this that weak spots in conventional defense must be eliminated. This means increasing the mobility and flexibility of the armed forces and significantly improving capability for rapid reinforcement. It also means more effective incorporation of existing reserves and in future increased utilization of the resources of modern technology to combat the second echelons.[39] On top of a reduction in nuclear weapons, there must not be an added weakening of conventional combat capability, measured relative to the posed threat.

With regard to the nuclear forces for Europe, the remaining systems must be restructured and modernized. That does not mean a circumvention of the INF agreement or the compensation of lost potential. In the framework of current strategy, the remaining weapons have to be adjusted to the existing threat and new weapons have to fill the gap if necessary to maintain the flexibility of NATO's strategy.[40]

The following may be offered as possible criteria for the future structure of the nuclear armed forces in Europe: options in the extended geographical area must be retained; total numbers must not be increased; options for modernization must be retained, if for no other reason than to permit reduction of battlefield systems; and all of the Alliance partners must share the costs and the risks.

The political objective of NATO must remain unchanged: to maintain a credible capability of deterrence with a sufficient minimum of nuclear weapons both in quality and quantity. As Lothar Ruehl notes:

The tendency on NATO's side has been to rely less on the early use of central strategic systems and of nuclear battlefield arms, and to reduce the part of the latter within the framework of Flexible Response....The question now arises whether this tendency will be reversed again in favour of nuclear battlefield weapons and short-range nuclear arms in general, or whether NATO will continue along the lines drawn up by Brussels, Montebello and Gleneagles decisions since 1979.[41]

It is my view that the Alliance should resolutely oppose any suggestion of restricting nuclear weapons to the role of counter- deterrence, that is, of keeping the nuclear option solely to deter Soviet use of nuclear weapons.[42] Any such restriction would be equivalent to tearing the cornerstone out of the edifice of Alliance strategy, and would unleash talk of denuclearization, with all that this implies for the existing strategy of deterring war.[43]

On the military-strategic side, one issue stands out: How to maintain credibly and effectively the viability of the strategy of Flexible Response in an area of crucial importance for Europeans, that of Deliberate Escalation, designed to terminate a conflict. After all, to reiterate the point, it is not as if the Soviet Union has given up its options of being able to strike any target in Europe with nuclear weapons. It still has systems of every type and range-capability in more than adequate numbers. This means that the requisites of deterring Soviet operations remain unchanged.

For longer-range intermediate options, there are air- and sea-based systems such as those in the U.S. and British forces now, or scheduled to be introduced in coming years. These include SLCMs, ALCMs, and SLBMs.[44] For the remaining sector of NATO's military potential, namely the shorter- range intermediate aircraft, the short-range missiles, and artillery, proposals for modernization and restructuring emerged from the Montebello meeting, the results of which were confirmed in 1986.[45] These proposals include as main items a replacement system for the LANCE and stand-off missiles for aircraft, both scheduled for the mid 1990s.

IMPACT ON NORTH AMERICA: A EUROPEAN PERSPECTIVE

At first glance, the INF Treaty would seem to have no great or direct impact on the defense of North America. After all, the weapons systems affected are in Europe, and have primarily posed a threat to European territory in both east and west. Warsaw Pact INF forces posed no threat to the North American continent, nor did the NATO ones constitute any threat to Warsaw Pact countries *from North America*.

In connection with the NATO two-track decision, the Soviet Union expressed the view that a launch of these medium-range missiles would be considered the equivalent of a strategic attack, and would be responded to on this level.[46] This illustrated that the Soviet Union did in fact feel threatened by these weapons (i.e., deterrence was obviously credible) and that it recognized that these weapons contributed to the strengthening of extended deterrence.

These two advantages have now been done away with. The agreement restricts the range of options, the very thing that "flexible response" requires if it is to work. This weakening of the strategy affects the whole Alliance and not just one part or one "pillar." Therefore, all NATO members — including Canada and the U.S. — must be cognizant of these effects and not simply dismiss the voices of concern from Europe.

The recently begun debate over the issue of a new Alliance strategy has given impetus to strengthening of the European pillar. Let us not dwell on whether this awakening and obviously growing resolve is based on European fears that the U.S. might reduce its Alliance commitments. Rather, the essential thing seems to be that European self-assurance and self-confidence can only be convincingly formulated in the Alliance if Europeans are able to speak with one viewpoint if not with one voice.[47] Were this to happen, the two-pillar concept, advocated as long ago as the Kennedy Administration, could become a reality.

In this context, one must examine the North American pillar of the Alliance. Traditionally, European analysts have held this to be synonymous with the United States. But Europeans should also ask, how does Canada fit in? The fact is often obscured that North America is home to a second Alliance partner, which makes an essential and not insubstantial defense contribution in Europe. To be sure, the transformation of NATO will affect Canada, and adjustments will be needed. Currently, Canadian security policy appears to have become more North American in orientation, especially in its maritime dimension, as the 1987 White Paper demonstrates.[48] Canada, as do other countries, currently wrestles with the dilemma of matching its security commitments with its capabilities. As it does so, it may face trade-offs between its North American and European roles.

What all Alliance members must in any case prevent — Canada of course above all — is a situation in which Canada, in coping with its dilemma, becomes caught in the middle, finding itself forced to withdraw from its European roles. At present it is not possible to assess the decidedly negative impact such a decision might have on the Alliance as a whole.

What could the Europeans do to minimize the Canadian sense of isolation — a mood that will likely grow in the post-INF environment? In this context, some consideration might be given to a report published by the Canadian Institute of International Affairs, which proposed to ask the European allies to help defend North America by stationing a multinational fighter squadron in Canada. Although the military value of such an initiative might seem slight, its symbolic value could be significant, for it could underline the concept of the strategic unity of NATO.[49] This goal would be as attractive to many in

Canada as it would be in Western Europe. It could also result in Canada serving as a bridge of sorts between the two pillars of the Alliance in the future. This could allay fears of decoupling, but it must be clear that it would have a price-tag, which both sides of the Atlantic Alliance must be prepared to address.

When all is said and done, while there may well be a military importance of the Canadian Arctic as part of NATO defense strategy, the front line of North American security remains in Europe. The Western Alliance is first and foremost threatened by the strong arsenal of the Warsaw Pact forces built up in Eastern Europe, and secondarily along the Northern and Southern European flanks. To maintain and improve defense capabilities in this area must continue to be the goal of NATO, all the more so in post-INF Europe. A self-assured Europe will no doubt assert its security interests more firmly; to this the U.S and Canada will have to adjust, for while they each have their own readily understandable security interests, neither can close their eyes to trends in European security.

CONCLUSION

The INF Treaty has re-kindled the debate over a new strategy. However, this debate is pointed in the wrong direction. True, the fundamental and established principles are to be retained: a capability for flexible and appropriate response, the principle of forward defense, and political solidarity. Also retained are all the various types of responses.[50] There will likely be some shifts in emphasis, with conventional defense becoming more important. However, the nuclear threshold for preventing war will remain, and it must continue to be incalculable for a potential adversary. The means of carrying out deliberate escalation have been curtailed by the Treaty; therefore, adjustments must be made in regard to the remaining conventional and nuclear forces.[51]

A military strategy designed to prevent war of any kind must not be abandoned simply because one element is removed for political reasons.[52] I have stated that the intermediate-range nuclear weapons involved in the INF Treaty are highly effective instruments; nevertheless, doing away with them should not pose any insurmountable problem. The question is less one of whether we need a new strategy and more one of asking how we can have both credible deterrence and effective arms control and disarmament.

Increased cooperation and collaboration among the Europeans is possible, for economic reasons alone, as well as because of growing pressure from the United States for burden sharing within the Alliance.[53] At the same time, steps toward arms control and disarmament must not run counter to NATO's paramount objective of enhancing security. Any measures undertaken by

NATO, even those related to arms control and deterrence, must further this objective.

In this context, the point should be reiterated that the purpose of nuclear weapons from the outset has been to offset the conventional superiority of the Warsaw Pact. In future negotiations over arms control and disarmament, it is therefore necessary to eliminate the reason for the existence of NATO's nuclear weapons. It is not sufficient, and may be dangerous, to treat the symptoms rather than the cause. This means eliminating the conventional superiority of the Warsaw Pact, and hence its capacity for invasion, must be a *sine qua non* of Alliance security policy. Only then could or should further steps in the area of nuclear weapons be tackled. For at least the short-term future, Europe and North America cannot do without nuclear weapons in Europe as a guarantee of deterrence, even if recourse to such weapons does involve political, military, and, as it always has, ethical and moral problems. Purely conventional deterrence is inconceivable.[54]

Notes

[1]Der Bundesminister der Verteidigung, Informations- und Pressestab, *Das INF-Abkommen und seine Verwirklichung in der Bundesrepublik Deutschland*, Material fuer die Presse (Bonn), 18 March 1988, 2-3.

[2]Karl Kaiser, "Koennen die Sowjetpanzer jetzt ungehindert rollen?" *Die Welt* (Bonn), 27 February 1988.

[3]This section is a comprehensive representation of the basic principles of this military concept. For the constituent elements, the following sources have been used:

Der Bundesminister der Verteidigung, *Weissbuch 1970 - Zur Sicherheit der Bundesrepublik Deutschland und zur Lage der Bundeswehr*, (Bonn, 1970).

_____, *Weissbuch 1971/1972 - Zur Sicherheit der Bundesrepublik Deutschland und zur Entwicklung der Bundeswehr, (Bonn, 1971)*.

_____, *Weissbuch 1973/1974 (Bonn, 1974)*.

_____, *Weissbuch 1975/76 (Bonn, 1976)*.

_____, *Weissbuch 1979* (Bonn, 1979).

_____, *Weissbuch 1983 - Zur Sicherheit der Bundesrepublik Deutschland (Bonn, 1983)*.

_____, *Weissbuch 1985 - Zur Lage und Entwicklung der Bundeswehr (Bonn, 1985)*.

[4]Hans Ruehle, "Welche Strategie braucht die NATO?" *Neue Zuercher Zeitung*, 29 February 1988.

[5]Bernhard Gravenstein, "Militaerstrategisches und operatives Konzept der NATO," in Gerhard Hubatschek, ed. *Strategie fuer den Frieden* (Herford: Busse Seewald, 1986), 145.

[6]Kaiser, "Koennen die Sowjetpanzer jetzt ungehindert rollen?"

[7] Gravenstein, "Militaerstrategisches und operatives Konzept der NATO," 152-53.

[8] Ruehle, "Welche Strategie"; Eckhard Luebkemeier, "NATO-Strategie - modifiziert angewandt," in Hartmut Buehl, ed. *Strategiediskussion* (Herford-Bonn: Verlag E. S. Mittler und Sohn, 1987), 133.

[9] Presse- und Informationsamt der Bundesregierung, *Aspekte der Friedenspolitik* (Bonn, 1981), 13-14, 23-24; Sam Nunn, "Warnschilder und Wegweiser fuer den Nordatlantikpakt," *Europaeische Wehrkunde*, no. 3/88, 159.

[10] Bundesminister der Verteidigung, *Weissbuch 1983*, 77-78.

[11] "Kommuniqué der Sondersitzung der Aussen- und Verteidigungsminister der NATO am 12.Dezember 1979 in Bruessel," in Guenter Walpuski, ed. *Verteidigung + Entspannung = Sicherheit* (Bonn: Verlag Neue Gesellschaft, 1984), 189-91.

[12] The Montebello Decision, Annex to the Final Communiqué of the Autumn Ministerial Meeting of the NATO Nuclear Planning Group (NPG) Montebello, Canada (27 October 1983), *NATO - Final Communiqués 1981-1985* (Brussels: NATO Information Service, n.d.), 106-7.

[13] Bundesminister der Verteidigung, *Weissbuch 1983*, 166-68.

[14] Ruehle, "Welche Strategie."

[15] Helmut Kohl, "Ost-West Gegensatz: Nicht das letzte Wort der Geschichte," *Europaeische Wehrkunde* (Muenchen), no. 3/88, 136; Lothar Ruehl, "The Nuclear Balance in the Central Region and Strategic Stability," *NATO's Sixteen Nations* (August 1987), 19.

[16] Ruehl, "The Nuclear Balance," 20-21.

[17] Presse-und Informationsamt der Bundesregierung, *Streitkraeftevergleich NATO - Warschauer Pakt 1987* (Bonn, 1987), 40.

[18] Werner Kaltefleiter, "Die Taeuschung mit der scheinbaren Nulloesung," *Europaeische Wehrkunde*, no. 5/87, 249-50.

[19] Siegfried Thielbeer, "Ist der Westen von Nuklearwaffen entbloesst?" *Frankfurter Allgemeine Zeitung*, 5 December 1987.

[20] Werner Kaltefleiter, "Gefahren der atomaren Abruestung - Das erhoehte Risiko fuer Europas Sicherheit," *Europaeische Wehrkunde* (Muenchen), no. 2/88, 80.

[21] Ibid., 78.

[22] Ludwig Schulte, "Wandlungen des Risikokalkuels - Stabilitaet durch SDI?" *Europaeische Wehrkunde*, no. 12/87, 674.

[23] Lothar Ruehl, "Balance ist unverzichtbar," in *Information fuer die Truppe*, ed. Bundesministerium der Verteidigung (Bonn), no. 2/88, 7.

[24] Christoph Bertram, "Das Wunder von Washington," *Die Zeit* (Toronto Edition), 25 December 1987, 3.

[25] Christoph Bertram, "Nulloesung: Nicht das letzte Wort," *Die Zeit* (Hamburg), 24 April 1987 (unless stated otherwise, all references to *Die Zeit* will be the Hamburg edition).

[26] Admiral Dieter Wellershoff, "Der Weg der Bundeswehr in die Zukunft," in *Festschrift zur Entlassung der Absolventen des Jahrganges 1985 des Verwendungslehrgangs Generalstabs-/Admiralstabsdienst der Fuehrungsakademie der Bundeswehr*, ed. Bundesministerium der Verteidigung FueS I 7 (Bonn, January 1988), 20.

[27]In 1981, K.-Peter Stratmann suggested such a concept: K.-Peter Stratmann, *NATO-Strategie in der Krise?* (Baden-Baden: Nomos Verlagsgesellschaft, 1981), 242-43. In 1986, he repeated this suggestion: K.-Peter Stratmann, "Aspekte der sicherheitspolitischen und militaerstrategischen Entwicklung in den neunziger Jahren," in Gerhard Hubatschek ed. *Strategie fuer den Frieden* (Herford: Busse Seewald, 1986), 353.

[28]Erklaerung der Ministertagung des Nordatlantikrates am 12. Juni 1987 in Reykjavik, in *Bulletin* (Bonn), ed. Presse- und Informationsamt der Bundesregierung, no. 59, 16 June 1987, 518.

[29]Christoph Bertram, "Brandmauern darf es nicht geben," *Die Zeit* (Toronto Edition), 19 February 1988.

[30]Kohl, "Ost-West Gegensatz," 136-7.

[31]Erklaerung der Aussenminister der NATO-Mitgliedsstaaten am 12. Juni 1987 (Ministertagung des Nordatlantikrates), *NATO - Brief*, no. 3/87, 32; Kommuniqué der Ministertagung des Nordatlantikrates vom 11. Dezember 1987, *NATO - Brief*, no. 6/87, 26.

[32]Presse- und Informationsamt der Bundesregierung, *Streitkraeftevergleich 1987 NATO - Warschauer Pakt* (Bonn), 37-40.

[33]U.S. Department of Defense, *Soviet Military Power 1987* (Washington, D.C.), 89.

[34]General John R. Galvin, "Allied Command Europe - Buttressing the Means," *NATO's Sixteen Nations* (August 1987), 16.

[35]Ruehle, "Welche Strategie."

[36]Richard Burt, "Singularisierung: Ein Produkt der Phantasie," *Der Spiegel* (Hamburg), 22 February 1988; François Heisbourg, "Nach dem INF- Abkommen von Washington: Fuer eine Weiterentwicklung der Grundlagen des Atlantischen Buendnisses," *Europa-Archiv* (Bonn), no. 5/88, 123-4.

[37]Henning Wegener, "The political framework and implications of the INF Treaty," *NATO-Review*, no. 1, February 1988, 15.

[38]Kommuniqué der Ministertagung des Verteidigungsplanungsausschusses der NATO am 22. Mai 1985 in Bruessel, in *Material fuer die Presse*, ed. Der Bundesminister der Verteidigung (Bonn), no. 22/1, 23 May 1985.

[39]Harald Kujat, "NATO-Strategie im Uebergang," in Hartmut Buehl, ed. *Strategiediskussion* (Herford-Bonn: Verlag E. S. Mittler und Sohn, 1987), 122-23; Bundesminister der Verteidigung, *Weissbuch 1983*, 151-52, 164-65.

[40]Frank C. Carlucci, "Amerikas Engagement fuer Europas Sicherheit," *Europaeische Wehrkunde*, no. 3/88, 156-57.

[41]Ruehl, "Nuclear Balance," 20.

[42]Helmut Schmidt, "Null-Loesung: im deutschen Interesse," *Die Zeit*, 8 May 1987.

[43]François Heisbourg, "Nach dem INF-Abkommen," 124.

[44]General John R. Galvin, "Es tut sich eine Luecke auf," (interview by Kurt Kister and Stephan-A. Casdorff), *Sueddeutsche Zeitung* (Muenchen), 13 February 1988; Paul H. Nitze, in "The INF Negotiations and European Security," United States Embassy (Ottawa), *Text*, 29 September 1987, 4.

[45]Nunn, "Warnschilder und Wegweiser," 159; Nuclear Planning Group, Luxembourg, 26-27 March 1985, *NATO-Final Communiqué 1981-1985* (Brussels: NATO Information Service, n.d.), 138-39; Kommuniqué der Nuklearen Planungsgruppe

der NATO (39. Ministertagung am 20. und .21 Maerz 1986 in Wuerzburg), *NATO-Brief*, no. 2/86, 35.

[46]Kaltefleiter, "Gefahren der atomaren Abruestung," 78.

[47]Sir Geoffrey Howe, "European Security Cooperation," *Survival*, (July/August 1987), 379-80.

[48]Canada, Department of National Defence, *Challenge and Commitment: A Defence Policy for Canada* (Ottawa: Minister of Supply and Services, 1987).

[49]Canadian Institute of International Affairs, Working Group of the National Capital Branch, *The North and Canada's International Relations* (Ottawa: Canadian Arctic Resources Committee, 1988).

[50]Ruehle, "Welche Strategie."

[51]Stratmann, *NATO - Strategie in der Krise?* 233.

[52]General Wolfgang Altenburg, "Zum Strategiekonzept Washingtons: Interview mit General Altenburg," *Sueddeutscher Rundfunk* II (Stuttgart), 13 January 1988.

[53]Der Bundesminister der Verteidigung, Informations- und Pressestab, *Pressespiegel* (Bonn), no. 12/88, 1-6.

[54]Erklaerung des NATO-Rats zur konventionellen Ruestungskontrolle: Der Weg nach vorn, in *Bulletin*, ed. Bundespresse- und Informationsamt (Bonn), no. 34, 7 March 1988.

2

Trends in Alliance Conventional Defense Initiatives: Implications for North American and European Security

Bruce A. Harris

The military forces we are building must be continually modified to keep pace with new weapons... We are at the very point, for example, of seeing a whole sequence of fundamental changes made in response to development of new types of arms. The tendency in recent decades to produce weapons of greater range, penetrating power, and destructiveness is accelerating. As a result the balance between men and materiel is bound to shift, probably reducing the ratio of materiel to men, increasing the complexity of equipment — as the price of its power.

General Dwight D. Eisenhower, Supreme Allied Commander,Europe, April, 1952

The North Atlantic alliance must meet the Soviet military challenge with continued modernization of NATO's military forces... Since Soviet modernization has shown no sign of slackening, there is no choice in this technological age when it comes to keeping up with the latest developments — we have to run just to stay even.

General John R. Galvin, Supreme Allied Commander, Europe, March, 1988

INTRODUCTION: THE ORIGINS OF CDI

The history of conventional defense improvement initiatives is as old as the Atlantic Alliance itself. In 1952 Supreme Allied Commander Europe (SACEUR) General Dwight D. Eisenhower recognized that improvements had to be tied to "the determination of people to achieve their defense, together, as rapidly and effectively as possible," while he cautioned "we must be careful that we do not prove that free countries can be defended only at the cost of bankruptcy."[1] Over the years, NATO has tried in many ways to wrestle with this problem; the most recent attempt is known in abbreviated form as CDI (or as it is often rendered, the Conventional Defense Improvement Initiative).

The tasking of the CDI is tied specifically to the December 1984 Defense Planning Committee (DPC) meeting wherein the Ministers:

> Invited the Secretary General and Defense Planning Committee in permanent session to come forward with proposals for coherent effort to improve NATO conventional defenses. This should, *inter alia*, include an early conclusion of ongoing work on a conceptual military framework, establishment of priorities for conventional defense improvements, harmonization of ongoing national efforts to improve conventional defense capabilities, the encouragement of current international efforts to coordinate defense procurement, Alliance-wide efforts to make the necessary resources available, optimization of use of available resources, and integration of the results into the planning process of the Alliance.[2]

Here was a definitive mission statement. The new Secretary General, Lord Carrington, with the assistance of U.S. Ambassador David M. Abshire and the SACEUR, General Bernard W. Rogers, quickly took on the task. The underlying rationale for CDI was readily evident. It had to recognize, in the face of real-world resource constraints, that Alliance-wide priorities would be needed because of difficult domestic resource considerations, and it had to work within the normal force planning system, not outside it. The Conventional Defense Improvements Report was formally adopted by NATO in the DPC in May 1985.[3]

Other factors affected the timing of the CDI and these can be traced to activity within the United States, especially the United States Senate. Buoyed by the increasing defense expenditures of the Reagan Administration and to a degree forgetful of the percentage decrease in spending compared to European allies in the 1970s, the Senate Armed Services Committee had renewed its interest in burden sharing. The 1984 Nunn-Roth-Warner Amendment sought to tie troop reduction in Europe to the Allies' ability to meet the objective of 3-percent real growth. The Amendment failed by a vote of fifty-five to forty-one but the message was received clearly in Brussels. Another factor involved the continuing debate over quantitative imbalances between NATO and Warsaw Pact forces and the narrowing of NATO's qualitative edge.

As General Rogers pointed out: "every SACEUR since the first has expressed a need for NATO to increase the number and improve the readiness of the conventional combat forces." He continued that "our Alliance can no longer afford *not* to take action to correct key deficiencies in our conventional forces, significant and sufficient improvements can be made at acceptable cost and, NATO's Conventional Defense Improvements (CDI) Initiative is a game plan by which the Alliance can fulfill this long-standing requirement."[4] The CDI focuses on agreed deficiencies thereby permitting discussion on the resolution of priority of tasks. The specific CDI package approved at the 1985

May Ministerial session of the DPC addresses the areas of force planning, sustainability, exploitation of technology, and long-term planning. This last concern implicitly recognizes the value of earlier longer-term approaches and provides for forecasting as far as twenty years into the future. This approach is able then to take into account the long lead time necessary to identify and integrate new technologies into defense structures. CDI also emphasizes the need to strengthen the Alliance's armament development and procurement. While several NATO organizations have begun to address this challenge and noted some success, the CDI provides a litmus test for competing systems, and again, most importantly, an agreed focus.[5]

One last aspect of the CDI bears emphasis. Not only does the CDI aim to extend the planning horizon, but it is complementary to the evolution of the NATO long-term planning process itself. The same Ministerial tasking for the CDI referred to an ongoing conceptual military framework. The Conceptual Military Framework (CMF) is a product of the efforts of the Military Committee and the Major NATO Commanders (MNCs) who wished to be able to examine projected capabilities, planning requirements, and shortfalls for the year 2000 and beyond.

NATO FORCE PLANNING/LONG TERM PLANNING

NATO's current force planning procedures began in the early 1960s but were formalized in 1966. NATO force plans are reviewed annually and projected for a period of five years. NATO Force Goals are developed every second year — the target set for the Alliance six years ahead encompassed the period of the next two annual force plans. A Military Committee appreciation of factors likely to influence the Alliance for the next planning review period is used by Ministers to issue guidance to the MNCs for the preparation of Force Proposals. In turn, the MNCs submit completed Force Proposals by country to the Military Committee which forwards them to the DPC. The Defense Review Committee (DRC) of the DPC compares the Force Proposals to Ministerial Guidance to ensure that there is an element of "challenge" to each member nation. The DPC eventually approves a set of Force Proposals for adoption as Force Goals. The DRC, various NATO staffs, MNCs, and individual countries negotiate differences between Force Goals and Country Plans. The end product is the five-year forces plan agreed at Ministerial level and adopted as a commitment of forces by each country for the first year of the plan and general planning for the balance of the period. This is just a general overview and omits extensive staffing procedures but the scope of collaboration and consensus is clear; so is the reality that, in principle, NATO can adopt a particular force goal for a country, but that country cannot be forced to comply.

The process described is for the short- to mid-term. The CMF, however, looks both at a twenty-year assessment of the threat *and* the required force improvements and thus, dovetails into the CDI because of its ability to influence individual nation's long-term country plans. The value of this process is the link to better armaments production which is part of the materiel response to perceived battlefield deficiencies. It is the logical progression of moving from an overall CMF, to the CMF of the Major NATO Commander, to a focus on areas of interest, to specific guidelines, to documentation of mission requirements, and back to the established Force Proposal system itself.[6] The intrinsic value of the CDI/CMF package is thus established. However, other issues and events influence the CDI and serve to raise its importance even higher. The first of these issues is strategy.

NATO STRATEGY: STILL VALID?

NATO defense policy was founded and continues to be based upon the doctrine of deterrence. Strategic concepts have been formulated and necessary resources determined to achieve and maintain a deterrent posture. The evolution of NATO strategy is well known. Initially, the Alliance operated under a nuclear tripwire strategy of massive retaliation and, with the accession of the Federal Republic of Germany, a politically sensitive, forward defense posture. Massive retaliation evolved as Soviet nuclear capabilities improved and the importance of in-theater nuclear weapons was recognized. Nuclear parity, conventional force increases, and limitations of massive retaliation prompted the adoption of a flexible response strategy and recognition of the NATO Triad. Forward defense, flexible response, and the concept of "first use" — retaining the option to use nuclear weapons in response to conventional aggression — define NATO strategy today.

Early debate regarding flexible response and, especially forward defense, centered on military aspects of the problem. Does the Inner- German Border represent the most defensible terrain? Should forces not trade space for time to wear down the enemy? Is an area defense better than a mobile defense? These questions, however valid, really were not about strategy but doctrine or tactics. Critics of NATO strategy in a broader context were often unable to offer viable alternatives and thus failed, in the main, to gain a real constituency. This is no longer the case.

Many of Western Europe's center and left parties now have an alternate vision of NATO strategy, particularly regarding the role of nuclear weapons.[7] The British Labour Party, for example, favors better use of reserve forces, emphasis on improved defensive weapons, and above all, an explicitly defensive strategy. The West German SPD similarly supports a non-threatening, defensive posture and would urge both NATO structure and weapon systems for that end. The leaking of a 1985 SPD defense discussion paper suggesting cuts in the length of military service and abandonment of inherently offensive weapons such as tanks caused a political storm but at least offered insights into the debate. Finally, the Danish Social Democratic Party has advocated a defensive posture that would abandon forward defense for a defense in depth from Danish territory.[8] There appears then to be no single socialist defense view but rather what has been described as "a socialist defense syndrome — a range of themes taken up by the parties to varying degrees."[9] This syndrome includes rejection of nuclear deterrence, a shift toward conventional weapons, non-offensive NATO forces, weapons and deployments, importance of arms control and distrust of U.S. good faith in negotiations, admixed with varying degrees of anti-Americanism.

The response to the socialist syndrome is not all political. Proposed "alternative strategies" have elicited a studied response by defense analysts. The feasibility of Danish and West German proposals to implement a defensive defense is under scrutiny with early analysis indicating that logistical and personnel problems alone will mitigate against a defense in depth, particularly as enunciated for Denmark.[10]

Another alternative, unarmed neutrality, is dismissed by most Europeans as utopian and unrealistic. Armed neutrality along the lines of the Swedish or Swiss models is more attractive, but only to a minority. The option of non-provocative defense receives greater consideration. Proponents of this essentially favor passive resistance: mass civil disobedience wherein the invader is denied victory by the conquered through non-cooperation and subversion of occupying forces.[11] A variation on this theme calls for a massive resistance movement patterned after partisan-style warfare. A last approach to non-provocative defense calls for a light, highly mobile militia which attacks forces in a war of attrition.[12] Defensive defense is receiving perhaps the greatest attention of all the alternatives to the status quo. Proliferation of less expensive anti-tank weapons to replace expensive, sophisticated armor platforms, and expansion of ground-based air-defense systems to supplant fighter-bomber aircraft are very attractive to economically stressed domestic audiences. So too, is the idea of relying on larger reserves and territorial forces rather than massive active forces. Other features of defensive defense include smaller, more mobile forces, better use of terrain (especially obstacles and barriers) and specialization of missions among Allied forces.[13] What must be recognized by NATO is that elements of defensive defense are very attractive and in a democracy their proponents may eventually carry the debate.

A series of recent articles has done much to further the contemplation and possible adoption of alternative strategies.[14] At the same time, however, a perception has arisen that future variations of strategy may, in fact, lean toward a more aggressive defense. Confusion between the United States Army doctrine of Air Land Battle, which devotes much discussion to "Deep Battle," and

NATO's Follow-on Forces Attack (FOFA) fuels criticisms claiming that, at a minimum, NATO is adopting United States doctrine without regard to Europe's unique geopolitical situation; in the extreme, the claim is made that NATO seeks to abandon defensive deterrence. The Soviet Union has done little to discourage this view. How accurate is either claim? Air Land Battle and FOFA do have similarities, but they were developed independently. FOFA does not mean pre-emptive strikes or NATO ground forces attacking across borders, heading deep into enemy territory. FOFA is more the evolution of air interdiction in consonance with counter- attack defensive theory and thus is a logical response to changes in Soviet doctrine emphasizing larger, more mobile attack forces. FOFA is not designed to replace the nuclear option but to reinforce conventional doctrine and is consistent with flexible response.[15]

One should realize also that individual nations implementing forward defense "defend forward" differently. While all forces would, in wartime, come under Allied Command Europe (ACE) for command and control and would follow ACE policies, procedures, and doctrine, at corps level in the Allied Forces Central Europe theater, each nation would defend differently; forces might employ mobile, area, positional, or combination defenses. The rationalization of these defensive doctrines would obviously be in ACE's interests, but the absence of rationalization does not necessarily imply defective, weak, or even "aggressive" postures. That said, it is nevertheless the case that *some* proposals have been mooted recently with a distinctly offensive tenor. The most controversial of these would have NATO, which for years has emphasized conventional defense, adopt instead a "conventional, retaliatory offensive military strategy."[16] The premise is that the Soviets have for too long been allowed the luxury of an offensive posture due to NATO's own defensive one. If NATO adopts a more offensive doctrine, then the Soviets would be forced into a more defensive orientation, accompanied by a greater expenditure of resources on land defensive systems.

However much they may differ, all these alternative strategies have been forcing NATO members to review both Alliance and national doctrines; nevertheless, flexible response and forward defense will continue to provide the basis for at least short- and mid-term planning. In this context, then, the CDI stands as a viable resource program for the support of NATO strategy.

EMERGING TECHNOLOGIES

Emerging technologies often are perceived as "doing more with less"; the "more" means increased firepower and mobility, the "less" fewer personnel. In reality, equipment costs are often so high that fewer systems can be purchased, leading to a phenomenon sometimes referred to as "structural disarmament." The debate within the Alliance over new technology has been described "as one between Europeans who dismiss the new technology as a typical American response to a serious problem — "a fix-it through a gimmick" attitude — and Americans who regard that view as Europessimism — a weary defeatism that real world problems are insoluble."[17]

Many Europeans, however, living in close proximity to a nuclear threat, do support conventional defense improvements and are sensitive to the impact of new technologies in an historical context. Indeed, major European allies fully recognize the danger "of being caught between the technological superpowers — the United States and Japan — and of falling behind in the transition to a new world economy based on rapidly-developing information technologies."[18] Their response has been encouraging. Rather than reverting to previous forms of European economic nationalism, these countries appear to be developing a new, cooperative technological-development community, or perhaps even a transeuropean structure involving American and Asian enterprises in joint technological projects.[19] This latter prospect raises issues of technology transfer and patent protection, but the potential benefits are there— benefits not lost on the Soviets.

Questions remain, however. "Leap-ahead" technology is more costly in terms of risk and funding but offers the greater payoff. Cruise missile technology certainly has presented a more difficult challenge to a defender and the so-called "stealth" technology promises the same effect. Incremental improvements are important to reduce risk of technology gaps in defenses when "new" systems typically take from ten to twelve years to advance from drawing boards to the field. Even Secretary of Defense Frank R. Carlucci understood that under the best circumstances advanced conventional munitions would be limited in number, employed most profitably in the early stages of conflict, and, at best, allow for an early shift to standard weapons from the stockpile.[20]

Political parties now willing to propose alternative strategies and thus alternative technological approaches are major players in budget deliberations. Because studies conducted by independent European and American defense analysts often recommend advanced communications systems, radar/target locating, conventionally armed missiles, and "smart" weapons, parties have been quick to seize on portions of these studies to support their own favored strategies.[21] The social implications are similarly complex. While technology promises better products, cheaper manufacturing and less cost, unemployment continues to be a major concern, especially in Europe. Further, the unemployed are either concentrated in age groups under twenty-five or over fifty. The former lack adequate technical education while the latter, often displaced by technological change, lack both training and the "youth" to compete.[22] An interesting sidelight to the political and social issues is the problem of arms control and "smart" weapons. Real nuclear arms reductions may lose their momentum as technology demonstrates that the same effect can be achieved by conventional means. Thus, as one critic points out, "it's quite possible that the Soviets could agree to and abide by a treaty requiring them to scrap a large portion of their present nuclear force — and yet, continue the drive to increasing strategic superiority."[23] All of these "additional" factors tend to confuse rather than clarify examination of CDI programs.

BURDEN SHARING

Monetary costs of technological development and, in essence, of CDI lead naturally to the issue of burden sharing. This emotional topic includes the 3-percent goal, the concept of the "two-way" street, and the issue of sovereignty versus solidarity in the Alliance. General Eisenhower, in his first annual report as Supreme Allied Commander, stated, "it would be fatuous for anyone to assume that the taxpayers of America will continue to pour money and resources into Europe unless encouraged by steady progress toward mutual cooperation and full effectiveness."[24] Almost every NATO Final Communiqué includes favorable comments on progress made in burden sharing but invariably states that much more needs to be done and nations must strive to achieve 3-percent real growth. While there is recognition that individual members (primarily in the Southern Region) need more assistance than they can render, it is ironic that some of these same countries (Turkey, Greece, Portugal), judged to have a relatively low ability to contribute, rank in the top three or four places in the Alliance under several different criteria that seek to measure defense expenditures as a percentage of gross domestic product.[25]

The danger in the burden-sharing debate is the tendency to look at the subject in isolation, in an effort to pressure or "grade" national contributions. Risk reduction, in this case referring to Alliance cohesiveness or propensity toward devisiveness, is therefore tied to the fact that as one analyst declares, "efforts to make determinative judgments about the fairness of the burden are doomed to failure — much less to change the allocation of burden in a dramatic way."[26] Especially regarding CDI, it is perhaps more important that members continue to contribute rather than that they bicker over whether a specific goal is or is not met. At the same time, Europeans must realize that changes in American policy toward a more isolationist stance would not necessarily be reversed if Europe increased spending, which in fact might be taken in Congress to buttress the argument that Europe simply does not need so much American support.

Statistics are *not* necessarily indicative of success in the Alliance when the larger objectives of well-being and national prosperity are kept in mind. As one analyst suggests: "improving the military burden-sharing balance within the Western consortium is clearly a necessary, but not sufficient prerequisite to assuring our collective, future well-being. There are many opportunities to improve our political-burden and leadership-burden sharing — national and international economic-burden sharing."[27] The term itself, burden sharing, may be pejorative.[28] In respect of CDI, there may well be wisdom in a consensus effort that considers limited resources and focuses on the larger issues of conventional force improvements and readiness and allows perspective to be gained in defining "contribution."

THE VIEW FROM WASHINGTON

Zbigniew Brzezinski and Henry Kissinger, both former National Security Advisors, have long been active in the debate over United States strategy. While Kissinger has examined NATO strategy and its implications on United States global strategy, Brzezinski has looked at United States global strategy and sought to assess its impact on Europe.[29] Recently, both men joined a bipartisan presidential commission to review long-term defense requirements. The unanimous report, titled *Discriminate Deterrence*, appeared at a time of increased tensions in Central America, reductions in federal budgets, and a general raising of consciousness of the American public regarding long-term national goals.[30] The report reaffirmed the need for United States troops in Europe, the maintenance of nuclear deterrent forces, and the pursuit of policies to block Soviet expansion in the Third World. However, it also stated, "we should emphasize a wider range of contingencies than the two extreme threats that have long dominated our alliance policy and force planning: the massive Warsaw Pact attack on Central Europe and an all-out Soviet nuclear attack."[31] Other highlights of the report include: rejecting reliance on the threat of a full-scale nuclear exchange; supporting emerging technologies to substitute for nuclear arms; recognizing that the bipolar world is becoming multipolar; developing highly mobile, versatile military forces less reliant on overseas bases; placing greater emphasis on conventional arms control; and emphasizing steady growth in defense and security assistance budgets — as opposed to "feast or famine." Finally, the commission recommended retaining burden sharing, forward deployed forces, reinforcement capability of active and reserve components, and support for the highest quality military personnel.

The reaction to "Discriminate Deterrence" throughout the Alliance has been mixed. As with "burden sharing," so too with "discriminate deterrence"—the term has quickly become value-laden. Many Europeans interpret it to mean that the United States is now backing away from the NATO Triad, particularly the strategic nuclear guarantee. Others see the report as further pressure on Europeans to undertake expensive conventional rearmament programs. Still others are encouraged by the apparent support for arms control, significant because much of the commission's membership is considered very conservative.

Finally, some see the Third World emphasis as pressing NATO to reopen the issue of "out-of-area" — outside traditional NATO boundaries — operations.

Criticism within the United States of the commission's report seems to center on "its failure to deal seriously with the economic underpinnings of national security."[32] This argument focuses on the growing disparity between strategy and available resources, the danger of over-reliance on high technology, and the apparent unwillingness of allies worldwide to help protect Western interests. The call is for "an equally serious and high level study integrating national security strategy with the economic realities faced by these United States."[33]

"Discriminate Deterrence," however, is a commission report *not* an official change in United States policy. In fact, basic United States grand strategy and military strategy are unchanged.[34] Nevertheless, in an attempt to increase the efficiency and effectiveness of defense planning, Secretary of Defense Carlucci formalized a process whereby the United States "is to gain and maintain a long-term united military advantage over the Soviet Union by pitting enduring American strengths against enduring Soviet weaknesses."[35] Thus far, a Competitive Strategies Council has been formed composed of a Competitive Strategies Steering Group and subordinate Competitive Strategies Task Force. The first task force on global conventional war (with a focus on the European theater) has recommended four initiatives:

- *Countering Soviet Air Operations*: NATO should enhance offensive capabilities against Soviet sortie generation by using unmanned aircraft against operating bases and air infrastructure. Integrity of NATO's air and ground operations should be improved.
- *Countering Soviet Penetration of NATO Forward Defense*: an asymmetric force capability of highly mobile, long-range platforms coupled with advanced target acquisition and command and control capabilities which out-range Soviet artillery and multiple launcher rocket systems should be developed.
- *Stressing the Warsaw Pact Troops Control System*: Soviet tactical operations must be frustrated by blocking preplanned options. Then, at the operation level, NATO could use deception, special operations, and direct attack to counter the Warsaw Pact's ability to plan and execute operational activities.
- *Countering Soviet Global and Multi-theater Operation*: United States forces must develop a capability for large-scale joint and combined conventional offensive military campaigns to exploit Soviet weaknesses in fighting long, multi-theater conflicts.[36]

The improvements to military capabilities linking the four initiatives are unmanned systems, area munitions, extended range tube-launched projectiles, rapidly deployed barriers, precision-penetrator warheads, and "smart" sub-munitions. These capabilities are to be further enhanced by extensive use of automatic data-processing, intelligence fusion, electronics miniaturization, low-observable technology, and better command, control and communications. In sum, the Competitive Strategies approach allows for focus in a fiscally constrained environment. It ties United States national programs into NATO's Conventional Defense Improvement Initiative.

A supporting program called the Balanced Technology Initiative (BTI) is designed to exploit technologies that have the potential of providing significant advances in conventional force capabilities. The BTI is particularly interesting because its original direction came from the United States Senate, which directed the Pentagon to take 200 million dollars from the Strategic Defense Initiative and earmark it for promising future technologies and concepts in conventional force improvement. BTI differs from the American CDI program in that CDI is decentralized to the Services while BTI is centralized in the Office of the Secretary of Defense. Nevertheless, a special effort is being made to ensure that BTI and CDI complement each other without duplication of work. Because current and projected funding for BTI is higher than CDI, industry both in the United States and abroad is interested in the opportunities BTI presents.

As previously mentioned, much of the impetus for both BTI and CDI has been provided by the Senate and especially, the Senate Armed Services Committee. Two Senators, Republican Dan Quayle and Democrat Sam Nunn, have been in the forefront of conventional defense improvements and both sponsored specific proposals in the Congress.

Quayle proposed a NATO Defense Initiative (NDI). Composed of three parts, the fifteen-year plan calls for modernizing NATO's nuclear forces with artillery shells of greater range and accuracy, a longer range replacement to the Lance missile, increased survivability for dual-capable aircraft, and air-to-surface nuclear standoff missiles; strengthening conventional forces by deploying an extended air-defense system, improved longer-range battlefield fire support systems, and pre-prepared terrain barriers; and finally, employing sea-, air- and ground-launched nonnuclear cruise missiles. The cruise missiles and improved C^3I would permit deep strikes against Warsaw Pact airfields, air defense units, and other key facilities as well as "chokepoints" such as tunnels, bridges and rail centers.[37]

Senator Nunn can be accurately described as a major figure in United States defense strategy and policy. As Chairman of the Senate Armed Services Committee, he has been in a position to urge the expenditure of scarce resources along specific guidelines and does so frequently. As noted previously, he co-sponsored an amendment to withdraw American forces from Europe if Alliance members did not demonstrate greater participation in burden sharing. The amendment failed but not before a clear signal had been sent to Europe and in great part, the CDI has been a response to Senator Nunn's concerns. However, the Senator, along with support from Republicans William Roth and John Warner, sponsored and had passed in 1985 the so-called "good" Nunn Amendment. This legislation is aimed at bringing some coordination to the NATO nations' separate programs of developing and fielding weapons systems. Concerned that NATO armies employ four types of heavy tanks (none with compatible ammunition), seven battlefield communications systems (none interoperable), and eleven different anti-tank weapons in service or under development, Nunn wished to offer incentive for NATO members to design systems together. The amendment, with requested funding at 239 million dollars for the first two years, identified projects for fielding in the 1990s which clearly recognize the budgetary realities of the next five years. Developed after close discussion with NATO Allies, twelve Memoranda of Understanding have been signed on projects ranging from a stand-off airborne radar demonstrator system for a surveillance and target acquisition program to a multi-function information distribution system. Thirty-two additional projects have been declared eligible for 1988 funds.

There is a downside to the Nunn Initiative. Within the United States budget, "cooperative monies" are only provided for each project for two years. After that time, the individual Services must incorporate funding requests into their own budget submissions. Although great care has been shown in providing initial money to projects of agreed priority and supportive of CDI, the Services could cut a program and thus undermine a NATO partner's efforts. Further, there is some criticism that the European role is more of a subcontractor than full partner. For their part, some Europeans fear that the Nunn Initiative may prove a potential distraction from intra-European cooperation.[38] The solution to this last difficulty may be to avoid purely bilateral programs, thus ensuring that at least two or more NATO nations are already participants and able to carry on if the transatlantic bargain becomes tenuous.[39]

In reviewing the issue of burden sharing in the United States one is struck not only by the depth of feelings but the breadth; articles on the topic no longer appear just in Washington, or New York, but in newspapers across the country. The discussion centers on the large, quantifiable direct costs of American commitments overseas, the apparent negative correlation between high military spending and national productivity, and the struggle of American industry to remain competitive.[40] The market for American military materiel is shrinking. Often, the loss of a large, single-sale contract can mean the difference between profit or loss for a company. Illegal transfers of sensitive technology and revelations of arms sales used as an instrument of foreign policy have done little to bolster confidence in the international market.[41] While emphasis is still placed on diplomacy and restraint in respect of burden sharing, the fudging of statistics and the pointing of fingers remain evident. Everyone is sensitive as well to a Congress that passes a Nunn Amendment but follows with a Gramm-Rudman-Hollings Act. As noted by Patrick Wall, past president of the North Atlantic Assembly, the United States is trying to address its deficit problem by an act "akin in some respects to the suggestion that one can avoid drowning by holding one's breath."[42] The central concern is that provisions of the act will automatically come into force requiring fairly drastic budget cuts and with them, perhaps, the loss of critical programs. Timing is important here because some systems that come on line in the next five years promise significant fire-power improvements while saving personnel, for example the NATO multiple-launch rocket system. The specter of troop reductions is quickly seen as the end result of "failed" burden sharing.

"Flesh and blood," said NATO Secretary General Lord Carrington, referring to the 326,000 United States troops stationed in Europe, "count for more than abstract deterrent concepts."[43] Former Secretary of Defense Weinberger has stated, "even the hint that the United States would seriously consider major unilateral troop withdrawals from Europe is potentially damaging to the leadership we are committed to provide in the defense of freedom and deterrence of aggression."[44] Richard Burt, American Ambassador to West Germany, has written that "the real threat to the Alliance is the unhealthy symbiosis that is emerging between the left-wing critics of the Alliance in Europe, and critics on the right in the United States."[45] Ambassador Burt addressed the three major arguments put forth for troop withdrawal: cost savings, stiffening of European resolve, and declining strategic importance of Europe.

Monetary savings appear to be illusory. Redeployment would be expensive, German host nation support funds would be lost, and redeployed forces could very well be demobilized and thus lost for global commitments. The issue of stiffening European resolve by a pull-out ignores the enormous contributions that Europeans already make for their own defense. Strong advocates of European defense also see an American unilateral withdrawal as supporting the political parties in Europe who would seek an accommodation with the Soviet Union. Finally, discussion of the declining strategic role of Europe confuses the issue of "most likely conflict" with "most dangerous conflict." "Western Europe remains the biggest strategic prize," argues Burt, who observes that "we do face threats in other regions, and we must of course deal with them. But to weaken our capabilities in the most crucial theater simply to strengthen them elsewhere is bad strategy."[46]

However, it is important to recall that the level of U.S. troops in Europe has not been constant. The impression is given that the United States has always maintained a figure of approximately 326,000 troops in Europe and that even a withdrawal of 10,000 to 20,000 troops would be devastating. The facts speak otherwise. Between 1950 and 1955 the United States, despite commitments to United Nations forces in Korea, increased forces in Europe from 122,000 to 418,000. Troop strength had gradually declined to 263,000 by 1970 but this was due to force deployments to Vietnam. However, with this figure a great deal of debate was generated by the series of Mansfield Resolutions (1966-70) and Amendments (1971-75) which sought, as a reflection of isolationist sentiments, to withdraw 100,000 troops from Europe. In the 1980s, operating under the Stevens' European Troop Ceiling Amendments, forces topped 352,000 and have recently stabilized at 326,000. A troop reduction therefore of 25,000 would be a return to 1975 levels and would not necessarily weaken NATO politically or strategically.

In summary, the United States component of North America is wrestling with strategic policy questions, planning alternatives, competing research and development initiatives, technological debate, burden sharing, and allocation of forward deployed forces. All of these issues, unique to America's superpower status, affect the NATO Alliance. The CDI may provide solutions to some of these problems.

THE VIEW FROM OTTAWA

The other major player in North America is Canada. Until the late 1960s, Canada maintained a force of one air division and one infantry brigade in Europe. As a result of the foreign and defense policy reviews of the first Trudeau government (1968-1972), these forces were cut in half, a general spending freeze was imposed and essentially non-military "sovereignty protection" roles were emphasized. Confirmed in the 1971 White Paper on defense, these changes were based upon an optimistic view of the international environment, one where a stable East-West balance of power coupled with arms control would reduce the role of armed forces. These were years, moreover, during which Ottawa's attention was drawn toward domestic and international economic issues as well as problems concerning national unity.

The next White Paper was not issued until 1987. In it, Perrin Beatty, Minister of National Defence in the Progressive Conservative government of Prime Minister Brian Mulroney, noted that:

> For much of the 1960s and 1970s, Canada's security and our defence relationship with the other democracies were given a low priority by the Federal Government. The Forces were cut in size and much of their equipment was allowed to become obsolete. As a result, Canada's security and sovereignty were seriously weakened and both our allies and potential opponents received mixed signals about our reliability as a NATO partner.[47]

Defense debates in Canada, as in the United States, sometimes deal with the familiar issues of strategy, long-range planning, technology development, burden sharing, and force deployments but more often focus on "what to buy." Canada has more recently added the issue of continued participation in NATO, concerns over Arctic sovereignty, and neutralism. The White Paper addresses all of these issues using as a point of departure the fact that Canadian defense policy will remain based on collective arrangements within NATO and a continental defense partnership with the United States. Key initiatives of the new defense policy include: creating a three-ocean navy, reinforcing surveillance capability, strengthening territorial defense, improving the credibility of Canadian contributions to Alliance deterrence in Europe, revitalizing the Reserve Forces, and building a solid foundation for future defense.

As this chapter deals with NATO's CDI, a closer examination of actions designed to improve the credibility of Canada's contribution to the Alliance is appropriate. There are seven components of Canadian European conventional force proposals. First, is the cancellation of the admittedly unsustainable commitment of the Canadian Air-Sea Transportable (CAST) Brigade and two fighter squadrons to Northern Norway. The exercise of the CAST Brigade in 1986 confirmed what many had suspected; despite extensive planning and the best military efforts "to make it work," severe problems remained. It took weeks to deploy the entire force and successful resupply and further reinforcement over the lengthy line of communication will be problematic. The fighter squadrons have the same limitations. While they can be deployed quickly, they can be better used as part of larger formations operating from more survivable, permanent facilities. Because the largest Canadian force is deployed in NATO's central region, the desire is to consolidate forces there. Problems of sustainability would still exist but would be reduced in scope. Therefore, the overall commitment would be more credible. The consolidation of two brigades would provide the base for a division-sized force. Initial negotiations with NATO have begun with Norway's need for a replacement-reinforcing force a top priority. West Germany has tentatively offered to provide one battalion to Norway but remaining ground forces plus the air squadrons are open issues. In fact, some Canadian critics of the plan support consolidation but argue that Northern Norway faces a greater threat of flank envelopment and thus, they argue, Canada could contribute more by withdrawing from the Central Region, where Canadian forces are a relatively small military force, and becoming fully dedicated to Norway.[48] As a further alternative, though one without much support, it has been suggested that perhaps Canada should contribute forces to SACEUR's Strategic Reserve rather than permanent forward deployment. These forces could pre-position equipment in the United Kingdom and subsequently be used throughout ACE, depending on the situation. The arguments against this course of action center again on the difficulty of supporting forces for contingency deployments and the potential negative signal sent to the Alliance by pulling out historically forward deployed units.[49]

The second initiative is closely related to the first and involves pre-positioning of former CAST-BG equipment and supplies in the Central Region. Pre-positioning is an effective method for reducing reinforcement time as troops can deploy by air without waiting for sealift. Of course, not all of the equipment of the former CAST-BG, previously focused on winter warfare, is appropriate for the Central Region. If the force is to be similarly equipped as an in-place force, then mechanized equipment will need to be purchased. One drawback to this is that a second set also needs to be provided for at-home training. Pre-positioning, therefore, is not a cheap solution but one well accepted by the Alliance as demonstrating true commitment. The alternative is that the force not be mechanized but become straight infantry, or something approaching that. These light forces can play a significant role in combat in built-up areas and in heavily forested regions, both characteristic of Central Europe. The two air squadrons previously designated as Rapid Reinforcement for Northern Norway would shift to the Central Region and join the three squadrons already there. They will be able to draw support from existing infrastructure and stage from hardened shelters.

The third goal is to re-equip Canadian armored regiments with new main battle tanks. The Army tank purchased in the 1970s was the *Leopard C1*, then state-of-the-art mounting a 105-mm gun. However, all major Central Region forces are now equipped with *Leopard II*s (FRG), *Abrams M1A1*s (US), or *Chieftains* (UK). All mount a 120-mm gun on a stabilized platform with night-vision capabilities. Canada is currently looking at both the *Leopard II* and *Abrams M1A1* as a successor tank.[50]

A fourth challenge involves the ACE Mobile Force (Land). Employed as a rapid-reaction force throughout ACE, this is an important asset of SACEUR to demonstrate NATO solidarity and resolve. Canada has long provided a battalion group to the formation. While unable since 1968 to support the battalion group's deployment to the Southern Region because of extended lines of communication, Canada has promised commitment to the Northern Region and will continue to do so. As one of the possible areas of employment is in Northern Norway where the previous CAST-BG operated, much of the equipment pre-positioned for that force will be left for the battalion group.

The fifth and six initiatives are related to the consolidation of Canadian force commitments to NATO. The forward-deployed mechanized brigade in Southern Germany is not fully structured and in times of tension some 1,400 additional personnel would be moved from Canada to bring the unit up to full strength. The Canadian Brigade Group from Calgary is the resource pool used to reinforce Europe. Also, the Militia, which contains many specialist units for combat support and combat service support, provides key replacement personnel for the Europe-based brigade. Thus, the White Paper emphasizes maintaining and improving both the Canadian Brigade Group and the Militia. The other initiative would increase personnel strength in Europe, especially in logistics and medical-support cadres. Additional air-defense units are needed for forward stationing and other assets to support potential divisional operations are more effective if present in peacetime.

The seventh and last initiative deals with another component of reinforcement, airlift. Canada has only forty-eight tactical transport aircraft and five strategic-transport aircraft. These aircraft too are older models requiring increased maintenance and spares. The need for a modern aircraft transport fleet is quite evident not only to support reinforcement during periods of tension or actual hostilities but also for peacetime exercises and support of other Canadian forces participating in peacekeeping activities around the world.

All of the above initiatives reflect a coherent approach to meeting Alliance commitments. They are, of course, related to and in large measure dependent upon the other major defense-improvement categories. For example, the three-ocean navy concept bears on NATO because the Atlantic navy has a definite role in sea lines of communication (SLOC) protection. As another example, reinforcing surveillance capability affects NATO because of strategic intelligence gathering and also SLOC protection. Finally, improvements to the Reserve Force are extremely important. Canada is coming to realize the military, economic, political, and social benefits of a properly constituted and equipped Reserve Force. NATO countries have long relied on Reserve Components and fully subscribe to a Total Force Concept.

Debate over the White Paper is spirited and generally runs along political party lines. The New Democratic Party (NDP) response, *Canadian Sovereignty, Security and Defence*, agrees with much of the Government's basic factual analysis but, not surprisingly, offers different solutions. Consolidation of forces for the NDP represents the opportunity to return Canadian troops home, better "to meet Canadian sovereignty and security needs."[51] The NDP would invest substantially in military forces with the aim of assuming total responsibility for the conventional defense of the northern approaches to North America. The NDP thus favors gradual withdrawal from NATO but is divided internally as to whether this means withdrawal from the integrated military structure or from the Alliance itself.

Other defense analysts are starting to focus on the areas of general agreement and are looking for a more distinctively Canadian contribution to collective defense, which they believe is still absent from current proposals. One writer argues that "an assessment of geostrategic circumstances, which must override all our policy considerations, suggests that an enhanced naval capability, together with the development of strategically mobile forces, based in Canada would be the most satisfactory vehicles to bolster Canada's commitment to NATO in the eyes of our allies."[52] His solution is to have "as a first step, Canada acquire the capacity to deny control of the northwest quadrant of the Atlantic to enemy forces."[53] He urges more extensive anti-submarine assets and advanced minesweepers. He would anchor the sea denial effort on Iceland with Canadian Forces replacing planned United States reinforcements of a Marine Expeditionary Brigade. Canadian CF-18 and *Aurora* squadrons would take over air-defense and surveillance tasks, respectively. "Such commitments would be within Canadian strategic reach, logistically, economically, and in terms of power."[54]

The key to the realization of any of these courses of action for Canada is funding. The White Paper recognizes that it provides only a blueprint and sets the direction of defense policy. The bricks and mortar, however, must be found within a fifteen-year planning framework. Contained in this construct will be a five-year funding plan which is to be reviewed each fall to establish firm budgets for the following five-year period with planning guidance for the remaining ten years. This picks up from NATO's CMF and more closely resembles the NATO Force Goal process. However, the White Paper says, "the Government is committed to a base rate of annual growth in the defense budget of two percent per year after inflation, for the fifteen-year period. Increased resources over those provided by this planned funding floor will be necessary in some years as major projects forecast in this White Paper are introduced."[55] This statement engenders two immediate thoughts regarding NATO. First, despite Canada's endorsement of the NATO 3-percent goal, it appears that this goal may only be achieved at odd years depending on the introduction of major programs. The counter argument is that 2 percent is *base*; but, in the budgetary world it is difficult to exceed consistently a bottom line. The second thought is related to the first. What happens if the "bumps" in funding do not occur? A change in government, adjustments in priorities, and underestimates in funding costs are all possibilities, particularly when long-term plans are in effect.[56]

The White Paper discusses at length the "commitment-capability gap" and is, in essence, the attempt to eliminate the discrepancies over time. Fiscal reality precludes any type of quick fix. The danger is that half-measures may be taken in the absence of clear national will. The sovereignty-versus-security issue is just one area of concern. As one writer points out there is concern that "the new Canadian emphasis on continental defense will be seen in Europe as the first step toward greater North American isolation. Sovereignty and security are not identical. Indeed the search for the former may lead to decline of the latter."[57] This should be Canada's fundamental concern.

A final issue from the Canadian perspective that undoubtedly has an impact on the NATO CDI and Alliance cohesion is neutralism. While the concepts of neutrality and nonalignment were examined during the 1968 defense policy review, they were quickly discarded.[58] However, a number of public figures—including some retired general officers, diplomats, and historians—have reopened the neutrality debate.[59] Public debate has become more broadly based and the proposals more sophisticated. Neutralists argue that nonalignment is important in reducing tensions and lowering the risk of war. This certainly has widespread appeal and more moderate variations of this theme are gaining visibility in both the Liberal and New Democratic Parties. The reaction of NATO and the United States to a neutral Canada would be expectedly strong. As one analyst states, "the question then is: are Canadians willing to pay the price?"[60]

LOOKING AHEAD

Given the conventional defense improvement initiatives of the 1980s, the Alliance-wide debates over strategy, emerging technology, burden sharing, and Alliance cohesion and the special views of North American and European pillars, what lies in store for Canadian and American defense policies?

One author says that "the players share a sense of high stakes, historic turning points, unparalleled opportunities, and awesome dangers."[61] While dramatic, this claim also happens to be, in my opinion, accurate. To be sure, the positive signs abound. The signed Memoranda of Understanding of the Nunn Amendment, the dovetailing of national programs under the NATO CDI priorities, and the CMF are encouraging. The resurgence of French interest in European defense, individual national initiatives such as Britain's proposal to create a 5,000-man airborne antitank brigade and Spain's desire to provide a helicopter-supported airborne unit to the Franco-German brigade, Belgium's proposal to host a NATO fighter-pilot training program at an airbase soon to be vacated due to the INF agreement, are all favorable omens. The appointment of former West German Defense Minister Manfred Wörner to succeed Lord Carrington as NATO Secretary General is a milestone as it fully recognizes West Germany's contributions to the Alliance.

In the area of armaments planning, so directly related to conventional force improvements, genuine progress also appears evident. Under CNAD, a new NATO Conventional Armaments Review Committee has approved and distributed the Terms of Reference for a two-year trial of a NATO Conventional Armaments Planning System (CAPS). The CAPS process is designed to identify armaments-related military requirements for the long-term, link these requirements to the Long-Term Force Proposal/Long Term Force Goal process, develop national armaments goals, and finally, produce a NATO Conventional Armaments Plan (NCAP).[62] The CAPS establishes an annual Armaments Planning Questionnaire (APQ) akin to the DPQ. Both documents together will produce a more accurate picture of conventional force improvements.

There is increasing discussion about a more formal European pillar in the Alliance, perhaps based upon the existing EUROGROUP and/or the Western European Union (WEU). The forthcoming further liberalization of economic relations within the European Community in 1992 may give increased impetus to greater defense collaboration. At the same time, major problems and difficulties continue among the European members of NATO making closer security cooperation far from easy or automatic. Thus while the Alliance may well be moving toward some kind of new transatlantic bargain, the situation in Europe remains unsettled.

The North American environment is similarly unsettled. Canada has issued a bold White Paper. However, while Alliance leaders generally agree with Defence Minister Beatty's assessment of sixteen years of neglect of Alliance obligations, many would recall the halving of Canada's European forces in 1968 just at the time of agreement on "future tasks of the Alliance" and the adoption of flexible response. Optimists may see the White Paper as a direct response to the latest NATO Conventional Defense Initiative and an opportunity for Canada to dovetail her interests once again with her allies; but the reality is that few specific CDI proposals are receiving "full implementation" as reported in the Canadian DPQ with the majority listed as "implementation with some exceptions" or "under consideration." A number of initiatives are characterized as "no implementation or implementation with significant shortfalls." The White Paper itself, as a long-term plan, remains dependent on fiscal resources. The conventional improvements for Europe, for example, the purchase of new tanks, are high-dollar programs. If nuclear submarines are purchased and the actual cost exceeds estimates, the likelihood increases of fewer tanks being purchased or European force consolidation being delayed. Canada may be perceived as continuing to do less than expected of a full partner. Domestic calls for Canada to ask European allies to help defend North America by stationing a fighter squadron in the Canadian North carry little weight under current circumstances.[63]

At the same time, the United States is clearly headed for a four- to five-year period of austere budgets. Secretary Carlucci readily admitted that he expects to see a "smaller military force."[64] Senator Nunn has once again mentioned troop reductions in Europe, this time tied to conventional force reductions agreements.[65] A major selling point of new technology continues to be personnel savings. Some troop cuts, either phased in small increments in the near- to mid-term or more dramatic in the long-term, seem a logical outcome of one or more of these factors.

Calling attention to the deficiencies of one or more Alliance members will do little for collective defense. Innovative proposals in the areas of expanded civil reserve mobility assets, harmonization of doctrine, force mission specialization, a "NATO basing rights" concept (as opposed to bilateral arrangements), and expanded training of geographically restricted, European forces in North America, pre-positioning of materiel designed to be used by all NATO forces, and re-deployment of forward forces to meet actual war plans are just a few areas for investigation. The NATO Conventional Defense Improvement Program and complementary national efforts represent a window of opportunity on the high side of the NATO conventional force improvement curve. The first signs and sounds of this window closing are in evidence.

Notes

[1]Dwight D. Eisenhower, "First Annual Report to the Standing North Atlantic Treaty Organization" (Paris: Supreme Headquarters Allied Powers Europe, 1952), 34.

[2]North Atlantic Treaty Organization, Defense Planning Committee, 4-5 December 1984, in *NATO Final Communiqués 1981-1985* (Brussels: NATO Information Service, n.d.), 127.

[3]NATO, Defense Planning Committee, 22 May 1985, in ibid., 140.

[4]General Bernard W. Rogers, "NATO's Conventional Defense Improvement Initiative - A New Approach to an Old Challenge," *NATO's Sixteen Nations* 31 (July 1986), 14.

[5]The Conference of National Armaments Directors (CNAD) is the most visible of NATO organizations tasked to make cooperation in arms development and procurement as advantageous as possible. Subordinate groups deal with functional areas (air defense, communications and electronics) and specific services (army, navy, and air). The *HAWK* air defense program, *Sidewinder* missile program, *Tornado* multi-role combat aircraft, are just a few of the genuine successes of Alliance arms cooperation. Other organizations such as the Independent European Program Group (IEPG), EUROGROUP, and Western European Union work to complement NATO efforts but the results overall are mixed.

[6]Interview, Moray Stewart, "Improving NATO Planning," *Defense Attaché*, no. 1, (1986), 32.

[7]See, for example, Michael Stuermer, "After INF, Review NATO Doctrine," *Wall Street Journal*, 30 December 1987, 19; Harlan Cleveland, "Strong European Defense Without Nuclear Arms," *New York Times*, 15 March 1987, 25.

[8]For an excellent review of Socialist defense strategy, see Jonathan Marcus, "A Socialist Defense Strategy for Europe," *Washington Quarterly* 10, no. 4 (Autumn 1987), 76-97.

[9]Ibid., 93.

[10]David Gates, "Non-Offensive Defence: A Strategic Contradiction?" Occasional Paper No. 29 (London: Institute for European Defence and Strategic Studies, 1987).

[11]Gene Sharp, *Making Europe Unconquerable: The Potential of Civilian-Based Deterrence and Defense* (Cambridge, MA.: Ballinger 1985).

[12]David Gates, "Area Defense Concepts: The West German Debate," *Survival*, 29, no. 4 (July-August 1984).

[13]Stanley R. Sloan, "Non-Provocative Defense and NATO," *National Defense* 71, no. 423 (December 1986), 24-28.

[14]General Cornelius de Jager, "NATO's Strategy," *NATO Review* 34 (October 1986), 9-14; Vice-Admiral J. J. R. Oswald and Wing-Commander R. McKendrick, "Flexible Response — Is There an Alternative?" *RUSI Journal* 131, no. 1 (March 1986), 20-25; and Matthew Goodman, "Two Europes: Air Land Battle Versus Alternative Defense," *Defense & Disarmament News* (December 1985/January 1986), 3-5. A most thorough article in support of forward defense is Philip A. Karber, "In Defense of Forward Defense," *Armed Forces Journal* (May 1984).

[15]General Bernard W. Rogers, "Follow-On Forces Attack (FOFA): Myths and Realities," *NATO Review* 32, no. 6 (December 1984), 1-9.

[16]See Samuel P. Huntington, ed., *The Strategic Imperative: New Policies for American Security* (Cambridge, MA: Ballinger, 1982), for the earliest exposition of the offensive military strategy. The impact of this proposal can be partially judged by the fact that the United States Army War College held a special conference in July 1983 to

discuss it. The result was Keith A. Dunn and William O. Staudenmaier, eds., *Military Strategy in Transition: Deterrence and Defense in the 1980s*, Studies in International Security Affairs and Military Strategy (Boulder, CO: Westview Press, 1984). Huntington's vigorous defense of his theories in 1984 fueled the FOFA controversy.

[17]Roger Fontaine, "Emerging Technology: Is it Right for NATO?" *Washington Times*, 2 June 1986, 6.

[18]Bruce L. R. Smith, "A New Technology Gap in Europe?" *SAIS Review* (Winter/Spring 1986), 219. While Smith's article relates specifically to the Strategic Defense Initiative, his research on European progress toward technological cooperation is informative.

[19]Ibid., 236.

[20]United States, Department of Defense, *Support of NATO Strategy in the 1990s*, A Report to the United States Congress by Frank C. Carlucci, Secretary of Defense (Washington, D.C.: U.S. Government Printing Office, January 1988).

[21]General Andrew J. Goodpaster, et al., *Strengthening Conventional Deterrence in Europe* (Boulder, CO: Westview Press, 1985). See also Andrew J. Pierre ed., *The Conventional Defense of Europe: New Technologies and New Strategies* (New York: Council on Foreign Relations, 1986).

[22]Frederick Bonnart, "NATO and High Technology," *Military Technology* 10, no. 4 (April 1986), 13.

[23]Gregory A. Fossedal, "When Smart Technology Outpaces Arms Agreements...," *New York City Tribune*, 22 August 1986, 9.

[24]As quoted in Eisenhower, "First Annual Report to the Standing Group North Atlantic Treaty Organization," 7.

[25]United States, Department of Defense, *Report on Allied Contributions to the Common Defense*, A Report to the United States Congress by Frank C. Carlucci, Secretary of Defense (Washington, D.C.: April 1988), 90, 101.

[26]James B. Steinberg, "Rethinking the Debate on Burden-sharing," *Survival* 29, no. 1 (January/February 1987), 70.

[27]Leonard Sullivan, Jr., "Allied Burden Sharing: Another View," *Atlantic Community Quarterly* 24 (Spring 1986), 79. Sullivan supports the argument that European Allies are not pulling their share, but recognizes the danger of simple statistical valuations. For a view supporting European contributions see Jonathan Paul Yates, "Burden Sharing in NATO: Myth and Reality," ibid., 24 (Spring 1986), 67-72.

[28]Jack A. LeCuyer, "Burden Sharing: Has the Term Outlived Its Usefulness?" Ibid. 24 (Spring 1986), 63-65.

[29]Henry Kissinger, "A Plan to Reshape NATO," *Time* (5 March 1984), 20- 24 and Zbigniew Brzezinski, "Getting Our Global Strategies Together," *Washington Times*, 15 January 1987, D-1.

[30]Fred C. Iklé et al, *Discriminate Deterrence*, A Report of the Commission on Integrated Long-Term Strategy (Washington, D.C.: U.S. Government Printing Office, January 1988).

[31]Ibid., 2.

[32]Ernest Conine, "A Strategy Study Worth Another Look," *Los Angeles Times*, 2 February 1988, II.

[33]Ibid., 7.

[34]United States, The White House, *National Security Strategy of the United States*, (Washington, D.C.: January 1988), 25-35 and United States, Joint Chiefs of Staff, Military Posture FY 1989 (Washington, D.C.: U.S. Government Printing Office, January 1988), 2-6.

[35]*Military Posture FY 1989*, 93.

[36]United States, Department of Defense, *Annual Report to the Congress*, FY 1989 Report of Secretary of Defense Frank R. Carlucci (Washington, D.C.: U.S. Government Printing Office, February 1988), 115-18.

[37]United States, *Congressional Record - Senate* (21 December 1987), S18877-S18879. Senator Quayle's estimate of $75 billion mirrors a figure quoted by Representative Les Aspin, Democrat, who is Chairman, House Armed Services Committee. However, Aspin would use the money for a ten division force build-up. See Les Aspin, interviewed by David Brinkley, George F. Will, Sam Donaldson, 20 September 1987, in ABC News *This Week with David Brinkley*, Transcript, American Broadcasting Companies, Inc., Washington, D.C. There is little evidence of any support for conventional force build- up.

[38]Jesse Schulman,"Nunn Initiative Spurring NATO to Cooperate, Cut Arms Costs," *Atlanta Journal & Constitution*, 22 March 1987, 33; David Dickson, "Europeans Wary of U.S. Offer on Military R&D," *Science* (18 April 1986), 314; and Dan Beyers, "In Push for Joint Ventures, Programs May Get Funds," *Defense News*, 8 February 1988, 6.

[39]Dickson, "Europeans Wary of U.S. Offer on Military R&D," 314.

[40]For example, Christopher Layne, "Defense Dollars: Our Allies Can Pull Their Own Weight," *Chicago Tribune*, 20 January 1988, 15; Gilbert A. Lewthwaite, "Europeans Foresee U.S. Pressure to Boost Defense Share, But Don't Offer Much," *Baltimore Sun*, 25 February 1988, 4; and Tyler Marshall, "Defense Outlays Give NATO Needed Muscle," *Los Angeles Times*, 31 July 1988, 1.

[41]Paul Mann, "U.S. Weapon Export Sales Face Waning Demand, Rising Competition," *Aviation Week and Space Technology* 126, no. 6 (9 February 1987), 134-135.

[42]Patrick Wall, "Europe Holds Its Breath on G-R-H," *Sea Power* 29, no. 5 (April 1986), 62, 69.

[43]As quoted in David Buchan, "Carrington Puts Stress on US Role in Europe," *Financial Times* (London), 18 September 1987, 2.

[44]Caspar Weinberger, "US European Troop Withdrawals," Speech presented before the Denver Rotary Club on 22 January 1987 (Washington, D.C.: Office of the Secretary of Defense, Public Affairs, 1987).

[45]Richard Burt, "America Needs Troops in Europe," *Washington Post*, 22 March 1987, C-2.

[46]Ibid.

[47]Canada, Department of National Defence, *Challenge and Commitment: A Defence Policy for Canada* (Ottawa: Minister of Supply and Services, 1987), 111. (Hereafter cited as White Paper.)

[48]General Gérard C. E. Thériault, "Whither the Alliance? What Price Security?" presented at the Foreign Policy Conference, Canadian Foreign Policy: Preparing for the 21st Century, Canadian Institute of International Affairs, 25-27 March 1988, Ottawa, Canada.

[49]The source for this alternative proposal is a recent interview with a former senior defense official who was personally aware of active discussions in this area at the highest levels. This assessment is corroborated by other defense experts.

[50]In the same period of time as NATO allies fielded one new tank, the Soviet Union has fielded at least three new tanks and is working on a fourth. The future Soviet tank is allegedly to mount an automatically loaded, 135-mm gun and incorporate the latest armor technology.

[51]Derek Blackburn, M.P., *Canadian Sovereignty, Security and Defence* (Ottawa: The New Democrats, n.d.), 22.

[52]Paul George, "New NATO Role for Canada," *International Perspectives* (November/December 1987), 9.

[53]Ibid.

[54]Ibid., 10.

[55]Canada, Department of National Defence, White Paper, 67.

[56]Senior DND and External Affairs personnel are sensitive to queries regarding funding issues, as well they should be. However, too often their response to Allies' questions is to take refuge behind national closed doors. Yet,Canada's response to NATO's Annual Defense Planning Review Questionnaire requires substantive financial data. The questions will not simply go away.

[57]Charles F. Doran, "Sovereignty Does Not Equal Security," *Peace & Security* 2, no. 3 (Autumn 1987), 9.

[58]Jocelyn Coulon, "Another Path for Canada?" *Peace & Security* 2, no. 1 (Spring 1987), 8-9.

[59]See, for example, Gwynne Dyer and Tina Viljoen, "The Defence of Canada," production of CBC/National Film Board of Canada, 1986. This television series emphasized the need for greater Canadian independence and the alternatives available in defense policy.

[60]Coulon, "Another Path for Canada?" 9.

[61]Smith, "A New Technology Gap in Europe?" 236.

[62]North Atlantic Military Committee Memorandum, Subject: Meeting of the NATO Conventional Armaments Review Committee (NCARC), 23 February 1988, 1-20. Enclosures include Terms of Reference and Trial Guidance for CAPS. The NCARC has received strong support from a recent CSIS study. See David M. Abshire et al., *NATO: Meeting the Coming Challenge - An Alliance Action Plan for Conventional Improvements and Armaments Cooperation* (Washington, D.C.: Center for Strategic and International Studies, 1987), viii, 32-33.

[63]Jeff Sallot, "Experts Want NATO Forces in North," *Globe and Mail*, 22 March 1988, A8.

[64]As quoted in *Defence Daily*, 29 January 1988, 145.

[65]Lawrence L. Knutson, "Nunn Would Cut Troops in Europe," *Philadelphia Inquirer*, 7 February 1988, 5.

3

The Contemporary Defense Debate in Canada

John Young

To write off neutralist sentiment in Canada as crankish or aberrational is a major misinterpretation of the public mood in the 1960s.

James Eayrs, November 1960[1]

Discussion of Canadian foreign policy has of late been much enlivened by the introduction of the concepts of neutrality and non-alignment.

Geoffrey Pearson, April 1987[2]

INTRODUCTION

As these observations by two of the country's keener students of domestic debates on national and international security issues attest, neutralist sentiment in Canada has peaked during two distinct phases of the American-Soviet relationship in the post-World War II era: those periods marked by heightened tensions from 1959 to 1962 and from 1979 to 1985 subsequent to the generalized public accreditation of perceptions that the Soviet Union had achieved a viable strategic nuclear retaliatory capability. In the discussion that follows, I will argue that a relation of cause and effect links these domestic and international phenomena. As well, I seek to demonstrate that at the core of Canadian debates on the relative merits of alignment and neutrality lie opposing threat assessments. The theme that relations of power in the international security domain condition systems of political thought is woven against the backdrop of government, pressure-group, and parliamentary threat formulations so as to better show how those formulations or definitions have undercut Canadian commitment to alliance mechanisms predicated on the concept of extended nuclear deterrence.

Eurocentric multilaterism has been an integral component, if not the bedrock, of the West's postwar international security regime. Current trends in intra-NATO relations, prompted in large part by the same generic forces that have inspired neutralist thinking in Canada and pointing to the eventual emergence of a two-pillared North Atlantic collective-deterrent mechanism, augur ill for the Canadian national interest as that notion has been generally understood, and are already working to exacerbate Canadian skepticism with regard to the ongoing efficacy of organic Western solidarity in the security field. Should the next swing of the pro-neutralist pendulum occur in the context of a quasi-exclusionary bilateral U.S.-Canadian collective-deterrent relationship, Canada's postwar self-perception as an honest yet allied broker in international security affairs could be subjected to stringent testing. Quite plausibly, the ultimate resolution of the Canadian alignment-versus-neutrality debate will be determined by the fashion in which the stresses attending that testing are resolved. In particular, this calling to account of the carefully nurtured internationalist persona of the country is likely to attend any breakdown of the American-Soviet détente that is now in progress.[3]

Notwithstanding government-sanctioned support for the two-pillar notion on both sides of the Atlantic, there are a number of eminently sound reasons for holding that the tensile strength of the transoceanic strategic link is inversely proportional to the degree of free-standing autonomy of its North American and European support structures. The latter, quite to the contrary of the metaphor invoked, remain upright because they lean on the transversal span. Since it is the bridge that supports the pillars, the forces of continentalism are, and have been since NATO's formation, in essential contradiction with Atlanticism. The Canadian founders of the Alliance understood this well, and strove to promote a thoroughgoing Atlanticist orientation within NATO.[4] Under concerted pressure from the very beginning, this orientation is now experiencing especially strong lateral strains.[5]

It is in this West-West context of incremental fissiparousness, then, that the internal debates on the merits of Alliance membership take on the full measure of their importance for Canadians. Although the arguments on both sides of this frequently acrimonious dispute tend to focus on the possible ramifications that its resolution would have for the existing international security regime, there can be no doubt that Canadians have a distinctly national stake as well in its outcome and, during fluid and relatively amorphous phases such as the present one, in its particular contours.

It is my contention that the Alliance disengagement debate within Canada retains its ongoing relevance despite the overwhelming defeat in the 1988 federal election of the only one of the country's three major political parties formally opposed to a predominantly Atlanticist collective-defense commitment.

In the pages that follow, the incipient linkage between the intra-Alliance debates on the "widening Atlantic"[6] and the Canadian domestic debate on NATO-participation is set out in an effort to clarify what is most assuredly an intriguing political phenomenon: intermittent public mooting of de facto neutralism as a live policy option within a nation that has "grown up allied" and that has been said to incorporate a commitment to alignment as an integral component of its political culture.

NEUTRALIST SENTIMENT IN CANADA: THE DISPOSING EFFECT OF GLOBAL RELATIONS OF POWER

The approximate 25-year hiatus between high points in neutralist leanings in Canada would seem to suggest, at least at first glance, the utility of an explanatory analysis that focuses on generational change. Such a prism has been employed, to good effect, in the cases of several NATO-Europe and Warsaw Treaty Organization countries.[7] But explanatory approaches derived from attitude surveys distinguishing among age groupings have tended to capture representations of step-phased evolutionary change rather than cyclical movements in opinion. Indeed, that is what the multi-nation study of the European successor generation (referred to immediately above) achieved and, moreover, was designed to accomplish. Similarly, after carefully weighing the available data on American public opinion across generations with regard to a closely related topic, relative support for containment policy, Ole Holsti concluded that "there is little in these survey results to indicate that the inevitable replacement of one generation by its successor will yield significant changes in public opinion ... generational differences may not be the most fruitful place to look for the dynamics of change."[8]

While there are elements of evolutionary generational change that do appear to be operative in the Canadian case,[9] the periodic waxing and waning of neutralist sentiment points to some larger, more encompassing, phenomenon in the conditioning environment as a plausible driving force. To some analysts of current debates on national and international security issues in Canada, this observation might suggest the need for an indigenous theory of political cycles along the lines of those developed by Arthur Schlesinger and Albert Hirschman[10] for the American historical experience. Filling that need is not my purpose in this chapter, but it does bear mentioning in this context that Schlesinger's scheme, on closer scrutiny, reveals a decisive dependency on external pressures rather than on internally driven action-reaction sequences in society-ordering choice hierarchies, while Hirschman's emphasis on economistic individual goals cannot be transferred to a domain that is essentially political in nature.

One could, of course, forego any attempt at explanation and offer a primarily descriptive account of the more recent wave of anti-Alliance thinking in Canada; there is certainly an ample literature to employ for that effect. If reference to the previous blip on the meter of Western-Alliance fidelity were required to complete the description, recourse might be had simply to various formulations expressing the homespun wisdom of that American wordsmith, Yogi Berra, to the general effect that "it's *déjà vu* all over again."[11] But that would leave us without a testable hypothesis susceptible of yielding insights into the political "puzzle" at hand.

Academic specialists in international relations, especially those interested primarily in political relations, frequently seek recourse to a tripartite division in their search for causal origin: human nature; the internal structure of states and domestic politics; and, the interstate system envisaged in its global dimensions. In an already classic modern statement of this procedure for first-cut approximations of the real world, Kenneth Waltz referred to these categorizations as first, second and third images respectively.[12] They are not exclusionary prisms by any means, since all three elements quite obviously push and pull in various combinations within an ongoing interactional matrix, but it is nonetheless useful to have some clear notion as to why one of these levels of analysis should be favored over the other two.[13]

Third-image conceptual modeling has been chosen here as the most appropriate means of analytical entry since it allows for immediate integration of what still appear to be the salient factors in international political equations, the coexistence of overarching and subtending relations of power. "Still" is used advisedly here in recognition of the many assertions that have been made defending the view that nuclear weapons, and more importantly, nuclear duopolies and oligopolies involving plausible adversaries have worked revolutionary effects in the international system's ordering principles. This putative truth, however, can be seen more accurately as a normatively mediated prescription rather than as a descriptive summary of nuclear-era international politics. It must cede before the manifest political leveraging of the nuclear threat that has been a constant since 1945.[14]

The most recent exemplar formulation of a system-level explanatory framework for conceptualizing international political relations accords preeminent importance to the distribution of relative capabilities among the interstate system's principal units at any given time.[15] In following on that approach, a reasoned search for the primary disposing influence in the present instance should focus on the Soviet-American dyad, and by logical extension, to those polarizing states' alliances. It is no state secret that cyclical swings between phases of relatively different levels of reciprocal tension have been part and parcel of the U.S.-Soviet relationship from the collapse of the Grand Alliance to the present. These swings and phases have been described and accounted for by numerous students of international security.[16]

A generally accredited shorthand chronology might read as follows: 1947 to 1954 — deteriorating relations, Cold War; 1955 to 1958 — uncertainty, some hopeful signs of greater mutual accommodation punctuated by major setbacks; 1959 to 1962 — deteriorating relations; 1963 to 1979 — cathartic Cuban Missile Crisis invigorates cooperative relations, highpoint of détente roughly 1973 (despite Prague Spring suppression and Vietnam), gradual downturn from 1975; 1979 to 1984 — breakdown of détente, "Cold War II"; and, 1985 to the present — improving relations. It is possible to quibble over some details of this pattern but a correlating pendulum movement for the dependent variable has been clearly identified, with high-tension phases located from 1959 to 1962 and from 1979 to 1984. It is in the nature of the process of course that the post-1957 downturns followed upon hopeful phases, tending to accentuate mutual and third-party perceptions of missed opportunities, wilfully inspired discord, or abuse of trust.[17] Whether in sorrow or in anger, reactions in the troughs were marked by acrimony and bitterness. More importantly for Americans and their allies, what came to be designated as Mutual Assured Destruction had begun to be perceived as a fact of life. If you could still run but no longer hide, what collective-defense good did extended nuclear deterrent regimes provide?

Quite understandably in terms of third-image (or "structural-realist") appreciations of international politics, it was in this qualitatively different context of a more generalized existential threat that American security managers and political leaderships first gave their benediction to the two-pillar concept. At the same time, and for many of the same reasons, the political class in Canada began to think seriously, and give voice to, alternative conceptions of what might be more appropriate security structures for the country in the new circumstances.[18] Official American sponsorship of the two-pillar idea and the much more generalized public mooting in Canada of neutralist thinking during the first downturn in the MAD era were but two faces of the same coin. In national security terms, that coin represented the devalued currency of a thoroughgoing Atlanticist acceptance of equality of risk.[19]

Canada's situation in respect of both East-West security in general, and relations with the superpowers in particular, occasions debate of a nature that has been and remains at once normative, institutional, and geopolitical. The first component, expressing the perceptual filtering process by which the contours of East-West relations are mediated by belief systems and value hierarchies, has undergone major change since the early 1950s. On the basis of extensive survey data, Don Munton has concluded for instance that: "During the cold war period most Canadians had essentially positive perceptions about the U.S. and essentially negative perceptions of the USSR. It is no longer so. Perhaps most striking of all in the 1987 survey is an evident tendency on the part of many individual Canadians to be negative about both superpowers' policies."[20] The second, encompassing Canada's NATO affiliations and its joint defense arrangements with the United States, has been subject to convolution over time, from the heyday of the bomber era, through the Diefenbaker era's fiascos,[21] through fitful but far from earnest consolidation during the Liberal tenure, to current distancing (or at least diffidence) on such American-sponsored concepts as the Strategic and Air Defense Initiatives, advanced cruise missile (ACM) development and testing, and the forward Maritime Strategy.[22] The third, deriving from the country's geographical position between the Soviet Union and the United States in polar projections, or the proverbial "ham in the sandwich" metaphor, has varied as a function of technological change in weapons systems and surveillance and warning infrastructures, of evolution in strategic doctrines, and of changes in the East-West power equation especially at the level of strategic deterrent forces, including basing and deployment modes.[23]

These normative, institutional, and geopolitical linkages in the Canadian-Alliance nexus would provide prima facie grounds for supposing that there might well be a relationship of cause and effect operating between the independent and dependent variables identified in this discussion: high tension phases in American-Soviet relations and greater degrees of generalized public legitimacy in Canada for a neutralist orientation. As I argue below, examination of the rationales put forward by supporters of withdrawal from NATO offers confirmatory evidence of the validity of a connective link between the two phenomena. For the moment, a working hypothesis to express this link can be formulated: neutralist sentiment in Canada varies as a function of the perceived degree of central-system war proneness, especially when conditioned by mutual assured retaliatory capabilities. This proposition is entirely consistent with the reasoning of Stephen Walt's persuasive "balance-of-threat" theory with respect to Alliance formation and participation,[24] and its predictive content would include the projection that neutralist leanings in Canada will be attentuated in periods of détente in central theater political relations.

It will be understood from earlier commentary that Canadian perceptions of the East-West divide are conditioned by perceptions of superpower relations. The complex of cross-cutting influences in the European security matrix, for all intents and purposes, do not form a constituent element of Canadians' cognition of the postwar security environment.[25] Thus, the only proviso that would need to be added to the hypothesis explored here involves some allowance for a time lag between the onset of perceived downturns in central theater security relations and the reactive Canadian pro-neutralist groundswell. It is during this phase of what cyberneticists and systems theorists would call "information processing" by the systemic unit that domestic reordering of threat perceptions occurs.

Similar account should be taken for phased adjustment to renewed détente and improved East-West relations, during which time alignment predispositions are reasserted amid declining but still vigorous anti-Alliance rump constituencies. Those constituencies do and will retain a certain degree of residual strength, deriving from what can only be described as an irreducible ideological prism predicated on the twin tenets of an absolute rejection of nuclear weaponry for whatever purpose (including the deterrence of war), and a persistently skeptical view of the goals and methods of American foreign policy. Accordingly, their proselytizing efforts will pay dividends when real-world referents start to provide some plausibility to the world view to which they so assiduously adhere. That the first MAD-era détente coincided with the American phase of Vietnam-centered warfare in southeast Asia lent a measure of credibility to the apostolic message of the true-believing neutralists in Canada.[26] This may account for the relative, if diminished, staying power of neutralist thinking among the public during the later 1960s and the 1970s and, consequently, the wider swath cut by the neutralist arc during "Cold War II." But both phenomena are also consistent with generalized public accreditation of the Soviets' progressive consolidation of strategic equivalency. This leads me to suggest that neither the "ugly-American" nor the "ugly-American-and-ugly-Soviet" theses are persuasive as explanations for the direction of neutralist-versus-alignment trendlines in Canada. It can be posited therefore, "Vietnams" and "Afghanistans" notwithstanding, that progressively deeper indentations in the Canadian support base for NATO are to be anticipated if the recent pattern of Soviet-American rivalry is restored *and* if their mutual-war-avoidance strategies continue to be predicated on nuclear deterrence. Moreover, the growth of the neutralist constituency should be the greater for the rapidity with which the tension-détente cycle revolves.

THE FIRST NEUTRALIST TURN: 1959-1962

The Soviet Sputnik launch of 1957 posed new dilemmas for NATO, resulting from the specter of American territorial vulnerability.[27] These would prove resistant to speedy resolution.[28] After a decade of hauling and pushing on both sides of the Atlantic, the catch-all deterrent concept of "flexible response" seemed to offer the best compromise possible for an Alliance confronted with fragile interior lines of resupply in conventional war scenarios and the political imperative of refusing to trade space for time in its operational plans and declaratory policies. Adopted in 1967 as the Alliance's doctrinal catechism, flexible response has retained its status against all alternative strategies primarily because it allows honest men and women to agree to disagree in a high-stakes environment and because uncertainty and doctrinal amorphousness is a virtue in deterrent policies predicated on the threat of nuclear reprisal. Natural geographic disadvantages and the West German-American compact of equality of risk that lies at the heart of the Western Alliance can be managed but not altered, except of course by the actions of the potential adversary.

The purposeful open-endedness of the flexible response doctrine, in attenuating the divisive tendencies inherent in extended-deterrent regimes under conditions of strategic nuclear parity, has served the Alliance well. It has helped especially in facilitating the management task of maintaining internal cohesion in the face of the centrifugal forces that drive two-pillar or "dumbbell" thinking.

The history of the flexible response issue demonstrates that even the most trying postwar strategic dilemmas are amenable to creative solutions by informed and determined political leaderships. Unfortunately, those qualities of leadership were lacking in Canada at the turn of the decade[29] immediately following Soviet acquisition of an ICBM capability. As a divided Cabinet careened from one security policy crisis to the next, Canadian defense policy-making became effectively rudderless and unduly subject to external, primarily American, influence.

While reactive national impulses did amplify the existential fears that the new strategic context had awakened,[30] the attention of the country was now focused as it never had been at any prior moment of the postwar period on the West's instrumentalities of nuclear-era security politics.[31] NORAD and NATO headed this blacklist primarily, but not exclusively, for reasons deriving from the newly perceived linkage of those mechanisms to American policies beyond the geographical scope of NATO, particularly to the degree that those policies were seen to involve the leveraging of the nuclear threat for politically aggressive goals,[32] and from a concern for what was seen to be the fragile stability of the nuclear standoff.[33]

It was in the radically new strategic context of reciprocal American and Soviet vulnerability to nuclear attack, then, that public interest in neutrality, understood throughout this discussion as a disposition to seek "a general alternative to alliances and alliance policy,"[34] reached levels of political saliency. The triggering and sustaining force that drove this revision of Canadian imaging of the postwar international security environment, it bears emphasizing, was a reordering of the threat assessment as a result of heightened tensions between the superpowers.[35] Relative both to high-tension phases in pre-MAD East-West relations, when Canadian political authorities had been prepared to contribute willingly to American-led responses to aggressive breaches of the postwar status quo,[36] and to pre-MAD and MAD détente phases, Canada became a most reluctant ally indeed. It was in this domestic context that a Canadian Prime Minister and a Canadian political executive, alone among NATO member states, and even though joined to American strategic systems through NORAD, could find it expedient to decline to back the U.S. position during the initial days of the Cuban missile crisis. In fact, it required a mutiny of sorts by the country's naval authorities for the ordering of supportive Atlantic patrols. The Cuban crisis revealed that de facto neutrality within de jure alliance could have concrete policy ramifications, of import moreover for the security interests of Canada's formal allies.

Residual traces of neutralist sentiment remained subsequent to the emergence of the détente that followed in the wake of the missile crisis, but they were never considered sufficiently broad-based to merit the kind of commentary that had been accorded disengagement advocacies of just a short time before. Apart from some university-based voices, including those of expatriate Americans,[37] inspired by attitudes of Cold War revisionism, the détente-era brand of Canadian neutralist thinking was largely confined to the new Trudeauite Liberal elite[38] and the NDP.

Previously identified with the New Democrats' view of foreign policy issues, and indeed with their domestic political agenda as well, Pierre Trudeau had been catapulted to power to manage and resolve a national-unity crisis, not to restructure the country's security policy. The aura of contrivance that surrounded the Liberal Party's approach to Alliance issues was not to dissipate until the launching of what became known as the Prime Minister's "Peace Initiative" in the midst of the second MAD-era downturn in Soviet-American relations.[39] Given the altered international environment, it is hardly surprising that Canadians rallied as at no previous moment to Trudeau's conception of the requirements for comity in East-West relations.

The NDP's espousal of neutralism during the post-1962 détente period, for its part, inversed Acton's dictum regarding the corrupting nature of power, the Party having no serious chance of being obliged to implement its new policy. In later times, when they sensed their main chance for an electoral breakthrough, and significantly enough during the détente phase that had begun in 1985, the New Democrats put the NATO-withdrawal question as far out of partisan contention as the Party's internal cohesion would permit. Now, not one but two victories at the polls, say NDP leaders, would be required for democratic authorization to leave the Alliance.[40]

THE SECOND NEUTRALIST TURN: 1979-1984

In-house researchers at the Canadian Institute for International Peace and Security (CIIPS), itself a child of Canadian consternation and alarm during the most recent cycle of high tensions between Washington and Moscow,[41] offered the following remark in 1986:

> Canadians are, and have long been, firm supporters of the NATO alliance and Canada's participation in it. Approval of the alliance has typically been substantial since the NATO treaty was signed in 1949, and there is no evident current trend toward a decline. A recent Goldfarb survey found 85 % supporting continued Canadian participation in NATO, and those more knowledgeable about international affairs tended to be most supportive.[42]

About a year after that summary assessment was issued — and it is in no way atypical of opinion-survey commentary on support levels for NATO — CIIPS commissioned and funded "the most extensive national survey conducted on attitudes to the superpowers, peace and security in terms of the range of questions it comprises."[43] In it, the sample group was asked to indicate the extent to which they agreed or disagreed with this statement:

Even though Canada is a member of NATO, I tend to think of Canada as being neutral between the two superpowers.[44]

The breakdown in the responses is shown in table 3.1.

Table 3.1
Public Perception of Canadian Neutrality

Level of Agreement		Response (percentage)
Totally disagree	1	8
	2	6
	3	12
	4	7
	5	11
	6	7
	7	10
	8	14
	9	8
Totally agree	10	17

Source: Don Munton, *Peace and Security in the 1980s: The View of Canadians* (Ottawa: Canadian Institute for International Peace and Security, 1988), 59.

Thus, a majority of Canadians (56 percent) tended either to see Canadian policy stances on American-Soviet issues positioned on middle or perhaps independent ground (or, conceivably, simply on irrelevant or non-existent ground), or to have given expression to normative imaging of the country's international persona in the great power context that is reflective of a disposition for non-partisanship in the major international security issues of the times. Unfortunately the question was formulated in such a manner that even critical judgments on systematic fence-sitting could be incorporated under the pro-neutralist masthead, so caution is in order when interpreting response patterns to "the" neutrality question in the survey.

Nevertheless, if the replies are taken at face value, then the generally high levels of support reported for Alliance adhesion in most polling grossly overstate the firmness of Canadian commitment to NATO. If only the three degrees at each end of the CIIPS response scale are considered, 39 percent of Canadians think rather strongly that their country is and should be neutral as between the Alliance's guarantor and the state that is conventionally seen as providing its very rationale,[45] while only 26 percent take the contrary view.

What is more, the new détente or at the least the end of deteriorating relations in the central dyad had already been noted (35 percent and 52 percent respectively) at the time of polling.[46] A few months earlier, in April 1987, the Department of External Affairs (DEA) commissioned a survey by the same polling organization, The Longwoods Research Group; this also showed 48 percent of Canadians as perceiving a warming trend over the course of the previous year, although fully 50 percent had remarked no change, whether for the better or the worse, in East-West relations.[47] The extent of neutralist sympathy abroad in the country, even after perceptions of the spirit of the November 1985 Geneva Summit had begun to make inroads within the collective consciousness, bears testimony to the philosophical shallowness of the Canadian public's attachment to Western collective-defense mechanisms.

In periods of heightened great power tension, the fragility of Canadian support can become remarkable indeed. For example, the telecasting, during Sunday evening prime time, of a three-part series on Canada's defense policies that culminated in a call for an exemplary national rejection of the postwar alliance structure shook the firmness and consistency that is said to characterize the Canadian public's disposition for alignment. Despite this National Film Board production's patent tendentiousness and warmed-over Cold War revisionism,[48] Canadians were so swayed by its neutralist plea that the Mulroney Government deemed it appropriate to try to set the historical (and contemporary) record straight.[49] A follow-on NFB production vaunting the merits of Scandinavian (and generally Nordic) neutrality, has never been telecast. Nor has its precursor paean been retelecast. One can, moreover, safely assume that neither will see network time in the near future. Both, however, are favored by the country's Cold War II-era peace movement and are screened on a regular basis in classrooms and various other settings, where their message is largely quarantined from counter-argument.[50] Since tracking public opinion on security issues is just beginning in Canada,[51] it is extremely difficult to demarcate shifts in attitude trendlines with the precision that most researchers would consider desirable. Thus, my citing of such incidents as the telecasting of the pro-neutralist NFB film and the reactions it provoked are but part of what, of necessity, must be a corpus of largely circumstantial evidence.

Despite the regular reporting of massive public support for alignment, that support has become largely an expression of Alliance formalism and significantly underplays the policy-relevant force of neutralist sentiment within the country. A majority of Canadians, for instance, would "accept defeat and Soviet control of Europe" rather than sanction the use of nuclear weapons to arrest an aggression. A majority thinks that Canada should become a nuclear weapons-free zone, even though the survey question was prefaced by the suggestion that "such a policy would weaken the western alliance and cause serious problems with Canada's allies, especially the United States." Fully 81 percent believe that nuclear weapons testing should be totally banned. Sixty-eight percent think that "Canada should refuse to allow further cruise testing," although here a leading question was asked that falsely implied that the United States was not pursuing arms reductions. Sixty-five percent believe that Western Europe should take "more responsibility for its own defence" and that the Canadian Government should "press" that view. Only 23 percent of Canadians favor an "increase in the size of our armed forces in Europe," while 29 percent say that Canada's force commitments to Europe should be reduced (10 percent) or completely withdrawn (19 percent). Yet, 58 percent believed that "the Soviet military threat is constantly growing and represents a real, immediate threat to the West." Only 4 percent dissented strongly from that view of Soviet capabilities, and only 7 percent thought, in response to another question, that "the Soviet Union and its allies" were militarily weaker than "the United States and its allies," while 31 percent saw clear military superiority on the Soviet side.[52]

Clearly, this opinion profile reflects a highly vitiated form of commitment. Majoritarian patterns show that the Alliance's strategy of flexible response is not supported, that the task of raising the nuclear threshold should fall on others, that a species of decoupling "dumbbell" or two-pillar thinking is preferred, and that Canada should oppose "neither-confirm-nor-deny" nuclear weapons transiting in its own jurisdictional areas.[53] There is a rejection of the principle of equality of risk, a rejection of increased burden-sharing beyond specifically Canadian needs, an ambivalence toward the goals and purposes of the West's leading power, and a defeatist passivity in the face of a perceived Soviet military superiority.

These indices of neutralist tendencies in Canadian attitudes have never come close to putting the country's membership in the Western Alliance at risk, for as the late John Holmes remarked "[Canada] can only resign once"[54] and there has been a pragmatic acceptance in the MAD era — at least to this point — that, whatever the membership-fee circumstances require, that minimum tariff should be paid: legitimate neutrality or non-alignment simply does not have any cost-benefit persuasiveness.[55] The Canadian contribution to the Alliance relative to other members need not be reiterated here, but it should be noted that, if left to its own devices, any Canadian Government would have been tempted to further reduce the country's European commitments, as the Conservatives evidently were in 1985,[56] as a result of domestic political ramifications stemming from the renewed tensions in the Soviet-American relationship.[57] As Jockel and Sokolsky have observed, "NATO has the Canadian commitment it deserves,"[58] and if Canadian forces are still in the FRG it is not by Canadian inspiration. This example merely serves to demonstrate that the neutralist heuristic has tangible and important effects on policy choice. It has substantive content. It is a political reality of impressive force that weighs heavily, as David Easton would say, in the "authoritative allocation of values for (Canadian) society."[59]

The range of specific programs and initiatives that gave texture to the new Cold War of the early 1980s and to which Canadians responded has been covered quite thoroughly in the literature.[60] Suffice it to say here that Canadian nerve-ends were agitated for the most part by the doctrinal adjustments, operational planning, procurement targets and R&D programs of their principal ally, rather than by, say, *Oscar I*-Class SSGNs, *Akula*-Class SSNs, *Backfire* bombers, European-theater OMGs, or even SS-25s and SS-20s. This asymmetry in judgment, needless to say, is far from being a predilection exclusive to Canadians among the Western allies.

Be that as it may, Canadians have convincingly demonstrated that they are reluctant participants, via alliance structures, in MAD-era hardball. In periods of declining mutual confidence in superpower relations it would appear that perceptions accredit the view that Western deterrent mechanisms actively contribute to nuclear war proneness rather than to war-avoidance. This seems to have been the case in the years leading up to the final shattering of the détente process in 1979, as well as throughout the tense years of the early 1980s.[61] Similarly motivated discomfiture was evidenced in the early 1960s.

This earlier period, it should be recalled, was characterized by publicly conducted debates in the United States from about 1956 onwards concerning the need for greater discrimination in the choice of options for the use of force to advance policy objectives. The doctrine of massive retaliation had given way to notions of graduated escalation by 1958, but fiscal conservatism continued to support continuity in action policy. During the presidential election campaign of 1960, the notion of the precursor American variant of flexible response gained currency, so much so that it was given doctrinal status in 1961. It is important to remember that the potential use of theater and tactical nuclear weapons was never separated doctrinally from the increasing emphasis on conventional capabilities. Indeed, the mooting of selective nuclear use was integrated within a burgeoning literature on the theory of limited war. This meant that nuclear fire could be expected to be brought to bear, if required, in regions where core Soviet national interests were not at stake. Thus, discussions of limited nuclear options meshed with North-South issues. The new doctrine did, to be sure, encompass a very heavy dose of damage-limitation capability in the central-theater scenarios, and it accredited the use of the nuclear threat for its efficacy in leveraging political issues in the NATO-WTO context.[62] The major context, however, in which contemporary Canadian debates on Alliance disengagement became linked (not sympathetically) with the Kennedy administration's willingness "to bear any burden" was in respect of U.S. policy toward the developing and non-aligned world — what would later be termed the Third World.

Both James Eayrs and Peyton Lyon identified this East-West versus North-South tension in the first round of the alignment-neutrality debate. Eayrs commented that:

Subservience to Washington, our readiness to follow the American line on such matters as recognizing Communist China and admitting it to the United Nations, on French policy in Algeria, and above all our military preparations in Western Europe and on our common continent - all this seemed fatally to impair any useful role we might play as confidant and trusted partner to those nations to whom all such policies appeared, in the words of Jawaharlal Nehru, as "provocative instruments of Western imperialism." If this was in fact the problem, the solution was at least simple. Canada should demonstrate its faith to the newly independent nations by cutting its ties with the West, and particularly with the leader of the West. To win the trust of neutrals, it is argued, it is necessary to become neutral ourselves.[63]

Lyon, writing in 1962, referred to this issue as "the most controversial in the contemporary discussion of Canada's foreign policy." Of particular relevance to my analysis, given its thematic recourse to structural-realist relations of power as explanatory first causes, are Lyon's comments linking Alliance-disengagement argumentation to Canadian threat assessments:

Two of the objectives of foreign policy, secure peace and freedom, are in a class by themselves; the avoidance of all-out war has become virtually a condition of survival; freedom is not valued equally by everyone ....Circumstances can arise in which men have to choose between peace and freedom ....Canadians differ widely about the seriousness of the challenges to peace and freedom; we do not even agree if the primary source of danger is Soviet imperialism or the nuclear arms race itself.[64]

Here then, as reported in astute summaries of the neutralist advocacy during the initial turn of the cycle, was identified the essential core of the issue: opposing evaluations as to the effect of Alliance mechanisms on global security and its regional subsets. These contending viewpoints on the nature of the threat came center-stage once again during the second neutralist turn. Both are sustained by the manner in which national and international security interests are blended into one indistinguishable concept, even by governmental and parliamentary authorities.

For a recent instance, reference could be made to the final report of the Special Joint Committee of the Senate and of the House of Commons on Canada's International Relations. The Committee introduced its "peace and security" assessment with an open-ended portrayal of the Canadian national security interest, observing that:

The close connection between Canada's security and the prevention of conflict between East and West, particularly the prevention of nuclear war, is uncontested. We see practically no point in thinking of national security as distinct from international security. We start from the assumption that the threat to Canada is one and the same with the threat to international stability and peace.[65]

The primary threat to Canadian security is clearly the outbreak of nuclear warfare between East and West according to this assessment, but there is a subsidiary conventional threat definition attached in some undefined manner to the preeminent menace. This approach allows the crucial policy choices as to how best the threat might be met and countered entirely unencumbered.

This amorphousness enabled the parliamentarians to accord equal legitimacy to both alignment and neutralist thinking, although some normative distinction might be seen in patterns of majoritarian support for the alignment stance:

> Although there is little disagreement on the objective, the choice of means to promote it produces some cleavages. Most accept the basic proposition that in a nuclear world, international stability and peace are best preserved by deterrence. Many argue, however, that the enormous build-up of nuclear weapons goes far beyond the real needs of deterrence. They want Canada to impress more forcefully upon both superpowers the absolute necessity of reaching agreements for the massive reduction of nuclear weapons and for an immediate comprehensive ban on nuclear testing, to mention only two examples. Some would argue that Canada can do this more effectively outside all military alliances. Others, who are in the majority, want Canada to remain in its alliances, arguing that if security is to be enduring, it should encompass an active defence of democratic values held in common with other western nations. They feel, however, that membership in the Western Alliance should not prevent Canada from taking independent initiatives to strengthen the safety and security of the world.[66]

The Department of External Affairs, responded to the parliamentarians with another ambiguously formulated threat definition: "Canada's security rests, first and foremost, on the maintenance of the strategic balance between East and West."[67] Whether "strategic" referred to the nuclear equation inclusive of French, British, and dual-key NATO systems or to American and Soviet long-range systems or, indeed, to the entire spectrum of deterrent capabilities was not specified. The Government's supportive text suggests the last-mentioned possibility, but the semantic content of this official version of the currently authorized definition invokes the nuclear threat given the nature of the parliamentary formulation to which it was responding.

This tendency of officially sanctioned threat assessments to become reduced to nuclear equations within clouds of semantic ambiguity constitutes the principal conceptual impediment that Atlanticists within Canada have to overcome in promoting alignment in phases of Soviet-American tension, since NATO is and will likely long remain a nuclear alliance, for the same reasons that it is essentially a maritime alliance. R. B. Byers reported along these same lines in one of the finest syntheses of contemporary Canadian security issues and problems on record, and observed: "The deterioration of East-West relations has dismayed Canada: deterrence is under attack; arms-control efforts are deemed insufficient; Canada's rationale for support of SDI research is questioned; cruise-missile testing remains controversial. The list goes on. Yet the government remains in strategic limbo."[68]

One particularly illustrative case that demonstrates how supporters of NATO are placed in a no-win situation if the focus of contention can be directed to the nuclear issue occurred during a conference on Canadian defense policy held in November 1986 and organized by Edmonton chapters of the Council of Canadians and the Canadian Physicians for the Prevention of Nuclear War.[69] A Department of National Defence (DND) spokesman was asked: "This meeting has to do with Canadian sovereignty. Would you please identify for us Canada's enemy — not the enemy of our allies, but Canada's enemy? Would you identify the specific hostile acts against Canada that form the basis of that identification?"

The reply respected officially authorized threat assessments: "Canada's enemy today is the potential for a nuclear war. There is no one country that stands to be an enemy to Canada. An enemy of Canada at the present time is a conceptual threat."[70] The conference concluded by passing a number of resolutions, including a call for the establishment of an independent commission to study alternative security policies, "including the possibilities of non-alignment and neutrality." It defeated another that resolved that Canada "continue to work within its alliances and elsewhere to promote both nuclear and conventional arms control."[71] In his introduction to the published proceedings, Mel Hurtig began by commenting that "because Canada is geographically located between the superpowers, Canadians are in particular danger. In any serious military confrontation between the Soviet Union and the United States, Canada would become the incinerated meat in the nuclear sandwich." Hurtig then mentioned an "eloquent proposal for Canadian neutrality" that had been presented, gave his support to former Canadian Ambassador to NATO George Ignatieff's rallying cry of "no incineration without representation," and concluded that "one point is clear," namely the official DND spokesman's dictum that "Canada's enemy today is the potential for a nuclear war."[72] This particular sequence of events and interactions captured the essential features of the second Canadian neutralist turn of the MAD era.[73]

The fundamental target of Canadian neutralism is really extended nuclear deterrence under conditions of strategic parity, not alliances per se. As one critic of NATO's purposes and strategy has written: "The heart of strategic doctrine is an understanding of the nature of deterrence — the conditions that are most likely to deter the use of nuclear weapons. Deterrence, for those interested in getting rid of all nuclear weapons, is not a synonym for military balance or strategic equivalence or symmetry or any other term implying power balances or stalemate. Neither is nuclear deterrence a synonym for nuclear intimidation, as in the case of extended deterrence."[74] Nor is this attitude simply the preserve of the activist anti-nuclear constituency, but rather seems quite pervasive among the attentive public.

Combined with the fact that about 40 percent of Canadians consistently report when polled that they have never even heard or read about NATO previously and that a significant minority of the remaining 60 percent cannot articulate its purposes,[75] it is clear that public opinion surveying that focuses exclusively on the desirability of Alliance membership exaggerates support levels, and significantly so. Canadians seem to hold to a very abstract conception that alignment is a positive virtue per se, but when their views are scrutinized more closely there is much discordance in their perception of NATO. Indeed, most of the Alliance's tenets do not seem to be well-regarded.

In periods of high international tension, threat definitions that center on the outbreak of nuclear war, as is the case in Canada, serve to exacerbate these residual doubts since in most deterrence-failure scenarios there is at the least a declaratory intent to encompass nuclear first use in response patterns. It is difficult not to conclude that, benefitting as they would as North Americans from targetting immunity in the event of a failure in the structure of deterrence confinable to the European theater, Canadians' pecking order in threat assessment is antithetical to the fundamental precepts of the Atlanticist collective-defense contract. Further, Canadians do not seem to want to do more in terms of conventional-force contributions, unless of course those additional forces can serve specifically Canadian purposes as well. Thus, functional duality in force tasking seems to be within the realm of voluntaristic possibility. But on the whole, Canadians, taken collectively, would appear to have become fair-weather allies. The extensive public expressions of neutralist sentiment, however vicarious, during downturns in the relations between the great protagonists of the hour serves to bring all of this residual and latent skepticism to the fore. Thus, there appears to be a step-scaled process underway as the tension-détente cycle proceeds — a process that is conducive to the progressive growth of the Canadian constituency for neutralist modes of thought. Since Canada is absolutely incapable of implementing a credible neutrality in the traditional, or more restricted, sense of the term, the end product is merely translated into the kind of "entry-fee" participation that has characterized Canada's membership in NATO for almost two decades now.

CONCLUSION: THE "WIDENING ATLANTIC" AND CANADIAN ATTITUDES TO NATO

Pierre Hassner has remarked that "foreign policy is by definition supposed to counteract uncertainty and inevitability."[76] This formula is sometimes rendered in the vernacular as "negotiate but keep your powder dry" or, a recent favorite, "trust but verify." In these more populist versions, however, the contingent and unavoidable have traded ranks in the word order. Policymakers and diplomats negotiate to make structural trendlines work to advantage. They maintain fallback positions as a hedge against the unanticipated.

Although successful diplomacy values both decisiveness and caution, it adapts itself to structural change more than it invests in backing-and-filling maneuvers. Let us assume for the purposes of the argument that this characterization of the requisites for efficacious foreign policymaking is well-founded. It would follow, in that case, that the principal and priority task on the current Canadian security-policy agenda centers on the accurate reading of the major structural changes that are now underway in East-West and West-West relations.

It is known, for instance, that the ratio of Soviet GNP to the combined GNPs of the United States, the EEC, Japan and the PRC declined from a 1960 level of 28 percent to 12 percent in 1986.[77] Thus, to borrow a phrase of some familiarity in Ottawa, "It is a fact, not a matter of interpretation, that the West is faced with ..."[78] a Soviet economy in free-fall. This phenomenon appears to be something more than merely contingent.[79] Most would agree that this bodes well for, at the very least, short- to medium-term superpower détente. Reciprocal efforts to that end can be expected on the part of the United States for a number of reasons, but including a structural component as well.[80]

As for relations between NATO-Europe and the United States, continentalism would seem to have the high ground over Atlanticism in both the economic and military domains.[81] The United States has demonstrated for many years that it would be quite prepared to fulfill a strategic reserve role with respect to European security if circumstances allowed.[82] Those circumstances are now discernible.

In an analysis of Soviet-American relations that has taken on added persuasiveness with the passage of time, Raymond Aron once observed that third-party evaluations of Soviet-American relations tended to exaggerate degrees of hostility and to pass over the implicit solidarity that nuanced the adversarial component of their relationship. He claimed that a shared proprietary interest in the nuclear duopoly and the desire to avoid war with one another overrode discomfiture in the face of limited relative gains on either side.[83] Let us assume, again for the sake of the argument, that Aron understood great-power security relations better than Canadian neutralists do.

If these elements are brought together, it could be argued that the prospect of East-West détente coupled with West-West economic competitiveness and functional security specialization, involving an increasingly conventionalized European theater (but one whose security remains predicated on a North American-based strategic nuclear arsenal), literally invites an ongoing and state-of-the-military-art Canadian Forces commitment to NATO-Europe. Progress in "two-pillarism" would require more not less attention to Canada's traditional interest in security multilaterism.[84] The prospect of prolonged détente, counterintuitive though it may seem, should increase domestic support for NATO. The trend to a conventionalized theater, with a form of minimalist coupling to U.S. strategic systems, should serve to undercut objections to extended nuclear deterrence. Under those conditions, even downturns in Soviet-American relations would not provoke the kinds of alarms within Canada that past tension phases have created. It may even begin to be perceived that NATO and the WTO form one "collective-security" system, and that it is in the Soviet interest that the United States remain committed to guaranteeing European security. With time and the instructions of experience, these kinds of cross-cutting interests may become more discernible.

On the other hand, the ultimate Canadian response to the changes in prospect might be to consolidate the CF in a "home guard." Given the motivations and rationales of the two national debates on the merits of alignment to this point, the 1959-1962 and 1979-1984 periods of domestic debate may well begin to seem benign when compared to those that lie ahead, for Canada would then have become exclusively associated with a continentalist joint-defense program closely linked of necessity with the U.S. strategic nuclear deterrent and its accompanying doctrines, force postures, deployment modes, and crisis-management functions.

Notes

[1] James Eayrs, "The Nostrum of Neutralism," in James Eayrs, *Northern Approaches: Canada and the Search for Peace* (Toronto: Macmillan, 1961), 168-76.

[2] Geoffrey Pearson, "Alignment or non-alignment?," in Claude Bergeron et al., eds., *Le Canada et la neutralité militaire* (St-Jean, Que.: Actes du colloque du programme d'études stratégiques, Collège militaire royal de Saint-Jean, April 1987), 16-21.

[3] For an insightful analysis of the internal logic of the tension- détente cycle, see Lawrence S. Hagen, "Contemporary Strategic Relations and the Dissolution of Detente," in Lawrence S. Hagen, ed., *The Crisis in Western Security* (London: Croom Helm, 1982), 9-26.

[4] For testimony regarding this point from non-Canadians, see, Theodore C. Achilles, "The Omaha Milkman: The role of the United States in the negotiations," in Nicholas Sherwen, ed., *NATO's Anxious Birth: The Prophetic Vision of the 1940s* (New York: St. Martin's Press, 1985), 30-41; and Nicholas Henderson, *The Birth of NATO* (Boulder, CO: Westview Press, 1983).

[5] For Canadian government-funded thinking on the new context in West-West relations, see, Albert Legault et al., *The Post-INF Situation: Canada's Position on Arms Control and the Security of the Atlantic Alliance* Extra-Mural Paper no. 50 (Ottawa: Operational Research and Analysis Establishment, July 1988); and George G. Bell et al., *After INF - What? Deterrence, Defence and Arms Control in the Post-INF Era* Extra-Mural Paper no. 49 (Ottawa: Operational Research and Analysis Establishment, July 1988).

[6] Andrew J. Pierre, ed., *A Widening Atlantic?: Domestic Change & Foreign Policy* (New York: Council on Foreign Relations, 1986). As Pierre notes: "In recent times there

has been some discussion of a "widening Atlantic." This concept is meant to indicate that perceptions and interests, as viewed on either side of the ocean, are pulling Europe and America apart."

[7]Stephen F. Szabo, ed., *The Successor Generation: International Perspectives of Postwar Europeans* (London: Butterworths, 1983).

[8]Ole R. Holsti, "Public Opinion and Containment," in Terry L. Diebel and John Lewis Gaddis, eds., *Containing the Soviet Union: A Critique of U.S. Policy* (Washington: Pergamon-Brassey's International Defense Publishers, 1987), 20-58.

[9]Don Munton, *Peace and Security in the 1980s: The View of Canadians*, Working Paper (Ottawa: Canadian Institute for International Peace and Security, January 1988).

[10]Arthur M. Schlesinger, Jr., *The Cycles of American History* (Boston: Houghton Mifflin, 1986); Albert O. Hirschman, *Shifting Involvements: Private Interest and Public Action* (Princeton, N.J.: Princeton University Press, 1982).

[11]Some readers of the draft of this chapter expressed doubt as to the authenticity of this quotation. For those who might share this incredulity, Yogi was reported to have said this on his televised film-review program, shortly after commenting that the movie "Biloxi Blues" "reminded me of being in the army - even though I was in the navy": Norris McDonald, "Mike Tyson, lucky Pierre, and more," *Whig-Standard* (Kingston, Ont.), 21 May 1988, 56.

[12]Kenneth N. Waltz, *Man, the State and War: A Theoretical Analysis* (New York: Columbia University Press, 1959).

[13]See, for example, J. David Singer, "International Conflict: Three Levels of Analysis," *World Politics*, 12 (April 1960), 453-461.

[14]See, for example, Barry M. Blechman and Stephen S. Kaplan et al., *Force without War: U.S. Armed Forces as a Political Instrument* (Washington: The Brookings Institution, 1978); and, the companion volume, Stephen S. Kaplan et al., *Diplomacy of Power: Soviet Armed Forces as a Political Instrument* (Washington: The Brookings Institution, 1981).

[15]Kenneth N. Waltz, *Theory of International Politics* (Reading, MA: Addison-Wesley, 1979).

[16]Some examples include Bernard A. Weisberger, *Cold War Cold Peace: The United States and Russia since 1945* (Boston: Houghton Mifflin, 1984); Fred Halliday, *The Making of the Second Cold War* (London: Verso, 1983); Andre Fontaine, *History of the Cold War*, 2 vols. (New York: Random House, 1969), trans. Renaud Bruce, and see also the as yet untranslated 3d volume, *Histoire de la détente (Paris: Fayard, 1982); Daniel Frei and Dieter Ruloff et al., *East-West Relations*, 2 vols. (Cambridge, MA: Oelgeschlager, Gunn & Hain, 1983); and, for a broader view, T. E. Vadney, *The World since 1945* (Harmondsworth, Middlesex: Penguin, 1987). For a clear-eyed analysis of the convolutions of the central Soviet-American-FRG relationship during the 1970-1980 period, see Kjell Goldman, *Détente: Domestic Politics as a Stabilizer of Foreign Policy*, Research Monograph no. 181 (Princeton, NJ: Woodrow Wilson School of Public and International Affairs, Center of International Studies, Princeton University, February 1984).

[17]See, in particular, Frei & Ruloff, Vol. 1: *A Systematic Survey*, 275-83.

[18]For representative examples of public acknowledgment of the new fact of life within Canada at the time, see John Gellner, "Active Air Defence is Obsolete," *Canadian Aviation* 33 (November 1960), 49; David MacIntosh, "Could we stop Russian missiles?"

Saturday Night 73 (24 May 1958), 8-9, 40-41; and W. H. Pope, "Let the Russians use the DEW Line too," *Maclean's Magazine* 72 (5 December 1959), 10 and 60-61.

[19]For a discussion of the U.S. decoupling strategy, see Earl C. Ravenal, "Extended Deterrence and Alliance Cohesion," in Alan Ned Sabrosky, ed., *Alliances in U.S. Foreign Policy: Issues in the Quest for Collective Defense* (Boulder, CO: Westview Press, 1988), 19-40.

[20]Don Munton, "Superpowers and National Security," *Peace & Security* 2 (Winter 1987/88), 2-3.

[21]See, in particular, Joseph T. Jockel, *No Boundaries Upstairs: Canada, the United States and the Origins of North American Air Defence, 1945-1958* (Vancouver: University of British Columbia Press, 1987); for a good characterization of the tenor of those times, see Peter C. Newman, *Renegade in Power: The Diefenbaker Years* (Toronto: McClelland & Stewart, 1963).

[22]Clear-headed postmortems of the Liberal Party's management of Canadian security policy are in Douglas L. Bland, *The Administration of Defence Policy in Canada, 1947 to 1985* (Kingston, Ont.: Ronald P. Frye, 1987); and Michel Fortmann, *La politique de défense canadienne de Mackenzie King à Trudeau (1945-1979)*, Notes de recherche no. 20 (Montréal: Département de science politique, Université de Montréal); see the relevant sections in the 1985-86, 1986-87 and 1987-88 editions of *A Guide to Canadian Policies on Arms Control, Disarmament, Defence and Conflict Resolution* (Ottawa: Canadian Institute for International Peace and Security, second year of edition indication). A particularly useful account of the Canadian reaction to the SDI proposal is Gregory Wirick, *Canadian Responses to the Strategic Defence Initiative* Background Paper no. 1 (Ottawa: Canadian Institute for International Peace and Security, October 1985). On ADI, see Charles Tutwiler's chapter in this volume.

[23]This metaphor is a favorite of Canadian critics of NATO and, more particularly, NORAD. A leading NDP spokesman on defense issues, Leonard Johnson, has completed the allusion: "And you know what ham is, ... dead meat!" Based on a geopolitical reality, the image evoked has given new meaning to the term "middle power" and has become quite pervasive. For example, see David Cox, "Living Along the Flight Path: Canada's Defense Debate," *Washington Quarterly* 10 (Autumn 1987), 99-112. See David G. Haglund, "Fresh challenge from an old threat," *Forum* 2 (July-August 1987), 5-9; and Ronald Buckingham, *Satellite Surveillance and Canadian Capabilities* Background Paper no. 7 (Ottawa: CIIPS, September 1986).

[24]Stephen M. Walt, *The Origins of Alliances* (Ithaca, NY: Cornell University Press, 1987).

[25]Fabrice Blocteur, *Etude comparative des quotidiens francophones et anglophones sur les questions de défense nationale* , Notes de recherche no. 21 (Montréal: Département de science politique, Université de Montréal, March 1988); and Isabelle Lasvergnas-Grémy, *L'Europe vue du Canada* (Montreal: Centre d'Etudes et de Documentation Européennes, Université de Montréal, 1976).

[26]The New Democratic Party (NDP) first adopted its NATO-withdrawal platform plank in 1969. Contrary to other Canadian political parties, the NDP is bound by its constitution to respect resolutions adopted at its national conventions. Bill Blaikie, the NDP's External Affairs critic, noted recently: "the policy ... had its origins in the Vietnam War ... where it was felt that NATO membership involved Canada in demands for allegiance not only to the world view of NATO in Europe but to the American global view of reality. This was something unacceptable." See Canada, House of Commons, 33d Parl., 2d Sess., Special Committee on the Peace Process in Central America,

86   *The U.S.-Canada Security Relationship*

Proceedings, Issue No. 3 (27 April 1988), 22. When informed by an expert witness that NATO had its American critics as well, but of a different ideological hue, Mr. Blaikie offered: "It is probably the strongest argument I have heard for NATO yet, that these neo-conservatives are against it." In this instance, however, the External Affairs critic only recalled a relatively minor element of the Party's objection to alignment in 1969. See, in this regard, Hugh Thorburn, "The New Democratic Party and National Defence," in Nils Orvik, ed., *Semialignment and Western Security* (London: Croom Helm, 1986), 169-85. Thorburn noted that "By 1969, as tensions mounted in Europe and NATO was committed to the use of tactical nuclear weapons in case of war, the NDP at its convention took the position that this confrontation should be reduced and eventually disappear." Other elements that influenced NDP thinking were also linked to MAD-conditioned security issues, such as concerns about BMD and MIRVing.

[27]For instance, the Soviets test-fired four ICBMs 8,000 miles within two or three miles of target in 1960. Coral Bell, *The Debatable Alliance: An essay in Anglo-American relations* (London: Oxford University Press, 1964), 78.

[28]On the complex of issues involved, the following texts offer helpful analyses: David N. Schwartz, *NATO's Nuclear Dilemmas* (Washington: The Brookings Institution, 1983); Hedley Bull, "European Security Alliances in the 1980s," in Arlene Idol Broadhurst, ed., *The Future of European Alliance Systems: NATO and the Warsaw Pact* (Boulder, CO: Westview Press, 1982), 3-18; and Kenneth A. Myers, ed., *NATO, The Next Thirty Years: The Changing Political, Economic, and Military Setting* (London: Croom Helm, 1980).

[29]See Richard Preston, *Canada in World Affairs, 1959-1961* (Toronto: Oxford University Press, 1964).

[30]See, for example, Kenneth McNaught, "Canada must get out of the arms race," *Saturday Night* 76 (10 June 1961), 23-26; Andrew Brewin and Kenneth McNaught, *Debate on Defence: Two Viewpoints on Canadian Foreign Policy* (Toronto: Woodsworth Memorial Foundation, 1960); Farley Mowat, "Canada joins the club," *Our Generation (Against Nuclear War)*, Vol. 1, No. 1 (Fall 1961), 8-13; and Ross Munro, "Let's keep A-bombs out of Canada," *Maclean's Magazine* 73 (7 May 1960), 8 and 83-5.

[31]See W. H. Pope, "NORAD, NATO, and the New Democratic Party," *Our Generation (Against Nuclear War)*, Vol. 1, No. 1 (Fall 1961), 23-32; David Grenier, "Some strange post-war Alliances," *Saturday Night* 75 (30 April 1960), 13-14; Blair Fraser, "Our real defence policy: Is it only to keep NATO happy?" *Maclean's Magazine* 72 (28 March 1959), 2; Peter C. Newman, "Atoms, NATO and NORAD: the coming election issue," *Maclean's Magazine* 74 (25 March 1961), 68, and idem, "The last days of NORAD," *Maclean's Magazine* 75 (21 April 1962), 18 and 63-6; James Eayrs, "Canada, NATO and nuclear weapons," *Survival* 3 (March-April 1961), 76-83; and Michel van Schendel, "L'atome, NORAD, le neutralisme, et M. Green," *Cité libre* 13 (juin-juillet 1962), 15-19.

[32]See, for instance, Kenneth McNaught, "Why we should not fight over Germany," *Saturday Night* 76 (25 November 1961), 12-14. For opposing views on this issue, see James M. Minifie, *Peacemaker or Powder-Monkey: Canada's Role in a Revolutionary World* (Toronto: McClelland and Stewart, 1960); and Peyton V. Lyon, *The Policy Question: A Critical Appraisal of Canada's Role in World Affairs* (Toronto: McClelland and Stewart, 1963).

[33]See, for instance, C. B. Macpherson, "Nuclear Arms for Canada: A strong case examined," in Dimitrios Roussopoulos, ed., *Our Generation Against Nuclear War* (Montreal: Black Rose Books, 1983), 133-39. [Reprinted from *Our Generation (Against*

Nuclear War) 2 (Fall 1962)]. Note the reprint year. The imprint of the MAD-era tension-détente cycle is engraved on the literature of Canadian neutralist thought.

[34]Harto Hakovirta, "The Soviet Union and the Varieties of Neutrality in Western Europe," *World Politics* 35 (July 1983), 563-83.

[35]See James M. Minifie, "Canada should be neutral," *Canadian Commentator* 3 (December 1959), 2-3; H. Pope, "Le Canada et le neutralisme," *Cité libre* 12 (mars 1961), 9-13; James M. Minifie, "In reply to Adlai Stevenson: Further defence of a policy of neutralism for Canada," *Canadian Commentator* 5 (April 1961), 10-12; no byline, "Canada: A weakening Ally?," *U.S. News and World Report* 54 (11 February 1963); and C. B. Macpherson, "Positive neutralism for Canada?" *Canadian Commentator* 7 (September 1963), 9-11.

[36]For the case of the Korean War, see Denis Stairs, *The Diplomacy of Constraint: Canada, the Korean War, and the United States* (Toronto: University of Toronto Press, 1974). Stairs is certain that the United Nations' imprimatur was essential for Canadian participation in the war. However, the point here is that parliamentary and media response was highly supportive of the Canadian political executive's decision to join in what was surely a "Western" cause that would require the sacrifice of Canadian lives in a far forward defense posture.

[37]For instance, see the published dissertation of John W. Warnock, a former member of the U.S. Foreign Service who took a teaching position at the University of Saskatchewan, *Partner to Behemoth: The Military Policy of a Satellite Canada* (Toronto: New Press, 1970).

[38]See Bruce Thordarson, *Trudeau and Foreign Policy: A study in decision making* (Toronto: Oxford University Press, 1972); Peter C. Dobell, *Canada's search for new roles: Foreign Policy in the Trudeau Era* (Toronto: Oxford University Press, 1972); and Charles Ritchie, *Storm Signals: More Undiplomatic Diaries, 1962-1971* (Toronto: Macmillan, 1987).

[39]See Michael Tucker, "Trudeau and the politics of peace," *International Perspectives* (May/June 1984), 7-10; Michael Pearson et al., "The World is entitled to ask questions: the Trudeau peace initiative reconsidered," *International Journal* 41 (Winter 1985/1986), 129-58; and Robert Miller, "Trudeau's peace crusade," *Maclean's Magazine* 96 (5 December 1983), 18-26.

[40]Canada, New Democratic Party, International Affairs Committee, *Canada's Stake in Common Security* (Ottawa: NDP, April 1988). See John F. Burns, "Canadian Leftists Drop Plans to Quit NATO," *New York Times*, 18 April 1988, A3; and Don McGillivray, "NDP seems subverted by mere whiff of power," *Whig Standard* (Kingston, Ont.), 18 June 1988, 10.

[41]See Gilles Grondin, *The Origins of the Canadian Institute for International Peace and Security*, Background Paper no. 6 (Ottawa: CIIPS, August 1986).

[42]David Cox and Mary Taylor, eds., *A Guide to Canadian Policies on Arms Control, Disarmament, Defence and Conflict Resolution, 1986-87* (Ottawa: CIIPS, 1987), 262.

[43]Munton, *Peace and Security in the 1980s*, 4.

[44]Ibid., 59.

[45]Joe Clark, "Leaving its Alliance is No Choice for Canada," *The Disarmament Bulletin*, Summer/Fall 1986 (Ottawa: Department of External Affairs), 28. In this reply to one of Gwynne Dyer's newspaper articles promoting neutrality for Canada, the Secretary of State for External Affairs noted: "Geography is not the paramount reason

we belong in NATO and NORAD. Freedom is. Those alliances, with all their imperfec-
tions, defend a system of free societies and — by maintaining strength in the face of
Soviet strength — help keep the peace."

[46]Munton, *Peace and Security in the 1980s*, 45.

[47]Canada. Department of External Affairs, *Canadians' Foreign Policy Attitudes*,
Communiqué no. 162, 14 August 1987, 3.

[48]For a similar assessment of the film, see G. G. Bell, "No time for silence!" *Forum*
2 (July-August 1987), 16-21.

[49]Gwynne Dyer had scripted and presented the narration of the film. The SSEA's
response, note 45 supra, publicly countered its premises and conclusions. Both he and
the MND, as well as departmental officials from both DEA and DND, made additional
interventions in this regard; for example, Joe Clark, "Canada and NATO," *Globe and
Mail* (Toronto), 4 December 1986 (Letter to the Editor); Perrin Beatty (MND), "Address
to the Empire Club," DND, 15 January 1987; W. J. Fenrick, "D Pub Pol (DND) Speaking Points for Gwynne Dyer Film Presentation," Carleton University, Ottawa, 17 March
1987; and N. Reeder, DEA, "Talking points for Carleton University Debate on
Neutrality," 17 March 1987.

[50]As Ian Carr, a former President of Physicians for Social Responsibility (1983-
1984), recommended to neutralist cohorts: "the advent of Educators for Social Responsibility is welcome ... our education must be accurate, up to date and phrased in terms that
folk in the highways and the byways can understand. Talk not of the possibility of fire-
storms in Canadian cities, but of bringing the furnace to the children, instead of the
children to the furnace." Ian Carr, "As through a glass darkly: The Canadian role in
shaping the future," in Thomas L. Perry and Dianne DeMille, eds., *Nuclear War: The
Search for Solutions* (Vancouver: Physicians for Social Responsibility, B.C. Chapter,
1985), 225-30. See Elizabeth Richards, *The Debate about Peace Education*, Background Paper no. 10 (Ottawa: CIIPS, December 1986).

[51]Munton, *Peace and Security in the 1980s*, 2-4.

[52]Ibid., passim.

[53]For the NWFZ debate, see Shannon Selin, *Canada as a Nuclear Weapon-Free
Zone: A Critical Analysis*, Issue Brief no. 10 (Ottawa: Canadian Centre for Arms Control and Disarmament, August 1988).

[54]John W. Holmes, "Canada, NATO, and Western Security," in John W. Holmes et
al., *No Other Way: Canada and International Security Institutions* (Toronto: Centre for
International Studies, University of Toronto, 1986), 122-39.

[55] See chapter by Douglas L. Bland in this volume; and John Halstead, "Canada's
Security in the 1980s: Options and Pitfalls" *Behind the Headlines* 41 (Toronto: Canadian
Institute of International Affairs, September 1983).

[56]See, for instance, United States, Department of Defense, Report to Congress, *Re-
port on Allied Contributions to the Common Defense* (Washington: DOD, April 1988);
Rod B. Byers, *Canadian Security and Defence: the Legacy and the Challenges*, Adelphi
Paper no. 214 (London: IISS, Winter 1986), 73; and Peter Gizewski, Michael Holmes
and Francine Lecours, *A Guide to Canadian Policies on Arms Control, Disarmament,
Defence and Conflict Resolution, 1987-1988* (Ottawa: CIIPS, 1988), 221-23. That the
September 1985 proposal to withdraw all Canadian forces from the FRG was made and
was vetoed by the U.K. and the FRG has been confirmed to the author by authoritative
Canadian and American sources.

[57]The Leader of the Opposition, John Turner, also sounded out the Europeans on this proposal to ascertain whether the Liberals could put forward a similar policy in response to the June 1987 White Paper. (Reliable sources in the Liberal Party to the author.) As for the NDP, immediate withdrawal from the central front forms part of the defense platform it took into the November 1988 election.

[58]Joseph T. Jockel and Joel J. Sokolsky, *Canada and Collective Security: Odd Man Out*, The Washington Papers no. 121 (New York: Praeger, 1986).

[59]David Easton, *A Framework for Political Analysis* (Englewood Cliffs, NJ: Prentice-Hall, 1965), 50.

[60]See, for example, Joel J. Sokolsky, "Changing Strategies, Technologies and Organization: The Continuing Debate on NORAD and the Strategic Defense Initiative," *Canadian Journal of Political Science* 19 (December 1986), 751-74; Douglas A. Ross, "American Nuclear Revisionism, Canadian Strategic Interests and the Renewal of NORAD," *Behind the Headlines* 39 (Toronto: Canadian Institute of International Affairs, 1982); John Barrett, "Arms Control and Canada's security policy," *International Journal* 42 (Autumn 1987), 731-68; Charles-Philippe David et al., *Canadian Perspectives on the Strategic Defence Initiative*, Issue Brief no. 3 (Ottawa: CCACD, July 1985); David Cox, *Trends in Continental Defence: A Canadian Perspective,* Occasional Paper no.2 (Ottawa: CIIPS, December 1986); and the "weather advisory" of Gerald Wright, "Canada and the Reagan Administration: Anxious days are here again," *International Journal* 36 (Winter 1980-1), 228-36.

[61]Munton, *Peace and Security in the 1980s*, 17-23.

[62]Five of the key statements of the period are in P. Edward Haley, David M. Keithly, and Jack Merritt, eds., *Nuclear Strategy, Arms Control, and the Future* (Boulder, CO: Westview Press, 1985), 62-91; a standard account is Lawrence Freedman, *The Evolution of Nuclear Strategy* (New York: St. Martin's Press, 1981). Characteristic of the thinking at the time was Thomas C. Schelling's comment, "With the development of small-size, small- yield nuclear weapons suitable for local use by ground troops with modest equipment, and the development of nuclear depth charges and nuclear rockets for air-to-air combat, the technical characteristics of nuclear weapons have ceased to provide much basis, if any, for treating nuclear weapons as peculiarly different from other weapons in the conduct of limited war," in *The Strategy of Conflict* (New York: Oxford University Press, 1960), 257.

[63]Eayrs, "The Nostrum of Neutralism," 172.

[64]Lyon, *The Policy Question*, 29, 42-3.

[65]Canada, Parliament, *Independence and Internationalism: Report of the Special Joint Committee of the Senate and of the House of Commons on Canada's International Relations* (Ottawa: Supply and Services, June 1986), 34.

[66]Canada, Department of External Affairs, *Canada's International Relations: Response of the Government of Canada to the Report of the Special Joint Committee of the Senate and the House of Commons* (Ottawa: Supply and Services, December 1986), 11.

[67]Ibid.

[68]Byers, *Canadian Security and Defence*, 69.

[69]See Jack Rosenblatt, *Soviet Propaganda and the Physicians' Peace Movement,* Mackenzie Paper no. 6 (Toronto: Mackenzie Institute for the Study of Terrorism, Revolution and Propaganda, 1988).

[70]The True North Strong and Free Inquiry Society, *The True North Strong & Free?* Proceedings of a Public Inquiry into Canadian Defence Policy and Nuclear Arms (West Vancouver, B.C.: Gordon Soules Book Publishers, 1987), 53.

[71]Ibid., 13-14.

[72]Ibid., 9-12.

[73]For variations on this theme, see Eric Shragge, Ronald Babin and Jean-Guy Vaillancourt, eds., *Roots of Peace: The Movement Against Militarism in Canada* (Toronto: Between the Lines, 1986); Jean-Guy Vaillancourt and Ronald Babin, eds., *Le mouvement pour le désarmement et la paix*, special issue of *Revue internationale d'action communautaire* 12/52 (Fall 1984); F. H. Knelman, *Reagan, God and the Bomb: From Myth to Policy in the Nuclear Arms Race* (Toronto: McClelland and Stewart, 1985); Simon Rosenblum, "Uncommon Security," in Penny Sanger, ed., *Canada and Common Security: The Assertion of Sanity* (Ottawa: The Group of 78, 1987), 11-13; Carole Giangrande, *The Nuclear North: The People, The Regions and the Arms Race* (Toronto: Anansi, 1983); Simon Rosenblum, *Misguided Missiles: Canada, the Cruise and Star Wars* (Toronto: James Lorimer & Company, 1985); and Ernie Regehr, *Arms Canada: The Deadly Business of Military Exports* (Toronto: James Lorimer & Company, 1987).

[74]Ernie Regehr, "New Approaches to Security," in Ernie Regehr and Simon Rosenblum, eds., *The Road to Peace* (Toronto: James Lorimer & Company, 1988), 104-28.

[75]Cox and Taylor, eds., *A Guide to Canadian Policies, 1985-86*, 281. For a contrary view of past levels of Canadian awareness, see Don Munton, "Canadians and their Defence," *Peace & Security* 3 (Winter 1988/89), 2-5. This latter view does not apply very stringent criteria.

[76]Pierre Hassner, "Europe and the Contradictions in American Policy," in Richard Rosecrance, ed., *America as an Ordinary Country: U.S. Foreign Policy and the Future* (Ithaca, N.Y.: Cornell University Press, 1976), 60- 86.

[77]Werner Obst, "The Kremlin looks West for help to pull itself out of the economic mire," *The German Tribune*, 1258 (18 January 1987), 5.

[78]Canada, Department of National Defence, *Challenge and Commitment: A Defence Policy for Canada* (Ottawa: Supply and Services, 1987), 5. The full sentence reads: "It is a fact, not a matter of interpretation, that the West is faced with an ideological, political and economic adversary whose explicit long-term aim is to mould the world in its own image." About seventeen months later, Margaret Thatcher pronounced the Cold War won and Marxism dead. Such are the vagaries of strategic forecasting.

[79]Paul Kennedy, *The Rise and Fall of the Great Powers: Economic Change and Military Conflict from 1500 to 2000* (New York: Random House, 1987), 488-514.

[80]David P. Calleo, *Beyond American Hegemony: The Future of the Western Alliance* (New York: Basic Books, 1987), 215-20.

[81]See Angela E. Stent, "East-West Economic Relations: An East-West or a West-West Problem?" in Steven Bethlen and Ivan Volgyes, eds., *Europe and the Superpowers: Political, Economic, and Military Policies in the 1980s* (Boulder, CO: Westview Press, 1985), 141-45; and Richard L. Rubenstein, ed., *The Dissolving Alliance: The United States and the Future of Europe* (New York: Paragon House Publishers, 1987).

[82]Robert E. Osgood, "The Diplomacy of Allied Relations: Europe and Japan," in Robert E. Osgood et al., eds., *Retreat From Empire? The First Nixon Administration* (Baltimore, MD: The Johns Hopkins University Press, 1973), 173-205.

[83]Raymond Aron, *Paix et Guerre entre les nations*, 6th ed. (Paris: Calmann-Lévy, 1968), 527.

[84]John W. Holmes, "The Dumbbell Won't Do," *Foreign Policy* 50 (Spring 1983), 3-22; and R. B. Byers et al., *Canada and Western Security: The Search for New Options* (Toronto: Atlantic Council of Canada, 1982).

4

Canadian Neutrality: Its Military Consequences

Douglas L. Bland

INTRODUCTION

A prominent American specialist in international relations has recently observed that "the best way to respond to inadequate strategic thinking is not simply with moralistic indignation but with better consequential analysis."[1] With Joseph Nye's advice in mind, I shall seek in this chapter to address some of the military consequences for Canada of a policy of neutrality, for it is my contention that advocacies of neutrality for Canada do indeed betray inadequacy of strategic conceptualization.

Building a practical defense policy upon such an ambiguous conceptual foundation as neutrality presents problems of both definition and objective. Strictly speaking, neutrality is a legal concept that only has relevance once a conflict has begun. As a peacetime strategy one is forced to ask: In respect of what or whom is it intended? How, for instance, should governments determine how much defense is "enough"? How would governments measure success? These questions, of course, are not limited in application to neutrality alone but are instructive in the sense that neutrality does not solve the problems of defense administration. Rather, it may only compound them.

The first problem in assessing the military consequences of a neutral Canada is to find some approach that would provide a relatively stable platform for a force model. Fortunately, the concept of neutrality has attracted much attention over the years from scholars, politicians, and lawyers — attention that has provided a body of "rules, duties and responsibilities" for neutrals and belligerents in most circumstances. Even though it is acknowledged that there are no iron laws of neutrality, the understandings and expectations about what neutrals and belligerents should do in peace and war provide a strong clue as to what is necessary in the way of force structure, and it is to these that we turn in our search for insight into the likely military consequences of a neutral Canada.

RULES OF NEUTRALITY

A state that remains neutral in an armed conflict has a large number of legal rights and duties.[2] Reduced to essentials, a neutral is obligated to take all practicable measures to maintain its independence and to prevent one party to a conflict from directing operations against another from or through neutral territory. Neutral territory includes land, internal waters, territorial seas and air space. It does not include outer space over its land mass. A neutral must take all practicable measures to prevent the air, land or sea forces of one party to a conflict from using neutral territory as a base of operations. It must also take all practical measures to prevent military aircraft and weapons, such as cruise missiles, from flying through its airspace, and land forces from crossing its territory. Under certain circumstances, warships may pass through the territorial seas of a neutral but, as a general statement, submarines must be surfaced on passage.

A state that is engaged in an armed conflict does, however, have the right to use force in self defense. In a hypothetical example of a Russian attack on the United States through Canadian airspace, it is, at the least, debatable whether or not the United States would be legally obligated to wait for Russian aircraft to cross the American border before committing its aircraft to combat. There are numerous cases in which states involved in an armed conflict have made incursions into neutral states using self defense as their legal rationale. These incursions are most likely to occur when the neutral has been unable effectively to implement its neutrality obligations.

In order to illustrate some of the military consequences of neutrality I shall construct a hypothetical model based on the general conditions and assumptions derived from the preceding interpretation of the customs and rules of neutrality. The central assumptions of my model are the following:

— Canada would be an armed neutral;
— Canada would be required to maintain surveillance and control of its territorial land, air, and sea spaces in peace and war in order to deny their use to actual and potential belligerents;
— Canada's capabilities to maintain surveillance and control would have to be demonstrated to the satisfaction of real and potential belligerents in peace and war; and
— Given that Canada has twenty-six million healthy, well-educated people, is one of the richest countries in the world, and would have no external obligations, it is assumed that other nations would expect

Canada to maintain a vigorous defense of its neutrality. Any other policy would be viewed as an abandonment of its responsibilities as a neutral and an invitation to belligerents to take self-defense measures in Canadian territory.

Neutrality, therefore, requires a Canadian strategy of deterrence to convince nations not only that Canada can defend itself but also to assure belligerents that their enemies could not take advantage of our neutrality. To paraphrase David Cox's description of the essential requirement of an effective policy for Canadian national sovereignty, what will be important to a neutral Canada is not what we think the Russians or the Americans will do, it is what the Americans think the Russians could do in Canada and what the Russians think the Americans could do in Canada.[3]

FORCE STRUCTURE: ARMY

The construction of a comprehensive force structure for any circumstance is a highly technical and complex business. Planners must not only construct obvious front-line units and equipment but must identify and quantify their immense supporting infrastructures.

All the interactive implications of building an essentially unique Canadian Armed Forces (CF) under a concept of armed neutrality cannot be considered here. It is possible, however, to address the major responsibilities and consequences of such a policy and draw from these inferences other support and infrastructure changes, beginning with the Army.

Three major defense needs have always influenced the structure of the Canadian Army. First, under the terms of the *Constitution Act 1867*, the federal government has sole responsibility for the defense of Canada. Provinces, on rejecting the "states" militia model of the United States, insisted, however, that they have unimpeded recourse to armed assistance if they need it. Under the National Defence Act, provinces have the right to request armed forces directly from the Chief of the Defence Staff (CDS) who must respond to such requests. The responsibility of the CDS to provide for "Aid of the Civil Power" must be accounted for in any force structure of the CF. Our history indicates that duties arising from this responsibility fall largely on formed army units.[4]

Second, Canada, even simply to display sovereignty, always requires an Army capable of conducting land force defense operations in all parts of the country. The organization and equipment of such forces depends upon assessments of threats. Since at least 1926, these have been restricted to the low end of the so-called "spectrum of conflict" and have only called for light scaled units. Our present operational assumptions might change if we believed that Canada as a neutral country must once again treat the United States as a threat.

The third factor conditioning the Army's structure has always been derived from Canada's sensible desire to fight wars when necessary as far from our shores as possible. Thus, the Canadian Army has always had a decidedly expeditionary focus. It is proposed by some that this be replaced by a neutral home-based concept of operations. On the surface it might appear that relieving the Army of its NATO and U.N. tasks would free resources to meet this new responsibility. This, however, would not likely be the case, because all three needs are now met concurrently by the same units. Except for troops actually deployed in Europe, there is no independent expeditionary force that could be disbanded without impairing the Army's ability to meet its first two responsibilities. In a neutral Canada the Army's present functions would actually have to be increased, and it would also have to provide significant support to the Air Force and the Navy.

The following examples of tasks and missions the Army would be required to continue to perform may help to illustrate the force structure the Army would need to serve a neutral Canada. Aid to the Civil Powers and Assistance to Civil Authorities would continue, at least at current levels. It is extremely unlikely, for instance, that the one operational formation in western Canada could be disbanded without comment from regional premiers. To do so would remove all soldiers west of London, Ontario. Similarly, it is not likely that the one Francophone brigade and the only operational formation east of the Ottawa River could be disbanded. Central Canada, that is Ontario, has at present some 5,000 soldiers scattered across an area as large as western Europe. Simply being prepared for contingencies that arise from time to time at the prisons in Kingston, Ontario, requires the stationing in that area of a battalion-size unit. Consequently, there seems little reason to believe that significant Army reductions could be made in any part of Canada.

The active air defense of Canada will be needed in peace and war. Since, however, airfields and aircraft are fragile things, often the best way to disable aircraft is to disable the airfields that support them. The defense of airfields, therefore, would become a major Army task. Each airfield in the North and South would require at least a peacetime skeleton force of 200 men and an additional air-defense battery of approximately 100 men. These units could presumably be filled out by the Militia during a crisis.

Near coasts and in territorial waters one main rule is that ships may travel through neutral waters or even remain in ports for up to twenty-four hours. After that time they must leave or be captured and interned by the neutral. The Army would have a coastal defense role to play in support of the Navy.

As a deterrent, and as a demonstration of our intent to enforce our neutrality, a defense system on each coast and at major ports would be needed. These systems, likely based on ground-to-air and ground-to-sea missiles, would require the development of several coastal defense regiments. Sweden, for example, has an elaborate coastal defense system based on five brigades of artillery to meet their small-scale problems. Though not a neutral, Norway has thirty fortresses, and some fifty artillery, mine, and torpedo batteries.[5]

In this regard, the St. Lawrence Seaway represents a unique problem. Certainly the use of the Seaway by American naval vessels in wartime would not impress the Soviets. The movement of merchant vessels destined for Europe would likewise also be discouraged. How would Canada address this problem? Certainly it would have to insist on some type of enforced inspection facility to control shipping on the St. Lawrence. Fortunately, the Citadel in Quebec is still in good shape and could, with modification, again serve our defense purposes.

What about the Great Lakes? Is the inland transportation of war materiel through the various locks a violation of the rules of neutrality? More soldiers might be required to guard these facilities as well.

Besides its responsibilities to the Navy and the Air Force the Army's more traditional functions of controlling our territories would remain. Currently, this need is only partly addressed by Canada's limited air mobile and air delivered (para) units. Nevertheless, the threat from raids is not too credible today given the enormous logistic problem the Soviets would face in launching such raids, and the large capacity of our American allies to assist us if we asked them.

As a neutral country, however, Canada may face new challenges. Canadian fears of an American land grab would have to be taken seriously not only by novelists but also by the Government. Therefore, it should be anticipated that the Army would respond to this challenge with two major undertakings.

First, the Army would increase its air-mobile and air-delivered capabilities. Even at light scales this requirement has many subordinate consequences for training, organization, infrastructure, and aircraft. Second, a northern base, long desired by some strategists, would become even more significant as a training and staging base for army patrols in Northern Canada.

Alaska would present an interesting problem for a neutral Canada. Certainly the Soviets would expect us in peace and war to restrict the transportation of all warlike materiel and supplies to and from Alaska through our territory. One must assume that we would establish a "land and be inspected" program to be enforced in peacetime by the Canadian Air Force.

In a crisis all transportation and communication between the continental United States and Alaska through Canadian territories would have to be closed and with military strength if necessary. We, however, should anticipate that the Americans might try to force open the Alaska Highway. It would be a major Canadian Army objective to deter them from such action. The establishment of a combat engineer brigade on the Alaska Highway with orders to deny the road to the Americans should ensure that it would never be available to them (or us, of course). The Americans could create an escorted air bridge to Alaska if they became convinced that the highway would be unusable and we might have to develop additional air defenses against such an intrusion.

No Army units would be allocated for U.N. peacekeeping duties. This model reflects the Swiss view that membership in the U.N. is inconsistent with the responsibilities of neutrals and, therefore, no Canadian peacekeeping capabilities are required. If, however, Canadians accepted a less ideal policy of neutrality than the Swiss then additional troops would be required for peacekeeping duties.

Neutrality would not reduce the need for a Militia in Canada. At least one would expect them during exercises and in crisis to perform specific roles such as home guards, civil defense agents, and reinforcements. A revitalized Militia would, of course, require stronger Regular Force Army cadre assistance and training.

The equipment needs of this new Army would change the present "Capital Equipment Program." Essentially, it would entail changing the Program objectives from maintaining general purpose forces to supporting lightly scaled units. The CF would likely let present stocks of tanks, self-propelled artillery, armored personnel carriers and their support equipment and supplies run down. In fact, since we do not manufacture any of these things, Canada may not have many other options. Besides, to strengthen our neutrality, Canada might want to develop further its own arms industry.

The new Army structure would require increases to some present equipments and the development or purchase of new ones. For example, additional purchases of all-terrain type vehicles, like the Volvo B202, would be necessary. We would require a major re-equipment of air-defense systems, and the development of coastal artillery. More surveillance systems would also be needed. Air portable and air base defense forces would require more equipment and transport aircraft to support them. To this list must be added the need to construct and maintain new infrastructures in the North and elsewhere in Canada for troops returning from Europe.

FORCE STRUCTURE: AIR FORCE

According to the *Encyclopedia of Public International Law* the air rules for a neutral are strict:

> A neutral's failure adequately to protect its airspace militarily or diplomatically can be regarded by a belligerent prejudiced thereby as a breach of the neutral's duties. The belligerent can then protest, claim war damages for resultant harm and, if a serious threat faces it from the neutral's airspace through violations of it by the belligerent's opponent, it can justify corrective military action as a measure of self-defence; depending on the scale of the threat, this could transmute that airspace into part of the region of war.

This legal interpretation presents serious consequences for Canada and calls up a particularly sophisticated Air Force structure. First, Canada would be required to develop or acquire a comprehensive air-space surveillance and control system covering the entire country. Second, we would have to acquire, deploy, and maintain aircraft to conduct intercept duties and to force, by one means or another, intruders to land. Third, as we move very rapidly into the era of cruise missiles, the CF would require the capability to detect, intercept and, if necessary, destroy their carriers. Finally, the CF would have to intercept and destroy any missiles crossing our territory en route to American or Soviet targets.

The aim must be to demonstrate a high level of competence to detect and intercept intruding vehicles. To convince both Soviet and American leaders that Canadian neutral territory would not be used as a covered approach by one against the other, an outwardly facing surveillance barrier would be needed. Also, an internal air-space surveillance and control system would have to be designed, constructed, and put into operation. The northern edge of a complete peripheral air-control system would presumably be available to Canada; that is, the North Warning System (NWS). The purchase of the whole system would cost approximately $6 billion today.

The NWS issue is complicated because the NWS will not be in operation until 1992. Any earlier hint that Canada would become neutral would surely cause the American government to reconsider its plans and as a result it may construct a U.S.-based and -controlled system elsewhere and with other technologies. In that case, Canada would have to develop and construct an NWS independently and likely without access to U.S. technology, materiel, instruments, technicians, or industries. Certainly, we could not expect American help in this project.

There is at present no Canadian warning network across the southern or coastal parts of the country but one would be needed to demonstrate our neutrality to the Soviet Union. Civilian systems in place and planned for the future are secondary radars that are designed to control "compliant" air traffic but not to identify unauthorized flights or to facilitate interceptions. The Transport Canada system, because of technical difficulties, cannot be converted to an air-defense role. A replacement of the PINETREE Line with primary radars would be required.

The requirements of neutrality would necessitate a significant increase in Canada's interceptor aircraft fleet. At its height in 1960 the active air defense of North America involved close to 3,000 interceptors, including 200 Canadian aircraft. These aircraft were supported by approximately ninety BOMARC and NIKE surface-to-air missile formations, some of which were deployed in Canada. Today Canada has only thirty-six aircraft dedicated to North American active air defense.

It is estimated that to give some semblance of air-space control several new air-defense bases would be required. Today we have only two such stations: Cold Lake, Alberta, and Bagotville, Quebec. New air-defense stations, for example, would be required at Goose Bay, Labrador; Summerside, P.E.I.; Trenton, Ontario; Winnipeg, Manitoba; Moose Jaw, Saskatchewan; Comox, British Columbia; in the Central Yukon; and at five locations in the far North. Obviously, all these airfields would require additional infrastructure to conduct sustained operations. As for aircraft, it can be assumed that a minimum of twenty aircraft at each base, or a total of 280 interceptor aircraft, would be needed. To this total must be added twelve as a training and maintenance reserve. In all an estimated 156 additional CF-18s would be needed for the Air Force.

Obtaining these additional aircraft would be the major difficulty facing this program. The cost of the extra 156 aircraft, approximately $5.5 billion in 1987 funds, may not be acceptable. We may also have difficulty in obtaining these aircraft from the present sources, especially if the Defense Production Sharing Agreement with the United States was terminated.

In addition to these costs there would be significant new infrastructure costs to support increased peripheral deployments. In this model, existing air stations have been used where possible but even these would have only limited capability to accept full-time fighter squadrons. The new Yukon and five northern airfields would have to be developed from scratch.

The Air Force of a neutral Canada would have to continue many of today's tasks. Search and rescue, transportation, training, and other surveillance duties of land and sea spaces would have to continue with some, like training, at increased rates. Canada would have no need to transport personnel and equipment over seas in support of NATO or the U.N. The CF, therefore, could reconfigure its 707 long-range transport fleet to meet other needs. Five aircraft, for example, could be freed to provide the frames for airborne refuelers to support the internal transit of fighter aircraft. It is estimated that four AWACS 707 aircraft plus two 707 command aircraft would be needed. These requirements would prompt a net increase of six 707s for the CF for air-space control in peace and war to supplement our transition ground radar stations and to meet threats developing from cruise missiles.

Our medium-range transport fleet today is based on twenty-six C-130 aircraft and an assortment of lesser machines. The Senate Defence Committee recommended in 1986 that the present Hercules C-130 fleet be increased from twenty-six to forty-five in the "medium term." The need for these aircraft for international service in support of NATO and the U.N. would be significantly reduced in this model.

There might, however, still be some requirement for international support to foreign aid and disaster relief. There would be a major increase in air-transport requirements inside Canada to support Army air-borne and air-mobile units and to resupply northern airfields. It is estimated that a neutral Canada, therefore, would require thirty-five aircraft. This increase of nine C-130 would cost $.3 billion (1987) and with this cost, of course, would come the usual increases in overhead and infrastructure.

FORCE STRUCTURE: NAVY

Neutrality at sea is a complex business. It involves the consideration of all aspects of sea usage including innocent passage, mercantile traffic, rights of inspection, control and surveillance as well as defense of territorial waters. Related to these aspects is the concern for ports and harbors and shore facilities.

Essentially, Canada would be required to ensure that our territorial waters remain free for use by all nations within the limits of the laws and customs of the sea. The rules of neutrality allow the passage of belligerents' ships through neutral waters. They must not, however, stay in neutral waters for more than twenty-four hours or take on materiel that could benefit them in operations. Vessels that do remain in neutral waters for more than twenty-four hours must be interned by the neutral power. Simply stated, Canada would be required to ensure that military forces of other nations could not use Canadian waters for the purposes of waging war.

These requirements raise unique problems for Canada. Our coasts are vast, well-sheltered, unpopulated and, therefore, hard to control. These factors call for the maintenance of a modern naval force capable of operation in all our territorial waters. Certainly Canadians would have to assume that our competence in sea control, as in the air, would have to be demonstrated and would likely be frequently tested by the U.S. and USSR. Sweden, for example, facing far fewer technical difficulties than Canada, has been notably ineffectual in enforcing its own coastal sovereignty.

One way to control access ways and major ports might be to use coastal batteries. Remote areas would require naval vessels, submarines, and attack aircraft for these purposes. How would we cope with special vessels such as nuclear-powered submarines? Without a similar capability this is a very difficult question, one that might best be left to the proponents of neutrality to ponder.

Inland waterways that we share with the United States are another difficulty. The status of the Rush-Bagot Treaty and the Great Lakes, the St-LawrenceSeaway, and the control of shipping in the Straits of Juan de Fuca may be subjects for new negotiations. The degree to which we could control waters that are of vital interest to the U.S. would surely provide a pretext for the USSR to pressure our defense policies and take advantage of Canada's neutrality.

It would be a mistake to assume that withdrawal from the NATO collective-defense arrangements would necessarily free naval resources for application to other defense responsibilities. The Canadian Navy under current NATO planning is by and large responsible for the defense of Canadian waters but it is common for critics to point out Canada's inadequacies in its NATO role as well as in the Arctic and Pacific territorial waters. These weaknesses are only overcome by our collective defense arrangements, but as a neutral, Canada's present naval force of twenty-six surface combatants, three submarines, and eighteen long-range patrol aircraft would reassure neither the U.S. nor the USSR that our waters were free of the other's forces. To attempt to be neutral with the present fleet would likely invite intervention from both.

FINANCIAL BALANCES

Ultimately, a policy of neutrality must address the question of costs and the balancing of Canada's present military capabilities against what would be needed for a reoriented defense force. Table 4.1 depicts the present defense budget broken down by "activities." It is also broken down into the three main Votes; that is, Personnel Years (PY), Operation and Maintenance (O&M), and Capital expenditures. It is the "net" figure that reflects the fact that DND, along with federal revenues, receives income from housing rentals, sale of meals, and certain other returns.

Table 4.2 illustrates the budget by percentages of activities. The point to note is that the discretionary budget lies almost entirely within the Capital-expenditure area. O&M tends to move with PY and Capital, so the only way to get more Capital out of this budget (without a discrete budget increase, of course) is to cut personnel and major capabilities. In this discussion it is important to acknowledge the low percentage spent on CF in Europe: 9.2 percent of the total budget. Table 4.3 gives a more precise breakdown of PY allocations.

Almost every unit in Canada is double- or triple-tasked for duties in Canada, and with NATO or the U.N. Therefore, cutting costs directed to one mission does not necessarily provide undiminished funds for other missions. For example, withdrawing from NATO would only free troops and capabilities actually deployed in Europe for those missions. More important, of the approximately one billion dollars spent on that activity, very little would be "saved" for new activities since more than 60 percent of that budget is spent for personnel salaries and the operation of equipment. Only by withdrawing the troops and disbanding them and storing their equipment would any saving accrue to Canada. However, in most cases neutrality would require Canada to redirect its efforts from NATO tasks to Canadian defense tasks in new regions.

Defense planners estimate that withdrawing *and demobilizing* Canadian troops now stationed in Europe might save some $30 billion over the next

Table 4.1: *Net Allocations, Defense Activities: 1987-88*

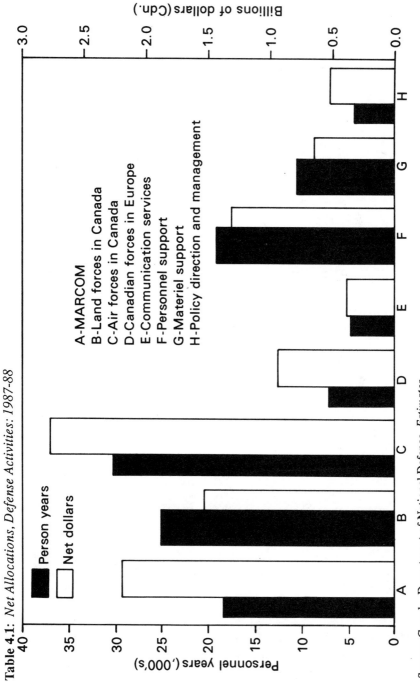

A-MARCOM
B-Land forces in Canada
C-Air forces in Canada
D-Canadian forces in Europe
E-Communication services
F-Personnel support
G-Materiel support
H-Policy direction and management

Source: Canada, Department of National Defence, *Estimates*

Table 4.2: *Net Allocations, Types of Expenditure: 1987-88*

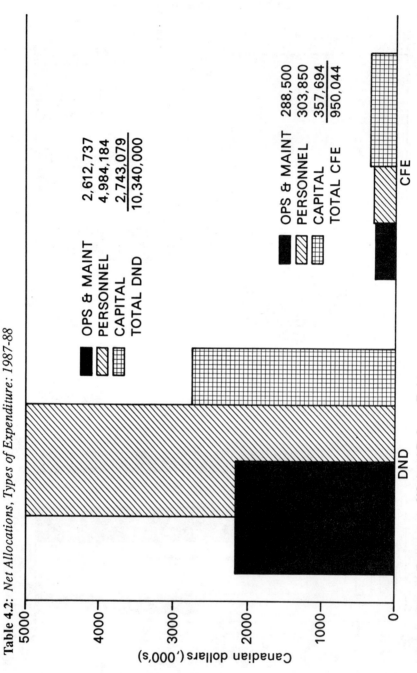

Source: Canada, Department of National Defence, *Estimates.*

Table 4.3
Net Allocations: Defense Activities 1987-88

	PYs	Net $(000)
Maritime Forces	18,107	2,199,727
Land Forces in Canada	25,129	1,526,426
Air Forces in Canada	30,354	2,776,175
Canadian Forces in Europe	7,171	950,044
Communications Services	4,794	398,432
Personnel Support	19,226	1,314,575
Materiel Support	10,601	652,476
Policy Direction and Management	4,271	522,145
Totals	119,653	10,340,000

Source: Canada, Department of National Defence, *Estimates.*

Table 4.4
Army Force Model

Formations/Equipments	Current	Neutrality Model
West	1 CBG	1 CBG
East	5 CBG	5 CBG
	CTC	CTC
NATO	4 CBMG	0
North	0	Arctic Base
Air Field Defense Battalion	0	12
Coastal Defense Battery	0	5
Engineering Regiments	4	7
Airborne Regiments	1	3
Militia	24,000(+/-)	40,000(+/-)
Tanks	114	0
APG	961	144
AVGP	460	900
ARTY - SP	50	0
- Air Portable	12	72
- LLAD (bty)	3	13
- Coastal (bty)	0	5

fifteen years.[6] Under neutrality there would be little possibility for disbanding these military units. Quite the contrary, we would have to increase the strength of the CF to protect our neutrality. There are not enough capabilities or costs going to NATO now to allow us to meet our requirements for neutrality simply by transferring our forces from one region to another.

Table 4.5
Air Force Model

Equipment	Current	Neutrality Model
Air Space Control		
North	NWS (Projected)	NWS
South	0	SWS
Interceptor Aircraft	36	292
Interceptor Air Stations	2	14
CC130 (Hercules)	26	35
CF137 (707)		
Transport	5	0
AWACS	0	4
C^3	0	2
Refuellers	0	5

Table 4.6
Maritime Force Model

Equipment	Current	Neutrality Model
Surface	26	35
Submarines	3	10 - 12
LRPA	18	36
Minesweeper/Hunter	0	9 - 13

Tables 4.4, 4.5, and 4.6 provide an outline of some of the comparative force requirements both under the current collective-defense posture and on the assumption of neutrality as I have modeled it.

Finally, Table 4.7 highlights some representative costs that would have to be met if Canada attempted to change strategies today. The allocation of O&M and PY funds to activities would change but the net effect would be a significant increase in defense spending.

Table 4.7

Typical Additional Resources to Attain Neutrality
(Fiscal Year 1986/87 Billions of Dollars)

	Capital Costs	Ten Year Operating Costs
North Warning System	$ 1.0	$ 0.7
South Warning System	?	?
Arctic Air Base	0.8	0.3
9 Transport Aircraft	0.3	0.2
4 Airborne Early Warning Aircraft	1.2	0.3
156 Fighter Aircraft	6.3	3.3
11 Low Level Air Defense Batteries	2.3	1.0
12 Frigates	6.7	1.4
7 Submarines	2.5	0.3
35,000 Military Personnel	---	13.5

Notes:

1. *General.* All costs are a very rough-order-of-magnitude and should be used accordingly. They represent added costs to DND of increasing the force by the elements shown.

2. *Source of Procurement.* For most of the elements listed, the capital cost is based on procurement from NATO allies (primarily U.S.). Should Canada become neutral, procurement costs could increase and the availability might decrease.

3. *Operating Costs.* Only the last element (35,000 military personnel) includes personnel costs.

4. *North Warning System.* These costs represent the U.S. share that we would absorb if Canada went along on this project.

5. *Arctic Air Base.* This would be an air base that would accommodate two fighter squadrons and a population of approximately 2,200 personnel.

These figures are in "accountant costs"; that is, they reflect fairly accurately costs for the people and real assets involved in this proposal. What is not considered here are what might be termed the intangible and lost opportunity costs to Canada and the CF if a policy of neutrality is adopted. Insofar as defense policy affects many aspects and issues in Canadian society a decision on strategic choices should not be made from budgetary concerns alone.

To support a policy of neutrality, defense spending might have to be maintained at 5 to 6 percent of the GNP (an increase of 2 or 3 percent and a great deal more during the transition phases). That represents an increase in resources that might well be spent on other things. National defense always necessitates a trade-off between guns and butter, but insofar as neutrality does not bring about any increase in the security already available through collective-defense arrangements, resources spent on neutrality represent a real waste and a loss of other opportunities.[7]

The present alliance system provides the CF, and thereby Canada, with significant returns that could not be available in a condition of neutrality. Military arts and sciences are rapidly changing. It is almost impossible for Canada, with a small defense budget and limited operational scope to keep up with the practical application of these changes. Each year Canadian and allied units visit each other's bases and take part in joint exercises. These cross-border mutual training arrangements save Canada millions of dollars annually and provide unequaled opportunities for Canadian service personnel to profit from our allies' experiences.

The Air Force conducts many of these visits and joint training exercises. The Maple Flag series of air combat exercises could not possibly achieve the same high standard if it were not for special equipments and challenges introduced by allies' aircraft. At Goose Bay, Labrador, Canadian air crews are exposed to the different techniques and equipment of British, American, German, and Dutch air forces. These experiences could not be duplicated in isolation.

At sea, Canadian crews and commanders are continually challenged and trained in cooperation with allied navies. We regularly exercise in the waters off allied coasts and use their training areas and facilities. Many of the highly sophisticated equipment and tactics of our potential foes cannot be duplicated for training purposes in Canada but we can gain experiences of them when we work with larger navies. These experiences would be lost to us as neutrals with the inevitable degradation of our military capabilities.

Of course, our land and air commitments in Europe provide the most important and cost effective training ground for the CF. Large-formation exercises using all the latest equipment and tactical concepts are common in Europe. By taking part in these exercises our soldiers and airmen, and especially our officers, gain experiences that are simply not available to them elsewhere.

Some might argue that the experiences gained from allies in a NATO context would be irrelevant to a neutral Canadian defense force. That, of course, is a narrow and incorrect assessment. Operational effectiveness is an important measure in any capabilities analysis. Certainly our inability to learn in friendly competition with others would degrade our operational effectiveness and this deficiency would soon be noticed by the U.S. and USSR. Closed in and isolated, the competence of the CF would wither away. No military force is of much value if it lacks intelligence upon which to base its plans and structure. A neutral Canada would have no immediate sources of military intelligence. Today Canada depends to a large extent on intelligence gained through NATO and from the U.S. and other allies. These sources would all be closed if Canada were neutral. Canada would be faced with either acting dumb or paying enormous sums to establish an independent intelligence network.

Neutrality would affect other aspects of our security as well. Canada's defense sharing agreements would be closed down and access to NATO, American, British and Australian defense consultations would be curtailed. All contacts with NATO and European defense agencies, industrial, scientific, and defense organizations would cease. All bilateral contacts on defense matters with the U.S., such as the Permanent Joint Board on Defense, would be canceled and all our defense-related treaties and arrangements with the U.S. and all NATO nations would have to be renegotiated.

One way out of the dilemma caused by a policy of neutrality that we were unwilling or unable to pay for would, of course, be to substitute nuclear defense for conventional defense. Presumably a strategy based on nuclear deterrence could work as well for a neutral Canada as it has for Canada in a collective-defense alliance.

Canada has the expertise and the materiel to construct both the nuclear warheads and the delivery systems it would require. To be sure, there would be some obvious political difficulties with such a strategy. We would have to develop a nuclear-release strategy (MAD or Flexible Response) that would be credible to those who might intrude into our territories. Domestic difficulties may arise when the government attempted to establish a testing area within Canada. A nuclear strategy for a neutral Canada might seem inappropriate to many. Nevertheless in the interests of completeness it is a policy option that must be looked at carefully, particularly as some non-aligned states, such as India, have flirted with similar ideas.

CONCLUSION

In order to provide a realistic framework for the discussion of neutrality in Canada and to establish a base line for a defense force model, a criterion based on the "rules and obligations" for neutrals must be established. That criterion has four main points:

— Canada would be an armed neutral;
— Canada would survey and control its territory so as to deny its use to belligerents;
— Canada's capabilities to control its territory would have to be demonstrated to the satisfaction of belligerents in peace and war; and
— Any neglect of Canada's responsibilities under the rules of neutrality would invite belligerents to take self-defense measures in Canada.

The final consequences of a military plan or defense policy can only be discovered by answering the following two questions: Will the policy work as a deterrent in peacetime and as a defense in conflict? Will Canada in the end be more secure in peace and war under conditions of neutrality than it has been under conditions of collective defense? In my view, the answer to both questions is no. No official should ever be allowed to propose policies without having to answer one further question: How shall this policy be implemented and what are its likely outcomes?

It remains to be seen when and how the proponents of neutrality propose that Canada should announce its new defense posture. Any attempt to enforce neutrality without the capabilities to do so would only invite challenges to it, and failures to meet these might well invite either armed intrusion or international ridicule, or both. If Canada declared that neutrality would be effective as soon as it acquired the capabilities, what would prevent the materiel suppliers of the present CF foreclosing on Canada immediately? In any case, building a neutral force structure would take at least ten to twenty years to accomplish.

Perhaps, Canada could secretly plan to become neutral, acquire the means over a number of years and then pop the surprise on its allies. Some obvious impediments to such an approach occur: it might be difficult for Ottawa to keep such plans secret, and allies in any event might wonder where all the new defense spending was going. How, indeed, could one manage an alliance and a neutral policy at one and the same time? Finally, how could Canada expect the world to stand still for ten to twenty years while it prepared its plans?

There is no way to implement a strategy of neutrality in the absence of capabilities. Even if sufficient capabilities were somehow acquired, there would remain the further question of whether neutrality would be a morally correct strategy for Canada? In the title of his film sketch on neutrality, Gwynn Dyer captured the essential problem for neutrals, "It is Harder than it Looks." For Canada, however, he understated the problem; not only would it be hard, it would also be more costly than collective defense, deceptive to Canadians, ineffective as strategy, and immoral insofar as it abandoned allies to fight for Canadian values.

Notes

An earlier version of this chapter was presented at a 1987 Conference on Canadian Neutrality, held at the Collège Militaire Royal in Saint-Jean Quebec. Conference papers have been published in a book entitled *Les choix geopolitiques du Canada - Les enjeux de la neutralité* (Le Meridien, forthcoming).

[1]Joseph Nye, *Nuclear Ethics* (New York: Free Press, 1986), 97.

2Most interpretations of "duties and roles" are drawn from Rudolf Bernhardt, ed., *Encyclopedia of Public International Law* vol. 4 *Use of Force in War and Neutrality*, (Amsterdam: North Holland Publishing Co., 1982). It was prepared under the auspices of the Max Planck Institute for Comparative Public Law and International Law at Munich. Assistance in interpretation was provided by the Judge Advocate General, the Canadian Armed Forces, Ottawa.

3Testimony of Professor David Cox, Queen's University, Kingston, to the House of Commons, Subcommittee on External Affairs and Defence, Minutes 8 March 1984, 3:33.

4Canada, Department of National Defence, *National Defence Act*, Section 236.

5International Institute for Strategic Studies, *The Military Balance 1985-86* (London: IISS, 1985).

6Interviews DND, Ottawa, April 1987.

7For a comparison of neutralists' defense spending as a percentage of GNP, see Sweden, Austria, Switzerland, *Military Balance 1985-86*.

5

"No East or West":
Canadian Churches and Collective
Defense in the 1980s

Roger Epp

Nuclear deterrence brutalizes friend and foe alike. None escapes this pervasive threat, and societies associated with perpetuating it cannot escape its moral burden. Nuclear deterrence is a judgement on our collective failure to meet our obligation to build peace and justice.

Above all, our attention to questions of war and peace is informed by the reconciliation that is promised us in the ministry, death and resurrection of Jesus Christ. In Him there is no East and West, no North and South — under His reign all are one. We do not, therefore, accept the division of the world into allies and enemies — and those who have been defined by others as our enemies, we regard as brothers and sisters whose welfare must remain our paramount concern.

> Statements by Canadian church leaders
> to the prime minister, 1988 and 1983[1]

INTRODUCTION: A NEW CANADIAN CHURCH ACTIVISM

In recent years, the major churches in Canada as elsewhere have adopted a more active and generally more critical approach to defense and foreign policy issues. If this new activism by Catholic and mainline Protestant leaders has become familiar throughout the West, and is nourished partly by increasing ties between them, it also has been defined in Canada within the context of a particular political culture and history, and with respect to a distinct range of issues. Thus, the Canadian churches have not spoken as fully as many of their American denominational counterparts to the morality of possessing nuclear weapons and threatening their use in deterrence, or first-strike, strategies. Instead, while rejecting nuclear weapons "without reservation" as "ultimately unacceptable agents of national security,"[2] they have devoted more attention, for example, to the testing of cruise missiles over Canadian territory and to the manufacture in Canada of nuclear weapons components. They have raised doubts about membership in a nuclear alliance. They have called on successive prime ministers to undertake independent initiatives for the sake of arms control and disarmament, and above all to prod United States policy — the indirect target of much of the churches' critique — in what are considered less provocative directions. Most recently, leaders of eleven denominations have issued a joint letter challenging both the "alarmist, anti-Soviet" tone and much of the related policy enunciated in the Canadian government's 1987 Defence White Paper.[3]

This chapter, in turn, constitutes an attempt to understand and to scrutinize the recent ecclesiastical activity within the realm of the study of politics and foreign policy, not theology or ethics, although it necessarily traverses such boundaries. My purpose is five-fold. First, I will be concerned to establish why and in what measure religious leaders, ideas and practices can be conceived as possessing political power in western liberal societies in general and Canada in particular, in what is widely assumed to be a secular age. Second, the essay will sketch out the central defense-related themes, assumptions, moral judgments and policy alternatives revealed in the pronouncements of major Canadian denominations and inter-church organizations. Third, I will examine at least some of the sources — international and national — of this activist critique of defense policy; in this regard, I will also explore the apparent tension between what might be called globalist and nationalist thrusts in the churches' statements. Fourth, some possible problems underlying those statements will be assessed. Foremost among them is the relative lack of a recognizable and rigorous framework, within which moral judgments are made and then addressed to the government and to Canadians outside the churches; and, the seeming difficulty in describing precisely what it is that national defense policy ought to defend, and from what, if by alternative means. Finally, the chapter will argue that, notwithstanding the quotations with which it began, the churches generally have not viewed themselves as being radically at odds with the Canadian government or the Canadian public over defense policy. Nor should they necessarily be viewed as such. To a rather surprising degree, their recent pronouncements borrow criteria from Canadian government policy and seek to place the churches within the mainstream of public opinion. It might be said, if anything, that church leaders have injected little of the transcendent into their critique. In any case, it will be argued that the mainline churches can be fitted into what has been described as the "voluntaristic" tradition in Canadian foreign policy — that is, the search for "moral opportunity" in the world from a position of relative physical security.[4]

RELIGION AND MORAL LEGITIMACY IN FOREIGN POLICY

If the much-publicized, much-contested 1983 pastoral letter of the U.S. Catholic bishops on war and peace achieved nothing else, it did serve to pose a puzzle for students of politics and foreign policy, who by their wide neglect had assumed religious factors were irrelevant to their work.[5] If, however, this was the case, why was it that the Reagan administration should have lobbied the Vatican, the bishops, and lay Catholics in the U.S. in an effort to modify the tone of successive drafts of the letter? Why should prominent strategic analysts have felt compelled to rebut at length the letter's "strictly conditioned," interim moral acceptance of nuclear deterrence? The best answer to the puzzle is that religious leaders may still, in some limited sense, speak from a privileged position as interpreters of morality; that the legitimacy essential to foreign policy — above all where it involves the taking and risking of life — may be contested partly on moral grounds comprising remnants of religious systems;[6] and, that particularly if the defense of the West is presented in terms of the defense of "Judeo-Christian civilization" and religious freedom against an atheistic evil empire, it matters whether the churches endorse such claims. This brief answer, however, requires further qualification drawn from contemporary analyses of religion.

As the outlines of social theory emerged in the nineteenth and early twentieth centuries around such major figures as Karl Marx and Max Weber, two central, essentially shared assumptions about religion also took root. On one hand, while religious ideas and movements had sometimes had a revolutionary social effect, institutional religion typically had fulfilled a conservative, functional role in support of the established order. On the other hand, religion was increasingly being stripped of whatever social force it once wielded by a process of secularization. To the extent that these claims have been modified in the face of the apparent persistence of at least some measure of religious belief and practice, it is in the direction suggested by Peter Berger. In short, Berger argues that religious belief has not disappeared but rather has been "privatized," while political issues increasingly are posed as mere matters of technical "problem-solving."[7] That religious belief has not disappeared completely is attributed to the failure of liberal capitalist ideology, atomistic and subjective, to construct its own moral ethos, giving meaning to daily experience and to the "basic risks of existence" — mainly suffering and death — within some larger reality.

What is equally clear, though, is that religion is no longer the source of legitimation, of that "socially objectified knowledge that serves to explain and justify the social order."[8] In other words, it no longer defines reality and the moral duties of individuals within it. Historically, Berger holds, religion has been so effective a means of legitimating social institutions because it could confer on them "an ultimately valid ontological status, that is, by locating them within a sacred and cosmic frame of reference."[9] This power bears particular importance,

> whenever a society must motivate its members to kill or to risk their lives.... Thus the "official" exercise of violence, be it in war or in the administration of capital punishment, is almost invariably accompanied by religious symbolizations. In these cases religious legitimation has the already discussed "gain" of allowing the individual to differentiate between his "real self" (which is afraid or has scruples) and his self *qua* role carrier (warrior, hangman, and what not).[10]

At present, however, despite religion's lingering presence in public rhetoric, it cannot fulfill what Berger calls its "classical task" of constructing a common framework of meaning.

In a similar vein, a continental sociologist has commented that religion "has become just one social factor among others in a context where secularization, tolerance and the separation of church and state have resulted in religious pluralism."[11] Religious accounts of reality and morality stand alongside secular accounts, and at that are widely ignored. Indeed, it has been suggested that when church leaders "wish to comment on social affairs they rely neither on revelation nor on holy writ. They set up commissions, often with considerable reliance on the advice of sociologists."[12] Their authority, too, is assumed to rest primarily in the persuasiveness of their arguments.

Yet, if religious blessing is not crucial, if it is situated no longer within a context of socially objectified knowledge, it would be a mistake to conclude that its force has been dissipated. The lingering presence of religious vocabulary in public rhetoric has been noted. Moreover, it is argued persuasively that because of the special historical linkages in the West between religion and morality — a result of the Christian preoccupation with sin — "the remnants of religion are, if receding, as yet in evidence."[13] In any case, the problem of political justification persists, and in the absence of new authorities religious leaders remain, to some extent, the interpreters of morality; their blessing can lend respectability to both an issue and one side of an issue. Thus defenders and critics of nuclear deterrence in the U.S., for example, have argued over the proper interpretation of the Catholic bishops' pastoral letter. President Reagan, unable to sway the bishops, immediately enlisted the active support of Rev. Jerry Falwell.[14] As prominent a figure as Zbigniew Brzezinski has taken to citing John Paul II, somewhat selectively, on the permissibility of deterrence.[15] Peace activists, meanwhile, vaunt where possible the endorsement of religious leaders and organizations. There appears, in sum, some measure of truth in this observation from a British perspective, made with regard to the recent debate over nuclear weapons:

> [T]he role of religion as a legitimator of political policy seems to have had a largely unexpected renaissance even in western secular societies, so that theology

is expected and encouraged to take part in the discussion, and strenuous efforts are made to recruit theological support for one side or the other.[16]

The case for such a renaissance is perhaps more readily made for the U.S., where the exceptionalist moral claims embodied in the polity have been both more overt and more overtly religious, than for Canada. At least historically, however, there are unquestionable links between religion, political culture and government policy in Canada. Space does not permit a full discussion here of this history, which properly would account, among other things, for important differences between a French Canada dominated by Catholicism and an English Canada affiliated mainly with Anglicanism or with Protestant denominations of British origin. In the case of English Canada, for example, it has been suggested that for the first two generations following Confederation, Protestantism was driven by a vision of the country as God's dominion; accordingly, it responded to the "threat" of non-British immigration with a "crusade to Canadianize the immigrants by Christianizing them" — that is, to assimilate them into "Anglo-Saxon values."[17] While the enduring effects on Canadian political culture of this crusade and the underlying vision are not easily traced, other, more tangible instances of ecclesiastical activity related to the concerns of this chapter can be identified. In World War I the churches "rallied without hesitation to the national cause."[18] They offered more than prayers, consolation and chaplains for the troops; ministers urged enlistment from the pulpit and sometimes served as official recruiting agents. Equally, in the reaction which set in against the war during the 1920s, the newly-formed United Church in particular was an important locus of interwar pacifism. When war did recur in Europe, the churches responded for the most part with support, but without the accompanying millennial fervor of the earlier conflict. In the aftermath of the war they have been described as staunchly supportive of the United Nations and less preoccupied with the Cold War and communism than their U.S. counterparts.[19]

Again, the relation of such attitudes to government policy — also committed to "liberal internationalism" and the UN in the post-war era — and to political culture is doubtless a complex one, demanding closer historical analysis. Most intriguing would be the possible influence of religion on what has been called the "long tradition of anti-militarism in Canadian political culture."[20] Whatever else can be said for Dean Acheson's unflattering depiction of Canada as "stern daughter of the voice of God," acting in world affairs with a sense of moral rectitude, the depiction itself also recalls Thomas Hockin's observation about the central role played by "sons of the manse" — Lester Pearson included — in giving foreign policy its internationalist thrust.[21]

Into the 1960s, the blessing of church hierarchies was still considered significant enough to merit attention in John Porter's classic elite-based study of Canadian society, *The Vertical Mosaic*:

In the light of their specialized "knowledge" religious bodies make pronouncements about the rightness or wrongness of economic, political, or military policy.
They can if they wish condemn decisions by other elites. Because of this power
of withholding their legitimizing approval, church leaders may be consulted
before decisions are made, or they may be brought into the decision-making
processes of other elites.[22]

That same decade, however, represents for others a pivotal period, when
the churches ceased to be "moral policemen" with special status as "the keeper
of the nation's conscience."[23] This judgment is confirmed by a recent, albeit
controversial, sociological study which argues that, for most Canadians, religion is neither "life-informing" nor the key source of their sense of what
issues are socially urgent. Moreover, whenever a religious group takes a moral
stance, it "does so in a cultural context that neutralizes the impact of its
claims"; such statements merely "are declared viewpoints and added like tiles
to the moral mosaic."[24]

Paradoxically, perhaps, the same study finds that "the religious establishment appears to be in better shape than ever,"[25] with greater social activism at the leadership level, for example, backed by larger research staffs. If
the corresponding messages are not always received positively in the pews —
the denominational rank-and-file will not even necessarily be familiar with the
stands taken by national leadership — there is again reason not to dismiss their
potential political import. The widespread public debate over the Canadian
Conference of Catholic Bishops' 1982 pastoral letter on the economy, involving everyone from the prime minister to labor leaders to economists, may be
instructive here; for these respondents, something other than theological
fidelity was deemed at stake in the bishops' statement. While to date there has
been no comparable debate around ecclesiastical activity in the sphere of foreign and defense policy, studies have suggested some degree of church
influence vis-à-vis Canadian policy during the Biafran crisis and, more
recently, in relation to Central America and human rights in general.[26] In
addition, the churches' response to the Defence White Paper has been deemed
important enough by at least one major newspaper columnist to earn an unre-
mitting denunciation of what he characterized as "moralistic rubbish."[27] In
Canada, too, however, church support can be claimed on different sides of
defense-related issues. Thus a senior official with the Department of National
Defence, for example, has appealed to the moral wisdom of Pope John Paul II
and the Anglican Bishop of London — their authority presumably attaching
to their roles — in arguing for continued reliance on nuclear deterrence.[28] In
sum, while the power of institutional religion should not be overstated, for the
reasons given, there is warrant enough for the survey that follows.

"LIVING IN SIN": NUCLEAR WEAPONS AND CANADIAN COMPLICITY

Any essay-length discussion of the churches and Canadian defense policy is necessarily selective. In this case, the emphasis will be on the articulated positions of the major churches over the course of the 1980s. This chapter does not account for all the activity undertaken by churches at the local and national level in the name of world peace: marches, vigils, visits to the Soviet Union, distribution of educational materials in the congregations, and so on. Nor does the essay claim to fit all churches into a single mold on defense questions, even though ecclesiastical champions of nuclear deterrence seem relatively rare in Canada.[29] Its focus will be the statements of major denominational and ecumenical bodies:[30] the Canadian Council of Churches, which embraces Anglican, United, Presbyterian, Lutheran and other smaller Protestant groups; the Canadian Conference of Catholic Bishops (CCCB); and, Project Ploughshares, a self-described "taskforce on disarmament and development" sponsored by the Canadian Council of Churches and supported primarily by churches and development agencies. One of a broad array of interchurch agencies established in recent years to speak to social issues, Project Ploughshares conducts research and monitors developments related to Canadian defense policy, military production and arms exports. Its personnel have contributed to the drafting of joint church statements, including the response to the White Paper.

The churches' positions are stated in various forms and fora. In some denominations, delegate bodies at periodic national meetings pass resolutions, typically expressing a concern to be communicated to the Canadian government. In the case of the CCCB, public declarations and pastoral messages — the latter meant to be read in congregations — are issued. On several occasions, church leaders have issued joint "open letters" to the prime minister. Indeed, the Canadian churches generally have stressed ecumenical cooperation against the tendency of their U.S. counterparts, for example, to speak denominationally to public matters. Finally, the aforementioned groups now appear on a regular basis before parliamentary committees dealing with defense and foreign policy. In some sense, then, the churches' public role has been facilitated by the increased emphasis on parliamentary review of foreign policy instituted during the 1970s. It is now expected — indeed assumed in the invitations to testify — that the churches will have positions to express. (As well, representatives may sit on formal consultative committees which include government officials and appointees of other societal groups; one such example is a committee established by the Ambassador for Disarmament.)

In turning to the substance of the churches' position, it should be said that the focus on the present decade constitutes more than the imposition of an arbitrary division for the sake of academic tidiness. Indeed, prior to the 1980s, what is striking is the virtual neglect of defense and security issues on the part of the churches (although it is true that the United Church General Council, for example, routinely passed motions opposing "war" at its biennial meetings in the 1950s and by 1960 was asking questions about the nature of Canada's alliances).[31] In this neglect, the churches would appear to have mirrored the broader inattention to such issues in Canadian society. Nonetheless, it is noteworthy that the emergent ecclesiastical activism of the 1970s under the banner of social justice did not address defense policy directly.[32] Further, when the churches began to do so in this decade, it was partly as a result of the spillover of more long-standing interests, including the relationship of global military spending to Third World development and, later, the effects of cruise-missile testing in the Canadian north on native peoples of the region.

It is possible, however, to identify at least two more immediate sources of this heightened concern of Canadian religious leaders with, in broadest terms, the nuclear arms race. The first is the election of Ronald Reagan as U.S. president and the belligerence that marked much of his first term in office, as manifested both in an openly skeptical attitude toward arms control negotiations with the Soviets and in what was widely perceived as a shift toward nuclear war-fighting and first-strike strategies. Thus the Canadian churches shared in, and responded to, the same sense of alarm that fed the U.S. freeze movement and mass demonstrations in Western Europe. Late in 1981, the CCCB issued a statement directed chiefly at the decision to proceed with development of the neutron bomb, but which in its introductory sentences reflected and addressed this wider, almost apocalyptic, public anxiety:

> Humanity seems to be rushing at breakneck speed to nuclear self- destruction. There is a growing sense among people today that the arms race is out of control. A global holocaust within this generation looms as a distinct possibility. The superpowers appear insensitive to the stakes involved, namely the annihilation of life on this planet which the Lord of Creation called good...[33]

In December 1982, the leaders of several major Canadian churches met with Prime Minister Trudeau for the first time to articulate their concerns. A year later, they praised his own "peace initiative" abroad and premised a lengthy statement with the comment that Canada had come to a crucial point in relation to the Reagan administration, which had shown itself to be "sharply out of step with North American and Western national security tradition" with its "dangerous, even suicidal, quest for military superiority."[34] This perception of a fundamental shift in American strategy, as will be clear, continues to inform the arguments of the Canadian churches.

The second source was the decision of the Canadian government to allow flight testing of the U.S. air-launched cruise missiles over its territory. On one hand, the decision was viewed as a final repudiation of the "strategy of suffocation" unveiled by Trudeau at the United Nations Special Session on

Disarmament in 1978. That strategy proposed, among other things, a comprehensive test ban and an agreement to stop flight testing of all new strategic delivery vehicles. For the churches it was to become the standard against which Canadian defense policy was measured and found wanting.[35] In this respect, in the words of the late Bishop Adolphe Proulx, spoken on behalf of the CCCB:

> the testing of the cruise missile in Canada has become a symbol of Canada's non-commitment to halting the nuclear arms race.... The cruise missile is a symbol of surrendering our sovereignty in determining our own defense and security policies. The cruise missile is a symbol of escalation and destablilization.[36]

On the other hand, it might be said in a perhaps perverse sense that the cruise missile was welcomed by some in the churches. As a senior United Church staff member has written, prior to the testing debate, "Canadians tended to cheer disarmament efforts from the sidelines" and never "defined their own security interests." From this view, too, the issue was symbolic: it served as the "avenue for entering the national and international debate on the best ways for building security for people in all countries."[37]

From the numerous statements issued since the early 1980s by the churches, thus motivated, it is possible to discern a broad analytical framework comprising three parts: a judgment of nuclear weapons and of "militarism" generally; the demonstration of Canadian complicity; and, the putting forward of alternative defense policies within a redefined vision of security giving greater emphasis to North-South disparities. Perhaps the churches' strongest denunciation of nuclear weapons is that found in the 1983 statement to the prime minister:

> [W]e must say without reservation that nuclear weapons are ultimately unacceptable as agents of national security. We can conceive of no circumstances under which the use of nuclear weapons could be justified and consistent with the will of God, and we must therefore conclude that nuclear weapons must also be rejected as means of threat or deterrence.[38]

Other, seemingly unequivocal condemnations of this sort might be cited. The United Church's General Council, for example, approved a resolution in 1984 supporting the declaration of Canada as a nuclear-free zone and stating a willingness to "live without the protection of weapons of non-discriminatory effect and mass destruction." It, too, committed church resources to the task of educating members as to "the urgency of delegitimizing nuclear weapons and the falseness of the deterrence option."[39] The Anglican Church's General Synod in 1983 delivered a similar judgment against nuclear and other weapons of mass destruction as "contrary to the will of God."[40]

Such condemnation, however, requires qualification. In the first place, it has always been accompanied in joint statements, as in 1983, by a recognition that the process of nuclear disarmament "can itself be destabilizing and fraught with danger" and should thus be conducted on a staged multilateral basis; the churches, they themselves caution, "have not called for unilateral, unreciprocated disarmament."[41] Second, the CCCB, when speaking on its own, has tended toward the position set out by John Paul II in 1982 and developed in stricter terms by the U.S. bishops: namely, that "the possession of nuclear weapons for deterrence can only be tolerated as long as progress is being made" toward the elimination by negotiation of all nuclear weapons systems.[42] Third, some of those who have spoken for the churches have drawn a qualitative distinction between mere retaliatory capability for strategic stability and those nuclear weapons and plans — "of an entirely different order" — which sustain war-fighting and first-strike options.[43] Ultimately, from this view, the problem remains that of eliminating all nuclear weapons; the immediate task, however, is to challenge those strategic doctrines which conceive of uses for nuclear weapons outside a simple deterrence relationship, as well as those weapons and defensive systems suspected of having first-strike potential. Thus, a church representative told a parliamentary committee that any strategic defense system involving Canadian airspace should be opposed, because it would undermine the doctrine of deterrence.[44] The first draft of the churches' response to the White Paper also calls on the government to clarify its definition of deterrence and strategic stability. Though cautioning against long-term reliance on "nuclear threat and counter-threat," the draft argues that Canadian imprecision "may be leading us, perhaps unwittingly," to direct support of war-fighting strategies and the "abandonment of basic deterrence."[45] That such an explicit statement of preference for mutual assured destruction, in essence, did not appear in the letter addressed to the prime minister may indicate that some church leaders do not like the matter put so plainly. Nonetheless, that interim preference informs some of the policy positions of the attached appendices, concerned that Canadian territory be used to enhance, not harm, strategic stability.

These qualifications and differences aside, there appears a more basic agreement as to why nuclear weapons are "ultimately unacceptable as agents of national security." First, they represent the most destructive element of a wider tendency towards "militarism" — that is, in broadest terms, the tendency to treat what are rightly political or social problems by military means — the overall effect of which is that the global problems of poverty and disease receive a disproportionate share of economic and intellectual resources. In this sense, the arms race is considered a cause of social and economic underdevelopment. As the churches' response to the White Paper put it: "Even if the world's obscenely growing stockpile of weapons is never detonated, it already produces victims on a grand scale."[46] Second, even if it is conceded that strategic stability may be better preserved in the short term by "basic deterrence," it is argued that nuclear weapons are inappropriate tools of defense, of preservation; instead, they merely destroy on a massive scale. Their power is so great "that there are no conceivable circumstances in which it could rationally be used."[47] The overall effect of nuclear weapons, moreover, has been to heighten not security but insecurity. Third, and perhaps most significant, nuclear arsenals threaten the very continuation of life on earth. Though this point is often made simply in terms of a threat to human survival, in other cases it is given a theological orientation. Whereas human beings are called to be stewards of the earth for this and future generations, the mere possession of nuclear weapons represents the arrogation of the power to destroy what God has created and declared good.[48] It raises "the distinct possibility of total human extinction, which would be the ultimate sin because it would be an act of mutual and total suicide."[49]

The second part of the churches' analytical framework is the demonstration of Canadian complicity in the nuclear arms race and the larger, global system of militarism. This judgment was stated perhaps most succinctly by the United Church's Committee on the Church and International Affairs in summarizing Canadian lack of innocence since 1945 in the manufacture of nuclear weapons: "By working on the periphery of the nuclear club, we have been living in sin."[50] On the whole, however, the judgment has been more qualified than this. In past meetings with prime ministers, church leaders have been careful to note what are deemed positive initiatives, among them the removal of nuclear weapons from Canadian soil and positions taken at the United Nations. As they also concede, it has been difficult to accuse previous Canadian governments of disproportionate levels of military spending.[51] On the other hand, the list of ecclesiastical suspicions about Canadian activity has lengthened during the 1980s. Mention has already been made of the symbolic character of cruise missile testing. To this could be added the following concerns: military exports, especially to the Third World;[52] manufacture of components, with government support, for such weapons as the cruise and MX, as well as increasing overall integration into the U.S. military-industrial complex, to the neglect of distinct national needs;[53] Canadian support for NATO's "twin-track" policy as part of its long-standing commitment to flexible response, which does not preclude the first use of nuclear weapons;[54] and, finally, Canadian participation in a North American air defense system, now "hardly the coast guard of the sky" once intended and perhaps even the "trojan horse" for a more destabilizing system.[55] It is on this latter point that the White Paper is criticized for its silence.[56]

Underlying this concern with complicity is the conviction — or at least the hope — that a more independent Canadian defense policy could contribute more effectively to the cause of global peace and nuclear disarmament. In the words of Bishop Proulx, "complicity with a superpower" is dangerous for the world because it hinders Canada from "playing the role it could have."[57] The implications of this position have been drawn most fully in the work of Project

Ploughshares, which explicitly has advocated the termination of NORAD and the maintenance of membership in NATO — albeit with the withdrawal of Canadian troops from Western Europe — only if fundamental reforms are implemented in Alliance policy.[58] Church leaders, however, have been somewhat more tentative on this point in their joint statements. In 1983, they did argue that Canada could not remain silent in the face of significant changes in American strategic doctrine, but only intimated that this should be done at the risk of its status as an "important ally."[59] In their 1988 open letter, church leaders address the alliance problem even less directly, though they do assert as a basic principle that Canada's security is dependent ultimately on an international order respectful of national sovereignty — not, by inference, on the strength of its military alliances.[60]

TOWARD A NON-PROVOCATIVE DEFENSE POSTURE

The final, and most recent, part of the churches' analysis is concerned with the presentation of alternative defense policies and of a redefinition of the concept of security. There are perhaps two major arguments involved here. The first is an assertion of the necessity of greater control of Canadian airspace, coastal waters, and territory, in order to contribute more effectively to strategic stability between the superpowers. Based on the principle that "Canadian territory should not be available to any other country for the purpose of attacking or threatening to attack a third country,"[61] this argument envisions surveillance capability sufficient to give such assurance to both the U.S. and the Soviet Union. The required capability, it is recognized, could only be achieved at considerable cost. Yet, as a representative of Project Ploughshares has argued, though the churches are reluctant to advocate increased military spending, they are anxious that Canada accept sovereign responsibility for knowing what is happening in and over its territory.[62] This capability, in any case, is restricted to passive or "non-provocative" forms of surveillance, interception and early warning: "It is the knowledge of certain detection that provides the deterrent, not the threat of interception."[63] Measures beyond this — for instance, an air defense system with combat capacity — serve only to diminish Soviet retaliatory confidence and thus to reduce strategic stability. Similarly, it is suggested, the nuclear-powered submarines called for in the White Paper would not contribute substantially more to Arctic surveillance than would passive acoustic means; yet, insofar as they could be integrated into the Americans' forward-based maritime naval strategy in the North Atlantic, they also would undermine strategic stability.[64] In all, the concern is to use Canadian territory and resources to restrict the nuclear options of both superpowers in crisis situations, and this in the name of old-fashioned deterrence:

If deterrence is to be the guide, *both* sides must be deterred.... In insisting on the mutuality of deterrence in transition to disarmament, we are not suggesting that there are no political or moral distinctions between the two sides, but rather acknowledging that since both have chosen weapons of global annihilation as their last resort, both must be subject to the discipline of deterrence.[65]

One final word may be in order here with respect to the churches' stated commitment to non-provocative defense. While the churches accord only a minimal role to military force in the pursuit of "common security," they do not advocate the full disarming of Canada. What they counsel is the "reduction of conventional arsenals to levels consistent with the state's obligation, within morally constrained limits, to protect the weak and preserve justice."[66] Again, while neither the churches nor Project Ploughshares have indicated what model of patrol aircraft and even submarine would meet these specifications — the need for both having been acknowledged by at least one representative[67] — they have called for the development of an indigenous defense-industrial base oriented to Canadian military requirements.

At the same time, the churches have situated their demands for a reassessment, but not a repudiation, of the national interest within a larger, globalistic vision of "common security." In their 1988 letter, they advise:

Governments must, as must we all, ultimately serve a common humanity, rather than only the national interest. Governments have an obligation to build peace with the building blocks of peace and justice.... The security of some must not be purchased with the insecurity of others.[68]

It is in this respect that the churches challenge distinctions of East and West, North and South. The reality of political-military divisions between East and West cannot be denied, at least in the short run, but "the people of the Soviet Union are brothers and sisters whose welfare is our concern." Further, there is "no moral or security justification" for the White Paper's characterization of the Soviet Union as an "eternal, unredeemable enemy." More importantly, the White Paper wrongly defines the world as dominated by the East-West rivalry, to the neglect of the "primary" or "most urgent and intractable world security problems" of the age. What is advocated in its place is a North-South view which stresses "indigenous threats to security — lack of adequate food, shelter, and health care, as well as a denial of fundamental human rights." From this perspective, the "chief threat to security faced daily by most of the people on earth is the threat to survival engendered by a world order that either will not or cannot meet basic human needs." In this context, then, "true security ... must be seen first and foremost as social and economic security."[69] While the church leaders do not suggest precisely how this alternative, North-South view should inform Canadian defense policy, it would seem to accommodate two of their long-standing concerns: stricter controls on military exports and continuing emphasis on peace-keeping activity under United Nations jurisdiction.

CRITICAL SOURCES: GLOBAL WELFARE AND CANADIAN AUTONOMY

If developments in the early 1980s provided much of the immediate impetus for the Canadian churches' concern with defense issues, leading to the critique described above, the position they have articulated can be said to share in wider theological currents worthy of at least brief consideration here. Admittedly, it is difficult to show clear lines of influence. Nonetheless, the churches' position parallels and, in some cases, is directly informed by a process of ecclesiastical rethinking on three prominent fronts: a heightened skepticism about war in general; a new sensitivity to Third World concerns; and, in Canada, a renewed appreciation of national sovereignty.

Within the Catholic and mainline Protestant churches, which traditionally have sided with a "just-war" rather than a pacifist interpretation of Christianity, the destructive conflicts of this century and the advent of nuclear weaponry have contributed to a basic re-evaluation of the moral status of military force.[70] This heightened skepticism may well have come at a point when, politically, it matters less, given the churches' declining influence. The change in ecclesiastical thinking on this problem has been both pervasive and relatively rapid, occurring chiefly in the post-war period. On the Catholic side, while the right and duty of states to protect their populations has been affirmed, the morally justifiable reasons for war were reduced to one — defense against aggression — even under the papacy of the strongly anti-communist Pius XII. His successor, John XXIII, in his famous encyclical, *Pacem in Terris* (1963), called for an "entirely new attitude" toward war and declared, in a much-disputed phrase, that "in an age such as ours which prides itself on its atomic energy it is contrary to reason to hold that war is now a suitable way to restore rights which have been violated."[71] Shortly thereafter, the Second Vatican Council committed the Catholic Church to "strain every muscle as we work for the time when all war can be completely outlawed by international consent."[72] Subsequent popes have continued to voice reservations about whether military force can still be an instrument of justice. National episcopal conferences have, with notable exceptions, reflected this shift in church teaching. The CCCB in particular quotes extensively from papal and other church statements in its judgments.

While the proclamations of the Protestant-dominated World Council of Churches are not similarly authoritative for individual adherents of member organizations, they reflect a skepticism about military force in the nuclear age broadly equivalent to that in recent Catholic teaching. The WCC's 1983

Assembly in Vancouver, for example, issued the following statement with the understanding that national churches would press its message upon their respective governments:

> We believe that the time has come when the churches must unequivocally declare that the production and deployment, as well as the use of nuclear weapons are a crime against humanity and that such activities must be condemned on ethical and theological grounds. The nuclear weapons issue is, in its import and threat to humanity, a question of Christian discipline and faithfulness to the Gospel.[73]

That the WCC has stopped short of a full-fledged pacifism is due partly to the arguments of those Third World members who suggest, sometimes by traditional just-war criteria, that violent revolution can be justified against the "structural violence" of political and economic oppression. Nonetheless, it has also evinced continued concern with "militarism" as a global phenomenon.[74]

If the primary theme of the post-war ecumenical movement has been the priority of Christian unity above national loyalties and conflicts, Catholic teaching too has declared the church's mission as not bound to any single political community or ideology. In both cases, this concern for the "whole human family" — nourished by greater transnational contacts — has been manifested perhaps most notably in a new sensitivity to issues of economic underdevelopment and political oppression. Within the WCC, this sensitivity has extended to the financial support of some national liberation movements through the controversial Programme to Combat Racism.[75] In Catholic teaching, the expressed general concern of recent popes has been developed further by Latin American bishops as a "preferential option for the poor."[76] In Canadian churches, the effect of these trends of thought over the past two decades is reflected in various ways: the establishment of new denominational and ecumenical organizations concerned with justice and peace; the annual sponsorship by local churches of workshops under the general banner, "Ten Days for World Development"; and, the making of statements by church leaders on issues of human rights abroad.[77]

Given this emerging globalist perspective, it may seem somewhat surprising that the churches should also be as strongly supportive of greater Canadian autonomy as their statements on defense policy suggest. There is, however, an explanation that brings together these different thrusts. While the churches' statements do not clearly make this connection, it has been made by several Canadian theologians in a way that serves to illuminate some of the assumptions underlying those statements. The link can be explained in this manner. Though the churches' activism with respect to foreign policy generally can be seen, in part, as a reaction against the shift toward "self-interested materialism" heralded in *Foreign Policy for Canadians* (1970),[78] their nationalism also recalls the type of internationalism ascribed to the same Trudeau government by Michael Tucker. In essence, Canada is regarded as a "mentor state,"

willing to take unilateral initiatives out of national interest but equally "on behalf of the world community."[79] Whatever the virtues of this description of
foreign policy under Trudeau, much of it does resonate in church statements
and more openly in recent writing on the theological status of the Canadian
nation. Where liberal Protestantism, most notably, tended in the inter-war
period to take up the cause of internationalism against the rivalry of nation-
states, it has rediscovered the value of nationalism — rightly defined — in the
face of increasing economic globalization and, with it, cultural homogeniza-
tion. In this context, abstract internationalism is said to easily "cloak the stark
facts of worldly irreconciliation" and injustice; what the present generation
"must learn intelligently to *fear*, if our culture is to survive with any quality,
is oddly similar to what the preceding generations taught us to *hope for*: One
World."[80]

Perhaps the clearest Canadian expression of this view, curiously reminis-
cent both of Hegel and of the same early nineteenth-century German roman-
ticism that has influenced the realist tradition in international relations, is a
self-proclaimed theological apologia for the churches' responsibility to uphold
nationalism "in the face of American encroachments."[81] Written in the mid-
1970s, its argument proceeds as follows. Since history has meaning as the site
of God's acting to achieve a purpose for mankind, and since nations are part
of historical reality, then nations share in this divine purpose and possess value
accordingly. A common humanity is refracted through particular cultures and
histories. Applied to Canada, this argument finds a nation "threatened by
absorption, culturally, economically, and politically by an American power
that shows grave evidence of serious moral decline." Yet, "history" has also
left open positive avenues to Canada that are not now open to the U.S., to the
extent it is given to militarism and materialism:

> In this time of United States sickness and travail it is foolish and indeed morally
> irresponsible to abandon Canadian sovereignty to the United States, not only for
> our sakes but ultimately for theirs and for the world's. Otherwise we shall scarcely
> be in a position to make a distinctive and useful contribution to a global society.[82]

While church leaders seldom put the point so clearly, and may not necessarily make "history" their principal reference, much of the above argument
has parallels in the statements on defense policy discussed in this chapter. It
is reflected further in the expressed opposition of some church bodies to any
free-trade arrangement between Canada and the U.S. Whether this ecclesiastical concern for Canadian sovereignty, partly on the basis of an assumed moral
superiority, has roots independent of the broader resurgence of nationalist sentiment since the late 1960s cannot be determined without further inquiry. It
appears, nonetheless, a rare occasion when a Canadian church leader declares
the nation-state to be an obsolete and inherently dangerous form of human
organization. Instead, the retention and affirmation of distinct national

identities is made the precondition of genuine internationalism. Greater Canadian sovereignty is less the problem than part of the potential solution in the nuclear age.

DEFENSE: OF WHAT, AGAINST WHAT, AND WITHIN WHOSE MORAL LIMITS?

Leaving aside the abstract and perhaps irresolvable issue of how much harmony and justice are possible in politics among nations, there are several lines of critical commentary that might usefully be raised in relation to the churches' statements on defense. At the level of policy analysis and recommendation, for instance, there is room for skepticism about the scope of influence likely to redound to a Canada extricated from NATO and NORAD (at what would be a considerable cost, diplomatically and otherwise). It is not clear that both superpowers, much less the major Western European states, would have an independent Canada play the mediating role envisioned by some church leaders. Even if the potential Canadian contribution to global peace is conceived less in diplomatic terms than in the capacity to give assurances to both superpowers about the use of Canadian airspace and thus to subject both to the "discipline of deterrence," this essentially neutral stance would be meaningless unless the Americans and Soviets agreed to respect it. (In any case, space-based detection could in future render Canadian airspace less vital to strategic stability.) Questions might also be asked about the churches' persistent association of defensive systems, particularly in relation to continental air defense, with first-strike capability and thus with strategic instability. This association feeds a somewhat surprising preference for mutual assured destruction (MAD) as the posture from which to move toward nuclear disarmament. While the moral basis of this preference will be treated below, it should be said here that the churches do not demonstrate why, presuming the nuclear powers indeed can be persuaded to dismantle their arsenals, MAD should be the logical way-station from which to do so. In wanting to warn against nuclear war-fighting strategies, the churches arguably may have given themselves too uncritically to the side of pure offense even as a supposedly transitional position.

In the churches' defense, in turn, it should not be forgotten that specific parts of their critique have also been raised by more "mainstream" strategic analysts. Not only the churches have had doubts, for example, about the renewal of the NORAD agreement in the context of U.S. "nuclear revisionism";[83] about the maintenance of a military presence in Europe;[84] about the decline of an indigenous defense-industrial base; and, about the acquisition of nuclear-powered submarines.[85] It was, indeed, no less eminent a strategist than Colin Gray who in the early 1970s suggested that in the absence of any direct threat the Canadian military faced a crisis of relevance; the guarantor of Canada's security, the U.S., was also its most probable political adversary.[86]

There are two perhaps more fundamental points on which the churches' position requires at least refinement and clarification. The first concerns their discussion of security. On one hand, the idea of security as something much broader than a military problem — as having economic, social and other dimensions — follows the helpful path charted in recent international relations theory by Barry Buzan.[87] There are compelling reasons why the security of nation-states is best conceived as multi-faceted and best considered in terms of regional or even global "security complexes," the U.S.-Soviet relationship being a prime example, wherein the security of those involved is in some sense interdependent. Thus the churches' argument that the "security of some must not be purchased with the insecurity of others" may be justifiable strategically as well as morally. The churches, however, having decided to speak to Canadian defense policy, neglect what is for Buzan the more elementary question (and one which is no less pertinent for strategists and policymakers): What precisely is the referent object for security? How can a nation-state, an "amorphous, multi-faceted, collective object," be conceived as such?[88] In particular, what ought Canadian defense policy to defend, if by alternative means? And from what?

The need for greater clarity on these points arises repeatedly in the churches' analysis. While they have cautioned that the preservation "of the ultimately transient institutions of nation states, even our beloved country, is not an ultimate value," and that, therefore, the means of defense are subject to moral limits,[89] they have not suggested far beyond this what moral or theological worth Canada should be given. This is, no doubt, a difficult exercise for those churches which have rediscovered in the post-war period the tension between allegiance to Caesar and to Christ. Nonetheless, what is it about Canadian shared values, if such exist, or Canadian institutions, however imperfect, that merits their defense and preservation? The churches and, more so, those theologians cited above come closest to at least a partial answer in their emphasis on Canadian autonomy vis-à-vis the U.S., for the good of both Canadian society and the world. Indeed, employing Buzan's broad definitions of security and the nation-state, it is possible to regard the U.S. as representing some manner of threat to Canadian institutions and ideas. Yet this is still primarily a negative statement of worth: a fear that closer integration into the American orbit will result in the loss of distinct, and presumably more humane, Canadian orientations. It remains to define those orientations and identify the threats they must confront. If the relative value of Canadian political institutions is linked, in part, to their ostensibly democratic basis — and the churches do desire "popular participation in decision-making" in all societies[90] — does this value represent something that is shared with other liberal democracies? If so, does it require some manner of common defense? This line of argument is not intended as a back-door affirmation of Canadian alliance membership. It does, however, without prejudging the answer, lead in the direction of the standard Canadian justification for NATO participation; Prime Minister St. Laurent in 1949 hailed the Alliance as essential to the survival of "Christian civilization" itself.[91] It is not necessary that the churches should share this judgment. Still, their argument begs the question: if, as they contend, the White Paper substitutes "jingoistic depictions of enemies" for "realistic threat assessments as the basis for defence policy,"[92] must it be incorrect to identify the Soviet Union as constituting some manner of threat, if not as an unredeemable enemy? Is the White Paper's analysis exaggerated or entirely misplaced? The churches' apparent reluctance to consider this question further might well arise from a concern not to give solace to any rigid, bipolar worldview. Yet even advocates of an alternative defense posture in Western Europe do not suggest that the Soviets pose no threat, military or political, to their societies; neither does much of the continental left.[93] Again, though the White Paper's assertion of a major Canadian security interest in the defense of Western Europe may stand in need of further demonstration, is it entirely misplaced?

As it is, the churches do admit a "vital interest" in Europe, but only insofar as the outbreak of war there would be catastrophic for the world.[94] In this way, their analysis tends to treat the problem of security in terms simply of preventing war rather than of describing what should be secured, of judging the means by which security has been pursued without assessing as carefully the purposes to which they are — or ought to be — directed. The Canadian churches are not alone in this tendency. It also marks the U.S. Catholic bishops' pastoral letter, and may be attributed in part to the increasing emphasis in recent just-war thinking given to the criteria of proportionality and discrimination.[95] This lack of clarity about the object of Canadian security leaves incomplete the churches' contribution to the debate over defense policy.

Against this criticism, it might be argued that the churches' nascent discussion of common security built on social justice furnishes such an object, along with a standard for assessing Canadian policy. To assert the primacy of a North-South perspective on security, however, is not to remove all remaining ambiguity. If nothing else, it demands clearer differentiation among referent objects of security. While the conditions the churches attribute to countries of the South represent undeniable sources of insecurity for the respective peoples, it is less clear how they relate to "Canadian" security. The churches do not argue that, if unresolved, these problems will one day lead the South to rise up militarily against the North. Neither would they want instability in these countries to be interpreted principally as an opportunity for the Soviet Union to expand its influence abroad and tilt the global balance of power against the West. While Canada may have a moral obligation and political reasons for seeking to alleviate the North-South gap, it is another question whether this problem should have been a priority in a White Paper intended to address security at a different level and, indeed, whether it is best conceived by Canadian policymakers at large in security terms.

The second fundamental point on which the churches can be prodded concerns the apparent lack of a rigorous, recognizable moral framework within which their judgments are made. In part, this lack is a function of the priority assigned to speaking ecumenically. When churches representing different theological orientations and ethical traditions concur on a joint statement on defense policy, it is perhaps not surprising that such concurrence will have been at the cost of more sustained moral argumentation. The task of achieving a common framework of foundational principles has, in essence, been made secondary to that of speaking to issues of the day. There is, however, a more substantive source of difficulty which is evinced too in denominational statements.

In simplest terms, the advent of nuclear weapons has generated a deep ambivalence about the entire just-war framework in those churches which traditionally have relied on some variant of it. Numerous church representatives have expressed a position close to that of Clarke MacDonald, former moderator of the United Church, for whom "the theory of a just war is absolutely put out of the picture by the presence of nuclear weapons."[96] Yet some of the same individuals utilize just-war categories, primarily those of proportionality and discrimination, in coming to a position essentially of nuclear pacifism.[97] The question of whether just-war arguments have been rendered inadequate in the nuclear age — or whether they ever accorded with Christian teaching — is best left to ethicists and theologians. For the purpose of this chapter, a word can be said about the implications of this ambivalence: namely, that the churches' search for an alternative ethic has led them perhaps by default in the direction of an unlikely consequentialism. If the prevention of nuclear war is sometimes presented in ecclesiastical statements in theological language — that is, as an obligation flowing from the command to be stewards of God's creation — it is also the immediate end in relation to which strategies, weapons and Canadian policies are judged. On this basis, a preference is stated repeatedly for "basic deterrence" against any perceived shift toward war-fighting doctrines and weapons. This interim preference, however, has not been accompanied by any wrestling with the dilemmas that would be raised within a just-war framework, among them, the moral status of targeting civilian populations and of threatening, for the sake of the deterrence relationship, to do what could not in conscience be carried out. In effect, though the churches would disassociate Canada from its nuclear alliances, they would still ask that others be prepared to do evil that good may come of it.[98] This sort of consequentialism is not foreign to liberal Protestant ethics (and it should be said that some of the most open statements of preference for "basic deterrence" have come from Protestant representatives); it is less easily accommodated by Catholic ethics or by the unconditional Christian pacifism of some other signatories of the churches' response to the White Paper. Moreover, while it does not represent the churches' entire position on nuclear weapons, which remain "ultimately unacceptable," the effect is that this ethical judgment comes to turn partly on matters of political judgment: what makes for strategic stability in the short term and what best facilitates the achievement of nuclear disarmament?

CONCLUSION: DETACHED PROPHETS OR "CONNECTED CRITICS"?

In a recent book, political theorist Michael Walzer sets out two alternative models of social criticism.[99] The first is that of the critic who pronounces judgment from outside a particular society. The second is that of the "connected critic" who is rooted within a society and challenges it in the name of values recognized and widely shared by its people. This connectedness does not guarantee success; Walzer's Old Testament archetype, the prophet Amos, could not turn his society around. Connectedness, however, means that the criticism may cut deeper because it arises from a knowledge of the values of those to whom it is addressed.

In their statements on defense policy, the Canadian churches have aspired to a role close to that of Walzer's connected critics. Although it has been argued compellingly that the churches should be viewed as a "counter-consensual" force on a range of foreign policy issues,[100] and although the White Paper's defenders may less enthusiastically endorse this description, such an emphasis obscures the extent to which the churches have sought to situate themselves in the Canadian mainstream. Undeniably, much of the impetus for their recent activism derives from wider theological currents and transnational ecclesiastical bonds. In their response to the White Paper, the churches attempt to identify themselves with the majority view of Canadians as reflected in public opinion surveys. To some extent, they see their task as articulating the moral concerns of that majority. Their representatives, moreover, do not necessarily consider the churches to be radically at odds with the Canadian government; if anything, they find agreement on at least part of the problem — "putting the brakes on" destabilizing U.S. initiatives — and differences largely on the extent and the most effective means of exercising Canadian influence in Washington.[101] Their joint statements, after setting out the basis of the churches' concern, are remarkably free of religious language, much less scriptural references. They do not call on the Canadian government to align its policies with revealed divine injunctions. Rather, the statements draw attention to previously articulated government positions, such as the strategy of suffocation, and ask that they be upheld in changed circumstances. They sometimes quote government ministers in support of ecclesiastical concern, for example, with the disproportionate share of global resources that is absorbed by the arms race. They accept the preservation of Canada as a good thing. They impart a view of Canada's present and potential place in the world that finds some parallels in the "mentor-state" internationalism ascribed to the Trudeau government through the 1970s. On this basis, they recommend that Canada take full responsibility for territorial surveillance in order to contribute to strategic stability between the superpowers. Finally, they concur with, but draw different implications from, the present government's position that, ultimately, Canadian security demands a stable, peaceful international order.

In sum, though it is possible to take issue with the churches' strategic and moral judgments, there is ample reason to situate them within the voluntaristic tradition that still, we are told, "runs so markedly through the Canadian psyche."[102] That tradition, for Thomas Hockin, "may be called an escape from the realities of power politics," but it is neither isolationist nor necessarily neutralist; at heart, it represents "an impulse to change the nature of international politics," by involvement in different international fora. Voluntarism "emphasizes the importance of working towards the *ought* of a better world order, rather than centring on ways in which the given international system can be exploited for national advantage."[103] The churches, if anything, have argued simply that the "search for moral opportunity" leads in new directions in an age of nuclear revisionism and North-South disparity.

By most measures, the churches have not experienced great success in their efforts to alter Canadian defense policy. Cruise missile tests have continued despite their protests. A decidedly pro-NATO, pro-NORAD White Paper was issued, its analysis focusing on East-West divisions, notwithstanding the concerns raised by the churches in the 1980s. If only on the issue of Alliance membership, majority Canadian opinion remains resolutely with the government. This seeming lack of influence can be attributed to several factors. As suggested above, religious blessing has lost what crucial character it once possessed; in Canada, moreover, such blessing is less actively solicited than it has been in the U.S. In any case, while religious leaders may still serve in some sense as interpreters of morality, they cannot define the moral agenda so much as speak to those issues identified for them as socially urgent. In this respect, it could be argued that the nuclear debate of the early 1980s never provoked in Canada a widespread existential moral dilemma of the same order as that in either the U.S. or Western Europe, where the visibility of weapons installations, among other things, made the sense of threat more immediate. The churches' lack of success might also be said to illustrate the extent to which Canadian foreign policy is formulated in isolation from domestic interests.[104] Finally, the fact that the churches' actual target is the U.S. government, and that this requires Ottawa not only to refrain from some action but to press specific concerns with Washington, makes success yet more elusive.

There is, however, one less apparent sense in which the effect of the churches' activity should not be discounted: namely, in the setting of parameters within which defense policy is made and articulated. Such impact is not readily demonstrable. Policy parameters, in turn, are not clearly discernible. Yet evidence of their existence can be found, for example, in the present government's decision against participation in the U.S. strategic defense initiative, in its unwillingness to accept any possible military dimension in the joint space-station program, and in the strikingly revised world view presented in the first annual update of the White Paper.[105] That the churches may have contributed something to those political and moral limits should not be overlooked.

Notes

[1]"Open Letter to Prime Minister Mulroney," February 1988, reprinted with appendices as *Peacebuilding: The Church Response to Canadian Defence Policy*, Working Paper 88-1 (Waterloo: Project Ploughshares, 1988), 3; "Therefore Choose Life: Statement on Peace and Disarmament," presented to Prime Minister Trudeau, December 1983, reprinted in *The Church and Nuclear Disarmament*, Working Paper 85-3 (Waterloo: Project Ploughshares, 1985), 1.

[2]"Therefore Choose Life," 1.

[3]*Peacebuilding*, 3-4.

[4]Thomas Hockin, "The Foreign Policy Review and Decision Making in Canada," in Lewis Hertzman, John Warnock, and Thomas Hockin, eds., *Alliances and Illusions: Canada and the NATO-NORAD Question*, (Edmonton: M. G. Hurtig, 1969), esp. 97-110.

[5]I have discussed this problem more centrally in "The Power of Moral Sanction: Toward a Modest Place for Religion in the Study of Foreign Policy," Occasional Paper no. 20 (Kingston: Queen's Centre for International Relations, 1987). The following paragraphs are drawn, in part, from pp. 20-22 of this earlier paper.

[6]On this point, I am in agreement with Robert W. Tucker's observation that, as war has become both a massive social enterprise and the object of greater popular suspicion, "when force is threatened or employed, the justification attending its threat or use is a matter of no small importance." Robert E. Osgood and Robert W. Tucker, *Force, Order, and Justice* (Baltimore: Johns Hopkins University Press, 1967), 196.

[7]Peter Berger, *The Sacred Canopy: Elements of a Sociological Theory of Religion* (Garden City, NY: Doubleday, 1967), *passim*; see also Bryan Wilson, *Religion in Sociological Perspective* (Oxford and New York: Oxford University Press, 1982), 27-52.

[8]Berger, *Sacred Canopy*, 29-30.

[9]Ibid., 33.

[10]Ibid., 44.

[11]Richard van Dulmen, "The History of Religion as Social Science," *Telos* 58 (Winter 1983-84): 23.

[12]Wilson, *Religion in Sociological Perspective*, 170.

[13]Ibid., 88.

[14]Haynes Johnson, "A Preacher for Peace through Strength, or, Maybe, the Bomb," *Washington Post*, 3 April 1983, A3.

[15]Zbigniew Brzezinksi, "The Strategic Implications of Thou Shalt Not Kill," *America* 154 (1986): 445-49.

[16]Duncan Forrester, "The Theological Task," in Howard Davis, ed., *Ethics and Defence: Power and Responsibility in the Nuclear Age* (Oxford: Basil Blackwell, 1986), 23.

[17]N. Keith Clifford, "His Dominion: A Vision in Crisis," in Peter Slater, ed., *Religion and Culture in Canada* (Waterloo, Ont.: Wilfred Laurier University Press, 1977), 24, 31.

[18]John Webster Grant, *The Church in the Canadian Era* (Toronto: McGraw-Hill Ryerson, 1972), 113-14; see also J. M. Bliss, "The Methodist Church and World War I," *Canadian Historical Review* 49 (1968): 213-33.

[19]Grant, *The Church in the Canadian Era*, 150-51, 167.

[20]Michael Tucker, *Canadian Foreign Policy: Contemporary Issues and Themes* (Toronto: McGraw-Hill Ryerson, 1980), 11.

[21]Hockin, "Foreign Policy Review," 151 n.7. The Acheson quotation is from his essay, "Canada: Stern Daughter of the Voice of God," in Livingston Merchant, ed., *Neighbors Taken for Granted: Canada and the United States* (New York: Praeger, 1966), 134.

[22]John Porter, *The Vertical Mosaic* (Toronto: University of Toronto Press, 1965), 460.

[23]Grant, *The Church in the Canadian Era*, 202, 204.

[24]Reginald Bibby, *Fragmented Gods: The Poverty and Potential of Religion in Canada* (Toronto: Irwin, 1987), 164.

[25]Ibid., 118.

[26]See, respectively, Donald Barry, "Interest Groups and the Foreign Policy Process: The Case of Biafra," in Paul Pross, ed., *Pressure Group Behavior in Canadian Politics* (Toronto: McGraw-Hill Ryerson, 1975), 117-47; Tim Draimin, "Canadian Foreign Policy and El Salvador," in Liisa North, ed., *Bitter Grounds: Roots of Revolt in El Salvador* (Toronto: Between the Lines, 1981), 103; and Robert O. Matthews, "The churches and foreign policy," *International Perspectives* (January/February 1983): 18-21.

[27]William Johnson, "Churches' critique is moralistic rubbish," *Ottawa Citizen*, 19 February 1988, A8.

[28]Lorne Green, "Maintaining Peace with Freedom: Nuclear Deterrence and Arms Control," *Points of View* no. 4, March 1987; see also General R. M. Withers' address to the 1983 Anglican Church of Canada General Synod, "The Mission of the Free World's Armed Forces: Peace Through Strength," in *Canadian Defence Quarterly* (Autumn 1983): 8-9.

[29]A minor exception is the conservative evangelical organization Heritage Forum, which in 1983 took issue with "left-leaning" mainstream churches on the issue of nuclear deterrence. See Michael McDowell, "Nuclear arms ensure peace, groups believe," *Globe and Mail*, 9 March 1983, 4.

[30]In terms of declared religious affiliation, 1981 census figures indicate that about 47 percent of the Canadian population is Catholic and 39 percent is Protestant. Of the latter group, the United Church accounts for about 16 percent and the Anglican Church for 10 percent. So-called conservative Protestant denominations constitute 7 percent. See the analysis in Bibby, *Fragmented Gods*, 47.

[31]Reports presented and resolutions passed at successive General Council sessions in the post-war period tell a more complex story than can be presented here. In 1948, the report of the Committee on the Church and International Affairs (CCIA) asserted that there was no more urgent task for Christians in the "new era of the atom" than to promote peace, and warned against "a mood of hysteria" or fatalism about war; yet, the report also declared Soviet expansion "the logical outcome of communist teaching and policy," which, in turn, was said to constitute a major challenge for Christian doctrine. In 1954, the General Council urged that the thermo-nuclear bomb be prohibited by international agreement. In 1958, it resolved that the time had come to renounce war as an instrument of national policy. But by 1960 and 1962 the CCIA and the delegate body both revealed divisions over nuclear deterrence, and concern over the direction of Canada's military alliances could not be translated into resolutions calling for withdrawal. In 1968, meanwhile, at the height of the Vietnam War, the General Council urged support for the Paris negotiations and demanded an immediate end to U.S. bombing of North Vietnam. It also expressed concern about war material sold to the U.S. by Canadian firms. See the *Record of Proceedings* of the respective Council sessions.

[32]Further evidence for this observation is found in two recent collections of church statements on a range of social issues: poverty, energy, native rights and northern development, refugees, human rights in the Third World, etc. — but not defense and disarmament as such. See John Williams, ed., *Canadian Churches and Social Justice* (Toronto: Anglican Book Centre/James Lorimer, 1984); Gerard Rochais, ed., *La Justice Sociale Comme Bonne Nouvelle: messages sociaux, économiques et politiques des évêques du Québec, 1972-1983* (Montreal: Centre Justice et Foi, 1984).

[33]"Canadian Catholic Bishops on the Nuclear Arms Race," reprinted in *The Ecumenist* (March/April 1982): 47-8.

[34]"Therefore Choose Life," 2.

[35]See, for example, "A Statement on Canada's Nuclear Weapons Policies," presented to Prime Minister Trudeau, December 1982, reprinted as Appendix F, in Robert Matthews and Cranford Pratt, eds., *Church and State: The Christian Churches and Canadian Foreign Policy* (Toronto: Canadian Institute of International Affairs, 1982). Reference to the strategy of suffocation also can be found in several of the statements collected in *The Church and Nuclear Disarmament*. The suffocation speech itself is found, among other places, in Larry R. Stewart, ed., *Canadian Defence Policy: Selected Documents, 1964-1981* (Kingston: Queen's Centre for International Relations, 1982), 279-84.

[36]Bishop Adolphe Proulx, Statement on the second testing of the cruise missile in Canada, 15 January 1985, in *The Church and Nuclear Disarmament*, 11.

[37]Bonnie Greene, Introduction to the section on disarmament and peace, in *Signs of the Times: Resources for Social Faith*, Vol. II (Toronto: United Church of Canada, 1984), 120.

[38]"Therefore Choose Life," 1. The statement was signed by Catholic, Anglican, United, Presbyterian, and Lutheran leaders, and by the president of the Canadian Council of Churches.

[39]*Record of Proceedings*, 30th General Council, 1984 (Toronto: United Church of Canada, 1984), 57-8.

[40]Reprinted in *The Church and Nuclear Disarmament*, 6.

[41]"Therefore Choose Life," 1.

[42]"Disarmament and Security," CCCB submission to the House of Commons Standing Committee on External Affairs and National Defence (SCEAND), 16 February 1982, reprinted in *The Church and Nuclear Disarmament*, 8. In a speech to the UN Second Special Session on Disarmament, John Paul II judged deterrence acceptable "not as an end in itself," but as a step toward a "progressive disarmament." The speech is reprinted in *Origins* 12 (1982-83): 81-7.

[43]Ernie Regehr, research director, Project Ploughshares, in testimony before SCEAND, *Minutes of Proceedings and Evidence*, 32nd Parliament, 1st session, 16 February 1982, 152.

[44]Bonnie Greene, member of the executive committee, Project Ploughshares, testimony before the Special Joint Committee on Canada's International Relations, *Minutes of Proceedings and Evidence*, 33rd Parliament, 1st session, 19 July 1985, 28.

[45]Draft of an open letter to Prime Minister Brian Mulroney, 31 July 1987, 9. Neither the draft nor the other statements of interim preference for "basic deterrence" cited above indicate which nuclear weapons would be countenanced in such a strategic posture.

[46]*Peacebuilding*, 2. See also, for example, "A Statement on Canada's Nuclear Weapons Policies," #12; CCCB, "Disarmament and Security," 9-10.

[47]*Peacebuilding*, 2-3. See also, for example, CCCB, "Disarmament and Security," 8.

[48]"Therefore Choose Life," 1; "A Statement on Canada's Nuclear Weapons Policies," #26.

[49]United Church Committee on the Church and International Affairs, Report to the 30th General Council, *Record of Proceedings*, 444.

[50]Ibid.

[51]"A Statement on Canada's Nuclear Policies," #6-7, also cited in *Peacebuilding*, 2.

[52]See, for example, "Therefore Choose Life," 4.

[53]This dimension, as well as that of arms sales to the Third World, is explored at length in Ernie Regehr, *Arms Canada: The Deadly Business of Military Exports* (Toronto: James Lorimer, 1987).

[54]"A Statement on Canada's Nuclear Policies," #20-22.

[55]The quoted comments are those respectively of Simon Rosenblum and Ernie Regehr, both of Project Ploughshares, in testimony before SCEAND, *Minutes of Proceedings and Evidence*, 18 November 1985, 14-15.

[56]*Peacebuilding*, Appendix III, 8.

[57]Bishop Adolphe Proulx, testimony before SCEAND, *Minutes of Proceedings and Evidence*, 18 November 1985, 13.

[58]The full range of Project Ploughshares' positions has been collected under the label of "common security" in a recent internal document, "Policy/Action Proposals." The conditions stated for continued Canadian membership in NATO are: adoption of a no first-use policy; denuclearization of Europe; transarmament to a non-provocative force

structure; and, planning for dissolution of NATO and the Warsaw Treaty Organization. The ultimate goal is "replacement of regional alliances with global collective security institutions." Regehr, meanwhile, has testified before SCEAND on Project Ploughshares' behalf against renewal of the NORAD agreement. *Minutes of Proceedings and Evidence*, 18 November 1985, 6-11.

[59]"Therefore Choose Life," 2.

[60]*Peacebuilding*, 1.

[61]Ibid.

[62]Ernie Regehr, testimony before the Special Joint Committee on Canada's International Relations, *Minutes of Proceedings and Evidence*, 10 April 1986, 130-31.

[63]*Peacebuilding*, Appendix IV, 9. See also Regehr's testimony, SCEAND, *Minutes of Proceedings and Evidence*, 18 November 1985, 6-11.

[64]*Peacebuilding*, Appendix IV, 10-11.

[65]Ibid., Appendix III, 8-9.

[66]Ibid., 3.

[67]Regehr testimony, Special Joint Committee, *Minutes of Proceedings and Evidence*, 10 April 1986, 130-31.

[68]*Peacebuilding*, 2.

[69]Ibid., 4.

[70]See, for example, Thomas A. Shannon, ed., *War or Peace? The Search for New Answers* (Maryknoll, NY: Orbis, 1980); Edward J. Laarman, *Nuclear Pacifism: "Just-War" Thinking Today* (New York: Peter Lang, 1984).

[71]John XXIII, *Pacem in Terris*, #126, reprinted in David J. O'Brien and Thomas A. Shannon, eds., *Renewing the Earth: Catholic Documents on Peace, Justice and Liberation* (Garden City, NY: Doubleday, 1977).

[72]"Pastoral Constitution on the Church in the Modern World," #82, reprinted in *Renewing the Earth.*

[73]"Statement on Peace and Justice," David Gill, ed., *Gathered for Life: Official Report of the VI Assembly*, Vancouver 1983 (Geneva: World Council of Churches, 1983), 137. The phrase quoted is from the report of a WCC panel following hearings on disarmament in Amsterdam in 1981. The panel, incidentally, included David MacDonald, former Conservative cabinet minister and United Church minister.

[74]Ibid.

[75]Darril Hudson, "The World Council of Churches and Racism in Southern Africa," *International Journal* 34 (1978-79): 475-500.

[76]Key documents of the Latin American bishops' important 1968 conference at Medellin, Colombia, are in *Renewing the Earth*, 549-79.

[77]Williams, "Introduction," *Canadian Churches and Social Justice*, 2-4.

[78]Matthews, "The Churches and Foreign Policy," 18.

[79]Tucker, *Canadian Foreign Policy*, 10.

[80]Douglas John Hall, "Introduction," in Graham Scott, ed., *More Than Survival: Viewpoints Toward a Theology of Nation* (Don Mills, Ont.: United Church of Canada/CANEC Publishing, 1980), 11-5. The emphasis is Hall's.

[81]Antonio Gualtieri, "Toward a Theological Perspective on Nationalism," in *Religion and Culture in Canada*, 510.

[82]Ibid., 516. Cf. in the same volume the critique of nationalist claims for moral superiority in Michel Despland, "Religion and the Quest for National Identity: Problems and Perspectives," 525-51.

[83]See, for example, Douglas A. Ross, "American Nuclear Revisionism, Canadian Strategic Interests, and the Renewal of NORAD," *Behind the Headlines* 39 (1982), no. 6.

[84]Joseph T. Jockel and Joel J. Sokolsky, *Canada and Collective Security: Odd Man Out*, The Washington Papers no. 121 (New York: Praeger/Center for Strategic and International Studies, 1986).

[85]James Eayrs, "Assessing the Ice-Pack Rationale," *Peace & Security* (Autumn 1987): 10-11.

[86]Colin Gray, *Canadian Defence Priorities: A Question of Relevance* (Toronto: Clark Irwin, 1972).

[87]Barry Buzan, *People, States and Fear: The National Security Problem in International Relations* (Brighton: Harvester, 1983).

[88]Ibid., 10, 13.

[89]"A Statement on Canada's Nuclear Weapons Policies," #5.

[90]*Peacebuilding*, 4.

[91]St. Laurent's comments are quoted in Hockin, "Foreign Policy Review," 150-1 n.6.

[92]*Peacebuilding*, 4.

[93]See, for example, Gene Sharp, *Making Europe Unconquerable* (Cambridge, MA: Ballinger, 1985); Andre Gorz, "Security: Against What? For What? With What?" *Telos* 58 (1983-84): 158-68.

[94]*Peacebuilding*, Appendix V, 12-3.

[95]I have made this argument, without challenging the bishops' judgments, in "Des Armes en Temps de Paix? La Dissuasion Nucléaire et la Menace Soviétique dans le Cadre d'Analyse de la Guerre Juste des Evêques Catholiques Américains," *Etudes Internationales* 19 (1988): 33-55.

[96]Clarke MacDonald, chairman, Project Ploughshares, testimony before SCEAND, *Minutes of Proceedings and Evidence*, 18 November 1985, 17; see also, for example, Proulx's testimony before SCEAND on the same date, *Minutes of Proceedings and Evidence*, 24.

[97]Dennis Murphy, general-secretary, CCCB, testimony before SCEAND, *Minutes of Proceedings and Evidence*, 16 February 1982, 91. Murphy argues that the reasons given in traditional moral theology for a just war no longer hold amid the "radically different" situation of nuclear weapons, but this claim is based on their "undue proportion."

[98]Some important differences between just-war, pacifist and "survivalist" orientations are drawn in Stanley Hauerwas, "On Surviving Justly: An Ethical Analysis of Nuclear Disarmament," in Jill Raitt, ed., *Religious Conscience and Nuclear Warfare* (Columbia, MO: University of Missouri-Columbia, 1982), esp. 2-12.

[99]Michael Walzer, *Interpretation and Social Criticism* (Cambridge, MA: Harvard University Press, 1987).

[100]Cranford Pratt, "Dominant Class Theory and Canadian Foreign Policy: the Case of the Counter-Consensus," *International Journal* 39 (1983-84): 99-135.

[101]Interview with Ernie Regehr, April 1988.

[102]*Interdependence and Internationalism, Report of the Special Joint Committee on Canada's International Relations* (Ottawa: Supply and Services, 1986), 139.

[103]Hockin, "Foreign Policy Review," 106, 108, 95-96.

[104]Kim Richard Nossal, "Analyzing the Domestic Sources of Canadian Foreign Policy," *International Journal* 39 (1983-84): 1-22.

[105]Canada, Department of National Defence, *Defence Update,* 1988-89 (Ottawa: Supply and Services, 1988). The update, for example, grants much more significance than the White Paper to reforms in the Soviet Union and to prospects for arms control agreements. Though cautious, the update discerns a "warming trend in East-West relations".

PART TWO

North American Defense:
Cooperation or Discord?

6

The Permanent Joint Board on Defense, 1940-1988

Christopher Conliffe

INTRODUCTION: THE BOARD AND THE HISTORIANS

Any discussion of North American security, particularly in this the fiftieth anniversary year of President Roosevelt's 1938 speech in Kingston, must inevitably come around to the Permanent Joint Board on Defense (PJBD). The Board was not created until 17/18 August 1940, at Ogdensburg, but it was the first agency through which substance was given to the President's promise that the United States would not stand idly by if Canadian soil were to be threatened by any other empire. It immediately took on the prestige of its status as the senior bilateral defense agency, and of its first co-chairmen, and has retained it in large measure throughout its life.

An evaluation of the Board's effectiveness is fraught with danger, for the conceptual lenses through which the Board is examined will vary, and in all probability vary significantly, from one person to the next. A severe limitation is that although a modern agency is the subject of inquiry, the records for the most recent twenty-five years of its life are closed, and the discussion of this period must perforce be circumspect. In spite of these two drawbacks, an assessment of the PJBD is both valid and necessary. It is valid because every agency of government benefits from periodic external scrutiny, and it is necessary because as new documents are declassified every year, so earlier opinions on the Board need to be either corrected, updated, or confirmed.

Three authors have made substantial contributions to the literature on the PJBD. Colonel Stanley W. Dziuban did a study of military relations between Canada and the United States during the Second World War as a doctoral thesis submitted to Columbia University; this was published in 1959.[1] Dziuban succeeded in having the Board's thirty-three wartime recommendations declassified, when some of them were less than fifteen years old. In his review of Dziuban's book, James Gibson, then Dean of Arts and Science at Carleton University, drew attention to this service to other scholars.[2] Dziuban looked only at the first five years of the PJBD's life, and his judgments are positive; this is not surprising. In his view, the Board was immediately effective, for the arrangement struck at Ogdensburg was "masterfully designed to meet the needs of both leaders."[3] The arrangement was politically acceptable in the United States because it was limited to mutual defense, and the inclusion of the word "permanent" in the title, helped to counter any suspicion that the arrangement would hasten U.S. participation in the War.

The PJBD limited itself to planning the measures and the troop and material resources needed to defend northern North America, which functionally translated into the construction of naval, army, and air bases, and of the auxiliary road, communication, weather, radar and similar facilities required by the United States in Canada and Newfoundland.[4] In all of this the Board was effective. On the other hand, the existence of service attachés in both capitals, and the Canadian Joint Staff in Washington, had a limiting effect on the Board's work. It also had the inevitable effect of causing overlapping of effort and confusion as to responsibilities.[5] Another liability was that unsound recommendations which had not been staffed by the appropriate departments could go forward. The most significant aspect of the Board's wartime operation was the direct access by the Chairman of the United States Section to the President.[6]

David Beatty devoted his entire 1969 doctoral thesis, submitted to Michigan University, to the PJBD.[7] His contribution therefore goes beyond Dziuban's in two ways. First, it is more in-depth, and second, it covers a larger period of the Board's life. Beatty has looked at the Board from a variety of perspectives. In his opinion, the PJBD provided Canada and the United States not only with an agency for the joint study of defense problems, but with a symbol as well. The appointment of full members from the Department of External Affairs and the State Department was significant in that it lent PJBD matters a higher priority in the activities of each nation's political departments.[8] Using the 1953 agreement on the LORAN stations in Newfoundland as an example, Beatty credits the PJBD with acting as a clearing house in case of disagreement between the two nations over the exigencies of a particular defense project.[9] The Board frequently assumed this position, he says, and in fact an examination of the documents does support this view. In a particularly telling judgment, Beatty shows that in many of the bilateral Canada-United States defense agreements, the PJBD played a major role, not just in framing the terms of the understanding, but also in becoming a final board of review to consider, at a point in the future, the ongoing necessity of a particular defense project. In this way, the Board guaranteed its own permanence.[10]

Another of Beatty's judgments which may be supported with no difficulty is that the Board helped to modify, to some degree, the demands of the American armed forces. Through the Board, Ottawa was able to exercise a degree of political influence on the United States government, and thereby make Washington pay more respect to public opinion in Canada than would have been the case without the PJBD.[11] Another aspect of the Board's value lay in the fact that in working out political details of joint projects between countries, Board members were representatives of their governments from lower levels, rather than principals.[12] There are some surprises in and among Beatty's judgments. The establishment of NORAD was the result of Board activity, he says.[13] At best this is stretching the truth to its limit; at worst, it is misleading to the point of being false. This will be dealt with in more detail later in this chapter. Also surprising is the statement that the PJBD contributed indirectly to the building of NATO, through Dean Acheson, who for a brief period was Chairman of the American section.[14] An even bigger surprise is the opinion that the functions of the Board evolved rapidly during the years 1953-1958, and further, that the Board allowed the Canadian military members to exert greater influence on Canadian policymaking than would have been possible with only normal diplomatic channels. The Canadian government, without the Board, would never have allowed the Canadian military so much voice in decisions.[15] This can only be a reference to the birth of NORAD, and Joseph Jockel in his recent book has shown that the PJBD was largely bypassed when NORAD was created.[16] Beatty returns to the 1953-1958 period later in his book and claims that the Board's impact on government decision-making was appreciable in those years. Nearly every consideration involving military matters affecting the two countries had been discussed at some time by the Board.[17] That might be true in a most general way; but no recommendations were made after 1953, so what was the impact on government decision-making? He goes on to say that after 1958 the Board's recommendations fell dead, one by one, when they reached the Diefenbaker government, because the controversy over nuclear weapons brought PJBD activity into an eclipse which would not end for half a decade.[18] In the first place, there were no recommendations sent forward to the Diefenbaker government, and in the second place it was not controversy over nuclear weapons which brought the PJBD into a period of eclipse. The term is most appropriate, but its causes go deeper into the personalities involved.

Before leaving Beatty's assessments of the PJBD, it is appropriate to draw attention to his opinion that after 1960, Washington's interest in the Board waned.[19] This is an accurate observation which will be developed later. He also points out that the amount of business which the Board handled, and its effectiveness in transacting it depended heavily upon the state of relations between the two countries, at the time.[20]

C. P. Stacey is the third writer who has looked at the PJBD in a comprehensive way. In an article[21] and an information booklet[22] he has given it a concise treatment, but in his book *Arms, Men and Governments* the analysis is more complete. Stacey did, however, limit himself to the operation of the PJBD during the war years, and he sees the Board through the eyes of the historian. He does make a number of worthwhile points.

The formal recommendations did not constitute the entire record of the Board's work. The Board's meetings have always been characterized by informal discussions which are not reflected in the journals, and out of these discussions came a number of informal suggestions which went to one or both governments.[23] To this day, informal discussions which have no written record are a feature of Board meetings, and may well be the most important feature of the meetings. Similarly, informal or at least oblique suggestions seem to be preferred nowadays.

Stacey also brings out the Board's usefulness as a testing ground for ideas which one side wanted to try out on the other, and as a negotiating body which combined foreign service and armed forces members. By its very nature, the Board was an effective means of collecting and exchanging information. Because of the people to whom it reported, the Board was also able to expedite action, and keep attention focused on projects of importance.[24] These points apply during the war years. The first three can be used as valid yardsticks to judge the Board's performance at any time in its life. The fourth has long since ceased to have any relevance to the Board's activities. Colonel Stacey acknowledges that the work which the PJBD did during the war could have been done without the creation of the Board, but thinks that the Board did it more rapidly and with more goodwill.[25] A final and telling point is that some matters which the Board might have handled were routed through other channels. As an example, Stacey cites the Canol Project in the Northwest Territories.[26] The President was not above ignoring the agency which he had created; for example, Roosevelt directly communicated with Churchill over aspects of the defense of Newfoundland, a subject which had in fact been a primary interest of the Board.[27] This leads to the question that must be asked sooner or later, which is: just what did Roosevelt really want and expect from the PJBD? In a short article on the reaction of the Conservative Party to the Ogdensburg meeting, J. L. Granatstein reproduces the words of Richard Hanson, leader of the Conservatives. When he heard the news about Ogdensburg, Hanson went to see the Prime Minister, and in a letter to Arthur Meighen, Hanson said:

> We found out that the whole thing was Roosevelt's idea to help him out with Congress and give him a *quid pro quo* for anything he might do with Great Britain, but that there are no commitments whatsoever, and the only agreement is that of a Joint Study Board.... At any event King told me...that Roosevelt had asked for

the interview and asked for the joint board as window dressing which he can take to the Congressional leaders....[28]

If that is indeed an accurate reconstruction of the President's attitude to the Board, then it explains in part the way the President paid attention to the Board when it suited him, but also bypassed it if that was more expedient. It also does much to explain why, as Stacey says, the PJBD was most important during the period of United States neutrality, although he attributes its loss of importance to the increased level of military liaison between the two countries.[29] It also illuminates Beatty's statement that in establishing the PJBD, the President wanted the most freedom possible with regard to Congress.[30] Lest we forget, the President was fighting an election in 1940, and while he was sympathetic to the idea of the United States entering the war, the country he led was not and was moreover subject to the Neutrality Act of 1935. The conclusion therefore that must be drawn is that in spite of the inclusion of the word "permanent" in the Board's title, its usefulness in the President's eyes was short term, or at least its utility was to be immediate, and the future would be dealt with in the future.

Before turning to other ways of assessing the PJBD's effectiveness, it is necessary to acknowledge Hugh Keenleyside's contribution to the body of opinion on this agency. Keenleyside was the External Affairs member of the Canadian Section from 1940 to 1945, and so, unlike the three scholars whose evaluations have been outlined above, he is able to share an insider's point of view. He does, however, limit himself to what he calls a factual statement, and unfortunately he gives little or nothing that is not available elsewhere. He does bring out that early in its life the Board adopted a policy of studying on the spot the problem areas with which it was involved. Although he wrote in 1960, Keenleyside made the briefest of comments on the Board's postwar life, and offers the closing opinion that the period of real importance was concentrated in the activities of the Board's early years.[31] Keenleyside is wider of the mark in his book *Canada and the United States.* There he says that the PJBD, throughout the whole war, was the chief instrument for the direct coordination of the two countries' defensive military policies.[32] One suspects that the participant was not entirely objective.

There are a number of common threads which run through these evaluations of the PJBD. The first is that the most important time of the Board's life was during the war, and more particularly the first year of its existence. The second is that each section combines military and civil service membership under a civilian chairman. Third, the Board in theory at least, has access to the highest levels of government. Fourth, the members are ranked lower than their principals, and that leaves latitude and room for maneuvre at a higher level. Fifth, the Board has changed, or evolved, over the years, to take into account changing circumstances. Finally, the Board's position was not guaranteed, and so it has found itself and its activities overlapped by other agencies which have come into being to meet more specific requirements. All four commentators have, on balance, come down in favor of the Board, and think that it has been a flexible, effective instrument.

Many years have gone by since the literature examined above was written, and new documents have been made available for research purposes. In the next section of this paper, this material will be used to bring a more up-to-date perspective on the activities and effectiveness of the PJBD.

THE EVOLUTION OF THE PJBD

The life of the PJBD may be broken down into phases. To achieve this we will look at the PJBD through the men who made the history; the personalities of the Presidents of the United States and of the Prime Ministers of Canada, their particular orientation in their administrations, and the way they related to each other, as well as the personalities on the Board itself, and most importantly the Chairmen of the two sections. Applying these criteria, the following delimitation of the Board's life emerges:

Phase 1	-	1940-1945:	The War Years
Phase 2	-	1945-1950:	Uncertainty
Phase 3	-	1950-1953:	The Last Fling
Phase 4	-	1954-1959:	Decline
Phase 5	-	1960-1963:	Eclipse
Phase 6	-	1963-1988:	Limbo

Phase 1, 1940-1945: The War Years

To be involved in a war means to face an enemy. While the United States was not involved in a war in 1940, Canada was, and the threat to North America was perceived to be a real one. The primary concern was the potential loss of control of the North Atlantic which would leave Newfoundland, still a crown colony, and the Atlantic seaboard of Canada open to German attack. Another major concern was the system of locks at Sault Ste-Marie, which was thought to be vulnerable to sabotage or possibly air attack, launched from a ship in Hudson Bay, and the loss of which would have a serious effect on North American industry. The enemy therefore was real, if only hypothetically capable of making the attacks mentioned here. The potential targets were the North American homeland, and the defense of the continent was a task which could not be sidestepped. For the first time the defense of North America was seen to be geographically and militarily indivisible. The PJBD was the ideal agency to cope with the work at hand; as Colonel Dziuban said, it met the needs of both leaders;[33] but it also met the needs of both countries. The war years were a busy period in the Board's life; a total of thirty-three recommendations were made, covering a spectrum of concerns from basic defense plans through to the disposition of facilities erected during the war. Commentators are agreed that the first year of the Board's life was its most valuable, as much for the level of activity as for the fact that the United States was still a neutral at that time. However, once the Americans entered the war much of the requirement to have the Board disappeared. The high level of activity which had been set in 1940 and 1941 slowed down, and, in fact, the Board ended the war very quietly. Other agencies were becoming or had become increasingly involved in work that was more concrete than making recommendations, and the importance of the PJBD decreased accordingly. It was the war that brought about its creation, and it was the war that caused its initial decline.

Let us turn to the powerful personalities of 1940 who launched the Board and gave it much of its early impetus. Roosevelt, that pragmatic and farsighted President, did not carry out any consultation with either the War or the Navy Departments before he met King at Ogdensburg. He did not even tell them of his intentions.[34] By reaching an agreement with King in the way that he did, Roosevelt gave himself the most freedom possible with regard to Congress.[35] The first Chairman of the U.S. section, Fiorello LaGuardia, Mayor of New York, was a personal friend of the President. When two people enter into an official or formal relationship, a friendship can be abused all too easily. There is no evidence that either party did so in this instance. There is, however, evidence that LaGuardia on occasion used the direct access to the President conferred by his position on the PJBD to correct problems. Dziuban mentions this in passing; the direct access to the President permitted a quick cutting of red tape.[36] Keenleyside is more forthcoming. He may also be more inaccurate.

> The peculiar value of Mayor LaGuardia's membership on the Board was reflected on three or four occasions when, difficulties having arisen with United States service personnel, or failures by government agencies or officials to carry out approved Board decisions having been reported, the US Chairman flew off to Washington and utilizing his personal friendship with President Roosevelt — and supported by his political influence in a major State — found ready access to the White House. Invariably he returned to the Board with the desired directive in his pocket.[37]

The PJBD journals reflect one such occurrence. During what is now called the tenth meeting of the PJBD, on 29 and 30 July 1941, in Montreal, LaGuardia left after the first day to fly to Washington to confer with Roosevelt, and missed the second day. It is, of course, possible that he did the same thing between meetings. It doesn't matter, in effect. The point is that LaGuardia had access to the President, and is known to have used it. That door is most useful when it is used infrequently, which LaGuardia undoubtedly knew.

In July 1943, the Board met in Vancouver and visited sites through the northwest of the two countries. The members ended the meeting in Ottawa where a dinner was held on 14 July. Prime Minister King and President Roosevelt exchanged telegrams, and Roosevelt said that the Board was doing "splendid work."[38] By now, of course, the Board was less important to the President than it had been initially. At first he wanted freedom from Congress, but later he freed himself from the Board and bypassed it, as we have seen.

On the Canadian side, the PJBD was taken very seriously by Mackenzie King. The Ogdensburg agreement was entered in the Treaty Series. Appointments to the Canadian section were made by Order-in-Council. The first Chairman of the Canadian section, retired Colonel O. M. Biggar, was a lawyer who had been Judge Advocate General during the Great War of 1914-1918. He brought prestige, respect and a judicial mind to the Board. Although he was the nominal Chairman of the Canadian section from 1940 to 1945, Biggar in fact missed all of the meetings in 1944 through illness, and only attended one meeting in 1945, that of 10-11 April. He then resigned. His relationship with the Prime Minister was obviously not based on common bonds of politics and friendship, but from all appearances was based rather on mutual respect. It was no less effective for that. The Prime Minister did not see the PJBD as a means of circumventing Parliament. On the contrary, the Board's recommendations were submitted to the Cabinet War Committee for approval. The approaches on the two sides of the Board were different in this period, but worked well nonetheless. This period came to an end in 1945 for two main reasons. The first was the end of the war, and the second was the death of Roosevelt and the resignation of Biggar, which removed two key players from the original cast.

This first period is in many ways a microcosm of the Board's life. After an initial period of activity, the Board shifted to a position of increasing inactivity and lack of relevance, which reached its culmination at the end of the war when all enemies in the field had been defeated.

Phase 2, 1945-1950: Uncertainty

The uncertainty which gives this phase its title can be found at several levels. At the highest level, the governments of the victorious nations had to make a fundamental decision: was there still a threat to world peace, or was it safe to demobilize the huge number of men and women under arms, and convert from wartime to peacetime economies? Truman and other western political leaders were keen on cutting military expenditures. The United States alone possessed the nuclear bomb, which had proved its effectiveness, but for how long would the U.S. remain the world's only nuclear power? What direction should defense efforts take? In Canada, Mackenzie King, having followed Great Britain into the war with no hesitation, and having entered into a defense agreement with the United States, literally on the spur of the moment, began to return to a quasi-isolationist frame of mind. Did Canada want to continue its defense relationship with the U.S.? What would happen to defense agencies? Would the PJBD, which had ended the war in what might be described as a run-down maintenance mode, survive?

The Joint Chiefs of Staff of the United States came out of the Second World War sure of one thing. Their country would not be served a military surprise in the future. In a policy statement issued in October 1945, they said that "potential enemies" would be kept at a "maximum distance."[39] To accomplish this, a considerable network of installations was needed. They submitted their not inconsiderable list of desired sites to the Secretary of State that same October. They also arranged for military members of the U.S. Section of the PJBD to start talks with a view to revising the Canada-U.S. Basic Defense Plan. This was an attempt at cutting through uncertainty. Even before this was done, the Board members themselves had cut through the uncertainty and made a bold bid for self-preservation. At the fortieth meeting of the Board, held on 4-5 September 1945, they showed that they intended to take the adjective "permanent" seriously. The journal for this meeting tells us that:

...the question of Canada-United States postwar military collaboration does not appear to present any special difficulty. Both [sections] were agreed that the founders of the Permanent Joint Board on Defense advisedly inserted the word Permanent in the Board's title. This being so, there would seem to be no reason why the two countries should not, and every reason why they should, continue their collaboration of the past five years in matters of defense.[40]

It must have been gratifying to the members of the moribund PJBD to be approached so soon by the Joint Chiefs. The uncertainty was pervasive. As Jockel has pointed out, the Chiefs did not really have a clear idea of the specifics of what U.S. strategic policy should be, or of Canada's role.[41] Prisoners of their experience, U.S. airmen had come out of the war with a good understanding of offensive air operations, but a very imperfect grasp on air defense. Would the funds be made available? It is no wonder that military thinking was plagued by uncertainty.

The instructions of the Joint Chiefs of Staff were carried out at the November 1945 meeting of the PJBD. The Canadian section relayed the request to Ottawa, and was able to inform the U.S. section in January 1946 that Canada was ready to talk. At this same meeting the U.S. section gave a demonstration of a structural weakness on their side of the PJBD. Their uniformed members were not integrated into the U.S. military hierarchy.[42] The U.S. Army member, Major-General Guy Henry, tabled a paper which spelled out a series of principles of defense cooperation. There was plenty of evidence that this paper did not come from the Joint Chiefs, and that Henry, in over pride, had gone too far. It is enough to record that the PJBD was made to understand that its action in proceeding with Henry's paper was inappropriate. The point is that the uncertainty of the PJBD's future did not cause this structural weakness to be corrected. In fact the PJBD did submit most of Henry's proposals as two recommendations, numbers thirty-four and thirty-five, in April 1946. Number thirty-five was modified and re-submitted in November 1946, as recommendation thirty-six, as the original number thirty-five was not approved in Canada. By now the Military Cooperation Committee (MCC) had come into being. Here was an agency which must have made the continued existence of the PJBD even more uncertain, for it was an agency which could do much of the work which might well have gone to the PJBD. It had the added advantage of not being chaired by civilians. Nevertheless, on 12 February 1947 the two governments issued a joint statement in which they said that military cooperation would continue and the PJBD would be retained. The MCC, in fact, did take on the planning role. The situation in the world was changing, but the PJBD had become a sideshow. The construction of the St. Lawrence Seaway and the standardization of screw threads were among the items which occupied the members in May 1947. The PJBD was floundering, at a minimum it lacked direction, and the real work was being done elsewhere. The agenda items through to 1950 are remarkable. In February 1948 the Board "expressed the view that the standardization of screw-threads is the key to the whole problem of standardization."[43] A proposed exchange of air cadets, the admission of Canadians to West Point and Annapolis, and the temporary assignment of black engineers to Chimo are a few of the incongruous subjects discussed by the PJBD. The recommendations which came out of this period are of limited impact; 47/1 dealt with the transport of service personnel in the military aircraft of the other country, 48/1 concerned the St. Lawrence Seaway, 48/2 covered the procurement of military supplies, and, of more substance, 49/1 attempted to remove certain barriers to the implementation of joint defense measures. Finally, 50/1 dealt with taxation, customs and excise exemptions, post offices, and jurisdiction over U.S. personnel at the leased bases in Newfoundland. The Board was made aware of the planning being done elsewhere, but was not a participant in this period.

The Board saw uncertainty in its staffing, as well. The U.S. section had three Chairmen in a relatively short space of time. LaGuardia served until his death in September 1947, Dean Acheson served for a year, and Major-General Guy Henry, the former Army member, now retired, served from 8 December 1948 until 2 February 1952 in an acting capacity, and was then confirmed as U.S. section Chairman until he left the Board in 1954. LaGuardia does not appear to have enjoyed, with Truman, the relationship he had with Roosevelt. He could, perhaps, have clarified the Board's purpose after the war with Roosevelt; it is not clear that he even tried to with Truman. Dean Acheson was a significant appointment to the Board, but his stay was short and he went on to better things. Major-General Henry's appointment is probably the most in-

structive. This is the man who as a serving officer had attempted to circum-
vent the Pentagon and been admonished for his pains. Yet as a civilian he was
reappointed to the PJBD as Chairman of the U.S. section, but only in an acting
capacity.[44] A satisfactory answer for this has proved to be elusive.

On the Canadian side, the new Chairman was the retired soldier, General
A. G. L. McNaughton. Andrew McNaughton had both enjoyed success and
suffered disappointment in the recent past, when he was appointed to the PJBD
in August 1945. McNaughton had been the commander of First Canadian
Army in the U.K. but had been removed from command at a time when his expectations were to take his formation into active operations. During an extended period of leave in Canada, he had been offered the opportunity of
becoming the first Canadian-born Governor General, which he had accepted,
but the conscription question and the departure of Ralston from the King
cabinet led to a reappraisal. McNaughton became the Minister of National
Defence, but he failed to win a by-election in the riding of Grey North in
December 1944, and was beaten into third place in the General Election of
June 1945. This led to his departure from the Cabinet in August; it also killed
his chance of becoming Governor General. He held Bachelor's and Master's
degrees in science, conferred by McGill University. How does one interpret
his appointment to the PJBD? What did King expect? As we have seen, King's
instinct after the war was to retreat into quasi-isolationism, and Canada's
forces, the fourth largest in the world, were rapidly demobilized. King was
optimistic about Russian intentions with regard to North America. Why send
McNaughton to the PJBD if defense was to be so unimportant? This is more
intriguing when one looks at the other appointments which were given to
McNaughton, particularly in connection with the United Nations. Swettenham
has suggested that McNaughton was chosen to protect Canada's rights against
the United States; he recounts the horror of the representative of the Department of External Affairs at McNaughton's bluntness with the Americans.[45]
McNaughton was fifty-eight at the time of his appointment, and still both men-
tally and physically vigorous. With his scientific turn of mind, it is not surprising that the St. Lawrence Seaway project and the standardization of screw
threads were items which captured his imagination. More to the point,
McNaughton could speak to King freely and easily. That access was still there.

Mackenzie King, like LaGuardia, did not find his close relationship with
Roosevelt repeated with Truman. That was regrettable, for on one occasion, a
meeting at the White House on 28 October 1946, King failed to appreciate the
President's feelings on air defense.[46] The meeting was short and formal. It is
not the intent here to lay blame, but rather to show that personal relationships
between leaders inevitably affect the outcome of events. King left office in
November 1948, the last of the originals of the PJBD to go. He died in July
1950. In a way, it was McNaughton who provided the second generation continuity. Out of the uncertainty of the post-war years, clarification in a number

of directions was emerging. The Cold War, the Berlin blockade, the 1949 explosion of a Russian atomic bomb, and the Korean war in 1950 were bringing an end to drifting and uncertainty. The PJBD was about to enter a new phase.

Phase 3, 1950-1953: The Last Fling

It is evident from the title given to this phase of the Board's life that the PJBD played a more significant role than it had in the previous period. The President was the same man, the Prime Minister of Canada was new, but had over a year in office, and the two Chairmen were the same people. There is only one way in which enhanced effectiveness could have grown out of the Board itself, and that would have been by successful representations to the two principals. There is no evidence that any such thing happened. What did transpire was that the USAF and the RCAF started to see the problem of air defense as one best solved by means of collaboration; before this arrangement became entrenched, senior officers in other services as well as foreign service officers of both countries saw in the PJBD the agency which should be managing the U.S.-Canada defense relationship.[47] This realization brought new importance to the Board, for instead of being a sideshow it became an agency handling matters of substance. The number of recommendations — there were six in 1951 — is an indication of increased activity leading to positive action. The most important recommendations dealt with the bilateral extension of the somewhat rudimentary Continental Air Defense System and related air defense issues.

Before examining these recommendations, it is of interest to pause briefly and look at the way this phase opened. It started at the May 1950 meeting held in Toronto and Halifax. The Deputy Minister of National Defence, C. M. Drury, attended the session in Toronto. This in itself was different from past practice. Drury congratulated the Board on the recommendation of 12 October 1949 (49/1) which had resulted in the reciprocal purchasing program of Fiscal Year 1951. He also mentioned that his department was trying to forecast the lines of development of the three services for the next five years.[48] It was a gesture of respect and consideration toward the Board which could not have failed to have an effect.

The PJBD at its October 1950 meeting recognized that Russian aircraft posed a potential threat to North America, and the subject of U.S. interceptor flights was raised. In 1951 the Joint Chiefs of Staff referred to the PJBD a proposal for the extension of the Air Defense System, and asked for the Board's recommendation. The Board rose to the occasion; it received this request at the 10-11 January 1951 meeting and reconvened on 30-31 January and 1 February when it adopted the proposal as Recommendation 51/1. The implementation of this recommendation was not without its complications. Be that as it may, they did not in effect concern the PJBD, once the recommendation had gone forward. Recommendation 51/2 was a renewal of previous recommendations concerning the St. Lawrence Seaway, 51/3 dealt with Air Defense training exercises, and 51/4, adopted at the May 1951 meeting, dealt with interceptor flights and their flight paths over the other country. Canada imposed limitations on what U.S. aircraft could do in Canadian airspace; they could not engage enemy aircraft or force them to land. Unhappy with the recommendation, the Americans bided their time. Two further recommendations were adopted in 1951: 51/5 established the regulations for the cross-border movement of military aircraft, and 51/6 concerned itself with air defense mutual reinforcement in war, and command relationships. Both were adopted at the 11-21 November 1951 meeting.

Recommendation 52/1 was a naval matter, and concerned the visits of warships to ports and territorial waters of the other country; it was similar to Recommendation 51/5 of the previous year, but with respect to the navies of the two countries. The only other recommendation adopted that year, 52/2, recognized that electro-magnetic transmissions might be used as aids to navigation by an invader. The PJBD recommended that each government establish a system to alert persons owning such equipment if attack was imminent, and to either silence these sources or else operate them in a controlled manner. Finally, Recommendation 53/1 at last gave the USAF the right to shoot enemy aircraft over Canada.

It must not be assumed that the PJBD, because it was once again looked at with favor by the Joint Chiefs of Staff on the one hand, and the Department of National Defence on the other, was suddenly concentrating solely on matters of substance. It was doing nothing of the kind. It continued to wallow in an agenda which was a carry-over from the previous period. There are a number of things which emerge from an examination of this phase. The first is that the Board was as effective as other and higher level people wanted it to be. When it was ignored or bypassed, it resorted to make-work activity. The second is that the sections retained the capability to handle serious subjects with ease, and so it may be concluded that the Board remained a capable body. McNaughton was probably as good a choice for Chairman as any, for the times, for with his background in science and engineering he must have understood what was being proposed and what was required better than most. When it came to cost sharing and the actual construction work, his abilities as a hard negotiator would have come to the fore. The third is that the Board was most effective when an identifiable enemy — in this case, a potential enemy — whose capabilities were more or less measurable and against whom a military appreciation could be done, was present. It took away the uncertainty and reduced the vagueness and guesswork. Let it also be noted in passing that in a phase which saw real work done by the PJBD, and work which was primarily of benefit to the Air Forces of the two countries, both Chairmen were former

Army generals. There may be an element of irony to that, but there is not the slightest hint that their work was ever anything but objective. Finally, Eisenhower's election to the Presidency occurred in this phase of the life of the PJBD. His influence was to be felt, but that was to come in the next phase.

Phase 4, 1954-1959: Decline

The year 1954 started well for the PJBD, if not for Major-General Guy Henry. The American Secretary of Defense, Charles E. Wilson, wanted to enhance the importance and prestige of the PJBD, because he saw it as the means of achieving a closer defense relationship with Canada. In 1953 he had said as much to the U.S. section. In March 1954, he corrected the structural weakness to which attention has already been drawn, by integrating the U.S. section into the decision-making chain.[49] In November 1953, General Henry was eased out of his position as Chairman with a view to strengthening the U.S. section. The original candidate to replace Henry was Governor Dewey, whose appointment, because he was nationally known, would indicate the importance the Eisenhower administration attached to the Board. Dewey declined the appointment, however, and the Chairmanship went to Dr. John A. Hannah, the president of Michigan State University. Hannah was told to report in person to Eisenhower every three months, and more often if he thought it necessary. In addition to all of that, the USAF member was replaced by the Assistant Deputy Chief of Staff, Operations, USAF, Major-General J. E. Briggs. A Department of Defense Directive dated 3 May 1954 summarized it all very neatly. "Due to the importance this Department attaches to our relations with Canada, it is desired that greater emphasis be placed upon all phases of work of the Military Representatives of the U.S. section...with particular reference to the politico-military, financial, and public relations problems".[50]

This did not go unnoticed in Canada. On 1 June 1954, D. A. Golden, the Assistant Deputy Minister (ADM) at Defence Production, wrote to his minister, C. D. Howe, and brought him up to date on the adjustments to the American section of the PJBD. He included a copy of the Directive quoted above, and offered the opinion that the U.S. had beefed up its side of the PJBD (in quality, not quantity) because of the importance they attached to continental defense. On 19 June 1954, C. D. Howe wrote to Lester Pearson and asked that a member of Defence Production sit on the PJBD as an observer. This was agreed.[51] At this time Canada was developing the Arrow, and it is only natural to speculate that the PJBD became one of the channels through which attempts were made to interest the Americans in this product. There is nothing in the journals to bear this out, but one of the characteristics of the PJBD is that not everything that is discussed finds its way into the record.

After this promising start, it looked as though the PJBD would continue to play a significant, and even enhanced, role in the defense relationship between the U.S. and Canada. It was not to be. The Board was not given substantial work, and so routine items continued to fill its agenda. The Eisenhower administration, for all its show of using the PJBD, in fact not only ignored the Board but also reached decisions on North American defense without talking to Ottawa.[52] Air Defense was predominant, and the USAF and RCAF were working things out on a service to service basis. The major event of this phase, the creation of NORAD, was realized with no real input from the PJBD. The Board was aware of what was being proposed, because reports from the ad hoc committee of the U.S.-Canada Military Study Group (MSG) were read to it. Yet at no time did anyone on the PJBD recognize that here was something which should be the subject of a formal recommendation. In January 1957, at its 86th meeting, the Board heard that the MSG had forwarded the ad hoc committee's report on the integration of operational control of the continental air defenses of Canada and the U.S. to the Chiefs of both countries with two recommendations: first, that the conclusions be approved as basic principles on which the integrated control of air defenses be undertaken, and second, that the respective Chiefs take action to secure the approval of both governments for the integration of operational control, in accordance with the concepts contained in the ad hoc committee's report.[53] The Board noted this report "with satisfaction." It had also quite clearly abdicated its responsibility, and accepted its fate quietly. After the NORAD agreement had been approved, the Board said nothing about it, but at the end of the 89th meeting in January 1958, when the next one was being arranged, the USAF member invited the Board to Colorado Springs: "in view of the importance of the establishment of the North American Air Defense Command to our two countries," he said, "it would be most advantageous for the Board to acquaint itself with the operations of the NORAD headquarters located in the same city."[54] Before leaving the NORAD issue, it is worth jumping ahead to the 150th meeting of the PJBD. This milestone, observed in June 1978, provided the occasion for some unclassified remarks by the Secretaries and the two section Chairmen. With remarkable candor, the secretaries recorded that in the 1950s the Board was concerned in much of the planning for North American defense, but as the perceived threat to North America became more direct, such planning shifted more to the military staffs of both countries. The Board's role with respect to the establishment of NORAD was "facilitative." The U.S. Chairman said that the Board had played a constructive role in the (periodic) renewal of the NORAD agreement.[55] That was the ultimate irony; having stared at the major defense agreement of the 1950s and failed to put its hands on it, the PJBD subsequently made a meal of every renewal of the agreement.

The phase continued until 1959, when Gen. A. G. L. McNaughton resigned. McNaughton had been appointed by Mackenzie King, with whom he enjoyed excellent relations. He had also had no difficulty in his personal relations with Louis St. Laurent and Lester Pearson. It was different with Diefenbaker.

McNaughton had been a Liberal cabinet minister. By 1959 he had had enough of this particular Prime Minister; at the April meeting that year he announced his resignation from the Board, citing his heavy workload with the International Joint Commission as the reason. McNaughton made a bland farewell statement; this is in marked contrast with the statement he made when he left First Canadian Army. The inference is that he thought much of the Army, but at the time of his departure from it, not very much of the PJBD. Major-General Guy Henry wrote to McNaughton; of all the things he might have brought up, he selected the St. Lawrence Seaway Project,[56] which the PJBD had supported on several occasions, it is true, but which owed its realization more to other agencies than to the PJBD. Also of interest is the verdict of George Ignatieff. A man who has had little good to say about servicemen, either during or after their military careers, Ignatieff nevertheless made an exception in McNaughton's case, and in 1967 wrote a laudatory article entitled "General A. G. L. McNaughton: A Soldier in Diplomacy."[57] Ignatieff dwells on all of the international agencies in which McNaughton played a part, with the exception of the PJBD, about which not one word is said. This stunning silence cannot be attributed exclusively to Ignatieff's feelings on military people and agencies, for he was after all writing about a soldier. It is more likely that Ignatieff, who as Under Secretary of State for External Affairs had been in a position to judge, felt that the PJBD was an agency of no great consequence, and in which McNaughton's work was unimportant. Before leaving this phase of the Board's life, let us look briefly at two of the Canadian Army officers who were members: Major-Generals Sparling and Kitching. In what was essentially the age of the Air Force, neither said very much in the Board meetings, according to the record. Back in Ottawa, Sparling would forward the journal to the Chief of the General Staff with the terse comment that he might want to look at it. On one occasion, however, he drew Simonds' attention to a report on the BOMARC missile.[58] The two gunners would have understood that subject very well. Kitching, in a most useful book of memoirs,[59] does not mention the PJBD at all, and one suspects that his reasons parallel Ignatieff's. The Board's decline was complete.

Phase 5, 1960-1965: Eclipse

General McNaughton was replaced as Chairman of the Canadian section of the Board by Dana Wilgress, a former diplomat. Wilgress stayed with the Board for seven years. In his memoirs he says nothing about his relationship with Diefenbaker. His remarks on the Board are brief and inoffensive.[60] It is safe to assume that while Dana Wilgress and John Diefenbaker may have had a polite relationship, Wilgress was in no position to press defense issues. Diefenbaker had put the nails into one side of the PJBD's coffin; John Kennedy put them into the other side after his election. Whereas Dr. John Hannah had a good relationship with Eisenhower (they were both Republicans), he had none at all with Kennedy.[61] After a few years, he resigned in September 1963.

Not only did the two political leaders not have much of a relationship with their respective PJBD section chairmen, on the face of it, but they had none at all with each other, and this in retrospect did nothing to smooth out the various defense problems which they encountered. It has been suggested that the PJBD is a mechanism in place in case of an emergency.[62] When that argument is applied to the Diefenbaker-Kennedy era, it fails. Forasmuch as the two men did not get along, and forasmuch as they ran into a variety of defense-related problems, then surely a ready-made agency such as the PJBD, which combined elements of the defense and foreign services of both countries, was the ideal vehicle for solving problems in a dispassionate way and making pragmatic recommendations. It could not have been used in this way over the Cuban missile crisis, but had it been used before that, and some level of confidence established in the defense arena, that problem too might have been tackled differently. The point is that the Board, capable as it may be, cannot of its own volition assume any role whatsoever, and while it may be looked at as a mechanism in place in case of an emergency, it will not necessarily be used when that emergency presents itself. It wasn't in the Kennedy-Diefenbaker era, and it went from decline to eclipse. This phase was to end with Hannah's departure, John Kennedy's assassination, and Diefenbaker's defeat at the polls.

Phase 6, 1964 to the present: Limbo

When John Hannah resigned from the PJBD, he was replaced by Freeman Matthews who, like Wilgress, was a former diplomat. Johnson replaced Kennedy, and Pearson succeeded Diefenbaker. That many new players necessarily created a new phase in the Board's life. It does not, however, mean that anything spectacular started to happen to the Board, even though a recommendation, 64/1, was made, the first and last since 1953. The Board carried on with an agenda of essentially make-work items, and signs that it was busying itself with its own survival began to appear. The journal for the Board's 9th meeting, in May 1941, is less than one page of text, yet that is the meeting at which strategic direction by a U.S. commander of certain Canadian operational forces in Canada was discussed. In contrast, the journal for the 106th meeting of the Board, at which a long list of mundane items was discussed, is 56 pages long. It was the start of a trend. The Board found itself in a tricky situation. If it reported that it was wasting time over agenda items which were less than worthwhile, and went to more infrequent meetings, then it stood to lose even those items which came its way, and that would be a sentence of death. There are several indications that the Board was uncomfortable. Beatty, who interviewed Dana Wilgress either shortly after or shortly before Wilgress left the Board, said that the PJBD would probably play "a decreasing role in the future defense of North America," because of the number of integrated programs and military agreements in place even by 1963.[63] At the 150th meeting of the Board, in 1978, the secretarial statement recognized the same fact; planning which the PJBD used to do had been picked up by the military staffs of both countries. Beatty does not ascribe the comment quoted above to Wilgress, but in view of the opinion expressed by the Canadian Armed Forces Maritime Member (1965-1967), Rear-Admiral R. W. Murdoch, that the Board spent its time discussing pedestrian items,[64] it is not unlikely that Wilgress was in agreement with Beatty's statement, if indeed he was not its author.

The journals for much of this period are still classified, a fact which led to the term by which it is described: Limbo. There have been a few indicators, tied to personnel, which show that the PJBD is relatively unimportant. Freeman Matthews and his successor A. L. Borg both held office for six years, but after that the U.S. section Chairman has served for relatively short periods. The U.S. service members serve for two years, and many serve for less than that. Continuity is not a strong feature on the U.S. side. The Canadian section has been more stable, with only one short-term Chairman, Bud Cullen, who served for six months in 1984. For fifteen of the last twenty years, Pierre Elliot Trudeau was the Prime Minister of Canada, and his views on defense are well known. His support of the PJBD must be regarded as problematic. One can with safety conclude that Trudeau's respect for advice given to him by John Aird would be greater than his respect for advice tendered by George Hees, and the political differences of Trudeau and Hees are not a factor. It is unlikely that either chairman was required to offer serious advice to the Prime Minister. The Board is in Limbo.

CONCLUSION

The PJBD was the first agency through which President Roosevelt's 1938 undertaking, or promise, was brought to life. Its creation was something of a grandiose political gesture on the part of the President of the United States. Its structure and role were not well thought out. Its somewhat vague terms of reference, to study problems and make recommendations, did not give it the mandate it needed (and needs) to be the authoritative, senior bilateral defense agency. Its effectiveness has always been at the mercy of its principals. From the beginning, the motives of the President and the Prime Minister in bringing the Board into being, and their expectations of it, are open to interpretation. The President was in an election year and faced certain domestic problems, whereas King, that study in contrasts, wanted to assert Canada's independence from Great Britain, and this agreement with the U.S. was one way of demonstrating that independence. American and Canadian interests were not the same in 1940, and they are not the same today. If they were, was the

PJBD necessary? If they were not, could the Board possibly work? Was the PJBD meant to be a flour pill coated with sugar? The placebo is often as effective as a stronger drug, depending on the malady being treated.

In spite of its fundamental weakness of not having a clear role and more executive authority, the PJBD has on occasion been effective. Two periods in particular, the first and third as identified in this chapter, saw work which by any standard can be called effective. Expressed in more blunt terms, the conclusion is that the PJBD has been effective for only six of its forty-eight years. It has been dependent on external patrons for its major work. During the Second World War, those patrons were the President and the Prime Minister. In the early fifties, they were the Chiefs of the armed forces, who recognized the Board's utility and potential. Whenever these patrons elected to achieve their aims by other means, the PJBD was reduced to housekeeping or make-work activity. And yet, the Board is kept alive by conscious act; it could have been abolished after the second war, but was formally retained in 1947; it could have been abolished in the Diefenbaker-Kennedy era, but was allowed to survive. In spite of its ups and downs, and there have been more downs than ups, the Board has invariably been staffed with men of high calibre; the potential for effectiveness is intact.

For much of the Board's life, the most that can be said for it is that it has been useful. A lot of the time it has seemed to be a forum for the discussion of military trivia. From the beginning, the things that it has done, and does, could have been done by other means. Whether or not it will be used again, as it was in the early fifties, is a matter of conjecture. It was not used by Diefenbaker and Kennedy during the most difficult time in bilateral defense relations since 1945.

Every shade of opinion on the changing role and self-image of Canada from 1939 on has been expressed in recent years. Canada as a colonial possession, as the linch-pin between Great Britain and the U.S., as a middle power with some independence, and for those who don't agree with that, as a satellite of the U.S., have all been advanced as explanations for our current posture. One thing is integral to the changing Canadian orientation/alignment, and that thing is the military alliance. In abstract terms, therefore, its existence is more important than the practical and concrete achievements of the Board.

Notes

[1] Stanley W. Dziuban, *Military Relations Between the United States and Canada, 1939-1945* (Washington, D.C.: Office of the Chief of Military History, Department of the Army, 1959).

[2] James A. Gibson, review of *Military Relations Between the United States and Canada, 1939-1945*, by Stanley Dziuban, in *International Journal* 16 (Winter 1960-61): 78-79.

[3] Dziuban, *Military Relations*, 25.

[4]Ibid., 49, 52.

[5]Ibid., 51.

[6]Ibid., 90.

[7]David P. Beatty, *The Canada-United States Permanent Joint Board on Defense* (Ann Arbor, MI: University Microfilms, Inc., 1969).

[8]Ibid., 62.

[9]Ibid., 265.

[10]Ibid., 267.

[11]Ibid., 228.

[12]Ibid., 289.

[13]Ibid., 71.

[14]Ibid., 186.

[15]Ibid., 227.

[16]Joseph T. Jockel, *No Boundaries Upstairs* (Vancouver: University of British Columbia Press, 1987).

[17]Beatty, *Permanent Joint Board on Defense*, 280.

[18]Ibid., 281.

[19]Ibid., 101.

[20]Ibid., 298.

[21]C. P. Stacey, "The Canadian-American Permanent Joint Board on Defence," *International Journal* 9 (Spring 1954): 107-124.

[22]_____, *A Brief History of the Canada-United States Permanent Joint Board on Defence, 1940-1960* (Ottawa: The Queen's Printer for Canada, 1960).

[23]_____, *Arms, Men and Governments* (Ottawa: The Queen's Printer for Canada, 1970), 346.

[24]_____, "Permanent Joint Board on Defence," 121.

[25]Ibid.

[26]Ibid., 120.

[27]Stacey, *Arms, Men and Governments*, 348.

[28]J. L. Granatstein, "The Conservative Party and the Ogdensburg Agreement," *International Journal* 22 (Winter 1966-67): 74, citing Hanson to Meighen, 23 August 1940, R. B. Hanson Papers, Public Archives of Canada, Ottawa.

[29]Stacey, *Arms, Men and Governments*, 348.

[30]Beatty, *Permanent Joint Board on Defense*, 28.

[31]Hugh Keenleyside, "The Canada-United States Permanent Joint Board on Defence," *International Journal* 16 (Winter 1960-61): 74.

[32]_____, *Canada and the United States* (New York: Alfred Knopf, 1952), 370.

[33]Dziuban, *Military Relations*, 25.

[34]Ibid., 29.

[35]Beatty, *Permanent Joint Board on Defense*, 28.

[36]Dziuban, *Military Relations*, 90.

[37]Keenleyside, "Permanent Joint Board on Defence," 55.

[38]PJBD Journal, Meeting No. 29.

[39]Jockel, *No Boundaries Upstairs*, 6.

[40]PJBD Journal, Meeting No. 40.

[41]Jockel, *No Boundaries Upstairs*, 10-11.

[42]Ibid., 11

[43]PJDB Journal, Meeting No. 51.

[44]Guy Vernor Henry, manuscript memoirs. US Military History Institute, Carlisle, Pennsylvania. Extracts in Directorate of History, National Defence Headquarters, Ottawa, File PJBD 79/316, 100.

[45]John Swettenham, *McNaughton* (Toronto: The Ryerson Press, 1969), Vol. 3, 191.

[46]Jockel, *No Boundaries Upstairs*, 25-26.

[47]Ibid., 124.

[48]PJDB Journal, Meeting No. 60.

[49]Jockel, *No Boundaries Upstairs*, 79.

[50]Department of Defense Directive No. 5132.5, 3 May 1954, McNaughton Papers, File 291, Public Archives of Canada, Ottawa.

[51]Golden to Howe, 1 June 1954; Howe to Pearson, 19 June 1954, McNaughton Papers, File 291, Public Archives of Canada, Ottawa.

[52]Jockel, *No Boundaries Upstairs*, 79.

[53]PJDB Journal, Meeting No. 86.

[54]Ibid.

[55]PJDB Journal, Meeting No. 150.

[56]Guy Henry to Andrew McNaughton, 4 May 1959, McNaughton Papers, File 291, Public Archives of Canada, Ottawa.

[57]George Ignatieff, "General A. G. L. McNaughton: A Soldier in Diplomacy," *International Journal* 22 (Summer 1967): 402-414.

[58]Sparling to Simonds, covering note on PJDB Journal, Meeting No. 92, National Defence Headquarters, Ottawa.

[59]George Kitching, *Mud and Green Fields* (Langley, B.C.: Battleline Books, 1986).

[60]Dana Wilgress, *Dana Wilgress Memoirs* (Toronto: The Ryerson Press, 1967), 182-190.

[61]Beatty, *Permanent Joint Board on Defense*, 102.

[62]Ibid., 311.

[63]Ibid.

[64]Rear-Admiral J. W. Murdoch, telephone interview with author, 19 May 1988.

7

Canada and the Modernization of North American Air Defense

John Anderson

INTRODUCTION

On 18 March 1985, during the final session of the meeting of President Reagan and Prime Minister Mulroney — "the Shamrock Summit" — held in Quebec City on 17 and 18 March, an agreement was concluded between Canada and the United States, by which the governments of the two countries undertook to proceed with, and to share responsibilities for, a program to modernize major elements of the North American air defense system.[1] This chapter seeks to provide an account of the steps that led up to conclusion of that agreement and, more particularly, of the part played by Canada in bringing it about.

CONCEPT AND DEVELOPMENT

The period of time (lead time) between conception and system-wide implementation of a program to modernize the continental air defense system, which Canada and the United States had cooperated to put in place during the 1950s, was a relatively long one. The planning concept of a modernized air defense system for the continental United States, CONUS (i.e., the 48 states south of Canada), was approved by the American Secretary of Defense as a basis for expenditure on technological development in the late 1960s.[2] Comprehensive briefings on this concept were given to Canadian Forces planning staffs and to senior officials of the Departments of External Affairs and National Defence following completion of the first stage of the defense policy review initiated by Prime Minister Trudeau in his statement on 3 April 1969, affirming *inter alia* the intention of his government to continue Canadian cooperation with the United States in the defense of North America.[3] The concept comprised four main system elements on which full-scale development was to proceed. These were:

- *Over-the-Horizon Backscatter,* two OTH(B) radars to be installed in the northeastern and northwestern United States and to be capable of detecting and tracking bomber aircraft within a semi-circular zone extending from 500 miles from the radar site out to 1,800 miles, and providing surveillance at all altitudes well out from the Atlantic and Pacific coasts. A third OTH(B) radar to be sited centrally in the United States and to provide coverage of the southern approaches to that country was added later.
- A fleet of large, long-range aircraft equipped with an Airborne Warning and Control System (AWACS) combining a powerful radar, data processing and communications equipment, capable when in flight of fairly long-range detection of aircraft operating at all altitudes and controlling their interception by fighter-type aircraft;
- An *Improved Manned Interceptor* aircraft capable of operating with AWACS and engaging bombers at all altitudes;
- *Integration* in the interior of the United States of military and civilian (Federal Aviation Agency) airspace surveillance and aircraft/air traffic control systems into a single system, later called the *Joint Surveillance System (JSS).*

The planning concept for air defense modernization was approved at a time when ballistic missiles were clearly supplanting bombers as the major component of the strategic forces of the Soviet Union threatening North America.[4] Moreover, the debate of the 1960s in the United States regarding ballistic missile defense (BMD) had recently been resolved by the decision of the Johnson administration to proceed with a "thin" BMD system, *Sentinel,* the stated purpose of which was defense against third-party threats and accidental launches rather than against a full-scale Soviet missile attack.[5] The emphasis of the concept was on a compatible air defense system, which would be less costly to operate and maintain than the existing system, and which would, in particular, improve the warning of air attack. Its approval was accompanied by decisions to reduce substantially the current U.S. air defense forces, with cost savings to be applied to development and eventually deployment of the new system.

CANADA AND THE CONCEPT

The planning concept for air defense system modernization, at least as presented to Canadian audiences, did not include any specific measures to replace or to update the components of the existing continental air defense system most directly involving Canada. The future of the CADIN/PINETREE radars in southern Canada was not mentioned, nor was that of the Distant Early Warning (DEW) line radars, most of which were located in northern Canada. There was, however, some indication in the material presented that the possibility of continuous patrols by AWACS aircraft over the Canadian North was, at that time, being considered as a future means of fulfilling the northern surveillance functions of the DEW line. CONUS does not include Canada, and it was undoubtedly because Canadian-American consultations, and agreement by the Canadian government, were necessary before it could be expanded to take in the continent as a whole that Canadian-based installations were not initially included in the concept. There were perhaps other reasons. No Canadian financial contribution to development was being sought, but it would take several years to complete, during which the Canadian dimensions of a modern continental system could be taken up. There were doubts, which later proved well-founded, that a northern and northward-looking OTH(B) radar installation would be reliable. It was already evident that the CADIN-PINETREE line, although better than nothing, was too far south to permit defense of potential targets in the south of Canada and the northern states against Soviet bombers equipped with stand-off missiles, and its interceptor control function was foreseen as being performed, in the event of attack, by AWACS. In addition, the planning concept itself provided a basis, and its presentation to Canadian authorities a starting point, for bilateral consultations on future needs within the framework of the North American Air Defense (NORAD) agreement.

The defense White Paper of August 1971, *Defence in the 70s*, accurately reflects the interest which the modernized air defense concept attracted among those in Ottawa charged with responsibilities for national defense and the defense relationship between Canada and the United States.[6] OTH(B) radar, because of its expected capability to detect aircraft at long range and to keep a very large volume of airspace continuously under surveillance, and AWACS, because its long-range mobility would enable it to be used to deploy surveillance and, within the limits of the range of interceptor aircraft, control capability when required over much of Canada, "could," as the White Paper put it, "in future fulfill an important role in the surveillance of Canadian airspace in the North American defence context."[7] Whether or not an OTH(B) installation in the north could adequately cover the Arctic air routes was, however, uncertain. OTH(B) depends on the reflection of radar energy off the ionosphere. It was known that this was subject to disruption by electronic emissions associated with the Aurora Borealis, but the scale of the problem was not

apparent. Arrangements, briefly mentioned in *Defence in the 70s*,[8] had, therefore, been made to have Canadian and American defense scientists carry out
experiments to determine how well OTH(B) radar would operate in the Arctic
environment.

"Change in technology and the quickening pace of arms control discussions," the Minister of National Defence had written in his preface to *Defence
in the 70s*, "make this a particularly difficult moment for long-range defence
planning. It will be appreciated, therefore, that we have not resolved all out-
standing questions. In particular, there are a number of equipment options for
which analysis is not far enough advanced to permit decisions to be taken at
this time."

The analytical challenge was clearly one that the Canadian Forces, with
much of their major equipment at or reaching the later stages of obsolescence,
and the Department of National Defence (DND), had to meet. In the months
following the issue of *Defence in the 70s*, the first of a series of studies, called
policy reviews, was initiated. Their overall purpose was to provide, within the
policy context set by the White Paper, the in-depth analysis of major areas of
military operational responsibility necessary to support consideration by the
government of re-equipment proposals. Three such studies had been
completed before the end of 1974, when the widening disparity between well-
articulated equipment needs of the Canadian Forces and the size of the defense
budget led the government, at the instance of the Privy Council Office
(Secretariat to the Cabinet), to decide that a more comprehensive study, the
Defence Structure Review, should be undertaken.[9]

One of the studies completed was a review of air defense policy. The results of this study, carried out between May and December 1972, were incorporated in a report submitted to and approved by the Minister of National
Defence, as a basis for future planning and for submission of related equipment proposals to the Cabinet and the Treasury Board, early in 1973. Two
principal considerations lay behind the study. The first of these was to examine, in cooperation with the Department of Transport, the possibility of a
joint civilian-military system of airspace surveillance and control, similar to
that to be established in the United States, which would meet future requirements both for air traffic control and safeguarding the integrity of sovereign
airspace. The second was to assess the implications of future U.S. air defense
systems concepts on Canada's contribution to the air defense of North
America. On the basis of recommendations flowing from the study, the government directed the Departments of National Defence and Transport to undertake a joint study examining the feasibility of an integrated national airspace
surveillance and control system (INSACS). The government also agreed that
a short-term renewal of the NORAD agreement, due to expire in May 1973,
should be negotiated with the United States, in order to allow time for
maturation of U.S. plans for air defense modernization and for joint discussion

of future continental air defense requirements taking these plans into account.[10]

CANADIAN STEPS TO INITIATE JOINT PLANNING

In fact, U.S. plans had matured little by the time the question of renewal of the NORAD Agreement came up again in the spring of 1975. Although bombers were not included in the first strategic arms limitation agreement (SALT I), the Soviet Union had done nothing to build up its strategic bomber force. A new supersonic bomber, known in the West as the *Backfire*, had entered operational service. It was judged to have sufficient range to reach targets in Canada and the northern United States from bases in northern Russia on two-way (return) missions, and throughout North America, on one-way missions; but it was the majority view of Canadian and American intelligence analysts that *Backfire* was intended, and was based in the Soviet Union, for use against targets on the European and Asiatic periphery of Russia rather than as an intercontinental weapon system. There was, at the time, no evidence of Soviet development of a new intercontinental-range bomber, similar to the B-1 being developed in the U.S. The Anti-Ballistic Missile (ABM) Treaty, concluded by the two superpowers at the same time as the SALT I agreement had, for the time being at least, already ruled out deployment, by either side, of large-scale defenses against attack by ballistic missiles. Moreover the accord, reached between President Ford and General Secretary Brezhnev at Vladivostock in November 1974, set a common ceiling of 2,400 delivery vehicles each for Soviet and U.S. strategic offensive forces; and had, at least in principle, brought bombers within the framework of strategic arms limitations, making it unlikely that there would be much change in the very large preponderance of ballistic missiles over bombers in the Soviet strategic arsenal.

In the United States, development of the OTH(B) radar and the AWACS systems was proceeding — the former apparently less quickly than originally expected, the latter more or less on schedule. No decisions to procure and to deploy either system as part of the continent's air defenses had, however, been taken. The air defense of North America was, at this time, clearly not a high priority of the Ford administration or of the Pentagon.[11] By now neither the Canadian nor the American authorities anticipated large new investments in continental air defense much before the end of the decade and, in consequence, they agreed to renew the NORAD agreement, without change, until 1980.

Planning in the United States for introduction of the Joint Surveillance System (JSS), however, had been going ahead and by the later months of 1974 had generated a requirement for four discrete air defense regions in the U.S. south of the Canadian border. To accommodate this need, agreement was reached in the Permanent Joint Board on Defense (PJBD) to alter the regional boundaries under NORAD, such that in future, when the JSS became fully operational, there would be seven regions, four in the U.S. south of the border, two in Canada, and one in Alaska. Regions that previously straddled the border would be eliminated. The Canadian Government approved the new arrangement early in 1975, seeing in it an enhancement of Canadian sovereignty since, when it came into effect, all air defense operations in Canadian airspace would be controlled, at least in peacetime, from Canadian soil. The arrangement was not cost-free. New regions needed new control centers. As part, therefore, of the same decision, the government agreed in principle that the Department of National Defence should join with the United States Air Force in a contract to design and supply the necessary equipment for seven Regional Operational Control Centers (ROCCs). The cost for the two Canadian ROCCs was then estimated at around $70 million. The old Regional Control Center at North Bay would be replaced by new centers for Eastern and Western Canada.

In the history of Canadian defense policy, the year 1975 will probably be seen as the year of the Defence Structure Review. The government had authorized an increase in the Defence Estimates for 1975/76 to take care of urgent financial needs, but, beyond that, most major projects were held in abeyance waiting completion of the review.[12]

THE PROBLEM OF OBSOLESCENCE

At the same time, however, the future of the CADIN/PINETREE radar line was emerging as a significant issue at National Defence Headquarters in Ottawa. In 1975, the oldest of the radars were twenty-two years old. Although nobody was able to set an absolute limit to the life of a radar, it seemed probable that replacement radars would, before long, be required if the line were expected to continue operating well into the future. The air staff had put forward a project, the Surveillance Radar Replacement Programme (SRRP) to do so. There were advantages to be gained from going ahead with it. The existing radars were not only old, but they also incorporated old technology, which was becoming increasingly difficult and expensive to maintain. They were costly to operate by comparison with modern, highly-automated radars then becoming available elsewhere. The twenty-four radars still in service employed some 4,000 people, 60 percent of whom were military. New radars were expected to need as little as a tenth of that number.

The advantages expected to accrue from replacement of the CADIN/PINETREE radars at a cost estimated at around $500 million were not seen by most senior officers and officials at NDHQ as sufficiently persuasive to gain approval for the project, even after the financial outlook for the defense program had brightened as a result of government decisions in December 1975 flowing from the Defence Structure Review. The future military value of the line was uncertain. Indications from service-to-service contacts with the Americans, who contributed some 45 percent of the costs of operating it, were that a replacement was not considered necessary as part of a modernized continental air defense system and that if such a project were to be undertaken, they would see it as a Canadian responsibility. Apart from the radars covering the East and West coasts, the line was also suspect, except perhaps as part of a joint civilian-military system covering the most densely populated and travelled parts of the country, as a means of assuring the integrity of Canadian airspace. Detection and interception of a foreign intruder approaching Winnipeg would not have been a very convincing demonstration of Canadian sovereignty.

The INSACS study with the Department of Transport was not making very much progress. The requirements of the two departments both as to coverage and as to time of completion were proving less compatible than had earlier been thought. Beyond this, tests completed by the defense scientists had led to the conclusion that a northern OTH(B) radar installation would not provide sufficiently reliable coverage of the transarctic air routes. The Americans were now talking instead of an Enhanced Distant Early Warning (EDEW) line and hinting that they would look to Canada to pay part of the costs.

The situation, as it appeared to NDHQ in the early weeks of 1976, was not comfortable. It seemed possible that the defense budget would have to pay the full cost of replacing the CADIN/PINETREE line, that the resulting expenditure would not be seen by the American government as an effective contribution to modernization of the North American air defense system, and that the Canadian government would be pressed as well to make a sizable financial contribution to replacement of the DEW line. The time had come to talk to the Americans in Washington.

CANADA INITIATES A BILATERAL APPROACH

At the first meeting of the PJBD in 1976, a Canadian proposal was made to form a bilateral group, to be headed on both sides by a senior official responsible for defense policy matters, which would consider how the two countries should share responsibilities, including financial responsibilities, for modernization of the North American air defense system. The Americans, at the next PJBD meeting, agreed to this proposal. They then formed the *Ad Hoc Canada-United States Steering Group on the Sharing of Responsibilities for Modernization of the North American Air Defense System*, or, more briefly, but no less clumsily, the *Ad Hoc Canadian-United States Air Defense Responsibilities Sharing Steering Group*.

The Steering Group held its first meeting in July 1976 in Ottawa. Like the PJBD it had co-chairmen. The Canadian chairman was the Assistant Deputy

Minister (Policy) from the Department of National Defence. The American chairman was the Deputy Assistant Secretary of Defense for European and NATO Policy. Membership of the Group included senior representatives of the Department of External Affairs and the State Department and senior officers from the various staff agencies both in NDHQ and in the Pentagon. Starting with the second meeting the Commander in Chief of NORAD was invited to send observers.

It would be both tedious and inappropriate to try to follow in any detail the proceedings of either the Responsibilities Sharing Steering Group or of the Working Group which it set up at its second meeting. It had really only just begun working by the 1976 Presidential election in the United States. The defense priority of the Carter Administration, when it took office in January 1977, was to gain agreement for, and to launch, a NATO Long Term Defense Program. North American air defense modernization was even less of a prior- ity than it had been for the Ford Administration. Canadians and Americans had been brought together to discuss the subject but, as 1977 gave way to 1978, little had in fact come of the discussions. The Canadian concern about the fu- ture of the CADIN/PINETREE line was no nearer to being resolved. A further concern, as to whether or not the Canadian part of the ROCC program should be continued, had arisen in view of uncertainty as to what the control centers would control.

THE JOINT U.S.-CANADIAN AIR DEFENSE STUDY

A further Canadian initiative was taken. The Minister of National Defence, Barney Danson, proposed to the U.S. Secretary of Defense, Harold Brown, that the two defense departments commission, and split payment for, a study of continental air defense requirements to the end of the century. The study, it was proposed, should assess possible development in the air threat to North America and take account of new air defense technologies either already developed, such as AWACS, or which might be developed, such as space-based surveillance systems.

The result of this Canadian initiative was the Joint United States-Canada Air Defense Study (JUSCADS). The study was carried out, during 1979, by a team of Canadian and American specialists recruited for that purpose. An American, Peter Aldrich, head of his own systems analysis company and more recently Secretary of the Air Force, was proposed by Secretary of Defense Brown. The co-director was a Canadian, Brigadier-General John Collins. The final report of the study, which is not part of the open literature, was submitted to the two defense departments at the end of 1979.

There is no intention here to go into the details of the JUSCADS study.[13] It brought out clearly the deficiencies in the existing air defense surveillance and warning system and it analyzed and costed a number of possible system designs by which these deficiencies might be overcome. The major accomplishments of the study were, however, somewhat different. First, it brought consideration of modernization of the continental air defense system in Canada and the United States on to common ground and provided a point of reference for the defense establishments in the two countries. Second, it brought Canada and Canadian interests to the forefront in the further development of modernization plans and programs. Third, it placed before the authorities of the two countries the fact that they faced a fundamental choice either of proceeding fairly soon with a relatively conventional modernization program or of stretching out the life of the existing system, perhaps to the breaking point, while proceeding as rapidly as possible to invest in and to develop space-based surveillance systems.

The JUSCADS report was discussed in the Air Defense Responsibilities Steering Group at a meeting in Washington early in 1980. It was agreed that the report should be used as an analytical basis for preparation of a master plan for North American air defense modernization. It was decided as well that the master plan should be prepared by the U.S. Department of Defense both because it was under obligation to Congress to produce one and because the relevant technologies were American. The work was, however, to be done in close cooperation with the Canadian Forces and was to involve NORAD headquarters.

Drafts of parts of a North American Air Defense Master Plan (ADMP) were sent to Ottawa for comment in the fall of 1980. At this point the U.S. Presidential election of November 1980 intervened. President Carter was defeated and in January 1981 the Reagan Administration came into office.

It is normal for a new government, when it takes office, to spend some time reviewing priorities, programs, and budgets left by its predecessor. In the United States, where new appointments go deeper into the governmental apparatus than in Canada, the period of hiatus in on-going work following the installation of a new President is often quite long. It was, therefore, somewhat uncertain when the preparation of the ADMP would reach the surface in Washington.

Somewhat fortuitously, however, the NORAD agreement, which had been extended in 1980 for one year to enable the Canadian government to fulfill an undertaking to refer the question of renewal to the House of Commons' Standing Committee on External Affairs and National Defence, was due to expire in May 1981. The Standing Committee had reported in favor of renewal with relatively few changes for a further five years and both the Canadians and Americans were in favor of such a renewal. In addition, President Reagan had accepted an invitation to visit Ottawa in March 1981 and it was considered both feasible and desirable that an exchange of notes renewing the agreement be signed during the President's visit.[14]

North American air defense then became a matter for early attention by the new American administration. Moreover, the new U.S. Secretary of Defense, Caspar Weinberger, accompanied the President to Ottawa, giving the Minister of National Defence, Gilles Lamontagne, an opportunity to discuss air defense system modernization and the status of the master plan. The two ministers, in fact, used the occasion to issue a joint public statement on overall objectives to be achieved by a modernization program and Secretary Weinberger gave assurances that work on the master plan would be moved forward as quickly as possible.

Some weeks later, the Americans requested a meeting with the Canadian members of the Responsibilities Sharing Steering and Working Groups to present proposals prepared by the United States Air Force for a North American Air Defense Master Plan. The plan, as presented, envisaged a program to modernize the existing system, comprising a new chain of Long-Range "Minimally Attended Radars" and unattended (automated) Short-Range Radars, soon to be christened the North Warning System, replacing the DEW line. Over-the-Horizon (Backscatter) radar installations in the Northeastern, Northwestern, and central United States would provide long-range surveillance in areas of 180 degrees respectively off the East and West coasts of the United States, in an arc of 120 degrees covering the southern approaches to the United States (see Figure 7.1). Twelve additional AWACS aircraft would be procured for North American air defense purposes, and F-15 fighter aircraft would be available to re-equip regular force United States Air Force air-defense interceptor squadrons. For its part, Canada had already decided to modernize its air interception capabilities with the McDonnell Douglas F/A-18, designated by DND the CF-18.[15] A further presentation of its main features was made to the Chief of the Defence Staff, the Deputy Minister, and other senior staff at National Defence Headquarters. The master plan, with relatively minor changes, was then approved in the U.S. Department of Defense and was issued, early in 1982, to U.S. defense agencies. At about the same time, it was sent officially to National Defence Headquarters in Ottawa with a request for Canadian concurrence or considered comment on it.

After a careful review of the proposed master plan by the Canadian staff officers responsible for air defense planning and air defense requirements, National Defence Headquarters replied to the effect that overall the master plan was considered adequate to meet the military requirements for future air defense as they were foreseen in Canada. It was endorsed by the Canadian defense authorities, subject to further consultations regarding a number of Canadian concerns. The major Canadian concerns related, first, to the location of the easternmost radars of the proposed North Warning System; second, to the adequacy of OTH(B) as the sole means of continuous surveillance off the East and West coasts of Canada and the Alaskan Panhandle; and third, to inclusion within the master plan of forward airfields (Forward Operation

Figure 7.1
Proposed Warning System

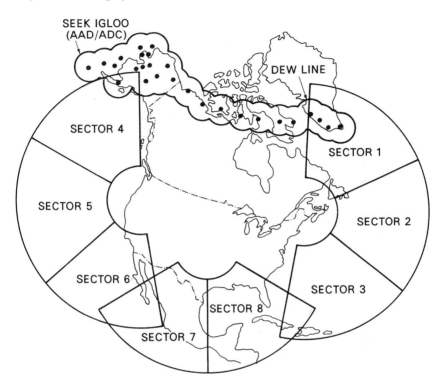

Source: Canada, Senate, Special Committee on National Defence, *Canada's Territorial Air Defence*, January 1985 (Ottawa: Supply and Services).

Locations or FOLs) to permit detached operation of interceptor aircraft within the radar coverage of the North Warning System, and of airfield facilities (Dispersed Operating Bases or DOBs) to support operation of AWACS aircraft in and over Canada.[16]

The first of the Canadian concerns arose from the fact that the master plan, as originally put forward by the Americans, envisaged emplacement of the easternmost radars of the North Warning System, as with those of the DEW line, in Greenland. The Canadian view was that this would leave the warning perimeter open to penetration, particularly at low altitudes by aircraft approaching over Baffin Bay and the Davis Strait, and, possibly, to outflanking, especially by cruise missiles launched by aircraft or submarines operating inside OTH(B) radar coverage. The Canadian proposal was to overcome these potential weaknesses in the warning system by siting the most easterly of the NWS radars in southern Baffin Island and on the Labrador coast rather than in Greenland. This proposal was, in due course, agreed upon by the Americans.

The second Canadian concern was motivated by the fact that the zones out to five hundred miles from the planned Northeastern and Northwestern OTH(B) installations, not covered by these systems, lay in large part off the East and West coasts of Canada. This was seen as posing difficulties for the conduct of identification missions by interceptor aircraft operating from Canadian coastal bases, especially in areas crossed by densely traveled civil air routes and, off the East coast, frequently penetrated by Soviet aircraft on long-range training and reconnaissance flights; since necessary surveillance data would be available only at considerable distance offshore and provided by systems primarily designed for warning of attack rather than for the control of interceptor aircraft. The Canadian proposal was to install modern ground-based radars on the Canadian East and West coast and in the Alaskan Panhandle, to back up OTH(B) by linking the coverage of the North Warning System on the East coast and U.S. air defense radars in Northwestern Alaska, on the West coast, with that of coastal radars of the U.S. Joint Surveillance System south of the border. This Canadian proposal, although it received support from NORAD Headquarters, was resisted in Washington. The United States authorities initially contended that, with procurement of the additional number envisaged in the master plan, sufficient AWACS aircraft would be available to meet offshore surveillance and interceptor control needs. Subsequently, when a review of U.S. defense program priorities in the latter half of 1983 led first to reduction and then to cancellation of procurement of more AWACS aircraft, the Americans responded by proposing additions to the OTH(B) installation in the central U.S. such that interior coverage, overlapping the zones left uncovered by the Northeastern and Northwestern OTH(B) installations, would be provided (see figure 7.2). While this proposal was welcomed by the Canadian staffs, there remained a doubt about the interceptor control capability of the OTH(B) system. The question of adequacy of the OTH(B) system to cover the East and West coastal regions and of the need for additional coastal radars was left open for later decision in the air defense modernization agreement of 18 March 1985.[17]

The third Canadian concern stemmed from the fact that it was implicit in the Air Defense Master Plan that the CADIN/PINETREE radar line, or most of it, would be shut down. Control of interceptor aircraft, which was the primary function of the line, would, in future, be carried out by AWACS aircraft. The relatively small number of AWACS aircraft and the high cost of operating them made it likely, however, that their availability, except in periods of high tension or actual conflict, would be restricted. Canada proposed that, in order to maximize the effectiveness of those available, dispersed operating bases should be set up in Canada (on existing air bases) to support AWACS operations in and over Canada. Canada also proposed that advantage be taken

Figure 7.2
Over-the-Horizon Backscatter Long Range Radar

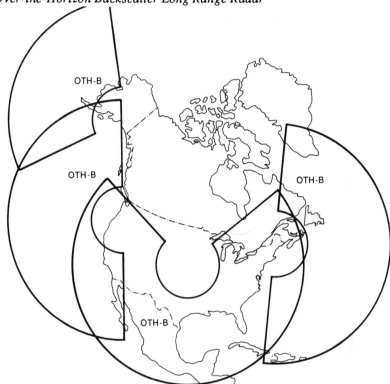

Source: Canada, House of Commons, Standing Committee on External Affairs and National Defence *Minutes of Proceedings,* 21 March 1985 (Ottawa: Supply and Services).

of inherent capability in the new Long-Range Radars of the NWS for control of interceptor operations, by building austere forward airstrips in Northern Canada to enable interceptor aircraft detached from more southerly bases to carry out identification missions within the coverage supplied by these radars. The Americans did not object to this proposal, but initially took the position that the facilities in question satisfied a Canadian rather than a joint requirement and should, therefore, be provided at Canadian expense. It seems likely that this position was dictated more by financial than operational considerations. The question of responsibility for costs of the FOLs and DOBs had not been settled at the time of conclusion of the agreement of 18 March 1985.[18] Agreement was, however, reached that the two countries would jointly determine what constituted "minimum essential upgrades" of "selected" FOLs and DOBs and "evaluate opportunities" for cooperation in their construction, "with a view to the United States contributing towards the cost." The results of the "evaluation" would be presented to the Air Defense Responsibilities Sharing Group by the end of 1985 and "be used as the basis for cost sharing negotiations."[19] In accordance with this undertaking, agreement was reached early in 1986 to share the costs of the FOLs and DOBs equally between the two governments.

It was the prevailing view in Ottawa that Canadian concerns and proposals respecting changes in, and additions to, the air defense master plan could better be dealt with in the context of negotiations to determine the responsibilities of the two countries for carrying out and paying for a modernization program. Recommendations to this effect were put forward to the Canadian Government in the latter part of 1982. The Government indicated its acceptance of the Air Defense Master Plan as a basis for negotiation, gave broad guidance as to the objectives to be sought in negotiations and directed that the results be brought before them for consideration, before any agreement was concluded.

For a variety of reasons, many of them extraneous to the subject matter of the negotiations, progress throughout 1983 and into 1984 was very slow. Factors that seemed to contribute to the slow pace included: President Reagan's announcement in March 1983 of the Strategic Defense Initiative;[20] a degree of preoccupation, thereafter, within the U.S. Defense Department with its implications; and toward the end of 1983 the review of defense program priorities mentioned above and the consequent changes in the master plan. On the Canadian side, a change of defense ministers in the summer of 1983 and the launching of Prime Minister Trudeau's peace initiative also diverted attention away from negotiations. In the first part of 1984, Canadian political events started to inhibit progress. Prime Minister Trudeau's decision to resign, the Liberal Leadership Convention, John Turner's succession as Prime Minister, and his decision to call an election created a situation in which conclusion of a major defense agreement with the United States was clearly unlikely.

In this way, an agreement on North American air defense modernization became a matter requiring early attention by the new Progressive Conservative Government, in September 1984. The intention of the two governments to proceed quickly with the negotiations was soon made clear. Robert C. Coates, the new Canadian Defence Minister and Secretary of Defense Weinberger, during a visit by the former to Washington on 8 October 1984, issued a joint statement that, *inter alia*, reflected this intention.

> The Ministers discussed plans for modernization of the North American Air Defence System. They agreed that every effort should be made to conclude expeditiously the negotiations now in progress regarding the modernization measures to be undertaken and the responsibilities to be assumed by Canada and the U.S. for the execution and funding of these measures. In this connection, they noted the particular capabilities of Canadian industry in northern construction and communications-electronics. These capabilities will be taken fully into account

in determining the portion of the joint modernization program to be contracted with Canadian industry.[21]

The last two sentences of this statement were important both in view of the position on employment taken by Prime Minister Mulroney during the election campaign and because they contributed to the agreement finally reached on the division of responsibilities between the two countries.

CONCLUSION

The announced intention to proceed quickly to complete the negotiations was given further stimulus when President Reagan accepted the Prime Minister's invitation to meet with him at Quebec City in March of 1985. Despite the slow progress earlier, the main elements of an agreement on air defense modernization were close to being settled. Such an agreement was thus seen as one of relatively few on which negotiations were sufficiently well advanced to make conclusion feasible at the Quebec City meeting. Remaining impediments were removed when the Americans proposed that Canada should take on the major responsibilities for managing work on the North Warning System to be done in Canada and should both undertake and pay for the provision of most new construction and for the necessary communications facilities, while the United States supplied the radars. Costs on this basis would be shared 60 percent by the United States and 40 percent by Canada. The Americans agreed that Canada should be responsible for operation and maintenance of the Canadian part of the North Warning System. The operating and maintenance costs would be shared on the same basis as the initial costs (60/40). The Americans had previously accepted the Canadian position on the location of the radars at the eastern end of the NWS and now agreed to the compromises regarding coastal radars and FOLs and DOBs discussed above. By the beginning of March 1985 an agreement acceptable to both governments had been reached. A year later, the two countries renewed the NORAD agreement, without change, for another five years.

Notes

[1]*Exchange of Notes and Memorandum of Understanding*, 18 March 1985, tabled in House of Commons, 21 March 1985.

[2]On the beginnings of bilateral air defense cooperation and the origins of NORAD see: Joseph T. Jockel, *No Boundaries Upstairs: Canada, the United States and North American Air Defence, 1945-1958* (Vancouver, B.C.: University of British Columbia Press, 1987) and Jon B. McLin, *Canada's Changing Defense Policy, 1957-1963* (Baltimore: Johns Hopkins Press, 1967).

[3]On the defense policy changes instituted in the early seventies see: Bruce Thordarson, *Trudeau and Foreign Policy: A Study in Decision Making* (Toronto: Oxford University Press, 1972); Peter C. Dobell, *Canada's Search for New Roles: Foreign Policy in the Trudeau Era* (London: Oxford University Press, 1972); J. C. Arnell and J. F. Anderson, "Program Management in the Department of National Defence," *Canadian Defence Quarterly* 1:2 (Autumn 1971); R. B. Byers, "Defence and Foreign Policy in the 1970s: The Demise of the Trudeau Doctrine," *International Journal* 33, 2 (Spring 1978).

[4]On the bomber threat to North America in the 1950s, see Melvin Conant, *The Long Polar Watch: Canada and the Defense of North America* (New York: Harper/for the Council on Foreign Relations, 1962).

[5]On the ABM debate in the 1960s, see *Anti-Ballistic Missile: Yes or No?*, A Special Report from the Center for the Study of Democratic Institutions (New York: Hill and Wang, 1968). At this time, the Canadian government was saying "no" to any involvement in ABM. In 1968, at Ottawa's request a clause was inserted into the NORAD agreement which specified that NORAD would not involve in any way "a Canadian commitment to participate in active ballistic missile defence." This clause was dropped from the agreement when it was renewed in 1981. Ottawa argued that the ABM Treaty and the fact that the United States had not proceeded with the one ABM system allowed under the Treaty had made the clause moot. The question of Canadian BMD involvement was to re-emerge with the launching of SDI. On the ABM clause, see James A. Everard, "Canada and NORAD: The Eroding Agreement," *Journal of the Royal United Services Institute* 127 (1984).

[6]Canada, Department of National Defence, *Defence in the 70s* (Ottawa: Information Canada, 1971).

[7]Ibid., 30.

[8]Ibid.

[9]The Defence Structure Review appeared to reverse the policy trend of the 1971 White Paper. See, Larry Stewart, ed., *Canadian Defence Policy 1964-1984: Selected Documents*, National Security Series, no. 1/82 (Kingston, Ontario: Queen's University Centre for International Relations, 1982), 39-59.

[10]On the post 1968 trends in Canadian defense policy, including those relating to air defense, see Danford W. Middlemiss and Joel J. Sokolsky, *Canadian Defence: Decisions and Determinants* (Toronto: Harcourt Brace Jovanovich, 1989).

[11]While the bomber threat had declined, the 1970s saw the development of two new weapons systems that would re-focus U.S. attention on North American air defense, the air- and sea-launched long-range cruise missiles (ALCM and SLCM). As the Congressional Research Service would observe in 1985, Pentagon planners had paid little attention to, and Congress had provided little money for, "defenses that could ward off ALCM, SLCM and bomber attacks against the United States." John M. Collins, *U.S.-Soviet Military Balance 1980-1985* (New York: Pergamon-Brassy, 1985), 54. On ALCMs see David Haglund, *Soviet Air-Launched Cruise Missiles and the Geopolitics of North American Air Defence*, Occasional Papers, no. 16 (Kingston, Ontario: Queen's University Centre for International Relations, 1987).

[12]For a review of the state of NORAD in the seventies, see Canada, Senate, Special Committee on National Defence, *Canada's Territorial Air Defence* (Ottawa, 1985).

[13]On JUSCADS and the Air Defense Master Plan, see Joel J. Sokolsky, "Changing Strategies, Technologies and Organization: The Continuing Debate on NORAD and the

Strategic Defense Initiative," *Canadian Journal of Political Science* 19, 4 (December 1986).

[14]The Reagan administration incorporated the ADMP into its strategic modernization plans. This prompted some Canadian analysts to argue that NORAD was going to be brought into a new United States approach to nuclear strategy which stressed warfighting over deterrence. See Douglas Ross, "American Nuclear Revisionism, Canadian Strategic Interests and the Renewal of NORAD," *Behind the Headlines* 39 (1982).

[15]The CF-18 would also replace Canada's fighter aircraft in Europe. See Frank L. Boyd, "The Politics of Canadian Defence Procurement: The New Fighter Aircraft Decision," in David G. Haglund, ed., *Canada's Defence Industrial Base: The Political Economy of Preparedness and Procurement* (Kingston, Ontario: Ronald P. Frye & Co., 1988), 137-58.

[16]The United States interest in the modernization of NORAD's air defense systems meshed with a wider effort to improve U.S. strategic command, control, and communications systems. See *Strategic Command, Control and Communications: Alternative Approaches to Modernization* (Washington, D.C.: Congressional Budget Office, October 1981); Jeffrey Richelson, "PD-59, NSDD-13, and the Reagan Strategic Modernization Program," *Journal of Strategic Studies* 6, 2 (June 1983); John C. Toomay, "Warning and Assessment Sensors," in Ashton B. Carter et. al. eds., *Managing Nuclear Operations* (Washington, D.C.: The Brookings Institution, 1987).

[17]*Memorandum of Understanding*, 18 March 1985.

[18]For the background to the 1985 agreement, see Canada, House of Commons, Standing Committee on External Affairs and National Defence, *Report on Canada-U.S. Defence Cooperation and the 1986 Renewal of the NORAD Agreement* (Ottawa: 1986). (Hereafter, SCEAND Report, 1986).

[19]Ibid.

[20]Possible links between NORAD and SDI touched off sharp debate within Canada as the 1986 renewal of the NORAD agreement approached. There were calls for the re-insertion of the ABM clause to preclude Canadian involvement in SDI. See, for example: SCEAND Report, 1986; G. R. Lindsey, et. al., *Aerospace Defence: Canada's Future Role?* Wellesley Papers, no. 9 (Toronto: Canadian Institute of International Affairs, 1985); David Cox, *Trends in Continental Defence: A Canadian Perspective*, Occasional Papers, no. 2 (Ottawa: Canadian Institute for International Peace and Security, 1986); idem, *Canada and NORAD, 1958-1978: A Cautionary Retrospective*, Aurora Papers 1 (Ottawa: Canadian Centre for Arms Control and Disarmament, 1985); Douglas Ross, *Coping with Star Wars: Issues for Canada and the Alliance*, Aurora Papers 2 (Canadian Centre for Arms Control and Disarmament, 1985); Sokolsky, "Changing Strategies"; Joseph T. Jockel and Joel J. Sokolsky, "Canada and Strategic Defense," in Wayne C. Thompson, ed., *Perspectives on Strategic Defense* (Boulder, CO: Westview, 1987).

[21]Canadian Embassy, Washington, Public Affairs Division, "Joint Statement by Robert C. Coates, Minister of National Defence and Caspar W. Weinberger, Secretary of Defense," 4 October 1984.

8

The United States and the Future of North American Air Defense

Charles M. Tutwiler

INTRODUCTION

For the last thirty years, Canada and the United States have shared in the responsibility for the strategic air defense of North America through NORAD. While some academics and politicians question the viability and need for Canadian alliance participation in today's global security environment, the Canadian government's support of NORAD remains firm. The exchange of Notes between Prime Minister Mulroney and President Reagan on 19 March 1986 confirmed this in extending the bilateral agreement for an additional five-year period effective 12 May 1986.[1] The agreement spells out the primary objectives of NORAD, namely to: assist each nation in safeguarding the sovereignty of its airspace; contribute to the deterrence against attack on North America by providing the capabilities for aerospace surveillance, warning, and characterization of aerospace attack, as well as defense against air attack; and should deterrence fail, to ensure an appropriate response against attack by providing for the effective use of the forces of the two countries available for air defense.[2]

Today, a number of developments are in motion that will shape the future of NORAD and its role in air defense.[3] Technological factors such as weapon size, range, and efficiencies; recent East-West progress in arms control including the signing of the INF Treaty and resumption of serious START negotiations; budgetary stringencies; and new political leadership in the participating countries — these are but a few of the obvious considerations at play. Many analysts now see new windows of opportunity being opened, in no small measure as a result of changes within the Soviet Union, where the current "glasnost" offensive has led some to conclude that the "threat" to the Western world has eroded and perhaps evaporated.

Admittedly, recent developments in the Soviet Union have resulted in *seemingly* major and dramatic shifts in domestic and foreign policy.[4] If these are real and concrete, it still remains to be seen whether they outlive their champion, Mikhail Gorbachev.

Many concerns will undoubtedly fuel the continuing debate over the best course for the West to pursue in dealing with the Soviet challenge over the next decade or so. This generalization is valid for the NATO countries as a whole; it is no less valid for the North American allies, Canada and the United States. While many in both countries will continue to disagree on the proper approach to peace and prosperity, the prospect remains that Canada and the United States might soon be grappling with problems relating to the defense of North America. As George Lindsey stated before the House of Commons Standing Committee on External Affairs and National Defence in late 1985:

> Future problems that will probably have to be faced before the end of the century include defence of North America against the air-launched cruise missile...,against the sea-launched cruise missile, and the use of new technology to defend North America against the ICBM and the submarine-launched ballistic missile.[5]

Canada can play a major role in this effort as a bilateral partner in NORAD, Lindsey went on to suggest in his testimony:

> these new technologies may...need the full cooperation of Canada...[and] to arrive at sensible continent-wide decisions would be [through] the excellent sharing of knowledge and experience that has been characteristic of NORAD since its foundation in 1958.[6]

Certain aspects of and proposals for improving continental defense of North America are currently under investigation on both sides of the border. This chapter examines one such proposal, the Air Defense Initiative (ADI). In the following sections, I shall briefly trace the evolution of continental defense cooperation; discuss the current and future status of ADI; and examine ADI's possible implications for Canada.

ROOTS OF CONTINENTAL DEFENSE

Concern over the possibilities of a Soviet attack against North America and the adequacy of defensive forces for protecting the continent from such an attack is not new. As early as 1949, in a Memorandum to the Joint Chiefs of Staff (JCS), the U.S. Air Force Chief of Staff, General Hoyt Vandenberg wrote:

> Since I became Chief of Staff, U.S. Air Force, I have been much concerned about the problem of air defense of the continental United States that would confront

us when the USSR had the A-bomb. I know you have shared this concern. Now the problem is no longer in prospect. It actually confronts us.

I will not review our mutual efforts to improve the position of the United States in respect to air defense. It is sufficient to observe that progress has been slow.[7]

The seriousness of JCS concern for air defense was brought into focus in a subsequent Memorandum for the Secretary of Defense stating:

The Joint Chiefs of Staff wish to advise you that the level of technological development in the field of air defense is insufficient to permit adequate air defense of the United States, either now or in the near future.

The Joint Chiefs of Staff have directed...a study to determine how best to set up a project with the urgency and priority of the Manhattan Project to improve the technological capabilities of air defense.[8]

Much has happened since this 1949 Memorandum was written, including the formation and growth of NORAD.[9] Even prior to the establishment of NORAD, however, it had been recognized in both countries that the air defense of Canada and the United States had to be considered as a single problem.[10] During the heyday of concern about continental air defense in the early 1960s, force structure grew to approximately 2,600 interceptor aircraft, 278 surface-to-air missile (SAM) units, and 480 radar installations.[11] Surely, it was felt, forces such as these could easily meet the challenges of continental defense.

The advent of Intercontinental Ballistic Missiles (ICBMs) with the capability to complete a non-interceptable, intercontinental trajectory in about thirty minutes resulted in both countries shifting emphasis to the ballistic missile area.[12] By the early 1970s, in light of the Soviet build up and relative concentration (some 90 percent of their nuclear forces) in these quick-strike weapons,[13] the logic behind the continued maintenance of a large air-defense structure in NORAD was questioned.[14] As such, NORAD forces were allowed to dwindle to mere shadows of their 1960s prowess. While the reduction in NORAD's interceptor aircraft still provided some capability against a modest force of Soviet bombers, these reduced numbers really only ensured that Soviet bombers would meet some resistance should they be launched against their North American targets.[15] As such, some deterrence to attack was maintained.

Under Canadian and U.S. cooperation, NORAD has undergone a facelift in the past few years, as John Anderson's chapter has explained. Even though the total number of modern interceptor aircraft remains well below the 1960s' level, current aircraft capabilities have been improved by several orders of magnitude as compared with a decade ago. Other upgrades in command and control, and surveillance, have likewise acted as force multipliers, dramatically improving overall efficiency of today's NORAD over that of a generation ago.

THE SOVIET SIDE

While some analysts have labeled recent Western defensive initiatives potentially destabilizing, the Soviet Union's preponderance of defensive systems brings to mind Dean Inge's observation that "it is useless for the sheep to pass resolutions in favour of vegetarianism while the wolf remains of a different opinion."[16] Conservative estimates routinely list the Soviet defense strength at some 2,250 modern interceptors (not counting 1,700 tactical counter-air interceptors); more than 13,000 SAMs; 10,000 early warning and ground-control interceptor and satellite warning systems; 12 AWACS-type systems; 100 anti-ballistic missile launchers; and nearly 300 attack submarines.[17] These defensive forces, most of which have undergone recent improvements, present an ever-increasing challenge to U.S. systems.[18] Consequently, the U.S. has attempted to take advantage of technology to maintain a credible, retaliatory deterrent force of bombers and cruise missiles to offset the Soviets' heavy investment in the defensive area.[19] Attempts at improving nuclear deterrence have been costly, both in a budgetary and a political sense.[20]

The formidable Soviet defensive force, combined with an offensive structure that continues to place a premium on quick-strike ballistic missiles, might lead one to query whether there exists a real "power" balance between the two countries. Analysis of the offensive forces alone can lead to the conclusion that neither side holds an overall advantage; offensive advantages in certain weapon systems, it is said, are offset by disadvantages in others.[21] However, because the United States relies so heavily on its air-breathing leg for deterrence, should not the formidable Soviet defensive systems be weighed in the "nuclear balance" equation? Might not their omission from such an equation give the Soviets an unfair advantage in force structure if arms control, as some believe, has really balanced both superpowers' offensive capabilities? George Will, for one, thinks it does, and suggests that defense is an important aspect of Soviet strength when viewed in a total force context. He writes:

> The ratio of Soviet warheads to US silo-based ICBMs may become even worse than it is (under START). Our least vulnerable weapon, submarine-launched ballistic missiles, will become more vulnerable: the agreement will create pressures to cut the number of missile-carrying submarines but there will be no limits on the number of Soviet attack submarines that can be deployed to track US submarines. Similarly, bombers will be limited but air defenses — we have virtually none; the Soviet Union has thick layers — will not be.[22]

Would improved defensive capabilities in the West then, better balance the defensive equation, ultimately resulting in improved deterrence and enhanced security for North America? If so, how might that be done? What, if any, role is there for Canada in this process?

ARMS CONTROL IMPACTS

U.S. proposals in the arms-control arena have attempted to diminish the threat to North America by seeking agreements that enhance security while reducing the risks of war.[23] Initial SALT agreements attempted to halt the Soviet expansion in ballistic missiles by limiting the missile numbers (SALT I) and later by reducing those numbers (SALT II).[24] Although SALT II "expired" in a sense in December 1985, it laid a foundation for the most recent START discussions between the U.S. and the Soviet Union. START, it is hoped by many, will reduce the total number of U.S. and Soviet warheads.

Success with the INF Treaty has demonstrated that the superpowers can compromise, thus hope of reducing certain aspects of the strategic arsenals is in the realm of possibility. Would such reduction, though, result in a restructuring of Soviet forces to compensate? Would existing NORAD capabilities enhance Soviet restructuring or provide incentives for so doing? Ronald Purver is dubious, at least on the first question, arguing that the Soviets' "recent arms control proposal for a 50-percent cut in strategic weapons, including bombers, suggests that they do not intend to place significantly greater reliance on their air-breathing leg in the future."[25] Others have suggested that "American defense and arms-control policies are threatening to push Moscow into a significant expansion of its cruise missile force. Were that to occur, the threat posed to Canada by these missiles, and the burden of defending North American airspace against them would grow enormously."[26] A few have even gone so far as to suggest that perhaps it has been such apprehensions that have driven Canada to vote against U.S. arms-control proposals better than half the time (55 percent) at the United Nations.[27]

The evidence seems to support the conclusion that the Soviets are indeed making strides in cruise-missile technology, both sea- and air-launched variants. Even the chief of the Soviet General Staff's Arms Control Directorate, General Nikolai Chervov, admitted in Washington in late December 1987 that the Soviets are developing their own sea-launched cruise missile with a range of 1,600 nautical-miles.[28] This, combined with their already existent ALCM, the AS-15, and a new supersonic intercontinental bomber, the *Blackjack*, suggests expansion in Soviet air-breathing capabilities.[29] Are arms-control initiatives, or perhaps such other kinds of efforts as the Strategic Defense Initiative (SDI), reducing the Soviet ballistic-missile threat, only to increase the onset and magnitude of the Soviet bomber and cruise missile threat, or is the enhancement of their air-breathing capabilities a Soviet attempt to leverage the West into bargaining away cruise missiles in future arms treaties? Some Canadians have already suggested that their government should convince the U.S. to negotiate strict limits on air-launched cruise missiles and ban deployment of sea-launched cruise missiles. This would obviate the need, they argue, for improvements to continental defense — saving Canadian taxpayers' money while maintaining the same relative level of security.[30] Senator Sam Nunn cautions against rushing into this type of strategic agreement, for it is his view that cruise missiles constitute the most effective means of protecting the NATO allies.[31] Assuming the Soviets continue to pursue cruise-missile deployments — and nothing suggests that they will not — it is likely that this will increase the complexity of NORAD's continental-defense mission.

It is no secret that Washington would like to see, through involvement in a variety of arms-control negotiations, "an orderly transition to a more defense-oriented world." Improved defenses, it is held, offer both a safer and more stable basis for deterrence and enhanced security for the U.S. and its allies.[32] Near- and long-term goals, particularly in the area of "total" continental defense, demonstrate this conviction. Among these goals is an attempt to acquire greater capability against the air-breathing threat of the 1990s; this aspiration is manifested in the Air Defense Initiative.

ORIGINS OF ADI

The near-term goals of strategic air defense in North America have been to improve the capability to detect and intercept current Soviet bombers and cruise missiles.[33] These goals are being met in part with Canadian help and support through modernization efforts focusing on improvements and up-grades to surveillance radar, interceptor aircraft, and command and control systems. While these efforts will answer today's needs, further efforts are re-quired to address future advances in Soviet weaponry.[34] The Commander of NORAD, General John L. Piotrowski, has voiced his concern over the emer-gence of a more formidable Soviet air-breathing threat, as evidenced by the "growth in the numbers and variety of Soviet bombers and submarines equipped with cruise missiles."[35] Can Soviet low-observable technology be far off? Should long-range security planners review that possibility today?

The U.S. is currently attempting to develop technology required to defend against anticipated Soviet growth in low-observable bomber and cruise-missile systems projected for the 1990s.[36] A Presidential National Security Decision Document (NSDD-178), issued on 10 July 1985, provided the U.S. national guidance in this area by requiring that a research effort be established, separate from but concurrent with the Strategic Defense Initiative, to investi-gate possible solutions to the future low-observable, Soviet air-breathing threat. The effort is to investigate technologies that would allow for a possible deployment decision to be reached at the same time as a possible deployment decision on SDI.[37] ADI answers this NSDD-178 directive. It directly comple-ments the defensive efforts of the SDI, for while SDI is designed to counter the ballistic-missile threat, ADI focuses on the air-breathing threat.[38] General Piotrowski sees ADI offering "some attractive prospects to supplement the defense of North America," and believes in reference to total defense of the continent that "most would probably agree that it's not particularly wise to build a house with a reinforced roof and then leave the doors and windows open to intrusion."[39] ADI thus will attempt to find ways of closing "the doors and windows" in concert with the national security strategy of "transition to a more defense-reliant world."[40]

To do this, ADI must be in tune with current fiscal realities. It must embrace cost-effective improvements in surveillance, command and control, and engagement. Ultimately, the air defense system must be able to detect, track, identify and negate systems such as higher-speed and lower cross-section bombers and air-launched and sea-launched cruise missiles threatening North American airspace.[41] This may be no easy task. The report issued in January 1988 by the Commission on Integrated Long-Term Strategy, entitled *Discriminate Deterrence*, noted the following, in the context of an advocacy for the speedy integration of low-observable systems into the U.S. force structure: "military vehicles that incorporate enough low-observable technology make existing radars rather ineffective. Replacing those radars with systems that can detect, track, and attack stealthy vehicles is technically difficult, expensive, and time consuming."[42] Does this mean that technological improvements must be a double-edged sword? The ADI will seek an answer to this question, by analyzing whether the technologies available might be applied effectively in the future — should a deployment decision be made. Colonel David Herrelko, USAF Deputy for Air Defense Initiative at USAF Electronics Systems Division, Hanscom AFB, Massachusetts has said:

> ADI is a conceptual development program to provide evolutionary growth in air defense to counter future strategic and tactical air breathing threats...The program investigates a broad spectrum of technologies while maintaining cognizance of current capabilities and proposed upgrades.

Significantly, in this same official's opinion, Canadian capability to support this effort cannot be overstated:

> it is in our mutual benefit to share [with Canada] in the research and development of advanced technologies for future surveillance, warning, communications and defense systems of North America.[43]

ADI APPROACH

As noted above, air defense is not a new issue. Today, there exists a variety of ADI and ADI-related technology programs that are or have been explored to improve air defenses. As the U.S. Defense Department's executive agent for ADI, the Air Force has attempted to capitalize on these efforts by focusing on those programs that might have applicability to improve the defensive capability of North America. To do this requires knowledge about, and some integration capability for, programs and efforts across Service lines. To better facilitate this focus, a multi-service coordinating mechanism known as the Interagency ADI Steering Committee was established and is chaired by the USAF. The overall result has been an attempt to leverage, through expenditures of relatively small amounts of money, billions of dollars spent or being spent in the area of air defense by tailoring the technology from these major efforts into a usable product for continental defense of North America.

Upgrading new systems when possible and capitalizing on new technology when required would appear to be the most affordable and sensible approach. While leverage may be achieved between many planned and ongoing research development initiatives, General Piotrowski envisions ADI to be "an affordable evolution of existing programs."[44] How can new technology be tied in affordably? What system architecture will be required? In September 1987, the Air Force contracted out to four U.S. company teams (two Canadian companies supported this effort) the task of generating an evolutionary approach to the problem of defense. Their final recommendations, submitted in late 1988, will generate preferred systems concepts, identify early critical technical issues, and outline a program of investment strategy.[45]

The teams have been working to generate a variety of postulated North American defense-systems architectures with varying levels of capability that build upon existing systems. Areas of focus have included surveillance, engagement, and battlefield management/command, control and communications.[46] The studies have also examined architecture effectiveness, at varying levels of force readiness, for a multitude of possible attack scenarios on North America. Postulated attacks ranged from a precursor cruise-missile, leading-edge attack to one that might be envisioned for total war.

Each team broke down the defense problem into three regions: 1) the prelaunch region, that area where the weapon carrier, bomber, or submarine has not released its weapons; 2) the weapons-launch region, the area where the carrier has released weapons; and 3) an inner region, an area where the target would be widely dispersed, multiple cruise missiles and/or penetrating bombers. Each contractor concluded that to negate efficiently the threat, wide-area surveillance was necessary to track and identify the offensive targets. Studies showed that if the weapon carrier could be identified and intercepted in the prelaunch region (i.e., before the carrier had an opportunity to release its multitude of cruise missiles) the problem of engagement and nullification of one larger target would be simpler than if many smaller targets had to be countered. In addition to wide-area surveillance, then, an effective long-range intercept mechanism was needed.

For those weapon carriers that could not be negated in the prelaunch region, more effort would have to be expended using advanced technology systems to negate the smaller missile targets. Once again though, wide-area surveillance capable of identifying and tracking cruise missiles, when linked properly to the command structures, could enhance the efficiency of the long-range intercept. Cruise missiles that could not be attrited in the weapons region would have to be dealt with in the inner region. In this area each contractor investigated a variety of defensive systems designed to counter this problem. The key to effective use of resources was to seek improvements in wide-area surveillance, an area the Air Force chose initially as one of the primary project goals.

SURVEILLANCE

In the area of surveillance, potential improvements and their cost effectiveness were investigated for such existing systems as the North Warning System (NWS), and Over-the-Horizon Backscatter OTH(B). Also investigated were space, airborne, and sea surveillance systems. While both space based radar (SBR) and infrared capabilities were examined, the contractor teams favored a SBR satellite constellation of two to three satellites with growth options to as many as twelve for the provision of world-wide surveillance. The advantage, of course, to a space-based system is that it could track on a real-time basis aircraft from their departure point throughout their route to landing. Major-General Lionel Bourgeois, Canadian Forces (CF), Director of NORAD Combat Operations Staff, suggested in May 1988 that two satellites could be placed in a polar orbit by 1994.[47] There has been a well-documented need for a space-based system that could track aircraft, ships, and land vehicles. An affordable system that could identify the originating country of an unknown aircraft and differentiate its flight path from the myriad of friendly civilian and military aircraft transiting the North American continent could greatly diminish NORAD's work load. The present NORAD technique of intercepting unknown aircraft to obtain visual identification is not only difficult, but expensive and impractical in a 1990s threat environment. The SBR concept understandably appears attractive — so much so that Lieutenant-General Larry Ashley (CF), Commander of Air Command, even suggests that with the advent of SBR technology, which will allow NORAD to peer down on Canada's north and accurately detect intruders, ground radar may be replaced.[48]

In addition to SBR, less exotic surveillance systems were also investigated. Contractors looked at a variety of large aircraft, airships, and remotely piloted vehicles, that could employ state-of-the art sensors and antenna systems capable of detecting low-observable cruise missiles. Variants on this idea ranged from an airborne system capable of just tracking, identifying, and relaying information to other engagement systems, to systems that could not only track, identify, and relay but actually engage the airborne threat. As early as September 1986, the USAF showed interest in the airborne surveillance aspect when they issued a "request for proposal" (RFP) for "preliminary design and development of an airborne radar...that would be capable of detecting and tracking air or sea launched cruise missiles with low-observable signatures."[49]

In light of recent and expected advances in Soviet SLCM capabilities, underwater-surveillance measures were also studied. Preliminary analysis indicates that an enhanced anti-submarine warfare (ASW) capability is critically required. With the North American continent being bounded by oceans, it is only logical to seek to counter possible Soviet SLCM attack. Additionally, acoustic quieting of Soviet submarines in recent years presents an ever-increasing problem and will require new technology in the non-acoustic area. Among the areas investigated in this connection were monostatic and bistatic sonar, towed arrays, and acoustic barriers. As well, possible detection options through submarine electronic emissions (radar and radio), magnetic anomalies caused by field effects of large metal masses, reflectivity in the sonic and electromagnetic area, and the dynamics of wave disturbances caused by submarine passage through water were explored.

ENGAGEMENT/BATTLE MANAGEMENT/COMMAND AND CONTROL

Several candidate systems are being investigated that range from the practical to the exotic. In the near-term, capability upgrades to the interceptor force include: radar, extended range capabilities, fire-control systems, and new air-to-air missiles (AAM). Radar upgrades contemplated would improve target detection (range and size), tracking accuracy, while at the same time reduce false alarms. Other improvements are likely to include resistance to ECM jamming, and adjunct systems capable of linking data from surveillance platforms to the interceptor's fire-control system. In addition to interceptor improvements, large aircraft platforms were reviewed. These airframes, by virtue of their larger transportation capacity, could provide extended loiter and range capabilities, carry a variety of equipment to key on existing surveillance systems (e.g., SBR, OTH[B], NWS) for target identification, and have available significant numbers of long-range AAMs for engagement. Additionally, with self-contained surveillance and tracking radar systems, self-directed engagements would be possible. Another approach could be a long-ranged SAM capable of being fired, if necessary, from U.S. soil and engaging enemy aircraft well beyond the North American land mass. Also discussed was a hypersonic glide vehicle carrying internal missiles that could traverse the North American land mass at multi-mach speeds, intercepting and disabling the target.

In the undersea world, enhanced ASW and armed P-3s could provide near- and mid-term solutions to the SLCM threat. Of course, point defenses such as

SAMs and armed orbiting aircraft in the inner region could provide the last line of defense.

Battle management/command and control studies are not yet complete. However, the groups are sensitive to the user needs. An attempt has been made to integrate all surveillance activity, insuring that all the operational control centers (ROCCS/SOCCS) receive timely and critical surveillance information needed for the effective employment of forces they control. Timely flow of this information is essential so that accurate and effective decisions can be made. Upgrades to ROCCS/SOCCS to better fuse data from intelligence sources with new sensor technology are being investigated. Also, survivable control centers and enduring communications systems are essential if credible deterrence is to be maintained.

In sum, a variety of threats, force postures, and strengths were reviewed against technology trade-offs and cost. Preliminary analysis indicates that a multi-layered defense system is advantageous in accommodating the most diverse threat. Wide-area surveillance can act as a force multiplier, increasing the efficiency of the force structure. Space-based radar provides unique advantages. It expands the depth of surveillance coverage and provides increased reaction time for efficient engagements of targets at extended ranges and altitudes. Additionally, SBR will complement existing systems such as OTH(B), NWS, PAVE PAWS (phased array radars), and ASW. Finally, enhanced ASW, airborne surveillance, and engagement systems are considered essential.

CANADIAN INVOLVEMENT

Major-General B. Morton (CF), Chief Air Doctrine and Operations, an officer who is intimately familiar with the possible political and military impacts of ADI on Canada, has remarked recently that "ADI is of great importance to Canada." Concluding that Canada could afford neither to stand idly by nor to go it alone in this area, Morton foresees technological advances taking place with or without Canadian participation — but in either case with likely implications for Canada.[50] In the 1987 Defence White Paper, *Challenge and Commitment*, the Government of Canada indicated its intention to participate in research on future air-defense systems in conjunction with ADI.[51] As of yet, however, no DND programs are specifically under ADI.[52] Some Canadian academics have suggested recently that while there have been collaborative efforts, Canada has yet to be formally invited to participate in ADI.[53] Is this the case? To what extent could or should Canada be involved in ADI? These two questions I pursue in this section.

The NORAD agreement has always provided Canada with an avenue for participation in those defense activities, such as ADI, that were "envisioned for NORAD's" future. The agreement recognized that "the closest cooperation between the authorities of the two governments" was necessary if the activities were to be undertaken in a "mutually satisfactory" way. Additionally, it emphasized the need for full and meaningful consultations to be carried out on a continuing basis.[54] Since the issue was first broached in April 1986, the commander of NORAD has strongly and continually recommended Canadian participation in ADI.[55] While most of the ADI activity is being pursued through U.S. resources, Canada's initial involvement in the program has been through Canadian representation on the NORAD staff.

Since August 1986, Canadian officers have been identifying requirements for the air-defense modernization efforts. In this capacity Canadians serve as members of the ADI Coordinating Committee, receiving updates on the latest technology developments in the program areas; as technical evaluators in preliminary research and development (R&D) proposals in Boston; and as members of the ADI Operations Requirement Panel, working Statements of Need for identified military missions. In an attempt to expand Canadian involvement, a Canadian officer has been assigned to the ADI program office near Boston since July 1988 to assist in the operational analysis of various ADI technology-development programs. Additionally, a scientific liaison position is also being sought and approval is pending for an officer to work as a technical advisor on ADI and related technology programs of Air Force Systems Command in Maryland.[56] Finally, in another ADI-related area, a Canadian has been assigned to the Joint (Air Force, Navy, Canada) Space Based Radar office in Colorado Springs.

Most recently, two Canadian-based aerospace companies, SPAR Aerospace and Canadian Astronautics, have been involved as subcontractors for the surveillance portion of ADI Architecture Studies being conducted in the U.S. Both companies have developed a variety of experience in surveillance systems. SPAR pioneered an infrared surveillance system, in part, under U.S. contract for the passive detection of ships, aircraft, and missiles. Canadian Astronautics has acquired knowledge and capabilities to include synthetic aperture, phased array, and space radar systems. Additionally, both have expertise in space-related communications systems.[57] There is much that Canadian industry can contribute to the ADI effort as the result of this experience.

Canada's involvement in space has been well documented and its demonstrated ability since the early 1960s to share and contribute in this area is noteworthy. In 1962 Canada put its first satellite into orbit, being only the third country at that time to have done so. Most recently, Canada built the arm for the NASA space shuttle and currently ranks fifth in space activities in the Western block.[58] Space is held to be increasingly important to Canada. In 1984, before a Senate Committee on Defence, the DND's Chief of R&D, Dr. Derek Schofield, foreseeing the need for Canada's involvement in space, noted that "it is becoming increasingly evident that space-based surveillance system is the technology that will be implemented in perhaps the late 1990s if we are to satisfy our national requirements."[59] Ottawa, as well, has seen a need for space technology, having earmarked $47 million over a seven-year period to develop a space-based radar-technology program. Two million dollars have been spent to date; understandably, Canadian firms associated with this effort are awaiting the release of more funds.

A Memorandum of Understanding (MOU) on the Modernization of the North American Air Defense System was signed on 18 March 1985. Among other things, it required the U.S. and Canada to establish an "effective means of cooperation" in research, development and employment of advanced technologies in primary mission areas of interest to NORAD. Cited were surveillance (including spaced-based systems), warning, communications, and defense-system areas. Additionally, the MOU stipulated that each country would have "continued opportunities" for participation in each other's developments.[60]

In an effort to improve cooperative research and development and implement the MOU, the CANUS Aerospace Advanced Technology Working Group (ADAT) was formed in 1986.[61] The ADAT brought together a wide variety of Canadian and American officials knowledgeable in R&D and interested in continental defense. The U.S. group was initially composed of Pentagon officials representing surveillance, international cooperation, defensive forces, and space-plans communities. Canadian membership was similarly balanced with appropriate representation from DND, External Affairs, and the Department of Regional Industrial Expansion (DRIE).

ADAT was chartered to develop and propose aerospace-defense R&D candidate projects and programs for joint participation to include coordinating approved proposals within each country's respective defense establishments. Additionally, ADAT members monitor the status and assist in the exchange of R&D information between national agencies when evaluation on the various projects agreed to and approved is needed. Finally, the ADAT reports through each country's national interface to the U.S./Canadian Permanent Joint Board on Defense and the Defense Development/Defense Production Sharing Arrangement Steering Committee. The ADAT provides Canada with one additional means to interact with the U.S. in ADI and related technology areas.

The first meeting of the ADAT working group was held in Ottawa on 20 November 1986; three subsequent meetings were held in 1987. U.S. discussions made it clear that virtually all areas of advance aerospace technology would be considered under ADI, and presented an ADI briefing that had recently been shown to the U.S. Deputy Secretary of Defense.[62] From the outset it appeared that Canadian ADAT representatives were concerned with technical information accessibility and desires for more management leverage over the ADI program. Even at the first meeting, the Canadian aerospace industry's voice was heard. ADAT members from External Affairs indicated that Canadian industry representatives frequently encountered difficulty gaining access to classified information in the U.S. regarding ADI programs. Access to technical libraries at Air Force Systems Command in Maryland and Electronic Systems Division in Massachusetts was also discussed as were ways to keep "Canadian industry apprised of potential air defense contracts" in the U.S.[63] Early on, Canadian representatives questioned the lack of Canadian representation on the interagency ADI Steering Committee, indicating that "Canada was interested in participation in all aspects of ADI including management."[64]

In the SBR area, the Canadian R&D representative advised the working group that SBR concept studies recently completed by Canada could be made available to the U.S. at a later date and expressed a desire to pursue joint development of SBR "regardless of Canadian involvement in other programs such as ADI." At this meeting, one SBR experiment proposal was even discussed and the consensus was that the proposal had potential. A Canadian Policy representative emphasized that the U.S. Department of Defense would have to sponsor the military requirement for the experiment, for without it Canada would not be prepared to commit funds or other resources.[65]

Subsequent meetings of the ADAT resolved the questions of Canadian membership on the ADI Steering Committee and eased Canadian access to ADI information. At the October 1987 meeting, the U.S. proposed that ADI be added to the ADAT project list and while this proposal is still under review by Canada, Canadian representatives did reiterate their country's desire to participate in ADI, both in research and technical as well as concepts and requirements areas.[66]

CONCLUSION: ADI AND THE CANADIAN DEFENSE DEBATE

Many critics of Canadian foreign and defense policy have adopted — for some time — a sanguine view of international politics; in their view, few if any states enjoy such a "comfortable" geo-strategic situation as does Canada. For some of these analysts, Canada's good geographic fortune leads to the questioning of the very purpose and need for ADI systems. Not a few have sought to highlight what they take to be the negative, indeed even sinister, side of the bilateral air-defense relationship.

Recent U.S. defense/security policy and arms-control initiatives, attempting to shift emphasis to a more defensive posture, have often been interpreted in Canada as driven by offensive considerations. Often singled out in this regard has been SDI, which has generated much uneasiness in the Canadian debate about bilateral defense issues in general. The furor over SDI has fueled the revival of some arguments, particularly the one that has Canada bereft of influence in matters of continental defense, its NORAD participation notwithstanding.[67]

Although SDI continues to command attention on the part of those who worry about continental-defense arrangements, ADI has begun to attract some critical notice, ever since the tabling of the 1987 White Paper. ADI is not SDI, but each has a mission complementing the other's. As well, ADI concentrates on technological areas of recent Canadian interest, and this too clearly upsets some critics. The Canadian military, for its part, is keenly aware of the possible beneficial impacts of ADI, particularly if space-based radar with the capabilities currently envisioned comes to fruition. While the U.S. continues to look forward to cooperating with Canada in the ADI program,[68] political considerations could ultimately result in the U.S. relying on its own resources to meet its national security needs. If it does, it will be in large measure due to a belief that Canada either will not or cannot demonstrate sufficient commitment to ADI.

Certainly Canada has shown a desire to participate in the ADI effort. Some in the U.S., however, believe that Canada is really only interested in ADI from the aspect of procuring advanced technology.[69] There can be little doubt that it would be advantageous to Canada's defense industry to obtain access to advanced technology such as that associated with ADI, especially if few resources have to be expended in its acquisition. In part because of the Defense Production and Sharing Arrangements with the U.S., the Canadian aerospace industry has done quite well of late; it exports a very high percentage of its production abroad — more than any other aerospace industry in the world — and is technologically sophisticated.[70] Moreover, it has had a reasonably high profile in space since 1962. It is in the context of both Canadian capabilities and Canadian interests that critical voices have been raised — and not just in the U.S. — about the relatively paltry sums Ottawa is prepared to allocate to military space research. One such voice is that of the president of the Canadian Institute of Strategic Studies (CISS), Brigadier-General (Ret'd) George Bell who in testimony before the Canadian Senate commented on the reluctance of the government to allocate more resources to this area:

> While it is recognized that a small amount of money is being provided for research in space-based radar and satellite communications..there is an urgent need for more positive action in the military space area if Canada is not to fall far behind its allies and is to avoid finding itself closed out of major military space research and development programmes...there is room for concern that Canada might ultimately be precluded from participation...[in certain aspects of U.S. activities]...if Canada is not seen to be making a positive and meaningful contribution to the space surveillance mission.[71]

It is probably correct to state that Ottawa's waffling on involvement with SDI (viz., no official governmental participation is permitted, but private-sector initiatives are encouraged) has been contributing to the perception, accurate or not, that Canada is not committed to active participation in the ADI project. Even if Canada had been officially committed to SDI, and announced itself all in favor of ADI, there would still be raised, in many American minds, suspicions about "free riding." To be sure, the "free riding" issue is as old as the alliance between the two countries. Lately, however, it is being linked to a more recent American concern, that of "burden sharing."

While numerous agreements have been signed between the U.S. and Canada indicating that sharing the burden of developing defense technology is a mutual obligation, there is anxiety on the part of some U.S. observers that Washington carries more than its share of the bilateral load. The Canadian government's recent announcement to spend approximately $1.2 billion (90 percent to be spent in Canada) over the next 15 years on the U.S. Space Station project is estimated to net Canada nearly $5 billion in commercial spin-offs and 80,000 person-years of employment.[72] No one can say, of course, whether this estimate will bear any resemblance to reality by the turn of the century; nevertheless, the mere mention of commercializing security — especially through the mechanism of "offsets" — has been known to stir frenzy on the part of many members of the U.S. defense community.[73]

In this connection, the stated desire of Minister of National Defence Perrin Beatty that Canada contribute more to collective defense may allay a good deal of the U.S. burden-sharing anxiety — at least in the sphere of air defense. Speaking on the occasion of the thirtieth anniversary of NORAD, Beatty discussed the Canadian cooperative commitment and his perspective on air defense, stating that "we will continue to make an equitable contribution to NORAD. And we consider it essential that our participation with the United States, in planning and research for the future of North American Air Defence also be equitable. NORAD is a partnership, an experience in sharing — sharing the duties, sharing information, sharing the risks and sharing the satisfaction that what we do is vitally important, even when it goes unnoticed by millions of those whose lives have benefitted by it."[74]

Even assuming the economic burden gets apportioned in a mutually acceptable way, the evolutionary aspect of a "total" ADI concept will require Canadian-U.S. cooperation, cohesiveness, and sense of common purpose. Possible requirements for forward deployments of aircraft and associated engagement systems, necessary improvements and possible growth of the interceptor force, and joint space surveillance activities may further exacerbate the Canadian political debate over sovereignty and independence — a debate that could strain the defense ties between the two countries. But the importance of effective continental defense to maintain deterrence cannot be overstated. In the long run, capabilities that grow from ADI will improve both the sovereignty of Canada and the security of North America.

Notes

[1]Canada and United States, *Exchange of Notes: Prime Minister of Canada and U.S. President*, 19 March 1986.

[2]Ibid., 4-5.

[3]For an excellent account, see David Cox, *Trends in Continental Defence: A Canadian Perspective*, Occasional Papers no. 2 (Ottawa: Canadian Institute for International Peace and Security, December 1986).

[4]Canada, *Defence Update 1988-89*; Presented to the House of Commons Standing Committee on National Defence (Ottawa: Minister of Supply and Services, 1988), 4.

[5]"Minutes of Proceedings and Evidence of the Standing Committee on External Affairs and National Defence," 33rd Parliament, 1st session, no. 33, Ottawa, 3 October 1985, 33:13.

[6]Ibid.

[7]JCS 2084, 16 November 1949, "Air Defense of the United States," files of the Joint Chiefs of Staff (JCS), HQDND Library, Ottawa, 1. In reviewing the logic behind the "slow" progress, General Vandenberg went on to write: "This is perhaps understandable since even though our intelligence agencies and our scientists officially estimate the Soviets could probably have an A-bomb by mid-1953, many thought it more likely they would not have the bomb for from 10 to 15 years thereafter."

[8]Ibid. (Enclosure Draft Memorandum for the Secretary of Defense).

[9]For a full appreciation of events leading to NORAD's formation see, Joseph T. Jockel, *No Boundaries Upstairs: Canada, the United States and the Origins of the North American Air Defence, 1945-1958* (Vancouver: University of British Columbia Press, 1987).

[10]Canada, *North American Air Defence Command: Agreement Effected by Exchange of Notes*, 12 May 1958. Letter from the Canadian Ambassador to the Secretary of State.

[11]George R. Lindsey, "The Strategic Defence of North America," *Issues in Strategy* (Toronto: The Canadian Institute of Strategic Studies, 1986), 4.

[12]Ibid., 9.

[13]P. Edward Haley, David M. Keithly, and Jack Merritt, *Nuclear Strategy, Arms Control and the Future* (Boulder, CO: Westview Press, 1985), 10.

[14]Edward J. Lacey, "The Air Defense Initiative: Vital Complement to SDI," *National Defense* Jul/Aug 1987, 81.

[15]David G. Haglund, *Soviet Air-Launched Cruise Missiles and the Geopolitics of North American Air Defence: The Canadian North in Changing Perspective*, Occasional Papers no. 16 (Kingston: Queen's Centre for International Relations, April 1987), 24.

[16]Quoted in William J. Yost, *Peace Through Security: A Total Defence Approach* (Ottawa: Conference of Defence Associations 1987), 163.

[17]Colleen Bollard, "Soviet Aerospace Almanac 1988," *Air Force Magazine* vol. 71, no. 3 (March 1988):73.

[18]U.S. Department of the Air Force, Office of the Secretary of the Air Force and Chief of Staff, *The USAF Report to the 100th Congress of the United States of America, Fiscal Year 1989* (Washington: USAF, February 1988), 10-12.

[19]Ibid.

[20]Cost is a relative term. While not "cheap," strategic nuclear forces only consume 7.6 percent of the total DOD budget compared to 55.7 percent for conventional forces. See *United States Military Posture Statement FY89 — Prepared by the Joint Staff* (Washington: JCS, 1988), 12.

[21]Jane Boulden, *Who's Ahead? Examining the Nuclear Balance*, Background Paper no. 12 (Ottawa: Canadian Institute for International Peace and Security, March 1987), 7.

[22]George F. Will, "Pink Sugar for the Tank — All Soviet Eggs Are in One Basket — The Quest for Politically Decisive Military Superiority," *Newsweek: Reagan in Moscow*, 6 June 1988, 80.

[23]United States, Department of State, *Security and Arms Control: The Search for a More Stable Peace* (Washington: U.S. Government Printing Office, October 1984), 7.

[24]See Henry Kissinger's discussion in *For the Record: Selected Statements 1977-1980* (Toronto: Little Brown and Company, 1981), 204-6. Here Kissinger describes the misperceptions that people had on the real object of SALT I. He says the U.S. in the early 1970s, and following the Vietnam War, could not muster the political support necessary to match the Soviets in missile numbers. The only option then for a secure world was to try to limit Soviet numbers through the SALT agreement. This is why he says the Soviets were given a numerical advantage in SALT I. Additionally, the agreement curtailed no American offensive programs. In his review of SALT he says "As one of the architects of SALT, I am conscience-bound to point out that — against all previous hopes — the SALT process does not seem to have slowed down Soviet strategic competition, and in some sense may have accelerated it. The Soviets worked hard and successfully to enhance the first-strike capabilities of their land-based ICBMs despite our restraint..."

[25]Ronald G. Purver, *Arms Control Options in the Arctic*, Issue Brief no. 7 (Ottawa: Canadian Centre for Arms Control and Disarmament, May 1987), 13.

[26]John M. Lamb, "Canadian-American Defence Relations and the Cruise Missile Problem," *Arms Control Communiqué* (Ottawa: Canadian Centre for Arms Control and Disarmament, November 1986), 1.

[27]This figure is based on a statement made by a representative from the Canadian mission to the United Nations, to the 14th Military History Symposium, "The Cold War and Defence," Kingston, Royal Military College, 24-25 March 1988.

[28]Peter Adams, "Soviet General Unveils Cruise Missile Plans," *Defense News* 14 December 1987, 1.

[29]United States, House of Representatives Committee on Armed Services — 99th Congress, "Dear Colleague Letter" (Washington: 16 June 1986), Congressman Les Aspin, Chairman of the House Armed Services Committee charged: "...they [the Soviets] are producing eight major new strategic systems, including two new ICBMs, two new bombers, two new SSBNs (ballistic-missile submarines), and two new SLBM. The U.S., in contrast, is only producing three such systems: one new ICBM (MX), one [sic] new bomber (B-1), and one new submarine (Trident)."

[30]Lamb, "Canadian-American Defence Relations," 3.

[31]Peter Adams, "Nunn: US Must Keep Longer-Ranged Missiles," *Defense News*, 23 May 1988, 1.

[32]Office of the President, *National Security Strategy of the United States* (Washington, January 1988), 17.

[33]United States, Department of Defense, Secretary of Defense Frank C. Carlucci, *Annual Report to the Congress — FY 1989* (Washington: U.S. Government Printing Office, February 1988), 239.

[34]Ibid., 240.

[35]In a presentation "Beyond INF: Why SDI and ADI Make Sense," AFCEA Ninth Western Conference, Anaheim, California, 26 January 1988, 7.

[36]*Annual Report to the Congress — FY 1989*, 239-40; Canada, Department of National Defence, *Challenge and Commitment: A Defence Policy for Canada* (Ottawa: Minister of Supply and Services, 1987), 56-57. The latter points out that "we [Canada] plan to participate in research on future air defence systems in conjunction with the United States Air Defence Initiative."

[37]Washington, ADI briefing supplied by Air Force Systems Command, "Overview the Department of Defence's Preparation for the Air Defense Initiative," undated, received February 1988.

[38]United States Air Force, "Statement of Work (SOW) ADI System Integration Study" (Boston: AF ESD/XR-2, 15 April 1987), 1.

[39]Piotrowski, "Beyond INF," 7.

[40]*National Security Strategy of the United States*, 17.

[41]USAF, "Statement of Work," 1.

[42]F. Iklé, A. Wohlstetter, Z. Brzezinski, H. Kissinger and others, *Discriminate Deterrence: Report of the Commission On Integrated Long-Term Strategy* (Washington, January 1988), 49.

[43]David A. Herrelko, in a letter to author of 22 April 1988.

[44]Piotrowski, "Beyond INF," 8.

[45]USAF, "Statement of Work," 2.

[46]Glenn W. Goodman, "ADI Program Advances Technologies for 1990s CANUS Air Defense," *Armed Forces Journal International*, January 1988, 55.

[47]In a presentation entitled, "The Air Defence of North America," AIRWAR 2000 Symposium, Canadian Institute of Strategic Studies, Toronto, 13 May 1988. (Hereafter cited as Bourgeois presentation.)

[48]In a presentation entitled, "An Airpower Strategy for Canada," ibid.

[49]Glenn W. Goodman, Jr., *Defense R&D Weekly*, September 1986, 2.

[50]In a presentation entitled, "SDI, ADI and Canadian Sovereignty," AIRWAR 2000 Symposium. (Hereafter cited as Morton presentation.)

[51]*Challenge and Commitment: A Defence Policy for Canada*, 56.

[52]Morton Presentation.

[53]Haglund, *Soviet Air-Launched Cruise Missiles*, 30.

[54]Canada and United States, *Exchange of Notes: Minister of National Defence/Secretary of State for External Affairs and U.S. Secretary of State*, 11 March 1981, 5.

[55]"Point Paper on Canadian Force Participation in ADI," NORAD Headquarters, Colorado Springs, Colorado, 22 February 1988, 1.

[56]Bourgeois presentation. Additionally confirmed through ADI project offices of USAF Electronic Systems Division and Air Force Systems Command, 10 June 1988.

[57]Ted Hallas, ed., "A Capability Guide: Canada's Aerospace Industry 1985-86" (Toronto: Aerospace Canada International, 1985), 46, 152.

[58]Presentation by Lieutenant-General, (Ret'd) K. Lewis (Canadian Forces), President of the Aerospace Industries Association Canada, entitled "Beyond 2000: Challenges for Canadian Industry," AIRWAR 2000 Symposium.

[59]Quoted in David Kattenburg, "The Air Defence Initiative," *Canadian Aerospace*, October 1987.

[60]Canada and the United States, *Memorandum of Understanding on the Modernization of the North American Defence System*, 18 March 1985, 2, 12-13.

[61]Information Sheet, "Aerospace Defense Advance Technology (ADAT) Working Group", 21 October 1987, Rome Development Center, provided by Air Force Electronic Systems ADI Office in Boston, upon author's request, 1.

[62]Minutes of a Meeting of the CANUS Aerospace Defence Advanced Technology (ADAT) Working Group (Ottawa: 20 November 1986), 5. (Hereafter cited as ADAT #1.)

[63]Minutes of a Meeting of the CANUS Aerospace Defence Advanced Technology (ADAT) Working Group (Washington: 14 January 1987), 4.

[64]ADAT #1, 4-5.

[65]Ibid.

[66]Minutes of a Meeting of the CANUS Aerospace Defence Advanced Technology (ADAT) Working Group (Rome, NY: 28 October 1987), 2.

[67]Joseph T. Jockel and Joel J. Sokolsky, *Canada and Collective Security: Odd Man Out* (Washington: Center for Strategic and International Studies, 1986), 58.

[68]Speech by MGen Logan (USAF), Headquarters Air Force Plans and Operations, before the CANUS Joint Board on Defence, February 1988.

[69]Interview with former Attaché officer to Canada, 8 April 1988, Colorado Springs, Colorado.

[70]Recent bilateral defense trade is discussed in Robert van Steenburg, "An Analysis of Canadian-American Defense Economic Cooperation: The History and Current Issues," in David G. Haglund, ed., *Canada's Defence Industrial Base: The Political Economy of Preparedness and Procurement* (Kingston, Ont.: Ronald P. Frye, 1988), 189-219.

[71]Testimony before the Senate of Canada, *Proceedings of the Special Committee of the Senate on National Defence*, 33rd Parliament, 2nd Session, Issue 10, Ottawa, 1 December 1987, 10A:5.

[72]*Globe and Mail*, 22 April 1988, A3.

[73]For a good discussion of the offsets controversy, see Frank L. Boyd, Jr., "The Politics of Canadian Defence Procurement: The New Fighter Aircraft Decision," in Haglund, *Canada's Defence Industrial Base*, 137-58.

[74]Quoted in Bourgeois presentation.

9

Ballistic Missile Defense, Arms Control and the Implications for Canada

Boris Castel

INTRODUCTION: THE HISTORICAL CONTEXT

We are now approaching the sixth anniversary of the historic launch of the Strategic Defense Initiative Program (SDI). In March 1983, in a rather unprecedented appeal from a U.S. President to the scientific community, Ronald Reagan took the lead in calling "upon the scientific community...to turn their talents...to give the U.S. the means of rendering nuclear weapons impotent and obsolete." The basic ethical concerns that underpinned the President's message — "wouldn't it be better to save lives than to avenge them?" — were rapidly obscured by objections of a technological and feasibility nature. Indeed since its inception, the SDI program had been intensely criticized, stirring bitter controversies that soon dominated discussions of American strategic-arms policy. Some held SDI to be another example of American technological functionalism, seeing in it the embodiment of the belief that technology could solve such problems as the dilemma of U.S. vulnerability to Soviet thermonuclear attacks.[1] Most criticisms were aimed, however, at the program's feasibility, with most experts concluding that comprehensive defenses are unfeasible because:

- the current defensive technologies are still in their infancy;
- the task of providing a near-perfect defense in computer realtime is too demanding; and
- the Soviets can rapidly develop effective and relatively inexpensive countermeasures to U.S. interception vectors.[2]

Partly in answer to these criticisms, SDI proponents ceased advocating comprehensive national population defenses and concentrated instead on more modest schemes that would give the American population only marginal protection and would protect in fact only selected military targets, like ICBM silos. Such a limited defense program (Phase I of SDI is often dubbed SDI II) is now the only scheme seriously envisaged by most military scientists and defense experts.[3] In addition, even the scaled-down version of Phase I has come under serious review and in its revised plan of 6 October 1988 even the Phase I Ballistic Missile Defense (BMD) budget was reduced by the Pentagon from \$115.4 to \$69.1 billion. Thus a pause in the BMD build-up program is expected and should be propitious to allow the incoming Bush administration, the Congress and hopefully the Canadian government to complete the preliminary strategic analysis to determine SDI's role in a broader international security context for North America.

In any case, the debate over strategic defenses on all its levels — scientific, technological, budgetary and political — is now part of the American policy landscape. Because of the momentum acquired by the SDI military and industrial complex, it is likely to remain so during the Bush administration.[4]

Two questions lie at the heart of this debate: Are ballistic missile defenses feasible? Are they desirable? A cursory analysis of these questions is a necessary backdrop to any study of SDI's implications for Canadian defense.

THE TECHNOLOGICAL CONTEXT: IS BMD FEASIBLE?

Strategic-defense systems are based on three components. The first is the tracking and discrimination system designed to detect and identify the targets. The second is the data-handling system feeding the information emanating from the sensors to the computers that control the interception machine. The third is the interception system itself: rockets, i.e., directed or kinetic energy weapons that actually impact on the target.[5] The public debate on SDI has so far mostly concentrated on the third and easiest part of the program, which is the design and the testing of the interception machine.

In principle, the interception of a ballistic missile can occur during any of the four phases of flight:

— the "boost phase" during which the rocket boosters propel the ICBM toward outer space;
— the "post-boost phase" following the burn-out of the rocket booster and during which the post-boost vehicle (known as the "bus") dispenses its warheads and any decoys or other penetration aids;
— the "mid-course phase" during which these warheads and decoys follow gravitational trajectories toward their targets; and
— the "terminal phase" during which the warheads re-enter the atmosphere on their way to their target.

A typical Intercontinental Ballistic Missile (ICBM) flight divides into three minutes of boost, five minutes of post-boost, twenty minutes of mid-course, and two minutes of terminal phase. Because of the curvature of the earth, Soviet missiles in boost phase can only be attacked by weaponry located high above the earth, or directly over Soviet territory. Early commitments of SDI planners on boost and post-boost phases depended heavily on proponents' claims that new and exotic technology could make these interceptions feasible. A recent study by a prestigious commission of the American Physical Society suggests that at least five years of intense study are needed before one can even assess the capabilities and degree of effectiveness of the exotic weaponry needed for boost and post-boost defense.[6] Essentially similar conclusions were reached after a two-year study by a panel of the Office of Technology Assessment, a nonpartisan Congressional research agency.[7]

Boost-phase and post-boost phase defenses are also, of course, seen as politically intrusive by the Soviet Union. They differ markedly from terminal defense in that they do strain the traditional concept of national sovereignty to which the Soviet Union seems particularly sensitive.

As far as mid-course and terminal defense are concerned, U.S. planners envisage using the same directed and kinetic energy weapons that were designed for post-boost phase, in addition to clouds of pellets or aerosols to destroy Soviet decoys.[8] During the brief two-minute terminal phase, U.S. defense planners envisage developing two varieties of rocket interceptors, one above and one within the atmosphere. Several of the mid-course and terminal interception schemes resemble the abandoned American Anti-Ballistic Missile (ABM) schemes of the 1960s, although SDI planners note that the technologies they incorporate, such as radars, computers, and interceptor missiles, have since become much more capable and efficient.[9]

Recently some recommendations of the U.S. Defense Science Board have also come down heavily in support of terminal and mid-course defenses.[10] The Defense Science Board which advises the defense secretary consists of prestigious scientists and engineers from academia and industry. Its recent proposals on a variety of Pentagon programs, such as the development of anti-armor systems and the management of the Pentagon's software systems have had a profound effect on Department of Defense (DOD) priorities and funding.

As far as SDI is concerned the Defense Science Board panel recommends deployment of ground systems in six progressive stages instead of the current plan that calls for the simultaneous fielding of a huge array of weapons, surveillance and targeting gear. In general, the panel eschews space-based weapons in favor of ground-launched anti-missile weapons, at least for the near future.

The first step envisioned by the panel would consist of deploying 100 ground-based rockets to achieve a limited defense against an accidental launch of ballistic missiles. This deployment would comply with existing treaties. The panel then recommends later installation of shorter, ground-based rockets in the Washington area to protect vital U.S. command posts. An improved version of the PATRIOT is one candidate, another is the high endoatmospheric defense interception system being designed for SDI. This step may also be achievable within the Anti-Ballistic Missile Treaty of 1972.

So far, my discussion on feasibility has largely ignored a possible *symbiosis* between strategic defense and arms control. This synergy equation has been intensively advocated recently. It was actually invoked fairly early in SDI's history by U.S. Air Force General Jasper Welch who used simple terms to declare:

> Look at what it would take to provide a strategic defense of the United States, and look at which we actually have available. The difference between what we need and what we have is about a factor of a thousand. If the Russians threw ten thousand warheads at us and we defended ourselves with the technology we now have available, we might expect to shoot down about ten of them. The Strategic Defense Initiative is supposed to give us the technology to make up the difference between ten and ten thousand. I am not saying that this is impossible, but it doesn't look reasonable. I don't expect any new technology to come along which would really improve things by a factor of a thousand. On the other hand, I can imagine that new technology might improve things by a factor of thirty. And I can imagine that arms control might be successful in reducing the offensive threat by a factor of thirty. If we could get a factor of thirty from strategic defense and another factor of thirty from arms control, we would have a factor of thirty times thirty which is near enough to a thousand. Strategic defense is too big a job for technology to do alone, but it is not too big a job for technology and arms control to do together[11]

Negotiated arms control has, for the most part, an admirable record of achievement. The Partial Test Ban Treaty of 1963, the Outer Space Treaty of 1967, the Nuclear Non-Proliferation Treaty of 1968, the SALT I and II accords in the 1970s, and, of course, the ABM Treaty were the product of difficult and prolonged negotiations. They have all enhanced U.S. security. Although in disfavor in the early 1980s because of such non-strategic issues as the invasion of Afghanistan and Soviet human rights violations, arms control is again the main item on the superpower agenda. In any case, one should examine the role that arms control can play in a transition to a world of offensive reduction and defensive build-ups. Indeed, if the U.S. and the Soviet Union simply appended strategic defenses to their offensive arsenals there might appear to be a considerable advantage to striking first during an escalating crisis. This apparent advantage to the first striker would certainly add to the potential for instability. An obvious solution to overcome one's adversary's strategic advantage is to increase one's offensive retaliatory capability. So unless the transition to a defense strategy is a negotiated one a BMD build-up by one superpower would be followed by an escalation of the arms race. Several studies involving various roles for arms control have been carried out recently. For instance, Wilkening and Watman have suggested in a recent RAND report[12] that crisis instability might be minimized if local, terminal defenses to protect nuclear retaliatory forces were built before a nationwide defense was attempted. The Soviets, however, have already announced that they plan to develop BMD countermeasures rather than build a defensive system. There seems, therefore, to be a great need for a negotiated policy to be undertaken before committing more extensive hardware projects to SDI.

THE POLITICAL CONTEXT: IS BMD DESIRABLE?

Several reasons are generally invoked in favor of SDI by its proponents. The main argument is the enhancement of deterrence that would result by better protecting U.S. strategic forces from attack. Development of a partial BMD can also diminish the value of Soviet ICBMs and Sea-Launched Ballistic Missiles (SLBMs) by decreasing their effectiveness, thus inducing the Soviets to bargain away these weapons more readily in arms-control negotiations.

Against these assertions, SDI critics outline the essential role that the ABM Treaty has played so far in protecting the effectiveness of U.S. ICBM forces by blocking the deployment of Soviet defenses. A relaxation, or abandonment, of the Treaty, which could follow from an SDI deployment, would sacrifice this protection. More American missiles might survive a Soviet attack (assuming the Soviet Union does not expand its offensive forces to offset U.S. defenses), but fewer would reach their targets in the Soviet Union. Any gain in ICBM survivability achieved by SDI must thus be balanced against this loss in target penetration due to increased Soviet defenses.[13]

Toward a Limited BMD: Implications for Canadian Defense

Let me now turn to the possible implications for Canada of a North American defense policy based on a symbiosis of limited BMD deployment and arms-control strategy.

The Limited BMD Aspect. I have so far developed a scenario assuming that the boost-phase defense system, politically the most intrusive to the Soviet Union, is also technically the most arduous and is therefore likely to cede place to the development of partial BMD based on mid-course and terminal defense. Those systems, which might be politically more congenial to the Soviet Union, are also those that can become technologically attractive as the development of sensors and computers moves ahead.

It is in that context that Canadian territory and airspace could well assume positions of increasing importance, particularly as the possibility of massive cruise-missile attacks becomes a key element in U.S. defense planning.[14] Of course the threat of such air-breathing and other non-ballistic delivery systems exists already; but limited BMD would likely place more emphasis on this threat than might otherwise be the case.[15]

In short, a scenario of increased tactical defense cooperation with the U.S. will perhaps confront Canadian defense planners as the limited BMD progresses. Within the Air Defense Initiative (ADI) the increased interdependence of Canadian and U.S. C^3I systems will create a situation where sound political judgment will have to be exerted to weigh the perceived gain in Canadian defense versus the degradation in sovereignty status resulting from joint military control over Canadian territory.[16]

The Arms Control Aspect. If the transition from the present offense-dominated strategic relationship to an offense-defense symbiosis is to be accomplished without destabilization, it must evolve in a climate conducive to arms-control negotiations. Unfortunately the history of arms control suggests that political realignment and political stability generally precede arms control. So while one can accept that the mutual possession of limited BMD may lead to greater crisis stability, substantial verification efforts will be required during the transition period. This is, of course, where Canada's political investment in arms control and its technological expertise could be called upon to play an important role.

It is true that up to now verification programs have been strictly unilateral in character. The reasons for that are largely technical and have to do with the fact that so far only the two superpowers have developed the sophisticated apparatus necessary to verify adequately compliance with arms-control agreements. This situation is rapidly changing, however, as the technologies of verification become available to an increasing circle of industrialized nations. It appears, then, that with or without the superpowers' approval the age of multilateral verification is coming — an age in which Canada could have a large role to play.[17]

Assuming an arms-control scenario requiring drastic cuts in both superpowers' ability to launch a first strike and inflict a disabling blow to C^3I systems, what should be the technical requirements for a workable verification program? One would envisage:

— the control of positioning of Anti-Satellite (ASAT) weapons;
— the detection of deployment of exotic new weapons designed to alter the agreed-upon BMD status; and
— the detection of significant deviation on the numbers of agreed-upon weapons and launchers.

Such an all-encompassing program is of course complex. There is, however, no necessity to envisage a multilateral verification program having to cover *all phases* of verification. Canada could focus on participation in an ASAT control program for instance. An ASAT arms race would be particularly destabilizing because of its effects on the C^3I and launch-detection capabilities of both superpowers. Because the U.S. relies more than the Soviet Union on satellites for both its domestic and intercontinental military communications, Canadian participation in ASAT control might be positively viewed by Washington. The only ASAT systems developed so far are those capable of destroying satellites in near-earth orbit (100-1500 km). An agreement halting developments of ASAT systems in geosynchronous and highly elliptical orbits would be particularly stabilizing. Since space-based ASAT weapons must remain in proximity of their targets for much of the time,[18] it is possible to design a series of ground- and space-based detectors that could identify killer-satellites designed to destroy communication and early-warning satellites.

In a major undertaking the Verification Research Program of the Canadian Department of External Affairs launched PAXSAT in 1986 — a research program designed to promote Canadian space technology in the process of arms control.[19] PAXSAT research has concentrated on two potential applications of space-based remote sensing: the space-to-space PAXSAT A which deals with verification of agreements regarding satellites and the space-to-ground PAX-SAT B, which focuses on agreements involving conventional forces. The Canadian satellites would draw on the technology developed for the civilian RADARSAT to achieve a seven-meter all-weather resolution imagery. This would be good enough to detect tank movements and thus useful to verify agreements like the 1987 Conference on Disarmament in Europe (CDE) ban on unannounced troop movements. By the late 1990s, the resolution of PAX-SAT imagery could be as good as one meter. Already, France and West Germany have expressed great interest in the project. It is to be regretted, however, that the importance of arms control is not more actively discussed in military declarations of future Canadian defense doctrine. For instance, the White Paper on defense makes no mention of allying arms control with ideas of future U.S. cooperation under the auspices of the Air Defense Initiative.[20] Canadian defense planners certainly recognize that a major part of verification consists of surveillance and that the technological developments of the two programs largely overlap. Thus, the development of a Canadian high-technology expertise necessary for participation in a multilateral verification program would also create the technological know-how necessary to monitor Canadian territorial sovereignty, a prospect to which future declarations of Canadian defense doctrine should pay close heed.

CONCLUSION

The nearly six years that have elapsed since the inception of the SDI program have summoned forth several studies on the political implications and the technological feasibility of the program. Most feasibility studies indicate that mid-course and terminal-phase defenses, largely inspired by the older ABM program, are likely to become operational a decade or more before boost-phase defenses, which rely on more exotic high-technologies. It is possible to imagine that, as the technology of sensors, microcomputers and data processors improves, a terminal-defense system may finally gain an advantage in cost-effectiveness over the attack. Of course, non-nuclear defense against nuclear attack will never be perfect or totally reliable, but it still may be technically sufficient to make multilateral nuclear disarmament possible. Also, mid-course and terminal-phase defenses are politically less intrusive to the Soviet Union and thus not as likely to strain the survivability of the ABM Treaty.

Several analysts have recently suggested that a symbiosis between limited BMD and arms control is likely to prove more stabilizing than either of these strategies in isolation. Evolution of a U.S. defense strategy based on limited BMD can involve Canada in at least two important ways.

First, Canadian territory and airspace would assume positions of increasing importance as the possibility of attacks by non-ballistic delivery systems becomes a more central element of U.S. defense planning. At the very least, the next decade is likely to bring the need for an evaluation of the balance between perceived gains in joint U.S.-Canada defense versus loss of sovereignty status resulting from sharing joint C^3I systems.

Second, Canada has recently developed the scientific and technological expertise to become an active member of a multilateral arms-control program. Such membership would be consistent with declarations of intent of several recent Canadian governments, and it could allow Canada to play a major role in promoting crisis stability, especially if it was articulated within the context of future military doctrines. Technological requirements for capability in arms control and military surveillance strongly overlap, thus providing an additional impetus for including more overtly arms control as part of future Canadian defense planning.

Notes

The Author is grateful to Dr. Jim Moore (Department of National Defence, Canada) and Dr. David Haglund for helpful comments and discussion.

[1]President Reagan's Speech to the Nation, 23 March 1983, reprinted in *Survival* 25 (1983), 3; John Tirman, ed., *The Fallacy of Star Wars* (New York: Vintage Books, 1984); idem, *Empty Promise: The Growing Case Against Star Wars* (Boston: Beacon Press,

1986); Steven E. Miller, ed., *The Star War Controversy: An International Security Reader* (Princeton, NJ: Princeton University Press, 1986); Charles P. David, *All-out Defence in the Nuclear Age*, Issue Brief no. 3 (Ottawa: Canadian Centre for Arms Control and Disarmament).

[2]George F. Jelen, "Space System Vulnerabilities and Countermeasures," in William J. Durch, ed., *National Interests and the Military Use of Space* (Cambridge, MA.: Ballinger, 1984); Greg Nelson and David Redell, "Could We Trust the SDI Software," in Tirman, *Empty Promise*; Richard L. Garwin, "The Soviet Response," in ibid.

[3]F. S. Hoffman, "BMD and US National Security," *Future Security Strategy Study* (Washington, 1984).

[4]*High-Technology Business* (SDI Survey, December 1987), 25ff.

[5]Kosta Tsipis, *Arsenal* (New York: Simon and Schuster, 1983).

[6]Report to the American Physical Society of the study group on Science and Technology of direct energy weapons, *Review of Modern Physics*, 1987, 51.

[7]United States, Office of Technology Assessment Report no. 13, Washington, D.C., 1988.

[8]Alexander Flax, "Ballistic Missile Defense: Concepts and History," in Franklin A. Long, Donald Hafner and Jeffrey Boutwell, eds., *Weapons in Space* (New York: W. W. Norton & Co., 1986).

[9]Gerald Yonas, "The Strategic Defense Initiative," in ibid.

[10]*Defense News*, vol. 3, no. 21, Washington, 1988, 1.

[11]Freeman J. Dyson, *Infinite in All Directions* (New York: Harper & Row, 1988).

[12]Dean Wilkening and K. Watman, *Rand Report* R-3412-FE/RC (Santa Monica, California, November 1986).

[13]Samuel Wells, et al, "Preserving the ABM Treaty," *International Security* 9, no. 2, 1984, 51ff.

[14]Ashton B. Carter, "The Relationship of ASAT and BMD systems," in F. A. Long et al, eds., *Weapons in Space*.

[15]A detailed analysis of the Air Defense Initiative can be found in the chapter by Charles Tutwiler, in this volume.

[16]J. W. Moore, *Canadian Participation in BMD Deployment: The Implications for National Sovereignty and Security*, Reprint.

[17]R. F. Cleminson, "The Feasibility of Space-based Remote Sensing in the Verification of a Treaty to Prevent an Arms Race in Outer Space," in *Modelling and Arms Control*, NATO ASI Series F v. 26, ff. 402.

[18]Carter, "The Relationship of ASAT and BMD Systems."

[19]PAXSAT Concept, Verification Brochure no. 2, External Affairs Publication.

[20]John Barrett, "Arms Control and Canada's Security Policy," *International Journal* 42 (Autumn,1987).

10

Nuclear Submarines for Canada: A Technical Critique

S. Mathwin Davis

INTRODUCTION

The purpose of this chapter is to examine the decision-making environment attending the mooted acquisition, by Canada, of nuclear-propelled attack submarines (SSNs). While this chapter's primary focus is the technical, logistic, and financial considerations relating to the 1987 Defence White Paper's selection of SSNs, it will also present a brief review of relevant background material. In this regard, the report of the Senate's Subcommittee on National Defence, entitled *Canada's Maritime Defence*[1] remains one of the better overview documents. The Senators, as would be expected, sought and received professional advice, from both naval and academic constituencies. Indicative of the thrust of the advice received by Canada's naval officials is the following statement:

> The nuclear submarine is very much the major warship or battleship of today...but there is nothing that frightens a nuclear submarine more than a conventional submarine. They are very quiet.... I do not think you should dismiss conventional submarines lightly....
>
> So there is a role for everything. If you want a bang for a buck, and if Canada wants to be able to go bang should the balloon go up, you will get a very fair return for a modest outlay from our conventional submarine.[2]

In their Recommendations, the Senators, taking note of the requirements for the protection of Canadian sovereignty and for a "full contribution" to NATO, applied the interesting constraint that the latter should involve only tactical anti-submarine warfare and not strategic surveillance missions.[3] To this point we shall subsequently return.

As a result of their deliberations, the Subcommittee considered extensively the sort of fleet that would be appropriate, noting that the only Government assessment for the desirable force level was a statement that "the Cabinet has determined a need for twenty-four frigates."[4] Following a study of a number of "models" they called for a mix of sixteen frigates, twenty conventional submarines, and thirty-six long-range patrol aircraft.

They did not ignore the Arctic but concluded that surveillance of the Northwest Passage could be provided by conventionally powered submarines (SSKs) stationed at the entrance and exit of the passage. Nevertheless, it was felt that if the frequency of nuclear submarine transits through the Passage rose significantly, Canada might have to consider obtaining nuclear submarines of its own.

THE ARCTIC AND THE SUBS

While not primarily related to maritime defense the sequence of reports following External Affairs' 1985 "Green Paper"[5] deserve brief consideration. In this regard the Department simply raised the issue of "priorities Canadians wish to ascribe to national defence, to making a substantive and cost-effective contribution to collective security and to enhancing Canada's international influence."[6]

To obtain a response to the "Green Paper" a Senate-House of Commons Joint Committee conducted extensive hearings across Canada and produced a lengthy report.[7] After calling for a study of long-term defense requirements they raised the issue of "A Northern Dimension for Canadian Foreign Policy" and, with regard to the Northwest Passage, recommended that "the possibility of equipping the Canadian Navy with diesel electric submarines be reviewed in the context of a general examination of the country's naval forces and more generally of Canada's defence policy."[8]

They shied away from "modern submarines" (presumably nuclear propelled) noting the possibility of "conventional propulsion systems" — as yet not proven — that would permit under-ice operations. As this Report was being published, the Department of National Defence (DND) was calling for proposals for a series of conventional submarines, preferably with some under-ice capability. External Affairs responded to the Report of the Special Joint Committee with a further publication recognizing that there is a link between defending the country and asserting its sovereignty.[9] Particular attention was to be paid to underwater defense in the Arctic, and a defense study was underway to carefully consider what type of new submarine would best meet the national requirements of Canada's defense policy.

Thus, in the political realm outside DND, the beginning of 1987 had seen the enunciation of: a need for substantial re-equipment of the Navy; some emphasis on the acquisition of substantial numbers of diesel-electric submarines; initiation of a discussion of sovereignty and security in the Arctic; and a tentative suggestion of the possible acquisition of nuclear submarines.

Harriet Critchley has described the threat to security by noting the potential of Soviet Sea Launched Ballistic Missiles (SLBMs), fired from their own Arctic waters, to reach all North American and NATO Europe targets. She notes also the earlier view that, "according to the levels of Western deterrence theory such a development stabilizes deterrence and is therefore desirable."[10]

With the increasing accuracy of SLBMs and the potential for both increased range and accuracy of Sea Launched Cruise Missiles (SLCMs) from Soviet SSNs, such an enhanced attack capability can be particularly destabilizing. Soviet ballistic-missile carrying, nuclear-powered submarines (SSBNs) and SSNs can, at will, "disappear" under Arctic ice for protection or in transit to Atlantic or Pacific waters. Since the Canadian Arctic Archipelago is clearly involved, Critchley concluded with the necessity for an adequate monitoring capability that would serve Canada's security interests as well as those of NATO.

Sovereignty is more diffuse and, in this study, may perhaps be restricted to a desire to know what is happening above, on, or under Arctic territory, including Arctic waters — ice-covered or not. In this aspiration the (comparatively) attractive Northwest Passage (M'Clure Strait, Viscount Melville Sound and Lancaster Sound) presents a difficult problem since the United States insists on regarding this as "international" rather than "Canadian internal" waters. This implies a freedom for U.S. SSNs to transit submerged — a right, of course, that would apply also to Soviet SSNs and SSBNs. A grudging acceptance has been achieved in the current Arctic Cooperation Agreement for Canadian consent to passage of surface vessels, e.g., icebreakers, but not, apparently, *prior* consent. This does not, however, apply to U.S. SSNs although "that traffic is said to be covered by secret military agreements."[11] Thus, from the underwater (or under-ice) aspect of Canadian sovereignty, there emerges a parallel and reinforcing requirement for under-ice monitoring. Indeed it may well be the view of the Government (or of External Affairs) that the sovereignty aspect presents the more persuasive requirement for nuclear submarines.

Critchley concluded that while the only satisfactory monitoring is by SSNs:

> given the very large area to be covered, the lack of choke points between the Kola Peninsula and the (operational) zones which could be monitored by NATO's navies, the uneven underside contour of the ice pack as well as ... the noise generated by the ice and the variations in water temperature — the cost effectiveness of this monitoring method is highly questionable.[12]

SUBMARINE ACQUISITION: CONVENTIONAL OR NUCLEAR?

Concurrent with the foregoing deliberations, it was evident that the Canadian *Oberon* conventional submarines would not have a life extending beyond the year 2000. Accordingly, a study was made of potential replacements, and in November 1985, Cabinet approved four conventionally powered boats, one of which was for the West Coast. The Canadian Submarine Acquisition Project Team developed a procurement sequence leading to a Request for a Proposal being issued for acquiring a varying number of boats, up to twelve. Eight apparently suitable European designs were suggested and a number of interested Canadian consortia presented themselves. However, it was not to be, for reasons I relate in the following pages.

In seeking to follow the decision process that led to the setting aside of conventional submarines in favor of nuclear, we must rely on evidence presented to, and discussions with, the newly formed (15 April 1986) Standing Committee on National Defence (SCND). This was the first Standing Committee of the House to be struck with an exclusive mandate for National Defence in over 17 years.[13]

However, information on some of the earlier events did not come until later in its activities. Thus, at a meeting in March 1988 the Minister of National Defence, Perrin Beatty, noted that: a project for replacement of *Oberon* class was initiated in 1980; Jean-Jacques Blais (then Minister of National Defence) suggested the acquisition of nuclear-propelled submarines; and in 1985, Erik Nielsen (Minister of National Defence) called for a review of the "nuclear option," indicating a willingness on the part of the Government to review strategic options.[14]

There was also a confirmation that, in November 1985, DND approached Cabinet with a request for four new conventional submarines following studies, during the previous twelve months, of the availability of conventional submarines.[15]

At SCND's first meeting one brief reference was made to the conventional submarines then being contemplated, noting that the concept was not yet at the stage of project definition, and that alternatives were being considered. A question was raised regarding the fitting of conventional, diesel-electric, submarines with the Canadian *Slowpoke* reactor. Somewhat confusingly, Harvie Andre, Associate Minister of National Defence, suggested that this was not one of the possibilities for the *Oberon* replacement, but was being studied in a separate context of whether or not it would be useful in the defense requirements in the North.

By the fourth Committee Meeting, there was a good deal of discussion regarding the *Oberons* and their potential replacements. It was established that it was important to have attack submarines "for the purpose of going after Soviet submarines that have penetrated through the two choke points in the North Atlantic." Vice-Admiral Nigel Brodeur responded: "The attack submarines, even the diesel-electric submarines, can serve a very useful role in those choke points."[16] In response to a direct question, reference was made to the Associate Minister's earlier observation that "we are looking at the possibility of some form of nuclear propulsion. The purpose of course, for Canada would be the possibility of under-ice operations."[17]

Here then, almost as an afterthought, came the first open suggestion of consideration of nuclear propulsion. The matter emerged again fairly soon with reference to the conventional's "limited capability to go under the ice" and a note of other closed-cycle systems "yet to be proven in a military submarine" which would permit the charging of batteries without surfacing. It was suggested that, if trials were successful, these latter systems could be available in the "not too distant future," with two to three years being mentioned.

The situation hardened somewhat at the Committee's next meeting when reference was made to a *Globe and Mail* article "Arctic may get nuclear subs by 1995."[18] In response, General Paul Manson (Chief of Defence Staff) said:

I really cannot answer that question directly because to do so would be to reveal a delicate analysis that is going on within the department right now as part of the submarine program. Right at this point in that program optional analysis is critically important.... I can say that to the extent that the article infers that the department is looking at the nuclear option, of course, that is right. I think it would be quite wrong for us not to look at it.[19]

This rather profound observation — that the nuclear option was being actively studied — excited no particular comment and, indeed, the Canadian Submarine Acquisition Project (CASAP) went forward on 16 July 1986 with inquiries relating to eight European designs for up to twelve conventional S/Ms. By December, however, the Standing Committee again began to take a particular interest in the submarine question. At the beginning of the month occurred a meeting to review Supplementary Estimates for National Defence with Paul Dick, the new Associate Minister of National Defence. Here was raised a key question as to the "basic strategy" on which CASAP was premised and this led to a somewhat more complex response. It was noted that there was a need to meet NATO commitments that would essentially replace the current *Oberons*, when their life expires, with similar submarines. However, Vice-Admiral Brodeur continued:

There then is another dimension, which is the dimension that is purely the defence of Canadian territory, Canadian waters, waters of national interest, which would require an additional capability on the part of those submarines. Of course, what I am referring to is the question of whether or not a conventional submarine is capable of operating under ice.[20]

This led to somewhat extensive questioning, primarily from Derek Blackburn, who had raised the basic strategy issue, and directed to whether or not Canadian submarines needed to go under the ice-cap or could "simply be waiting at choke points for Soviet entry or exit." It was emphasized that there was no evidence of Soviet submarines entering the Canadian Arctic — although they might well do so in the future. Brodeur stated that we must have, in the future, the capability to operate our submarines wherever we have waters of national interest, and that involves the three oceans, including the Arctic. He further asserted that "the only submarine we are aware of that is in production, in service, and has the ability is the nuclear-powered submarine." Dick reported to SCND that, as well as CASAP's conventional activity "with all the variety of options that were proposed, there is an entirely different committee working within the Department considering nuclear submarines." He suggested that, at some point, both groups would come together for a discussion on whether to go ahead with conventional submarines or look more seriously at the nuclear.

An outsider might perceive that there was already some serious "looking." At any event, the conventional proposals, upon which several shipyards were working, were now clearly in doubt. Perhaps, somewhat pessimistically, it was suggested that a decision would be made "in the latter half of 1987 or the first half of 1988."[21]

In mid-December, the new Minister of DND, Perrin Beatty, paid his first visit to the Committee. His statement noted that while the project definition phase for "modern submarines" had been initiated, "We will be looking into the possibility of an under-ice capability" and that decisions about type and number would be made by 1989.[22] In this regard, it was reported that the CASAP proposals required an indication of whether an under-ice capability was being offered, using some of the "hybrid" systems understood to be available. During further deliberations, the Minister drew attention (somewhat at variance with earlier reports) to the substantial number of SSNs armed with SLCMs that were utilizing the Arctic Archipelago — suggesting that looking at southerly choke points would not insure against entry from the North. At this point, he concluded that "no decision has been taken. We are simply ... canvassing opinions and trying to look at the feasibility of having a presence in those Arctic waters and what sort of trade-offs would have to be made."[23]

THE DEBATE QUICKENS

The national press now began to take an interest. The *Financial Post* reported the Minister's "enthusiasm" about nuclear propulsion and noted his visit, in October, to see the French *Rubis*.[24] The *Globe and Mail* noted Canada's "consideration of a continental naval defence pact with the United

States to counter a growing Soviet threat in the Arctic" but indicated that the Minister had suggested on 19 December that "a second option would be for Canada to acquire a small fleet of nuclear powered submarines capable of waging anti-submarine warfare under the Arctic ice."[25]

By the end of 1986, it was or should have been fairly clear to all interested that Beatty, at least, had an enthusiasm for — even a commitment to — the acquisition of nuclear-powered submarines. He believed, as reported in the *Toronto Star* in January, that nuclear submarines would politically be very attractive in reinforcing a claim to Canadian sovereignty.[26] The *Star* noted, however, that while there appeared to be increasing Arctic penetrations by U.S. submarines "no confirmed record of Soviet incursions was available." Politics, it suggested, would determine the choice of submarine.

At this point the Defence Committee held a lengthy session devoted to Arctic Sovereignty and Security. There were extensive initial briefings on these issues, during which it was established that, due to the extensive range of Soviet SLBMs (SS-N-20 and SS-N-23 at greater than 8000 kms) there was no apparent reason for Soviet ballistic-missile submarines to operate in or even near Canadian Arctic waters.

Thus, the threat under consideration would come from the seventy-two Soviet nuclear attack submarines, all potentially equipped with SLCMs. These would be likely to patrol off the east and west coasts, as well as the southern areas of the Canadian Arctic and would transit through Arctic waters. As well, they could be expected to patrol offensively (in combat) to intercept any U.S. or NATO submarines seeking to enter the Arctic Ocean through the Canadian archipelago. Better surveillance and control were required in all three oceans. Fixed underwater arrays would be suitable for the former capability but, for the latter "the most effective and versatile means would be submarines with a sustained under-ice capability."[27]

This implied nuclear propulsion, not only for Arctic operations but to provide a general operational capability "of the order of three times the value of conventional submarines." It was felt that the nuclear-powered submarines would signal Canada's intention to deter any intrusions into the Arctic, Atlantic, and Pacific approaches. Nuclear submarines would offer the only long-term solution to the defense of our Arctic maritime security, the underpinning of our sovereignty.

There ensued a good deal of repetitious discussion about operational probabilities, wherein two points of significance emerged:

> Given resources, we could put into the Arctic passages, at the choke points, a bottom based trip wire in real time, that would tell you that something had gone by. If you are significantly discrete in your knowledge you can identify what it is. That does not give you the ability to do anything about it, but you would know it had been there.

There is a 50% probability of finding open water anywhere in the Arctic, even in mid-winter, open water or first year ice which is less than three metres.[28]

In response to a direct question about costs, there was some hedging about whether it was sail-away, or program cost, or vessel life cost, or the cost of training facilities on-shore, which are vital to the operation of that system. With these reservations it was suggested, with some lack of clarity, that "we are talking about something in the order of $400M to $500M." Presumably this was per boat.

At this point, the DND thrust appeared to change somewhat, responding to the possibility that the current perceived threat (of SLCMs) could have been negotiated away. The pace of Committee meetings now began to quicken, with four being held in March. The Associate Minister reported that the parallel investigations, conventional and nuclear, were only just being brought together, and noted the possibility of enhanced propulsion systems for conventional submarines.[29] Also, it was established that the proposed *Polar 8* Icebreaker would have "no utility" from the viewpoint of Anti-Submarine Warfare (ASW). The seventh meeting was directed to a concern for Research and Development and reported that there was a good deal of information available with regard to the application of underwater acoustic surveillance in the Arctic Archipelago, i.e., a system that could ultimately be such that "you know something has gone by and you know which direction it has gone in." However, it was clarified that this capability did not presently exist, but that "we believe we could put such a system together in Canada."[30]

All this discussion had sparked more curiosity and, toward the end of March, the press could report that both French and British companies building nuclear submarines were becoming interested. More significantly perhaps, the report asserted that:

> The Conservative cabinet is currently mulling over the ramifications of Beatty's formal recommendation, submitted early in March to go with a nuclear fleet ...

> Beatty is pushing hard for final cabinet approval before June, in keeping with his pledge to produce a new White Paper on Defence Policy by spring.[31]

This article also raised the issue of the British-U.S. agreement that restricted each country's ability to export nuclear-related technology to a third country. Of further significance, it suggested that the nuclear activity had "put into limbo a separate procurement program to buy up to twelve conventionally powered submarines" — which would have cost about $4 billion (of which $1 billion was for "infrastructure"). By the end of March 1987, therefore, it was evident that DND, if not yet the Cabinet itself, were committed to nuclear submarines and it remained to be seen how contentious the decision might be.

The Committee, meeting with Joe Clark, the Secretary of State for External Affairs, toward the end of April, heard him respond that if nuclear powered submarines were considered they would "allow us to serve both sovereignty and security purposes in the Arctic, probably in that order at this time — sovereignty and security."[32]

By this time, the first independent analysis appeared, prepared by the Canadian Centre for Arms Control and Disarmament. This noted that while the Government may have had some concerns with regard to cost, it

> clearly feels under pressure from the public to do something serious about Arctic security and our claim to sovereignty over the region. At the same time, powerful bureaucratic interests in the Department of National Defence, not to say the military services themselves, have gathered behind the nuclear submarine option, giving it momentum.[33]

DND DECIDES ON SSNs

Indeed, momentum was the appropriate word, for this Communiqué concluded by noting that while the Priorities and Planning Committee had recommended the purchase of ten nuclear-powered submarines, a final go-ahead had not yet been given by the full Cabinet.

This analysis was repeated, at considerably greater length, in May and formed the basis for an Op-Ed article in the *Globe and Mail*.[34] In the latter, the decision process was perceived to have hardened somewhat, since it began with the statement that "Evidently the Federal Cabinet has decided to order a fleet of nuclear-powered attack submarines for the Navy."

That became abundantly clear with the introduction of the White Paper *Challenge & Commitment* on 5 June 1987. In a relatively brief speech Beatty noted "the growing strategic importance of the Arctic Ocean as an operating area for foreign submarines raising both security and sovereignty concerns for Canada."[35]

Indeed it was suggested that the cost of such a submarine would be "approximately the same amount" as for a modern air-defense frigate. The rather complex, and very significant funding pattern was identified, i.e.,

> During the 15 year planning framework of the White Paper, the Government is committed to annual real growth in defence spending which, except in fiscal emergencies, will not fall below 2 percent. Increased resources over those generated by this planned funding float will be provided as major projects forecast in the White Paper are introduced and implemented.

These "annual incremental resources" would be based on a "rolling five-year funding plan" to be reviewed each September — beginning in 1987. Opposition parties suggested that this 2 percent was less than adequate and, more significantly, that the acquisition of nuclear submarines would tend to destabilize the deterrent, as well as being an inappropriate unilateral military approach to the legal problem of sovereignty. As well, the specter of being drawn into the (also destabilizing) U.S. Forward Maritime Strategy was raised. Canada was urged to "not fall victim to the Minister's mindless lust for nuclear submarines." It was suggested that he had proposed spending up to $10 billion to protect our sovereignty against our closest ally.

Thus, it appeared that the nuclear submarine issue was likely to provoke some controversy. The *Globe and Mail*, both by Editorial and Column (in unusual consonance), decried the acquisition — achieved at the expense of cancelling the third group of eight frigates — as less than cost-effective, particularly since it was held that the initial cost (estimated at $7 billion) was likely to be exceeded, and there would be substantial on-going operating costs.[36] However, more serious considerations of the topic surfaced in a Standing Committee meeting convened to review the White Paper. While it took some time to come to a discussion relating to nuclear submarines, an interesting point arose with regard to the life of the Paper. The Minister noted that "one of the advantages of the five-year rolling plan we are talking about is [that] it will force us to revisit on a regular basis the assumptions on which all our defence strategy is based and, particularly the assumptions on which our procurement policy is based."[37]

During some later discussions regarding the relative safety of Western maritime nuclear reactors (very good) and Soviet (alleged to be very poor) Beatty noted the importance of a Canadian "presence" in the Arctic "to ensure that we have control over Canadian waters and that the vessels in those waters meet Canadian standards and Canadian policies."[38] On the whole, the meeting paid relatively little attention to this major acquisition and, indeed the topic was not to recur in this forum for several months.

It became clear that the choice would be between the British *Trafalgar* class and the French *Rubis*. Commentators noted that acquisition of ten to twelve of these submarines would give Canada the third largest fleet of SSNs in the West. Already, concerns were raised as to whether or not the U.S. would block the transfer, from the British, of U.S. nuclear technology.[39] This transfer could be prevented under the terms of the 1958 Anglo-U.S. agreement. As the summer progressed, interest in the potential competition accelerated.[40] By now, the academics had become involved and a set of "Comments on the White Paper" was produced by the Canadian Institute for International Affairs (CIIA) in a *Behind the Headlines* issue in September.[41] On the whole, while applauding the emergence of the paper, the pundits found little to favor. In this regard, David Cox noted that "this decision would have been unthinkable without the rationale of sovereignty assertion in the Canadian Arctic." He went on to suggest that this "notice of intent" would not guarantee implementation and that the overall acquisition program would require a 4 percent real growth rather than the 2 percent provided. Further, that if the nuclears were acquired, and some cooperative arrangement achieved with the U.S., this would not settle the sovereignty issue one way or the other.[42] Harald von Riekoff noted that the comprehensive paper and its financial support "attests to Perrin Beatty's leadership and political skill," but brooded that submarine costs were probably under-estimated and disturbing, in light of a probable 2 percent ceiling in real growth. He suggested that the diverging objectives of promoting security (against the USSR) and sovereignty (against the U.S.) could not both be resolved by nuclear submarines which "lack visibility, good communication and the response options enjoyed by surface vessels."[43]

However, momentum was beginning to build with the potential Canadian competitor organizations coming together, and with visits from the British *Torbay* in late October, and the French *Saphir* in mid-November. About this time also, there was a lengthy interview with the Minister.[44] This revealed some of the tensions between military and civil aspects of his department, since:

> At the end of the day you want one piece of advice on what the options are and that advice should come from the appropriate official. With regard to on-going financing, the Minister noted cautiously that Cabinet has to retain for itself the ability to approve particular items and to regulate the pace at which they become available.

Beatty stressed that the White Paper represented an optimal 1987 judgment, which would have to be adjusted as circumstances evolved. However, in response to a key question as to whether the decision for nuclear propulsion was irrevocable, he stated categorically that "there is no conventional technology that will allow us to do what we would like to do not only in the Arctic but also in the Atlantic and that will give us the advantages such as sustained speed and endurance that we would like to have." In response to cost considerations, he observed that "We simply can't afford to get into a program that's too rich for our blood. There is capable equipment out there for prices that we can afford. It's not our intention to go for a Cadillac model if we can do the job cost-effectively for less."

Finally, at this point, came a slightly sour note from a U.S. Congressman, Charles E. Bennett, in an Op-Ed piece in the *Globe and Mail*.[45] This posed the searching question as to whether the U.S. (by agreeing to share nuclear technology) should help create a fleet to monitor a claim to sovereignty over the Northwest Passage that the U.S. did not recognize. He concluded that the concurrent issues of U.S.-sanctioned nuclear transfer, and of sovereignty "raise the spectre of a tough political-military decision that could have long-term consequences for NATO and for the unique friendship the United States and Canada enjoy." He adjured both governments to give the matter careful study.

However, very shortly thereafter, it was announced that Britain and the U.S. *had*, in fact, reached an agreement that would allow the transfer of nuclear technology to Canada.[46]

November 1987 was marked by a growth of external interest in the submarine question. A paper prepared by the Canadian Centre for Arms Control and Disarmament, dealing with the first annual Cabinet review of defense expenditure, surveyed the various cost estimates that had been provided, both official and unofficial, and concluded that the program cost, including supporting infrastructure, was likely to be much greater than the generally accepted $8 billion.[47] It raised the issue of a need for further study of conventional submarines, probably with provision for Air Independent Propulsion technologies — earlier reviewed but "derailed by the political momentum favouring SSNs." The paper came to the supportive, but cautious, conclusion that:

> There is little question that Canada, with its long coastline and its NATO anti-submarine warfare role, requires a submarine fleet. However, the size of the fleet and the capabilities of the boats themselves will have to be determined, not exclusively but in large measure, by the budgetary constraints that Canadians traditionally impose on defence expenditure.

The worst outcome, the CCACD suggested, would be to start a program, with the essential massive infrastructure, that would, for financial reasons, be cut short after completing only a few submarines.

Shortly after this, a *Financial Post* conference in Ottawa reviewed the industrial implications of the White Paper. This produced some American questioning with regard to the submarine program. R. B. Pirie, former U.S. Assistant Secretary of Defense, suggested that NATO allies would have preferred Canadian expenditure on other programs, e.g., defense of Norway, and asked whether Canada would not be better off purchasing cheaper conventionally powered submarines.[48]

All this led the *Globe and Mail* to note that Beatty was now having problems both with his Cabinet colleagues, regarding the extent of funding involved, and with the U.S. Navy, regarding Canada's claim to the Northwest Passage.[49]

There was now a lapse, until a series of SCND meetings in February and March 1988, which were devoted to extensive reviews of the nuclear submarine program, concluding with a session at which the Minister appeared. Nuclear safety and the implications for Canada's stance on nonproliferation were given a thorough review.

It was established that the first vessel could be anticipated by 1996, with the bulk of spending after 1990. There were frequent references to cost, with an indication of how the accepted total of $8 billion had been achieved. Thus, the average cost of a *Trafalgar* in December 1986 was about $450 million and DND representatives advised that they had added some additional cost to that and said it would round out at about $500 million. The sail-away total was about $5 billion and the additional $3 billion was for support of various kinds (including MK 48 Torpedoes) but was based on the enhancement of existing facilities, i.e., not a "green field" approach.[50]

It was pointed out that while this was a very substantial sum, it approximated the cost for the eight ASW Frigates that had been planned, together with four conventional submarines to replace the *Oberons*. With the program extending for some 27 years, this would be an average annual cost of $300 million — "about half the monies now being spent each year for the Canadian Patrol Frigate."[51]

A spirited attempt by the Canadian Centre for Arms Control and Disarmament to present very detailed annual operating costs, leading to a program cost of some $15 billion, was fairly easily deflected.[52] The current cost estimates, DND officials asserted, followed government practice in major procurement programs and, in any event, it was neatly observed that the figures made a strong case for nuclear submarines since the annual operating cost of a *Trafalgar* submarine is about the same as the annual costs of one of Canada's current destroyers, the DDH 280. Thus, for the same annual cost it would be possible to operate with a much stronger, more credible, more balanced fleet that included nuclear submarines.[53]

Some further points that were given elaboration were:

— while the British *Trafalgar* had operated under the ice, the French *Rubis/Améthyste* had not. The latter, however, would be equipped with vertical "ice-picks," and testing at the experimental ice-tank in Newfoundland had suggested that these would be effective;
— the ability to provide underwater sensors was acknowledged and it was suggested that in ten years we might be able to look out into the (Arctic) Basin to know if something were coming towards our area;[54] and
— from General Manson, Chief of the Defence Staff: "There is no compulsion in the fact that Canada belongs to NATO to follow any strategy that Canada does not agree with; that is one of the fundamental concepts of the NATO organization."

In summation, therefore, following Erik Nielsen's call for a broader review of approaches in mid 1985, a Nuclear Submarine Option Study (NSOS) was conducted between October 1985 and March 1987.[55] Meanwhile, action was also taken on the intended procurement of conventional submarines, with requests for proposals being issued in July 1986. There were some references by DND officials to their capability at "choke points" in the Arctic, but a growing attention was being paid to possible acquisition of nuclear boats — particularly in support of sovereignty of the North.

These aspirations *appear* to have been enhanced by the evident commitment of Perrin Beatty, coming into office in June 1986. From this point there was growing attention to, and formal study of, the nuclear alternative, which was now being posed as a necessity for operations in the Atlantic and Pacific as well as in the Arctic.

Thus, the inclusion of nuclear submarines in the June 1987 White Paper on Defence was hardly a surprise, although their acquisition became a matter of considerable discussion. While public opinion was not vocal, academics in general were against the acquisition and both Liberal Party and NDP (particularly the latter) were opposed, largely on grounds of cost. There was general skepticism that acquisition could be achieved for program costs of $8 billion and, indeed, that the funding increase proposal of 2 percent real growth per annum plus special allotments would meet the overall defense program.

In light of all this, it is not surprising that DND announced a campaign to gain support for the nuclear acquisition.[56] Even one generally favorably disposed academic commentator, Rod Byers, noted that the "controversial" SSN program could face objections on a number of grounds, ranging from economic to ethical concerns.[57]

There can be no doubt that developments during the last three decades have demonstrated that the nuclear submarine is the ultimate submersible, whether in its major role as a carrier of ballistic missiles or in the almost equally significant guise of hunter-killer. The advantages are generally well understood and can be very simply enunciated:

— wholly independent of the surface, with high speed and endurance limited only by the ability of the crew;
— optimal hydro-dynamic form;
— excess of power for weapons, sensors, etc.;
— no large batteries required, giving more room for weapons, sensors, and crew; and,
— minimal noise (currently, but only attained after significant and expensive technical efforts).

This is, however, a somewhat complex and sensitive vehicle whose nuclear propulsion capability has demanded significant technical endeavors, both during construction and in subsequent maintenance. Thus, the following disadvantages should also be noted:

— size and shape of the reactor tends to produce a large submarine, probably presenting a more substantial target;
— requirement for noise attenuation necessitates sophisticated and costly mountings for machinery and equipment;
— crews need to be highly trained in a range of modern technologies (and are thus attractive to industry);
— much more sophisticated shore support (than is normally found) must be provided with special facilities and trained personnel; and,

— disposal of spent fuel may present ultimate problems.

All of these stringent requirements lead to high and growing costs. While the present *Los Angeles* SSNs of the USN are said to cost about $700 million, it appears that their successors, the *Seawolfs*, will complete at about $2 billion each.[58] This also applies to facilities ashore, for British and French experience with such facilities has shown that initial construction costs can amount to at least three times those of the actual building of a submarine, while the day-to-day running costs of the facility are twice those of surface ships.[59] It should, after all, be recalled that the introduction of the concept of SSNs into the USN was neither easy nor, three decades ago, particularly popular. For example, the Military Reform Caucus in the U.S. Congress had argued that the decision to rely exclusively on nuclear power was not reached on militarily or economically rational grounds, but instead had been a direct consequence of Admiral Hyman Rickover's ambitions and political power.[60]

ASSESSING ALTERNATIVES TO THE SSN

The discussion of the desirability of nuclear submarines has skirted conventional alternatives to these boats. Yet there do exist such alternatives, possibly ones employing Air Independent Propulsion (AIP) systems, about which one enthusiastic proponent has written that "it now seems possible that, by the turn of the century, new generations of cost-effective submarines will be replacing the cumbersome, complex, mechanically inefficient, manpower-intensive and noisy nuke."[61] In a similar vein, DND representatives appearing before the Standing Committee on National Defence heard one MP assert that "in a lot of scenarios that are relevant to Canada's defence needs, hybrid submarines and diesel-powered submarines may in fact be an asset."[62]

To support his contention, this parliamentarian listed several advantages he believed conventional submarines possessed:

— a cost of construction less than that of nuclears;
— lower operating and crew costs;
— less susceptibility to detection due to being smaller, and with lower thermal and magnetic signatures;
— less rotating machinery than nuclears and thus quieter;
— better adaptability to shallow water operations.

This was a reasonably well-informed catalogue that, indeed, was not significantly contended by the naval representatives. In addition, these characteristics were reiterated in a respected naval journal with added features of: robustness — generally simpler and therefore more easily repairable; political acceptability; and greater availability due to shorter overhaul time.[63] In sum, conventional submarines could be considered similar to, and in some respects, better than, nuclear submarines, with the exception of the fundamental difference in propulsion. The advantages of the SSNs are generally increased speed, vastly greater range, more power for sensors, and under-ice capability.

Two points, significant in the Canadian decision, deserve special consideration, cost and under-ice capability. The former is not easy to determine since it is rarely clear just what is being included. However, it would seem that an overall program cost of $4 to $6 billion for ten to twelve SSKs would be a reasonable figure, compared with current estimates for nuclear submarines of $8 billion.[64]

Under-ice capability is dependent on underwater range without surfacing and the data here are even more obscure than those for cost. German *Type XXI* boats of World War II could achieve 72 hours at 5 knots.[65] Suggested contemporary figures are 107 hours at 6 knots, and 120 hours at 4 knots.[66] Thus, for quiet surveillance work, it would appear that 100 hours at 5 knots might reasonably be expected. This could suggest a penetration of some 200 miles into the archipelago which would, at first glance, seem to be a respectable distance.

However, with appropriate Air Independent Propulsion there could be considerable improvement, perhaps 24 days at 7 knots, 38 days at 4.17 knots, and, 60 days at 4 knots.[67] Essentially, this would imply a month of patrolling at surveillance speed with some reserve for occasional higher speed sorties. All this, of course, takes no account of the alleged frequency of polynas or thin ice which should provide opportunities — with some lack of discretion — for charging batteries. This capability, certainly not comparable with nuclear performance, might well appear to be enough for Canada's sovereignty/security needs in the North.

A telling point is the present disposition of relatively new, or currently building, conventional submarines. A total of about ninety such boats are either in service or about to enter it, more than forty of them in NATO navies. Competent builders are doing business from Britain, France, the Federal Republic of Germany, Italy, and Sweden. Thus, there is no lack of competitive designs. A key point, however, will be the capability to achieve successful Air Independent Propulsion.

AIR INDEPENDENT PROPULSION

A continuing aspiration for those in the submarine fraternity who are not involved with nuclear propulsion has been the development of some means of power, even of auxiliary power, that can operate more extensively when submerged. The basic concept of the use of batteries to provide electric power is an obvious example of Air Independent Propulsion and better batteries might provide a reasonable solution for increased submerged endurance. However, they have a low power-to-weight ratio and, for the short and medium term, do not appear promising. As far as the proposed Canadian conventional program was concerned a concept of a nuclear battery was presented by Atomic Energy of Canada Limited. While this appeared to have some advantages, extensive development would have been required and the project apparently has been dropped.

There was an early attempt at AIP in World War II by the Germans, with the Walther turbine using hydrogen peroxide and liquid oxygen as fuel; it carried significant risks. The concept of closed-cycle diesel engines has been pursued for some time but with little actual research, and with the significant shortcoming of noise, which would destroy the SSK's principal advantage of near-silent operation. Currently there appear to be three alternatives moving into the stage of development and operation: fuel cells; the Stirling engine; and auxiliary nuclear propulsion.

Fuel Cells. These are a fairly old concept, being essentially the opposite of electrolysis and involving the production of electrical energy by the combination of hydrogen and oxygen in fuel cells to produce water and electric power. Since direct current is provided, it can be fed directly into the switchboard for use in main propulsion, "hotel" or sensor load, or for charging batteries. The operation is essentially silent, can take place at low temperatures and produces an amenable waste product. The German firms of Ingenieurkontor Lubeck, Howaldswerk Deutsche Werft, and Ferrostaal have been active in research and development during the 1980s with the operation of a test plant on a representative hull section. This led to a 350-hour performance test in 1986, monitored by the West German military, which was reported to have substantially exceeded requirements, with the system being cleared for sea trials. It was also reported that the German submarine U1, now in the course of a major refit, was to be lengthened to accommodate the new system with sea trials to begin at the end of 1987.[68]

Stirling Engine. This engine was developed in Sweden twenty-five years ago and involves the continuous high pressure combustion of diesel fuel and pure oxygen for electric power generation. It does not have the explosive, and thus noisy, characteristics of the diesel. This concept has also been moving ahead in the 1980s with testing, since 1985, in a full-scale submarine test section. It was announced that this unit, in a neutrally buoyant hull section, six metres in length, would be installed in a *Nacken* class submarine of the Swedish Navy during 1987.[69]

Claims have been made that a hybrid system, with half the battery replaced by the Stirling and its liquid oxygen fuel, would give five times the previous endurance underwater, with patrols of up to ten days including several attacks.

Auxiliary Nuclear. The intent here is to utilize a small nuclear power source that could provide *unlimited* endurance, with a limited submerged speed (about 6 knots) and maintain the batteries fully charged so as to provide a high speed capability for brief periods. An example is the Autonomous Marine Power Source (AMPS) being developed for naval use (AMPS-N) by ECS Energy Conversion Systems, a Canadian group.[70]

This involves a small and safe reactor, somewhat similar to the Canadian *Slowpoke* used at several universities, the latter being the only civil reactor so far licensed for unattended operation. The equipment can be installed in a self-contained "plug" about ten metres in length. Various components are being tested and it is reported that a land-based prototype is to be built in 1988-89, which could subsequently be installed in a hybrid submarine, sometimes referred to as an SSn. It would appear that this might be an innovation for the mid-1990s and a cost estimate of about $40 million increase for each conventional submarine has been suggested. In the conventional competition, where AIP proposals were invited "no one was prepared to bid on or to touch the hybrid option because it was too risky, too expensive and would not in the end produce useful capability."[71] More comprehensively, although without opportunity for informed debate, it was asserted that "hybrid propulsion for our boat was a very, very distant possibility. It had a very high degree of risk attached to it. It was not something we felt would come into production in the time frame we were looking at for introducing even the conventional submarines."[72]

TECHNICAL AND OPERATIONAL CONCERNS

In assessing the desirability of acquiring SSNs as an essential component of operations in the Atlantic and Pacific, it is instructive to review again the recommendations of the Senate Committee. The members asserted the need for Canada's maritime forces to be equipped to perform a sea denial role in waters over which Canada claims jurisdiction, and amplified this by calling for Canada "to make a full contribution to NATO at sea while maintaining the ability to act in defence of Canadian sovereignty and to contribute effectively to the defence of North America."[73] In this regard "full contribution" and "contribute effectively" are somewhat debatable concepts. However, the Senators offered some further guidance: "Canada's anti-submarine tasks [should] be confined to those of a tactical nature — defence against anti-shipping submarines and only such strategic surveillance missions as can be carried out with the same equipment."[74]

In considering alternatives to the current SSN program, it is possible that both the Senate's and the White Paper's recommendations could be achieved by manifesting a concern for the Arctic and a determination to adopt a more limited, perhaps even a coastal role in the Atlantic and Pacific. The term, coastal, should be given a generous interpretation and it implies those areas of the North Atlantic and North Pacific that are considered to relate to Canada's concept of its national jurisdiction. These objectives would have implications for Canadian maritime equipment.

In the Arctic. For the Arctic Archipelago, a reliable enhancement of underwater bottom-based sonar surveillance would seem eminently desirable and not unduly expensive (in comparative terms), perhaps costing as little as $100 million. While one *Polar 8* icebreaker would be a desirable and obvious presence, more than one would enhance the establishment of Canada's presence and authority in the Northwest Passage and adjacent waters. Reference is frequently made to the mystique of the submarine's uncomprehended and lurking presence. Thus the Falklands campaign, while demonstrating the effectiveness of one British nuclear submarine, also (perhaps less evidently) identified the extensive ASW measures required *by* the British against the *possibility* of action by conventional Argentine submarines.

It is my view that a "reasonably adequate" Arctic surveillance, which may well indeed, in such a hostile anti-submarine environment, be all that *can* be accomplished, could be mounted by the bottom-based sonar supported by one, or more, conventional submarines operating at appropriate choke points. They have been variously identified as Prince of Wales Strait, the Northwest Passage (Barrow Strait, Lancaster Sound), Robeson Channel, Kennedy Straits, Fury and Hecla Strait. These range in depth from less than 200 to 500 metres and in width from six to eighteen nautical miles. If this surveillance could be enhanced by some limited under-ice capability (as provided by Air Independent Propulsion) it might constitute as much demonstration of the principles of control as the situation demands.[75]

One must also, of course, consider the question of communication with submarines, whether nuclear or conventional. They can receive radio signals on Very Low Frequency (VLF) at a reasonable data rate and depth. Extremely Low Frequency (ELF) at *very* slow rates (i.e., measured in characters per minute) can be received worldwide at any depth. However, to transmit, either submarine must raise an antenna above the water or ice. This could well be a severe constraint with regard to the sort of Arctic operations presently being proposed by Canada, since it is "most unlikely that any such patrol would be carried out in peacetime or during a period of tension without effective two-way communications, i.e., implying operations in areas where open water is available."[76]

For "Blue-Water" Activities. Much has been made of the high speeds and endurance of the nuclear submarines. These abilities probably contribute significantly to the alleged three-to-one advantage of the SSN over the SSK. This point is encapsulated in an observation by the Canadian Institute of Strategic Studies that it is really the time/distance/volume of sea calculation which makes the SSN so much more effective than the SSK for blue-water operations. In a coastal defense role, of course, the SSN advantage is much less.[77] If the volume of ocean for Canadian operations was limited, this could again reasonably adequately, perhaps even *more* effectively, be met by smaller, cheaper, more numerous conventional submarines, particularly if these had the potential advantage of Air-Independent Propulsion.

Industrial Impact. A point not infrequently made with regard to the acquisition of SSNs is the amount of direct labor that would be generated — some 55,000 person years is quoted in DND briefing material. However, it is also asserted that only some 20 percent of this would be in fields relating to nuclear engineering. A conventional (or hybrid) propulsion system would entail its own labor requirement. Thus the overall size of the industrial impact of either nuclear or conventional vehicles would probably be of the same order.

CONCLUSION

Quite apart from the various technical and strategic considerations that surround the acquisition of nuclear submarines and which have been (to a greater or lesser extent) considered in this chapter, there are broader potential concerns that have not been reviewed here, but that will be addressed in the next two chapters, e.g., the erosion of the Nonproliferation Treaty, and the issue of the USN's Forward Maritime Strategy. Given all these apprehensions it is most curious that until April 1988, two years after its deliberations started, the Standing Committee on National Defence, meeting frequently, had heard no witnesses other than those supporting the nuclear option; and this, nearly a year after the decision had been announced (or, at any event, clearly indicated) and almost at the point where a selection of vehicle would be made. It is generally stated that this program (which is to be the subject of an annual financial review) is to last for twenty-seven years. It seems highly unlikely that such continuity could be sustained, especially in light of the announced opposition to nuclear submarines by the Liberal and New Democratic parties — an opposition that, in the Spring of 1988, appeared to be shared by the nuclear submarine fraternity in the U.S. Navy.[78] But even if the political will existed, would it be accompanied by financial capability? At this point there is, of course, the unknown quantity of what the SSN program will *actually* cost, but we must accept that, in the first instance, the funds expended on nuclear submarines are equivalent to those identified for the maritime procurement elements that had been canceled. Nevertheless, it seems safe to say that, for the procurement of the same number of SSKs there could be a saving, both in initial procurement and subsequent maintenance, of billions of dollars.

In conclusion, I believe that we should not commit ourselves to a massive program that could last half a century. Perhaps worse, we could become involved with a massive and expensive infrastructure that, through lack of political will, or unanticipated financial constraints, would end up supporting a smaller number of vessels than had originally been intended.

It would be more appropriate to enter into a phased program of conventional submarine acquisition, four to six at a time, so as to be able to take advantage of improvements in design and to respond to the political (and financial) perceptions of the emerging strategic balance, as it affects Canada. Such a graduated approach could facilitate an ability to respond to the potential developments in Air-Independent Propulsion. This latter would seem to be a field in which Canada could usefully sustain the auxiliary nuclear development activity, with a view to recapturing some of its earlier interest in the export of nuclear power plants.

Notes

I should like to express my appreciation to Rear-Admiral John Anderson, Chief, Submarine Acquisition, and his staff for their helpfulness in the preparation of this chapter.

[1] Canada, Standing Committee on Foreign Affairs, Subcommittee on National Defence, *Canada's Maritime Defence* (Ottawa, May 1983).

[2] Ibid., 16.

[3] Ibid., 12, Recommendation #9.

[4] Ibid., 43.

[5] Canada, Secretary of State for External Affairs, *Competitiveness and Security - Directions for Canada's International Relations* (Ottawa, 1985).

[6] Ibid., 39.

[7] Canada, Special Joint Committee of the Senate and of the House of Commons on Canada's International Relations, *Independence and Internationalism* (Ottawa, June 1986).

[8] Ibid., Chapter 10, 127 et seq.

[9] Canada, Secretary of State for External Affairs, *Canada's International Relations* (Ottawa, December 1986).

[10] W. Harriet Critchley, "Polar Deployment of Soviet Submarines," *International Journal* 39 (Autumn 1984): 828-65.

[11] Mark Nichols, "Arctic Compromise," *Macleans*, 25 January 1988, 12.

[12] Critchley, "Polar Deployment," 857.

[13] Harvie Andre, Associate Minister of National Defence, in his opening statement to the Standing Committee on National Defence (SCND); SCND *Proceedings* (33rd Parliament, 1st Session), Issue no. 1, 15 April 1986, 1A:2.

[14] SCND *Proceedings*, Issue no. 29, 7 March 1988, 29:5.

[15]"CASAP - Replacing the OBERON SSKs," *Canada's Navy Annual, Wings Magazine*, 1986.

[16]SCND *Proceedings*, Issue no. 4, 24 April 1986, 4:13.

[17]Ibid., 4:25.

[18]*Globe and Mail*, 2 June 1986.

[19]SCND *Proceedings*, Issue no. 8, 2 June 1986, 8:17.

[20]SCND *Proceedings*, (33rd Parliament, 2nd Session) Issue no. 1, 2 December 1986, 1:36.

[21]Ibid., 1:54.

[22]SCND *Proceedings*, Issue no. 2, 11 December 1986, 2:8.

[23]Ibid., 2:24.

[24]*Financial Post*, 15-21 December 1986.

[25]Jeff Sallot, "Canada Studies Treaty with US to Combat Threat of Soviet Subs," *Globe and Mail*, 20 December 1986, A1.

[26]Richard Gwyn, *Toronto Star*, 23 January 1987.

[27]SCND *Proceedings*, Issue no. 3, 27 & 28 January 1987.

[28]Ibid., 3:27-28. These observations were made by Rear-Admiral C. M. Thomas, Chief, Maritime Doctrine and Operations, who headed the team set up to investigate the possibility of acquiring nuclear submarines — and for which, as his other evidence demonstrates, he was a keen protagonist.

[29]SCND *Proceedings*, Issue no. 6, 17 March 1987, 6:16-17.

[30]SCND *Proceedings*, Issue no. 7, 24 March 1987, 7:32.

[31]James Bagnall, "Hungry Shipbuilders circle nuclear-sub battle," *Financial Post*, 23-29 March 1987, 1.

[32]SCND *Proceedings*, Issue no. 10, 28 April 1987, 10:11.

[33]Tariq Rauf and Dan Hayward, "Nuclear Powered Attack Submarines: Does Canada Really Need Them?" *Arms Control Communiqué* no. 36, Part I and no. 37, Part II, 15 May 1987.

[34]Rauf and Hayward, "Canadian Public Should Torpedo Nuclear Sub Idea," *Globe and Mail*, 14 May 1987.

[35]*Hansard Parliamentary Debates*, (33rd Parliament, 2nd Session), 6776-6783.

[36]"Why Nuclear Subs?" *Globe and Mail*, 1 June 1987; Jeffrey Simpson, "And Hold the Subs," *Globe and Mail*, 1 June 1987.

[37]SCND *Proceedings*, Issue no. 14, 25 June 1987, 14:22-3.

[38]Ibid., 14:44.

[39]Paul Koring, "Canada's Purchase of UK Subs Will Require Approval by US," *Globe and Mail*, 10 July 1987.

[40]Jonathan Manthorpe, "7B Contract Irresistible Lure for International Salesmen," *Ottawa Citizen*, 1 August 1987.

[41]Rod Byers, ed., "Challenge and Commitment - Comments on the Defence White Paper," *Behind the Headlines* (Toronto: Canadian Institute of International Affairs,1987).

[42]Ibid., 4.

[43]Ibid., 22. He goes on to observe, "To spend more than $10 Billon on nuclear submarines merely to register U.S. incursions into waters claimed by Canada would make it a rather extravagant telephone system."

[44]"Sovereignty and Security - Canada's New Defence Policy," *Canadian Business Review*, August 1987, 9-15. (Being the report of an interview of Perrin Beatty by David Cox.)

[45]Charles E. Bennett, "Tough Questions Rise to the Surface," *Globe and Mail*, 29 October 1987. (Congressman Bennett is Chairman of the Seapower Subcommittee of the House Armed Services Committee.)

[46]Jeff Sallott, "Accord opens the door for Canada to get nuclear subs, officials say," *Globe and Mail*, 5 November 1987.

[47]John Barrett and Tariq Rauf, "Can Canada Afford the Nuclear Submarine Program," *Arms Control Communiqué # 41*, 16 November 1987.

[48]Jeff Sallott, "U.S. Aiding Canadians in Sub-hunt, Envoy Says," *Globe and Mail*, 20 November 1987.

[49]Jeffrey Simpson, "Subs Under Attack," *Globe and Mail*, 25 November 1987.

[50]SCND *Proceedings*, Issue no. 25, 3 February 1988, 25:36.

[51]SCND *Proceedings*, Issue no. 28, 28 February 1988, 28:5.

[52]Dan Hayward, "The Missing Element in the Nuclear Submarines Costing Debate," *Arms Control Communiqué* no. 46, 24 February 1988.

[53]SCND *Proceedings*, Issue no. 29, 7 March 1988, 29:13.

[54]SCND *Proceedings*, Issue no. 24, 2 February 1988, 24:23.

[55]Private Communication from Captain (N) W. G. D. Lund, 28 March 1988.

[56]"A-Subs to be Promoted," *Globe and Mail*, 7 January 1988.

[57]Byers, "Challenge & Commitment."

[58]B. van Voors, "Murky Waters for the Supersub," *Time*, 25 January 1988, 30.

[59]Paul Beaver and Richard Sharpe, "New Members for the SSN Club," *Jane's Defence Weekly*, 9 January 1988.

[60]Norman Friedman, *Submarine Design and Development* (Annapolis: Naval Institute Press, 1984): 184.

[61]Roy Corlett, "The Modern Non-Nuclear Submarine," *Maritime Defence International* ll, no. 3 (March 1986): 71.

[62]SCND *Proceedings*, Issue no. 24, 2 February 1988, 24:36.

[63]D. Conley, Commander R. N., "Don't Discount the Diesel," *USN Proceedings* 113, no. 10 (October 1987).

[64]John E. Moore and Richard Compton-Hall, *Submarine Warfare - Today and Tomorrow* (Maryland: Adler & Adler, 1987), 287 n; Rauf and Hayward, *Arms Control Communiqué* no. 37; F. Robertson, "The New Submarine Project - Jackpot for Industry,"

Pacific Defence 14, no. 1 (July 1987); SCND *Proceedings*, Issue no. 4, 10 February 1987, 4:18 & 20.

[65]Friedman, *Submarine Design and Development*.

[66]Corlett, "The Modern Non-Nuclear Submarine"; F. Cranston, "Australian Navy Plans West German Type 200C Submarine," *Jane's Defence Weekly*, 7, no. 21 (30 May 1987): 1049.

[67]Moore and Compton, *Submarine Warfare - Today and Tomorrow*.

[68]Gunter Sattle, "Air-Independent Fuel Cell Propulsion Systems," *Defence*, 18 no. 6, (June 1987): 345-8.

[69]This is noted in the section relating to Submarines in the Swedish Navy in *Jane's Fighting Ships*, 475.

[70]R. J. Gosling, A. F. Oliva and K. B. Church, "The AMPS Nuclear Reactor Based Air-Independent Power Source for Diesel-Electric Submarines." Paper presented at R.I.N.A. International Symposium on Conventional Naval Submarines, London, England, 3-5 May 1988.

[71]SCND *Proceedings*, Issue no. 24, 2 February 1988, 24:20.

[72]SCND *Proceedings*, Issue no. 26, 11 and 23 February 1988, 26:27.

[73]Senate Subcommittee on National Defence, 40.

[74]Ibid., 40.

[75]E.J.M. Young, Commander, "Submarines for the Canadian Maritime Forces," *Canadian Defence Quarterly* 16, no. 1, Summer 1986.

[76]Peter T. Haydon, Commander, "The Strategic Importance of the Arctic Understanding the Military Issues," DND Strategic Issues Paper no. 1/87, March 1987, 15.

[77]Private communication to the author, 3 February 1988.

[78]Marc Clark, "Keeping Canada Out of the Sub-Club," *Macleans*, 11 April 1988, 12.

11

The SSNs and the Question of Nonproliferation

David G. Haglund

INTRODUCTION

When the Department of National Defence (DND), in the first half of 1987, was putting the finishing touches to the section of the Defence White Paper dealing with the proposal that Canada acquire a fleet of some ten to twelve nuclear-propelled attack submarines (SSNs), there could be no doubt among planners that the bold recommendations were bound to unleash a stream of opposition from a variety of groups.[1] Many, perhaps most, of the opposing arguments could be anticipated. After all, the Minister, Perrin Beatty, had participated personally in a series of well-attended defense round-tables in the half-year or so before the tabling of the White Paper, and the press had been full of defense-related stories for some months, in part as a result of DND's deliberate floating of trial balloons. So the criticisms of the proposal could be foreseen. It was, for example, taken for granted that the disarmament groups would reject the SSNs — indeed, the entire White Paper — because anything that promised to add to, refurbish, or otherwise enhance Canadian armaments they would hold a priori to be illegitimate.

Others, not so given to outright condemnation of weapons-systems merely because they *were* weapons-systems, could still be expected to reject the SSN proposal on a number of scores. Opposition parties in Parliament could hardly be counted on to embrace the initiative, and would likely direct their criticism not against a defense build-up per se, which their defense critics, at least, seemed to think long-overdue, but to the "opportunity costs" and budgetary implications of the SSN proposal. What might we not be able to do, they would ask, as a result of spending the money on the very expensive SSNs? Could we afford these boats, given the competing claims on the federal budget, not only from other precincts in DND, but from any number of other departments?[2] The arms-control community, as well, would likely have its criticisms, and doubtless these would be directed at the core concern of this community: could these vessels be deployed in such a manner as to destabilize the strategic balance? To many of those who put the question thusly, it was not too difficult to derive an affirmative answer: the SSNs, it was argued, would become a cog in the U.S. Navy's "forward strategy," which the arms-control community saw as anything but stabilizing.[3]

Perhaps the most unexpected objection to the SSNs, and the principal subject of this chapter, was the argument that the acquisition of nuclear-propelled vessels would have serious implications for nuclear nonproliferation. Indeed, to some who examined these implications, there seemed a real possibility that a Canadian SSN acquisition would so threaten the international nonproliferation "regime" that the future of that regime itself would be imperiled. Others, who did not necessarily adopt such a bleak perspective on the global nonproliferation implications of the SSNs, did nevertheless wonder what the effect of the proposal would be on Canada's own nonproliferation policy, for it struck them as inconceivable that that policy, arguably one of the world's toughest, would not be able to escape modification, at least in some respects. Whether the modifications were for the better or the worse was not, to these analysts, the major question; at issue was the matter of recognizing and seeking to gauge the effect the SSN program would have on the policy.

Because so little attention had been accorded, within the Department of National Defence, to the nonproliferation implications of the SSN program proposal, it came as no surprise that the department's initial response to criticisms leveled at this aspect of the White Paper was not particularly well-conceived. Early attempts to rebut the charge that the SSN proposal would endanger the international nonproliferation regime centered upon simply denying that the allegation could have any substance, as everyone knew that the Nonproliferation Treaty of 1968 (NPT), to which Canada is a signatory, only forbade non-nuclear weapons states (NNWS) from acquiring nuclear weapons. As the SSNs were not going to have anything but conventional torpedoes (and, possibly, Exocet missiles) as weaponry, it followed that the nonproliferation argument was baseless in this context.

This tack really did miss the point, however; for although there are probably many in Canada (including not a few undergraduates!) who seem to think the nuclear submarines are nuclear-*armed* vessels, those in the arms-control community who dwelt upon the nonproliferation argument obviously knew better.[4] What they feared, as I shall discuss below, was that Canada, held to be a consummate exemplar of nonproliferationist virtue, would be setting a worrisome precedent for other, less trustworthy adherents to the NPT, as well as for some NNWS that had never signed the Treaty. Better, these analysts argued, that Canada not become the first signatory to acquire SSNs; because while no one in the arms-control community may have fretted about Canada diverting nuclear materials from its SSN program to weapons-building purposes, could the same equanimity be displayed given the prospect of, say, Brazil or some other NNWS obtaining nuclear fuel or facilities for its SSNs?

After some initial period of confusion about the nonproliferation issue, DND finally began to coordinate this aspect of the SSN proposal with the major bureaucratic players in the realm of nuclear policy, the Department of External Affairs (DEA) and the Atomic Energy Control Board of Canada (AECB). Now the view in government is that there are indeed nonproliferation implications stemming from the SSN proposal, but that these implications need not be adverse for the nonproliferation regime. It is possible, say some who are monitoring the issue, that a *positive* precedent may be set by the Canadian SSN program. Thus the debate has become engaged, and a focus of much of what follows in this paper will be the question of whether Canadian SSNs, which now *all* seem to concede have a bearing on the nonproliferation regime, are likely to have a negative or a positive impact on that regime, and to what degree.

There is a second major nonproliferation issue associated with the SSN proposal, and this issue took not only DND by surprise, but the arms-control community as well. In the past few months there has been emerging a rather curious ally of sorts for the Canadian arms-control community — an ally that professes to be equally worried about the Canadian SSNs setting unfortunate precedents. This ally is the U.S. Navy (USN) and some of its Congressional patrons, and their concern is that, for a variety of reasons, a Canadian SSN capability will complicate matters for them. The reason that USN opposition becomes perforce a "nonproliferation issue" is that Washington has the authority, under the terms of a 1958 bilateral nuclear cooperation agreement between the U.S. and Britain, effectively to prohibit a British transfer of *Trafalgar*-class nuclear technology to Canada. It acquired this authority as a result of earlier American anxiety about the possible spread of nuclear weapons resulting from the dissemination of American nuclear technology to other countries. Thus U.S. nonproliferation policy may have an influence, however indirect in inspiration, on the future shape of the Canadian SSN program. As a recent article in a major Canadian newsweekly put it, "where Canada buys its submarines may ultimately be decided outside the country."[5] This possibility has arisen because the two major contenders for the SSN contract are Britain's *Trafalgar* and France's *Améthyste* update of its *Rubis* class submarine; and the French boat is not encumbered by any third-party control over technology transfer.

Despite being overlooked in the early stages of the SSN proposal, the nonproliferation question has attained a level of importance that has required policymakers to give it close attention. It is the purpose of this chapter to contribute to the ongoing debate over the manner in which nonproliferation concerns — whether of Canada, the global community, or the U.S. — can both be affected by and have an effect upon the Canadian SSN program. I begin this investigation in the following section with a summary of some relevant matters related to the functioning of the international nonproliferation regime.

THE CONTEMPORARY NONPROLIFERATION REGIME

Because the health of the nonproliferation regime is said by some to be so fragile that a Canadian SSN program would render its prospects even more problematical than they now are, it is necessary that some attention be accorded the current condition of that regime. In this section, I shall concentrate upon what might be termed the spine of that regime, the International Atomic Energy Agency and its all-important system of safeguards. It could probably be said of the nonproliferation regime that it is like Mark Twain, in that reports of its death seem to be premature; I prefer, however, to compare the regime to another 19th-century personage, Charles Darwin, because while Darwin may have been a valetudinarian, he still managed to produce an impressive body of work. Similarly, the nonproliferation regime, or more specifically, the IAEA, surely does have numerous problems confronting it, yet withal it seems to be one of the most effective international organizations that we have witnessed in the post-World War II years, with the possible exception of NATO and the Warsaw Pact.

Analysts will no doubt puzzle over the exact reasons why the IAEA should have been so relatively successful, given that the fate of most international organizations over the past four decades has been to be condemned to varying degrees of fecklessness. Realists will say that the IAEA works because — and only because — both superpowers see its continuation as in their interests; liberal-pluralists (sometimes confusingly called "neo-realists") on the other hand will see in the IAEA proof that the pessimism embodied by contemporary realist thinking on the prospects of international cooperation is misplaced. About this dispute, this essay will have little to say. Nor will it address the important but ultimately perplexing inquiry on the meaning and nature of international "regimes."[6] Whether or not international politics is in a state of transformation will not concern us here. What will concern us is the evolution and the working of the IAEA-centered nonproliferation regime, with that latter term being employed in the old-fashioned sense of a "prevailing system."

What is the contemporary nonproliferation regime? Briefly, it may be considered to be a set of operative assumptions, norms, and institutions that have arisen and been sustained because of a widespread concern over the possible spread of nuclear weapons beyond the handful of acknowledged nuclear-weapons states (the U.S., USSR, U.K., France, and China). In addition to this basal consensual understanding of the adverse implications for international security of nuclear proliferation, there is another expectation that has under-girded the current regime, namely that a compelling case exists for the dissemination of the peaceful application of nuclear energy.[7] Given this dual concern — to stanch the spread of nuclear weaponry but encourage the adoption of nuclear energy — there has been developed a series of institutional arrangements that collectively can be taken as the organizational apparatus of the regime. There have been: a) arrangements by suppliers, both on a bilateral basis and a multilateral one, to attach constraints on their exports of nuclear materials, facilities, and technology; b) two significant treaties, the NPT and the Treaty of Tlatelolco; and c) an international agency, the IAEA, which has been charged with the important task of administering and verifying safeguards on nuclear exports.[8]

In its evolution, the nonproliferation regime may be said to have gone through at least three major stages. The earliest, and by far most stringent, phase of global nonproliferation aspirations occurred in the first decade of the post-World War II period, when the United States attempted, through a policy of secrecy and denial, to prevent the spread of nuclear weaponry, even if that entailed prohibitions on the peaceful use of nuclear energy. This policy proved a failure, as both America's allies and adversaries would show themselves capable of developing their own nuclear weapons despite the U.S. embargo on materials and technology. The second phase began in late 1953, with President Dwight Eisenhower's "Atoms for Peace Proposal," through which Washington signaled a new willingness to stimulate peaceful international nuclear cooperation. This phase came to a rather abrupt halt in 1974, when India's detonation of a "peaceful" nuclear explosion, coupled with the proposed transfer of sophisticated fuel-cycle technology by both France and the Federal Republic of Germany to a group of countries then in the early stages of their own nuclear-energy programs, led to a rekindled American desire to impose tighter controls on nuclear exports — a desire shared by Canada as well.[9]

It would take the appearance of the IAEA, and the emergence of the two nonproliferation treaties of the late 1960s, to complete the institutional infra-structure of the contemporary regime. Of critical importance were the founding of the IAEA, which has been rightly termed the "organizational core of the nonproliferation regime,"[10] and the signing of the NPT. The IAEA, which is based in Vienna, was set up in July 1957. Its main function has been to administer safeguards on nuclear transfers, thereby ensuring that materials and facilities intended for civilian use do not easily get diverted for prohibited military purposes. Although the IAEA performs other functions, far and away its most important one is the administration of safeguards; as one source puts it, "IAEA safeguards have by now become an indispensable component of most other parts of the nonproliferation regime."[11]

IAEA safeguards enter into effect upon the conclusion of a safeguards con-tract between the Agency and states (or, in some instances, groups of states).[12]

Two main types of safeguards agreements exist: one is applicable to those states that have not signed the NPT, and permits Agency monitoring of only selected nuclear facilities; the other is applicable to NNWS signatory to the NPT and, in most cases, the Treaty of Tlatelolco, and applies to all their nuclear activities (i.e., these are "full-scope" safeguards). The relevant safeguard documents are, for the former, INFCIRC/66, and for the latter, INFCIRC/153. (INFCIRC stands for Information Circular.) The vast majority of IAEA safeguarding activities today are under the auspices of INFCIRC/153. Nevertheless, several NNWS that have not signed the NPT have some of their nuclear activities safeguarded on the basis of INFCIRC/66: India, Pakistan, Israel, South Africa, Argentina, Brazil, Chile, Cuba, and Spain.[13]

The essence of safeguards is to deter the diversion of nuclear materials to military purposes through the prospect of early detection. This deterrent element is supplied by the inspection role and capabilities of the Agency; but it is important to remember that the Agency itself cannot police violations, it can only report them. In other words, the Agency counts upon the cooperation of those states with which it has safeguard agreements to live up to the terms of the arrangements. In the apt words of one U.S. governmental report, the Agency is "a monitoring group responsible for sounding an alarm."[14] Whether the alarm bell functions at all has come into question among some parties of late, with the most dramatic show of non-confidence in the Agency's efficacy as a nonproliferation guarantor being the Israeli attack on the IAEA-safeguarded Iraqi Osirak reactor on 7 June 1981.[15] Developments in another NNWS, Pakistan, have also triggered some concern of late about the IAEA's capacity to limit the spread of nuclear weapons. Some time ago the Agency admitted that it could not guarantee that Pakistan's Kanupp reactor was being used for peaceful purposes only, an admission that came in the wake of concern about Pakistan's growing sophistication in the enrichment of uranium.[16] According to U.S. intelligence sources, Pakistan has been enriching uranium to weapons grade of more than 90 percent at its Kahuta plant, near Islamabad — and this, despite a pledge made to the U.S. not to enrich beyond 5 percent. Moreover, Pakistan is now said to be constructing a second enrichment facility, at Golra.[17]

To the worry about "normal" states getting access to nuclear weaponry has been added another concern, that of nuclear weapons or weapons-grade materials falling into the hands of terrorists.[18] Of particular relevance here is the prospect of plutonium, produced by commercial reactors in Europe and separated in that continent's reprocessing facilities, being stolen by terrorists to make weapons. A recent battle has been fought within the U.S. administration over the relative security threat posed by the increased commercial use of plutonium — a battle that has pitted the Department of Defense against State and some other departments. The Pentagon is especially worried that IAEA standards for safeguarding plutonium (as well as highly enriched uranium) are sufficiently lax as to make the danger of terrorist theft too considerable. Contrasted with this position is that of the State Department, which holds that current standards are adequate.[19]

If it can be said that the effectiveness of the IAEA is seen by some to be in question, it can also be said that the Nonproliferation Treaty, the other chief component of the regime, is itself subject to stresses and strains. The NPT was opened for signature on 1 July 1968, and entered into force on 5 March 1970. By August 1985, the eve of the Third Review Conference of the Treaty, some 130 states had ratified and acceded to it.[20] The Treaty's objectives are contained in its first five articles, which seek to check the spread of nuclear weapons to NNWS (Articles I and II), to ensure through safeguards that the NNWS do not engage in nuclear-weapons fabrication (Article III), and to promote cooperation for the purpose of achieving the peaceful use of nuclear energy under international monitoring (Articles IV and V). The Treaty also serves, through Article VI, as a goad to the nuclear-weapons states (NWS) to move toward arms reduction and, indeed, eventual nuclear disarmament.[21]

In a sense, the NPT represents an exchange of commitments between NWS and the NNWS, with the latter agreeing to renounce the acquisition of nuclear weapons in return for the former granting them access to their civilian nuclear materials, facilities, and technology. As it has not been lost on the NNWS that there is a certain asymmetry to the respective commitments made by the two categories of states, the NWS undertook to try to reduce and ultimately eliminate their own nuclear arsenals — or at least to say that they would. That is, the NWS pledge to stanch the "vertical" proliferation of nuclear weapons, as part of a general thrust to temper "horizontal" proliferation of these weapons. Until the recent INF accord between the U.S. and USSR, this latter commitment has seemed hollow indeed, something that has not gone unnoticed by several NNWS.[22]

Apart from the contentious issue of the practical and ethical workability of a nonproliferation regime that, through the NPT, continues to depend upon a two-caste division of states, there has arisen another matter of discord over the Treaty, one relating to the undertaking of signatories with nuclear capability to transfer their technology and materials to states wishing to develop civilian nuclear-energy resources. On the one hand there has been resistance by some NNWS to the notion that primary emphasis should be placed on safeguards, at the expense of the competing claim made, especially by the LDCs, for preferential access to nuclear know-how and materials. On the other hand, there has been a split among the ranks of the nuclear-supplier states — a split that pits some states (e.g., the U.S., Canada, Australia, and Sweden) desirous of making full-scope safeguards a condition of nuclear exports against other states (e.g., the U.K., Federal Republic of Germany, Italy, and Japan) that resist the mandatory imposition of such safeguards on their nuclear transactions.[23]

That the IAEA and NPT have represented relatively successful initiatives in the area of international law and organization cannot be denied. Nevertheless, it would be unwise to assume that their relative success, and consequently that of the global nonproliferation regime, will be as evident in future as it has been to date. For reasons related above, as well as for other reasons that I have not discussed, both the IAEA and the NPT have become subject to erosive forces in the past few years.[24] It is in the context of this erosion of the global nonproliferation regime that one must examine the Canadian SSN proposal, with specific attention being given to the argument that Canada, in acquiring nuclear-propelled attack submarines, would be establishing a *precedent* that must prove injurious to the regime. It is to this matter of precedent that I now turn, and in doing so I shall examine both the legal considerations involved in the Canadian SSN proposal and the degree to which Canadian nuclear-export policy has marked Canada as an exemplary state in the politics of nonproliferation.

A MATTER OF PRECEDENT, I: THE ARTICLE 14 ISSUE

To those who are most inclined to view the Canadian SSN proposal as inimical to the long-term future of the nonproliferation regime, one matter stands out above all the others as worthy of anxiety: the potential precedent that a Canadian nuclear-propelled submarine program might set for other would-be acquirers of SSNs. There are really two aspects of this concern. In the first place, no state has yet to avail itself of a provision in the safeguard agreements between the IAEA and the NPT NNWS signatories that allows the latter to withdraw from safeguards nuclear materials intended to be used for nonweapons, nonexplosive military purposes (e.g., submarine or other naval-propulsion reactors). Should Canada, as it appears likely, pursue this avenue, it would in so doing probably be setting a precedent; that much seems clear. What the *effect* of this precedent upon the regime must be, of course, is open to debate. Suffice it to say at this juncture that for those who view with foreboding the Canadian SSN program, the precedential effect upon the regime must be negative, and markedly so. What is held to be at stake is nothing less than the future credibility of the IAEA; for should any state have recourse to the provision in Article III of the NPT that sanctions the withdrawal of materials from safeguards for "non-proscribed" military purposes, then this "could result in the negation of the treaty's *raison d'être*, namely, to avoid the proliferation of nuclear weapons. The reason for this is simple.... The Agency would no longer be in a position to provide assurances that no diversion toward weapon manufacture ... was taking place, thereby weakening the credibility of IAEA safeguards."[25]

To be sure, no knowledgeable student of international nuclear politics thinks Canada would be taking material out of safeguards for the purposes of weapons-fabrication. However, those who do maintain the position that the Canadian SSN proposal must have *negative* precedential significance do so precisely because they view Canada as an exemplary nonproliferator. Thus, any derogation by Canada, it is argued, from the highest standards of nonproliferation would have the same chilling effect on the regime that an evangelist's lapse from probity must have on his or her followers. No NNWS, according to this view, should take advantage of Article 14, but least of all should Canada. One might call this the "Elmer Gantry" proviso, which is another way of saying that while it would be bad enough for the regime were Chad to announce a desire to obtain SSNs, it would be devastating for Canada to do so.

It is with these two related aspects of the precedent issue, then, that this and the next section will be concerned. In the pages that follow, I shall briefly analyze those considerations in respect of IAEA safeguards agreements that are currently attracting such attention, and then turn to an examination of both Canadian declaratory policy on nonproliferation *and* official practice regarding nuclear weaponry and nuclear-product exports. Although there is merit in the views of those who worry about the global nonproliferation implications of the Canadian SSN proposal, I shall argue in this section that it is by no means certain that the precedent that Canada might set in acquiring SSNs must be a negative one. Moreover, I will also try to show, in the subsequent section, that the exhalted status Canada has for some reason attained among nonproliferators is probably not warranted, at least not completely. The cynic might be excused for recalling, while contemplating Canada's nuclear-export and nuclear-arms experience, this famous epigram of La Rochefoucauld: "Our virtues are most frequently but vices in disguise."

Those who worry about the potential dire consequences of the SSN proposal would perhaps not see matters in this light, although they certainly would consider as a major vice any Canadian departure from the straight and narrow path of eschewing nuclear materials or technology for military purposes. They would not necessarily challenge the "legality" of Canada's so straying.[26] It is clear that there exist, depending upon one's interpretation of Canada's NPT adherence, some avenues for it (and other states) to pursue in legally applying nuclear products and facilities to non-proscribed military purposes. At the moment, there are two possible approaches Ottawa can make to the legal (if not the ethical) question of how to acquire SSNs yet remain consistent with the country's NNWS status.[27] On the one hand, Ottawa could simply argue that neither the NPT nor the IAEA are affected by the SSN proposal, for the good reason that both these institutions exist to prevent nuclear materials and technology from being diverted from peaceful to military purposes. Since the SSN program would clearly be military in intent, origin, and application, it would, according to this view, fall outside the ambit of both the NPT and the IAEA.

An alternative approach to the international legal issue, and the one that Ottawa feels more comfortable in following, is to take advantage of the provision in the country's safeguard agreement with the IAEA that allows, under certain conditions, nuclear material to be withdrawn from safeguards for permissible (i.e., non-proscribed) military applications. When Canada and other NNWS ratified the NPT, they agreed that they would conclude with the IAEA a safeguard arrangement that would, according to Article III(1) of the Treaty, be directed toward "the exclusive purpose of verification of the fulfillment of ... obligations assumed under this Treaty with a view to preventing diversion of nuclear energy from peaceful uses to nuclear weapons or other nuclear explosive devices." As I noted earlier, the basis for all the agreements reached between the IAEA and NNWS signatories would be INFCIRC/153.[28] This would not actually be the safeguard agreement per se that Canada would make with the IAEA; it would only be the model for that agreement. In Canada's case, INFCIRC/164, which came into force in February 1972, would spell out Ottawa's rights and responsibilities in respect of the IAEA under the NPT.[29]

Because some NNWS signatories, at the time the Treaty was being completed, had plans eventually of tapping nuclear power for their submarines and surface vessels (both the Italians and Dutch have been cited in this regard), a provision to this effect was included in the model safeguard agreement, INFCIRC/153. This, of course, is the celebrated Article 14, which has yet to be invoked by any NNWS signatory to the NPT. Canada bids fair to be the first to invoke this article, which would require it to satisfy the IAEA that non-proscribed military use of the nuclear material in question will not violate any Agency safeguard undertakings Ottawa may have already made regarding the same material, *and* that "during the period of non-application of safeguards the nuclear material will not be used for the production of nuclear weapons or other nuclear explosive devices."[30] *How* Ottawa will succeed in satisfying the Agency on these two matters will take some negotiations between it and the IAEA; *that* it will satisfy the Agency is not seriously in doubt.[31]

Those who fear Canada's taking the momentous step of invoking Article 14 base their case upon the conviction that in setting a precedent, Ottawa sets a bad precedent. It is possible that their assessment will, in retrospect, prove to have been correct; but this we have no way of knowing at the moment. What can be stated is that, logically, one could as well argue that the precedent will be a positive one. Alternatively, one could argue that the precedent will not really matter, one way or the other; in effect, the real significance of the Canadian precedent would be that it had no significance. Let us examine these latter two possibilities.

The current position of the Department of External Affairs, to which both the Atomic Energy Control Board of Canada and the Department of National

Defence also subscribe, is that if the resort to Article 14 is done well, it could have the effect of making the prospects of nonproliferation more, rather than less, tenable. To this end, Ottawa has been seeking, through bilateral agreements with both Britain and France, the two contenders for the SSN contract, to construct safeguard arrangements that would, it is hoped, have the effect of assuring both Canadians and the international community that even while the nuclear fuel for the submarines is out of IAEA safeguards it will still be safeguarded. The bilateral agreements contain a renewal of the respective parties' nonproliferation commitments, which in the case of France are not to be found in the NPT, to which it is not a signatory, but rather in such institutions as the London (or Nuclear) Suppliers Group, which established a code of conduct applicable to its members' nuclear trade.[32] The agreements will be legally binding in international law; they will be made public; and they will be consistent with Canada's current nonproliferation policy. The suppliers will monitor the nuclear material while it is in Canada, and Canadian officials will monitor it while it is outside the country.[33]

This attempt to secure a beneficial outcome for the nonproliferation regime as a result of the Canadian precedent assumes that what Canada does will be noticed by, and have an effect upon, other NNWS that, whether signatories or not to the NPT, might be tempted to acquire their own SSNs. This may indeed reflect reality; on the other hand, it is arguable that other countries with SSN dreams have already embarked upon fulfilling their visions quite independently of anything being done in Canada. In this event, then one could remark that the Canadian precedent will be neither good nor bad, but simply irrelevant. Is there any reason to imagine that Canada's invoking of Article 14 will have little effect upon other states, and therefore upon the global nonproliferation regime? Yes, and it inheres in the recent experience of at least two states that have announced ambitious plans of their own for SSNs. To the extent that these two states, India and Brazil, have made their plans quite independently of anything Ottawa has been considering doing — a logical supposition given the rather lengthy gestation period for both countries' SSN proposals — then it becomes extraordinarily difficult to argue that Canada's SSN program has set any precedent at all for the clearly identifiable would-be entrants to the SSN club.

Indeed, the Brazilian SSN program dates back to March 1979, long before the Canadian project was even a gleam in former Minister of National Defence Erik Neilsen's eye. Key to the Brazilian SSN project was the country's announcement, made in September 1987 by President José Sarney, that it had succeeded in developing the capacity to enrich uranium, thereby freeing itself from dependence upon foreign sources of enrichment for its sole nuclear power reactor, *Angra I*.[34] As well, and most importantly, solving the enrichment puzzle will allow Brazil, should it wish to, to build nuclear weapons. Even assuming that Brazil intends to keep its conditional commitment — made in the Tlatelolco Treaty — not to introduce nuclear weapons into Latin America, the country will have every reason to press ahead with its SSN program.[35] If it does, there is ample cause to expect that Argentina, so impressed during the recent Falklands/Malvinas War with the value of SSNs, will also speed up plans to acquire SSNs of its own. It is even possible, given last year's nuclear-sharing accord between Brasilia and Buenos Aires, that Brazil will assist its long-time rival in obtaining SSNs.[36] Alternatively, should the recent rapprochement between the two South American powers prove short-lived, then there would appear to be an even greater incentive to Argentina to proceed with SSNs.[37] In fact, Argentina's own enrichment program, centered upon the facility at Pilcaniyeu, predates Brazil's by a year and is thought to be somewhat more advanced.[38] It goes without saying that any Argentine breakthroughs in military nuclear technology will stimulate grave anxiety in the continent's third naval power, Chile.

For those in Canada who ponder the effect that SSNs might have upon nonproliferation, the South American cases seem a nightmare come true. If, as these critics of Canada's SSN program appear to believe, SSNs can serve to enhance the prospects of the bomb spreading (because of the likely, though not inevitable, association of weapons-grade enriched uranium with this class of vessel), then the "Southern Cone" countries epitomize the risks involved in nuclear-propelled submarines. However, given these same critics' insistence that the *Canadian* SSN program entails such danger for the nonproliferation regime that it should be halted immediately, it is difficult to avoid the conclusion that their argument suffers from a major logical fallacy — that of anachronism. SSNs may well, as the critics maintain, make the world less safe for nonproliferation; but it seems as if the Canadian program, far from being the *initiator* of an unfortunate chain of events, is at worst simply another stage of a process already begun — a process, furthermore, that will continue even should the Canadian SSN program be scrapped. If the cancellation of the Canadian SSN program would not have any effect upon arresting the proliferation hazards inherent in nuclear-propelled submarines, it is difficult to see how its *existence* impels the world toward greater proliferation risks. One cannot have it both ways: either the Canadian SSN program is somehow a logically necessary antecedent of the Brazilian (and Argentine) one, or it is not. If it is not, which appears to be the only sustainable conclusion, then in what exactly does the Canadian "precedent" consist?

Brazil does not expect to launch its first SSN before 1995.[39] Of more immediate concern, in the context of the SSN-proliferation link, is the recent acquisition by India of a nuclear-propelled submarine. The acquisition of this vessel, a *Charlie* class (in NATO designation) boat on lease from the Soviet Union, constitutes a precedent in its own right; for it makes India the first NNWS to acquire SSNs.[40] India is thus only the sixth country to have nuclear-propelled submarines, the others being the United States, the Soviet Union,

China, the United Kingdom, and France.[41] The lease of this boat, now called by the Indians INS *Chakra*, is expected to be followed by the outright purchase from the Soviets, in the early 1990s, of four *Sierra* class SSNs. Given India's rather infamous nonproliferation record, it might be thought that its acquisition of SSN capability would have triggered a good deal of anxiety among analysts who have been pondering the connection between SSNs and proliferation. Curiously, although some worry has been expressed in a variety of countries about the Indian démarche, in Canada at least the actual acquisition of the submarine has occasioned much less anxiety than have the *potential* Canadian SSNs — even though the latter will, assuming they get funded, not begin to arrive until the middle of the next decade. The relative lack of interest shown in this country in respect of the Indian SSN program is doubly curious, for the Soviets have argued that they are imposing a safeguards system that, in some respects, will bear the earmarks of the bilateral safeguard agreements Ottawa has concluded with Britain and France.[42] Thus it could be maintained that the ability (or inability, as the case may be) of the Soviets to safeguard the nuclear materials transferred to India may be of some relevance to both the Canadian case and to the international nonproliferation regime. Ironically, while it is evident that the Canadian SSN proposal cannot be seen as a precedent for the Indian program, it is possible that the latter might establish a precedent of sorts for the former.

A MATTER OF PRECEDENT, II: CANADA AS A MODEL NONPROLIFERATOR

Because neither Brazil nor India have signed the NPT, they obviously do not confront the Article 14 problem discussed above. In many ways, the Canadian "precedent" is largely based on the argument that the invoking of this article must adversely affect the nonproliferation regime, a contention whose logic I have sought to question in the above section. Beyond this concern, there is one other major element to the fear that a Canadian SSN program would imperil the nonproliferation regime, and it relates to Canada's reputation (at least in some quarters) as an exemplary nonproliferator. Certainly, not all who follow nonproliferation issues would share this assessment of Canada as a model state when it comes to inhibiting the spread of nuclear weapons; Ashok Kapur, for instance, heaps scorn on this image of Canada, which he considers to be a "crypto-nuclear state ... benefiting from the full protection of the Western umbrella."[43] And Ron Finch takes a stern and skeptical look at Canadian nuclear-export policy over the past forty years, concluding that "Canada has never produced an atomic bomb of its own, but it has played a major role in the proliferation of nuclear technology throughout the world."[44]

Although critics such as these can err in the direction of excessive condemnation of Canadian nuclear-export practices, they are at least refreshingly free of the Pecksniffianism that seems to infect much of the community of analysts — in this country and abroad — who seem to imagine that there has never been such an unblemished nuclear actor as Canada. All the more reason, lament this latter group, to condemn the SSN program, which to them plunges Canadian credibility among the nonproliferation faithful into depths of degradation usually attained by less noble states. Consider, for example, some recent testimony prepared by the Canadian Centre for Arms Control and Disarmament, before the Standing Committee on National Defence of the House of Commons. Were it not for the Canadian SSN program, the CCACD argues, Canada would be much better placed to denounce the recent Soviet lease of a nuclear-propelled submarine to India. "Today," notes John Lamb, the Centre's Director, "we'd be laughed out of the room if we as much as raised the issue with them."[45]

If Canada's record as a nuclear producer and exporter is not as bad as some of its reproachers may maintain, it certainly is far from being the paragon of nonproliferation sensibility that contemporary critics of the SSN program make it out to be (not to mention a few individuals in the Department of External Affairs).[46] Perhaps Aristotle's injunction that we must be virtuous, but must first secure a livelihood, is appropriately kept in mind in discussing the record of Canada in nuclear matters. Clearly, we are far from the nuclear Manuel Noriegas that the arch-cynics would have us be; also clearly, we are unlikely to be mistaken for Little Nell, however much many of the contemporary SSN opponents would wish it to be otherwise.

In truth, Canada's current policy on the export of nuclear materials and technology is remarkably strict — a strictness no doubt stimulated by our complicity in the 1974 Indian "peaceful" explosion, but a strictness nonetheless. Indeed, Canada's own policy on its exports is more restrictive than either the NPT or IAEA norms; for while the latter do allow for non-proscribed military uses of nuclear material, Canada's policy is to prevent its nuclear exports from being used for *any* military purposes.[47] At times this rigorous approach to nuclear trade can produce some illogicalities, as when Canadian uranium is kept out of use in U.S. nuclear-propelled submarines — vessels that provide a major portion of the nuclear umbrella under which successive generations of Canadian policymakers have happily sought shelter.[48] Such can be the pitfalls of excessive rigor; and in any event, U.S. nonproliferation policy is no more tolerant, evidently, of Canadian military applications of U.S. nuclear technology, as I shall relate in the next section.

For the moment, however, it might be useful, in attempting to place Canadian nuclear behavior in the proper context, to dwell upon three related issues that, individually and collectively, should serve to dispel some of the sentimentality attached to the image of Canada as being among the nuclear saints of the world. The first issue is that of nuclear weaponry. As everyone does or should know, Canada neither builds nor possesses nuclear weapons. What is perhaps forgotten is that Canada did play a part in the American atomic-bomb project during World War II, that Canadian uranium mines were an important early source of supply to the post-World War II U.S. nuclear arsenal, and that the Canadian Forces were equipped with nuclear weapons from 1963 until 1984, when the last nuclear-tipped Genie air-to-air missile left Canadian soil.[49]

Gone are the days when a Canadian politician can be caught heaping praise on nuclear weapons in public; but in the wake of the Hiroshima bombing, a Canadian cabinet minister, C. D. Howe, could and did announce with "particular pleasure ... that Canadian scientists and Canadian institutions have played an intricate part and have been associated in an effective way with this great scientific development."[50] Nevertheless, despite Canada's own renunciation of nuclear weaponry, it remains a committed participant in an alliance one of whose fundamental deterrent doctrines is that of the first use of nuclear weapons. Not only is Canada a member of NATO, but its role in NORAD has ineluctably been to lend support to the strategic nuclear retaliatory capabilities of the U.S. Air Force. Thus our rejection of nuclear weaponry can only be termed complete in a Pickwickian sense. Our membership in the NATO Nuclear Planning Group attests to the fundamentally ambiguous approach we continue to take to the question of nuclear weaponry.

The third issue concerns Canada's own tough policy regarding nuclear exports, one that, it will be recalled, prohibits the use of Canadian uranium (and other nuclear materials) for any military purposes. The SSN proposal raises, at the very least, the interesting prospect of Canada seeking to acquire from foreign sources that which it would not supply to those same sources. By this I mean that Canada would of necessity (at least in the early stages) be forced to import enriched uranium to fuel its SSNs, all the while that its own nuclear-export policy would remain one of prohibiting its allies from using its uranium for their own nuclear submarines. The Department of External Affairs remains committed to the notion that even should we import enriched uranium for military purposes, there is no necessary reason why we would allow our own nuclear materials to be used for similar purposes, even though the NPT allows such applications. We are, DEA officials insist, not going to deviate from our nuclear-export standards, Canadian SSN program notwithstanding. What this position overlooks, of course, is that for the past several years Canadian uranium already has been put, and continues to be put, to non-proscribed military purposes. In other words, we have permitted our own strict and self-imposed export standards to be violated. Given this, our own use of nuclear materials for non-proscribed military purposes hardly constitutes a significant departure from our nonproliferation policy, at least in logic.

In what way has Canadian uranium been employed for non-proscribed military purposes? In armor-piercing *conventional* shells made with depleted uranium, which is a by-product of the enrichment process, where the isotopic "mix" of natural uranium is altered to boost the proportion of U-235 from its naturally occurring 0.711 percent. Unlike the enriched product, depleted uranium contains a greater percentage of U-238 than is found in nature. The virtue of this substance, from the point of view of weapons manufacturing, is that it is incredibly dense and heavy, and possesses superior penetrating capability if made into shells.[51] Moreover, there are currently plans to install steel-encased depleted-uranium armor on the remaining batches of the main battle tank purchased for the U.S. Army, the M-1A1 Abrams. This new tank armor is thought to be impervious to Soviet antitank weaponry, and will be made from a mesh of depleted uranium that is two-and-a-half times as dense as steel. The first of the Abrams to be equipped with this new armor came off the General Dynamics production lines late last summer, and was deployed with the U.S. 7th Army in Germany at the end of the year.[52] Given the high level of Canadian imports that are being processed by the U.S. Department of Energy's enriching facilities — some 25 percent of the uranium hexaflouride enriched in the U.S. in 1986 — it is inevitable that there be a good deal of "Canadian content" in the depleted uranium that is sold to weapons manufacturers in the U.S.[53]

Thus Canada's nuclear-export practice, as opposed to its policy, is somewhat different from the stereotype maintained by those who see in Canada an exemplary nonproliferator. This does not mean that Ottawa intends to make it easier for NNWS to acquire the bomb; quite the contrary. It simply means that an SSN acquisition would not constitute the lapse from sanctity that many currently fear. A Canadian nuclear submarines program will mean, instead, that Canada has engaged in yet another military application — only this time directly — of nuclear materials.

THE OTHER NONPROLIFERATION ISSUE: U.S. POLICY AND THE CANADIAN SSNs

If the uproar over the implications of the Canadian nuclear-submarine proposal for the global nonproliferation regime took the Department of National Defence by surprise, the tangle into which the Canadian proposal landed as a result of *American* nonproliferation policy must have come as a shock. Indeed, not only were Canadian government officials initially unprepared for a problem to arise from this precinct of the nonproliferation realm, but so too were those members of the arms-control community who did so much to stimulate early debate on the SSNs and nonproliferation. The two sets of issues had this in common: in both, there was a clear relationship between the Canadian proposal and the question of nonproliferation. This similarity aside, there were some major differences in the manner in which the submarines and nonproliferation were interrelated. Perhaps the greatest difference was that in the instance of the American nonproliferation policy, it was the Canadian program that now found itself placed in the position of the "dependent variable"; that is, unlike the earlier concern over the extent to which Canada's program might affect the global regime, in this instance it was now the matter of the influence that American policy might exert on Canadian intentions that commanded attention of analysts.

As I noted earlier, American nonproliferation policy has been, by and large, much more restrictive than that of any other of the nuclear supplier countries over the past forty years. Although it may be the case, as some have maintained, that Washington has not consistently adopted a tough nonproliferation stance on all of its nuclear exports, it is evident that U.S. policy compares favorably with other exporters in the degree to which it has evidenced a commitment to preventing nuclear commerce from making it easier for other states to acquire nuclear weapons.[54] The centerpiece of American nonproliferation policy — and one that some analysts see as the subject of erosion under the current administration — is the Nuclear Non-Proliferation Act of 1978 (NNPA), which reconfirmed and extended into new categories Washington's restrictions on nuclear commerce, and its support for the IAEA.[55] However much renown this Act may have attained, it is a much older export arrangement, the 1958 U.S.-U.K. Agreement for Cooperation on the Uses of Atomic Energy for Mutual Defense Purposes, that is of critical importance to the contemporary Canadian SSN proposal. Also significant for the future shape of the Canadian program is a bilateral accord signed by Ottawa and Washington the following year, the 1959 U.S.-Canada Agreement for Cooperation on the Uses of Atomic Energy for Mutual Defense Purposes.[56]

The U.S.-U.K. agreement requires that Washington approve any transfer of American-supplied nuclear technology such as that contained in the *Trafalgar*-class submarines that Canada is contemplating buying; the bilateral Canada-U.S. agreement of 1959 would, in the event the *Trafalgar* were chosen, once again require American (in this instance, Congressional) approval before the United States could provide highly enriched uranium to Canada for fuelling the boats. In either case, it is clear that the Congressional branch, whatever the wishes of the Executive branch, can if it chooses exercise a most decisive voice on the direction of the Canadian SSN program. Washington cannot, as some seem to believe, exert any "veto" power over the Canadian proposal; but it can make it less likely that the *Trafalgar* and more likely that the French contender, the *Améthyste/Rubis*, will get selected as the Canadian SSN. Indeed, advertisements placed by the Canadian subsidiary of the French producer, SNA Canada, have cleverly drawn attention to two nonproliferation advantages possessed by their boat: it is unencumbered by third-party restrictions regarding transfer of sensitive technology; and for good measure its power plant uses uranium that is enriched to only 10 percent, as compared to the weapons-grade 95-percent fuel consumed in the *Trafalgar.*[57]

As late as the spring of 1988, it seemed as if the British boat were going to win the competition over the French one as Canada's nuclear-propelled submarine. Noted one reporter for a major Toronto newspaper in early April: "The conventional wisdom on Parliament Hill is that the British will win the competition, hands down."[58] It was felt by many, throughout the period between the unveiling of the SSN proposal in the 1987 White Paper on defense and the early spring of 1988, that the *Trafalgar* simply possessed too many operational advantages over the *Rubis* that military requirements would compel it to be the vessel of choice. Today, the mood among those who follow the Canadian SSN program is remarkably different; and the current conventional wisdom has the French craft as the clear winner in the battle. So confident are those directly involved with the French bid that the president of SNA Canada, Lawrence Herman, could recently announce that "I am prepared to say the British option is dead."[59]

What has wrought this transformation, in such a short span of time? Although not the only factor, by far the most significant reason for the dramatic alteration in the competitive prospects of the two contenders is the fact that, for reasons stemming in the first instance from U.S. nonproliferation concerns, the *Trafalgar* has come to be seen, whatever its operational merits may be, as a major political liability for the Canadian government. This is so because to get it, Ottawa must count ultimately on securing Congressional approval of the transaction. This poses serious problems for two understandable reasons. The first is that it is far from certain that Congress would grant such approval, even though the administration has shown itself in favor of allowing the technology transfer.[60] The second reason is that it is simply too embarrassing for Ottawa to have to put itself in the position of indirect mendicant in order to achieve an objective that has recently been billed as the single most important goal that the Department of National Defence has set: the acquisition of SSNs.

U.S. nonproliferation policy may be the *mechanism* for injecting an American influence over the future shape of the Canadian SSN program, but it is not the *motivation* for such intervention. Admittedly, as I noted above, the U.S. does remain committed to the objective of nonproliferation, and many in Washington do worry about the nonproliferation implications of nuclear-propelled submarines, no matter who possesses them. When in late April President Reagan came out in favor of allowing the transfer of *Trafalgar* technology to Canada, the State Department took some pains to point out how exceptional such an action was, one undertaken, in the words of Department official Charles Redman, "because of the unique circumstances involving the

United Kingdom and Canada, two of our oldest and closest allies. U.S. policy remains opposed to the transfer of nuclear submarines to other nations."[61]

Redman could have added that many in the U.S. Navy seem to be opposed to their transfer to Canada, as well; for the reality is that the Canadian SSN proposal has engendered some surprisingly firm opposition on the part of influential figures, both in the Pentagon and on Capitol Hill. Significantly, among the reasons adduced by the opponents of the Canadian SSN program, one encounters few objections based on the desire to maintain inviolate U.S. nonproliferation policy. Instead, there are several differing explanations these opponents have put forward in their bid to persuade either Americans or Canadians (sometimes both) to arrest Ottawa's campaign to acquire nuclear-propelled submarines.

Prominent among these explanations is one that links the Canadian SSNs to the oft-stated goal of protecting Canadian sovereignty in the Arctic. In this instance, it does seem that Ottawa — whatever its "real" justification for the SSN program — has convinced some Americans that its primary purpose is the sometimes-advertised one of safeguarding Canadian internal waters against prowling American submarines. Although it is often assumed that the main theater of operation of any Canadian SSNs would be the Arctic, in reality it is highly unlikely that normal peacetime deployments would call for much of a Canadian SSN presence in the north. As one senior officer in Maritime Command stated unequivocally on the day the White Paper was tabled in June 1987: "We would want these subs just as much if the Arctic did not exist."[62] Yet some in the U.S. (as, indeed, in this country) appear to think that the *raison d'être* of the SSNs is their ability to patrol under the ice in the Canadian Arctic. This American disquiet over Canadian sovereignty claims may not be the most important source of U.S. opposition to the Canadian SSN program, but it was the first such source to arise.

For instance, more than a month before the SSN option was officially announced with the tabling of the White Paper, the *New York Times* published a story that related the fears of some unnamed Pentagon officials that a "future Canadian government would use the existence of its own nuclear submarine force as grounds to challenge the passage of American submarines along the protected routes through the [Canadian] archipelago."[63] A few months later, Congressman Charles Bennett, the Chairman of the Seapower Subcommittee of the House Armed Services Committee, restated this concern, in an op-ed piece in the *Globe and Mail*. Asked Bennett, in reference to the fact that Canadian access to British nuclear technology could be impeded by Congress, "Should [the U.S.] help create a fleet that could be used to enforce a claim it doesn't recognize?"[64] This query was repeated in November by the American Naval Attaché in Ottawa, Captain Robert F. Hofford, who observed that many people in Washington were wondering why the U.S. should help Canada get military assets that could have "adverse implications" for the U.S. Navy.[65]

Directly or indirectly, the source of these fears could be fairly easily discerned in the presence of Admiral Kinnaird R. McKee, director of nuclear propulsion programs for the U.S. Navy. McKee, assisted by Senators John Warner and Jim Exon (both of the Senate Armed Services Committee), as well as by Congressman Bennett, has been instrumental in drawing attention on Capitol Hill to the Canadian SSN program.[66] Although the Admiral's worry about the Canadian sovereignty claim should not be dismissed (it would, after all, be entirely consistent with the USN's long-standing aversion to anything that threatened to circumscribe its freedom of maneuver), there are some other reasons that McKee is so passionately opposed to the Canadian program.

Foremost among these is the worry that an accident on a Canadian nuclear submarine could have disastrous consequences for the nuclear program of the USN itself. In a peculiar twist to the precedential argument I discussed in the early sections of this chapter, one now finds some in Washington speculating about the demonstration effect a Canadian nuclear accident could have for Americans and others. In a remarkably patronizing article published in the *Globe and Mail*, former Pentagon official Frank J. Gaffney claimed that the Canadian SSN proposal was "dangerous folly." What especially upset Gaffney was his perception that a Canadian SSN program would be so under-funded that it would have to cut corners on safety, for reasons of financial exigency. That, he argued, could "perpetuat[e] a catastrophe that would degrade public confidence and the operational flexibility of the NATO weapons systems critical to Western security."[67]

Another argument made against the Canadian nuclear submarines, and one that has an audience elsewhere in the Pentagon than the Navy Department, is the claim that the opportunity costs of the program are simply too high for the Western alliance. Senator Warner would like to see Canada spending its defense dollars building up its conventional forces, a view echoed with amplification recently by the *Economist*, which has its own preferences for how Canadian taxpayers' money should be spent: "[T]here are much better uses for [this] money: such as putting an armoured division or two into West Germany, instead of the lonely little brigade it has there now."[68] Closely related to this concern about opportunity cost is the argument that whichever boat Canada eventually did buy would be woefully obsolescent even before it entered service. Pentagon sources regard either the *Trafalgar* or the *Rubis* as being vastly inferior to the USN's *Los Angeles* class SSN — and the latter they even consider to be outmatched by the SSNs the Soviets will be deploying in the mid 1990s, when the first Canadian boat is scheduled to become operational.[69]

It has even been suggested that the USN has a "hidden agenda" in its opposition to the Canadian SSN project — an agenda having little or nothing to do with sovereignty, safety, opportunity costs, obsolescence, or nonproliferation. It is possible that the target of the USN's objections is situated in Washington, not Ottawa; for it may be that McKee and others are concerned about the effect that an additional ten or twelve SSNs in North America might have on their own struggle to win more dollars from Congress. This at least is the intriguing thesis of one defense analyst, who argues that:

> logically, one would expect the United States naval establishment, facing a major Soviet underseas threat, to welcome the addition of advanced submarine forces to western hemisphere defense.... United States naval leaders are concerned, however, about the effect on budget requests to the U.S. Congress of a significant added allied force in the hemisphere, for which they until now had the sole responsibility.[70]

CONCLUSION

Whatever the exact nature of the USN and Congressional unease with the Canadian SSN program, two things seem clear: the first is that, no matter how hard some in Washington huff and puff, they cannot blow down the Canadian SSN program. They can, and probably will, render the *Trafalgar* option too risky to take. If Canada does not acquire SSNs, however, it will be as a result of domestic political and economic considerations, not because of pressure from certain quarters in the United States.

The second is that the tempest over the Canadian nuclear submarines has generated some ill-will on the part of normally well-disposed communities in both countries. There is surely something more than a little curious about members of the Canadian defense community railing against American intrusions upon Canadian sovereignty; that kind of talk typically comes from quite another domestic constituency in this country. Two ironies arise here. The first has to do with the Canadian arms control community's serendipitous reliance upon some heretofore unsuspected allies, especially those in the USN. The second is that Admiral McKee and his colleagues may be engaging in self-fulfilling prophecies when they cite Canada's sovereignty objectives as a major (the major?) reason for their own opposition to the SSNs. Consider the following emotional commentary by one of Canada's defense analysts: "The important argument today," wrote *The Wednesday Report*'s Mike O'Brien,

> is no longer about doctrinal and economic aspects of SSN operations, but a question of sovereignty.... Some considerable damage is being done to Canada/U.S. relations. If Americans believe that the Canadian people can be driven to cure what the U.S. seems to think is SSN folly, they are misguided in their approach.... We are not Panama. We are not Central America.[71]

It would be yet another confirmation of the principle of the opposite effect if USN opposition were to provide a fillip for the Canadian SSN program, by rallying nationalists around the Department of National Defence.

Nonproliferation policy and law in the U.S., as I have mentioned, will have an effect upon the Canadian submarine program, even if it is not the effect intended by American critics of that program. However, what of the effect the Canadian nuclear submarines might have upon the nonproliferation regime itself? As I have argued, the claim that Canadian SSNs *must* do damage to that regime remains to be substantiated; it may turn out that critics of the Canadian proposal are right. It will require more than incantation to make this argument convincing. What must be taken into consideration are: a) the possibility that a Canadian "precedent" might have a positive effect on the regime; and b) the possibility that Canada's acquisition of SSNs will have absolutely no effect upon the global move (if that is what it is) toward SSNs. Above all, we simply need to know much more than we do right now about the impact of SSNs on the prospects of global nonproliferation.

It is a convention for essayists to conclude their analyses (especially if they are academics) with the observation that "further research is called for." In most cases, this means that the writer has run out of things to say, and cannot think of a graceful way to exit. In this instance, however, I would suggest that invocation of this convention is justified. For until we know a great deal more about the policies of various relevant countries concerning SSNs, it is simply impossible to pronounce judgment upon Canadian nuclear submarines and their impact on the nonproliferation regime.

Notes

[1]Government of Canada, Department of National Defence, *Challenge and Commitment: A Defence Policy for Canada* (Ottawa: Minister of Supply and Services, 1987), 52-55.

[2]For an analysis of the White Paper that raises these and other questions, see David Cox, "Living Along the Flight Path: Canada's Defense Debate," *Washington Quarterly* 10 (Autumn 1987): 98-112.

[3]See, for this view, Tariq Rauf and Dan Hayward, "Nuclear-Powered Attack Submarines: Does Canada Really Need Them?" *Arms Control Communiqué*, no. 36 (Ottawa: Canadian Centre for Arms Control and Disarmament, 15 May 1987). A lengthier version of the CCACD's negative assessment of the SSN proposal is found in Idem, "O Canada e os Submarinos Nucleares," *Política e Estratégia* 5 (April/June 1987): 211-23. Also see the letter to the editor written by Senator Philippe D. Gigantes, "Subs Are First-Strike Weapons," *Globe and Mail* (Toronto), 28 May 1988, D7.

[4]Some months after the White Paper's release, DND sought to temper some of the criticism through the publication of a pamphlet that, among other things, gave the reassurance (which evidently some seem to need) that in obtaining SSNs the government was not renouncing its policy of eschewing nuclear weaponry. See Government of Canada, Department of National Defence, *Facts About Canada's Nuclear-Propelled Submarines* (Ottawa: DND, n.d.).

[5]Marc Clark and William Lowther, "Keeping Canada Out of the Sub Club," *Macleans*, 11 April 1988, 12-13.

[6]A useful introduction to the current debate over the meaning and importance of regimes is Stephen D. Krasner, ed., *International Regimes* (Ithaca: Cornell University Press, 1983). Also central to this inquiry are Robert O. Keohane and Joseph S. Nye, *Power and Interdependence: World Politics in Transition* (Boston: Little, Brown, 1977); Robert O. Keohane, *After Hegemony: Cooperation and Discord in the World Political Economy* (Princeton, NJ: Princeton University Press, 1984); Oran R. Young, "International Regimes: Problems of Concept Formation," *World Politics* 32 (April 1980): 331-56; and Friedrich Kratochwil, "The Force of Prescriptions," *International Organization* 38 (Autumn 1984): 685-708.

[7]It should be noted that not all analysts (or, evidently, all governments) accept the argument that proliferation is inimical to security. The most well-known contrary statement is Kenneth Waltz, "The Spread of Nuclear Weapons: More May Be Better," *Adelphi Papers*, no. 171 (London: International Institute for Strategic Studies, 1981).

[8]Lawrence Scheinman, *The International Atomic Energy Agency and World Nuclear Order* (Washington: Resources for the Future, 1987), 21-39.

[9]Ibid., 16-21; and William C. Potter, *Nuclear Power and Nonproliferation* (Cambridge, MA.: Oelgeschlager, Gunn and Hain, 1982), chap. 2.

[10]Scheinman, *International Atomic Energy Agency*, 31.

[11]David Fischer and Paul Szasz, *Safeguarding the Atom: A Critical Appraisal* (London: Taylor & Francis, 1985), 7.

[12]The procedural basis of safeguards is discussed in International Atomic Energy Agency, *IAEA Safeguards: An Introduction*, SG/INF/3 (Vienna: IAEA, 1981); and Idem, *IAEA Safeguards: Aims, Limitations, Achievements*, SG/INF/4 (Vienna: IAEA, 1983).

[13]Scheinman, *International Atomic Energy Agency*, 129.

[14]U.S. General Accounting Office, "New and Better Equipment Being Made Available for International Nuclear Safeguards," GAO/NSIAD-84-46 (Washington, 14 June 1984), 4. Also see Hans Blix, "Safeguards and Nonproliferation: The IAEA and Efforts to Counteract the Spread of Nuclear Weapons," *IAEA Bulletin* 27 (Summer 1985): 3-7.

[15]For an analysis of both the Iraqi nuclear program and the Israeli raid, see Jed C. Snyder, "Iraq," in Jed C. Snyder and Samuel F. Wells, Jr., eds., *Limiting Nuclear Proliferation* (Cambridge, MA: Ballinger, 1985), 3-42. Although not a signatory to the NPT, Israel does belong to the IAEA.

[16]Pakistan's relations with the IAEA, to which it belongs, are discussed in Rodney Jones, "Strategic Responses to Nuclear Proliferation," *Washington Quarterly* 6 (Summer 1983); Idem, "Nuclear Supply Policy and South Asia," in Rodney W. Jones, et al., eds., *The Nuclear Suppliers and Nonproliferation: International Policy Choices* (Lexington, MA: D. C. Heath, 1985), 163-73; and Richard P. Cronin, "India and Pakistan," in *Limiting Nuclear Proliferation*, 59-88.

[17]Don Oberdorfer, "U.S. Asks Pakistan to Stop Producing Bomb-Grade Uranium," *Washington Post*, 23 July 1987, 37; Simon Henderson, "Pakistan Builds Second Plant to Enrich Uranium," *Financial Times* (London), 11 December 1987, 28.

[18]This concern is not recent, for in the early 1970s there was a short-lived spate of alarm about terrorists availing themselves of nuclear weapons to achieve political ends, in this case income redistribution. For this earlier fear, see Robert L. Heilbroner, *An Inquiry into the Human Prospect* (New York: W. W. Norton, 1975), 41-45. For a discussion of nuclear terrorism in the context of contemporary Middle Eastern politics, see

Robert A. Friedlander, "Terrorism and Nuclear Decisions," *Social Science and Modern Society* 23 (January/February 1986): 59-62.

[19]John H. Cushman, Jr., "Rising Nuclear Trade Stirs Fear of Terrorism," *New York Times*, 5 November 1987, 5; Daniel Charles, "DOD Sees Risk in Plutonium Trade," *Science*, 13 November 1987, 886; Cass Peterson, "U.S. to Allow Unrestricted Transfer of Plutonium," *Washington Post*, 22 April 1988, 4.

[20]M. I. Shaker, "The Third NPT Review Conference: Issues and Prospects," in David B. Dewitt, ed., *Nuclear Non-Proliferation and Global Security* (London: Croom Helm, 1987), 3. Article VIII(3) of the NPT calls upon the adherents to convene and review the Treaty's functioning every five years.

[21]The full text of the NPT can be found in Dewitt, *Nuclear Non-Proliferation*, Appendix A.

[22]For a critical, and sometimes biting, analysis of the asymmetrical nature of the NPT exchange of commitments, see Ashok Kapur, "The Future of the NPT: A View from the Indian Subcontinent," in Dewitt, *Nuclear Non-Proliferation*, 201-15.

[23]Contrasting export policies of the industrialized states are examined in Pierre Lellouche, "International Nuclear Politics," *Foreign Affairs* 58 (Winter 1979/80): 336-50; Erwin Hackel, Karl Kaiser, and Pierre Lellouche, *Nuclear Policy in Europe: France, Germany and the International Debate* (Bonn: Forschünginstitut der Deutschen Gesellschaft für Auswartigesamt, 1981); and John Simpson and Anthony G. McGrew, eds., *The International Nuclear Non-Proliferation System: Challenges and Choices* (New York: St. Martin's Press, 1984).

[24]A comprehensive treatment of the challenges facing the IAEA is given in Lawrence Scheinman, *The Nonproliferation Role of the International Atomic Energy Agency: A Critical Assessment* (Washington: Resources for the Future, 1985).

[25]Marie-France Desjardins and Tariq Rauf, "Opening Pandora's Box? Nuclear-Powered Submarines and the Spread of Nuclear Weapons," *Aurora Papers*, no. 8 (Ottawa: Canadian Centre for Arms Control and Disarmament, pre-publication edition of February 1988), 22.

[26]There is some confusion among anti-SSN advocates on the matter of the legality of the SSN proposal. Greenpeace's John Willis, for example, seems to think that the NPT requires that Canada not use or allow to be used nuclear material for *any* military purpose. See his letter to the editor, "A-Subs Would Put Treaty at Risk," *Globe and Mail*, 16 January 1988, D7. For a useful corrective to this, also by an analyst who opposes the SSN proposal, see John Barrett's letter to the editor, "Submarines Slip through Loophole," ibid., 30 January 1988, D7.

[27]This discussion of the legal aspects of the SSN project is based largely on interviews I conducted with IAEA and Canadian officials in Vienna and Ottawa between December 1987 and February 1988.

[28]International Atomic Energy Agency, *The Structure and Content of Agreements between the Agency and States Required in Connection with the Treaty on the Non-Proliferation of Nuclear Weapons*, INFCIRC/153 (Vienna: IAEA, June 1972).

[29]International Atomic Energy Agency, *The Text of the Agreements between Canada and the Agency for the Application of Safeguards in Connection with the Treaty on the Nonproliferation of Nuclear Weapons*, INFCIRC/164 (Vienna: IAEA, June 1972).

[30]Ibid., 5.

[31]From the Canadian side, the negotiating team will be made up of officials from DEA, AECB, and DND; from the Agency, the relevant actors will be the divisions responsible for External Relations, Safeguards, and Legal matters.

[32]For the NSG, see U.S. Congress, Office of Technology Assessment, *Nuclear Proliferation and Safeguards* (New York: Praeger, 1977), 220-23; Leonard Spector, *Nuclear Proliferation Today* (Cambridge, MA: Ballinger, 1984), 447-51; and Charles N. Van Doren, "Nuclear Supply and Nonproliferation: The IAEA Committee on Assurances of Supply," Report no. 83-202-8 (Washington: Congressional Research Service, October 1983), 60-65.

[33]Ken Romain, "Ottawa to Sign Agreements on Nuclear Subs," *Globe and Mail*, 15 January 1988, B5; Sharon Hobson, "Canada Completes Talks to Build Nuclear Submarines," *Jane's Defence Weekly*, 19 March 1988.

[34]Richard House, "Brazil Says Uranium Enriched," *Washington Post*, 10 September 1987, 29.

[35]Michael Kepp, "Brazil on Verge of the Atomic Bomb; Next Step Is in Hands of the Military," *Baltimore Sun*, 21 October 1987, 2. The conditionality of the Brazilian nonproliferation pledge stems from Brasilia's insistence that its commitment to eschew nuclear weaponry depends upon the Treaty of Tlatelolco being ratified by all Latin American countries. Brazil has ratified this 1968 regional nonproliferation accord, but Argentina has yet to do so. (Cuba has neither signed nor ratified the Treaty, and is not likely to do either.) See John Redick, "The Tlatelolco Regime and Nonproliferation in Latin America," in George Quester, ed., *Nuclear Proliferation: Breaking the Chain* (Madison: University of Wisconsin Press, 1981), 103-34.

[36]Michael R. Gordon, "Brazil and Argentina Start Nuclear Discussion," *New York Times*, 22 July 1987, 3.

[37]Whether the historical enmity between the two can be overcome is discussed in two recent articles written in conjunction with a symposium on Argentine-Brazilian relations held in Buenos Aires in April 1987. See Deodécio Lima de Siqueira, "Brasil-Argentina: Término ou Transformaçao do Conflito"; and Luis Santiago Sanz, "Argentina-Brasil: Término ou Transformaçao do Conflito," both in *Política e Estratégia* 5 (July/September 1987): 293-320.

[38]Enrichment levels, which refer to the proportion of a given unit of uranium accounted for by the fissile isotope, U-235, have reached 20 percent at Pilcaniyeu. Weapons-grade uranium would have to attain a level of about 90 percent; a similar level would be needed to fuel many SSNs (e.g., the British *Trafalgar* class). Brazil's Ipero centrifuge enricher should now be approaching the 20-percent level. Brazil also has an IAEA-safeguarded civil enrichment facility at Resende, built with German help; this currently has attained an enrichment level of 0.85 percent, and is intended ultimately to reach the 3-percent range that most civilian nuclear power reactors require for fuel. "In Search of Enrichment," *Economist*, 5 March 1988, 86.

[39]Richard House, "Brazil Steps Back from Race to Build Nuclear Weapons," *Washington Post*, 28 August 1986, E1.

[40]The Indian submarine, which is nearly twenty years old, is powered by one reactor. Its conventional armaments include fourteen torpedoes and a potential eight SS-N-7 cruise missiles, which have a range of thirty-five miles. "India's Leased N-Sub Said One-Reactor Type," *Washington Times*, 10 February 1988, 2.

[41]Paul Beaver and Richard Sharpe, "New Members for SSN Club," *Jane's Defence Weekly*, 9 January 1988, 11.

[42]The *Chakra's* fuel is weapons-grade, and the Soviets have assured Washington that they will strictly monitor the fuel while it is out of the Soviet Union on board the Indian vessel. Adam Kelliher, "India's Nuclear-Powered Submarine Causes Widespread Concern," *Ottawa Citizen*, 27 February 1988, B5.

[43]Kapur, "The Future of the NPT," 201.

[44]Ron Finch, *Exporting Danger: A History of the Canadian Nuclear Energy Export Programme* (Montreal: Black Rose Books, 1986), 13.

[45]Paul Koring, "Projected Role of New Submarines Naive Plan, Arms Expert Tells MPs," *Globe and Mail*, 11 May 1988, A4.

[46]A good example of the idealistic interpretation of Canadian policy is found in Douglas Roche, "Canada and the NPT: The Enduring Relationship," in Dewitt, *Nuclear Non-Proliferation*, 165: "Canada's record in its efforts to prevent the proliferation of nuclear weapons is indeed unique. Canada has a set of non-proliferation credentials which is shared by few other countries in the world. In non-proliferation — horizontal and vertical — Canada has led, and continues to lead, by example."

[47]For Canadian policy on nuclear exports, see James F. Keeley, "Canadian Nuclear Export Policy and the Problems of Proliferation," *Canadian Public Policy* 6 (Autumn 1980): 614-27; and Michael C. Webb, "Canada as an Insecure Supplier: Nonproliferation, Economic Development, and Uranium Export Policy," in David G. Haglund, ed., *The New Geopolitics of Minerals: Canada and International Resource Trade* (Vancouver: University of British Columbia Press, forthcoming).

[48]For a discussion of this, see David G. Haglund, "Protectionism and National Security: The Case of Canadian Uranium Exports to the United States," *Canadian Public Policy* 12 (September 1986): 457-72.

[49]For an analysis of Canada's experience with nuclear weapons, see Jon B. McLin, *Canada's Changing Defense Policy, 1957-1963: The Problems of a Middle Power in Alliance* (Baltimore: Johns Hopkins Press, 1967), chap. 6: "The Problem of Nuclear Weapons." Also see Tom Kent, *A Public Purpose: An Experience of Liberal Opposition and Canadian Government* (Kingston and Montreal: McGill-Queen's University Press, 1988), chap. 15: "The Nuclear Error."

[50]Quoted in Kyle McIntyre, "The Limits of the Functional Principle: Canada and Atomic Energy Policy, 1941-1949" (M.A. thesis, Royal Military College of Canada, 1988), 63.

[51]Among the ordnance in the U.S. arsenal that is composed of depleted uranium are the 20-mm. round for the ship-based anti-aircraft gun, Phalynx, and the 105-mm. anti-tank ammunition fired by the M-60 and M-48 tanks. Warren Strobel and Karen Field, "Uranium-Core Shells to be Sold to Jordan, Probably Two Others," *Washington Times*, 10 March 1988, 2.

[52]On the Abrams armor, see "Effort Disclosed to Improve Armor on Tank," *New York Times*, 15 March 1988, A20; George C. Wilson,"Tougher Tank Armor Developed by Pentagon," *Washington Post*, 15 March 1988, A4; and "M1A1's Uranium Shield," *Jane's Defence Weekly*, 26 March 1988, 573.

[53]In 1986, U.S. domestic utilities delivered 12.9 million pounds of foreign-origin uranium to the Department of Energy's enrichment facilities. This amount represented nearly 42 percent of U.S. utility requirements, and some 59 percent of *this* amount was accounted for by uranium originating in Canada. U.S. Department of Energy, *Domestic Uranium Mining and Milling Industry: 1986 Viability Assessment* (Washington: Energy

Information Administration, November 1987), 66. Uranium hexafluoride (UF$_6$) is an intermediate stage in the process of transforming uranium concentrate (U$_3$O$_8$) into enriched uranium.

[54]For an argument that challenges the notion of American nonproliferation preeminence, see Lawrence Scheinman, "The Case for a Comprehensive U.S. Nonproliferation Policy," in *Limiting Nuclear Proliferation*, 319-36.

[55]For a good analysis of the NNPA and of U.S. export policy, see Peter A. Clausen, "U.S. Nuclear Exports and the Nonproliferation Regime," in ibid., 183-212.

[56]Barbara Starr, "Reagan's Endorsement of Sub Technology Transfer May Pressure Canada," *Defense News*, 2 May 1988, 7.

[57]Michel Van de Walle, "Les Français misent sur l'économie de couts et l'indépendance technologique," *Le Devoir* (Montreal), 7 May 1988, B3. For an example of a SNA ad that prominently features the nonproliferation advantages of the French boat, see "Take a Deeper Look at the Facts," *Financial Post*, 9 May 1988, 41. But for a stinging rebuke to the French contender's nonproliferation claims, cf. John M. Lamb and Tariq Rauf, "Canada Sets Sail in Dangerous Water," *Globe and Mail*, 12 May 1988, A7.

[58]Carol Goar, "How France May Win Nuclear Subs Deal," *Toronto Star*, 7 April 1988, A23.

[59]Mathew Horsman, "French Claim Edge over British Sub," *Financial Post*, 17 May 1988, 4. Also see Giles Gherson, "Submarine Choices Evaporating," *Financial Post*, 18 May 1988, 13; and "La France croit avoir de bons atouts pour obtenir le contrat de sous-marins," *La Presse* (Montreal), 16 May 1988, B1.

[60]Bob Hepburn, "Reagan to Seek Okay for Canada's Sub Purchase," *Toronto Star*, 28 April 1988, A10; Jennifer Lewington and Ross Howard, "U.S. Won't Block Subs Plan, Reagan Says," *Globe and Mail*, 28 April 1988, A1. Also see Jonathan Manthorpe, "U.S. Vow to Canada May Aid French Sub," *Defense News*, 2 May 1988, 1: "One Canadian involved in the competition for the submarine fleet said last week it would be absolute folly for the government to hold itself hostage to the approval of Congress where there already has been vocal disquiet with the project."

[61]Herbert H. Denton, "Reagan: Canada Can Buy Sub Reactors," *Washington Post*, 28 April 1988, A1. Also see Michael S. Serrill, "Go Ahead Friend, and Dive Right In," *Time*, 9 May 1988, 47.

[62]DND briefing on the White Paper, National Defence Headquarters, Ottawa, 5 June 1987.

[63]Richard Halloran, "U.S. Suspicious over Canada Atom-Sub Plan," *New York Times*, 4 May 1987, 14.

[64]Charles E. Bennett, "Tough Questions Rise to the Surface," *Globe and Mail*, 29 October 1987, A7.

[65]John F. Burns, "Canada May Lose Nuclear Sub Plan," *New York Times*, 27 November 1987, 21.

[66]Jonathan Manthorpe, "Admiral Tries to Sink Canada's Submarines," *Ottawa Citizen*, 22 April 1988, A9.

[67]Frank J. Gaffney, Jr., "Could Canada's Subs Torpedo NATO Navies?," *Globe and Mail*, 12 April 1988, A7. For an impassioned rejoinder to this article, written by no less a figure than Canada's Ambassador to the United States, see Allan Gotlieb, "Canadian Sub Deal Will Go Forward," *Defense News*, 2 May 1988, 24.

[68]"Canada's SSN Buy Faces Opposition in US Congress," *Jane's Defence Weekly*, 26 March 1988, 551; "Arctic Antic," *Economist*, 7 May 1988, 14. Also see Anthony Cordesman's argument that the SSNs would "mortgage Canadian defence investment funds for a generation." Cordesman is a national security adviser to Senator John McCain, an Arizona Republican who is a member of the Senate Armed Services Committee. "True Cost of Subs Will Bleed Military Defence Expert Says," *Winnipeg Free Press*, 21 April 1988, 26.

[69]George C. Wilson, "Transfer of U.S. Nuclear Sub Technology Considered," *Washington Post*, 22 March 1988, 4.

[70]"From the Editor in Chief," *Journal of Defense & Diplomacy* 6, 3 (1988).

[71]Mike O'Brien, "Comment: Sovereignty Crisis," *The Wednesday Report: Canada's Defence News Bulletin*, 13 April 1988.

12

Parting of the Waves? The Strategy and Politics of the SSN Decision

Joel J. Sokolsky

INTRODUCTION

When both the *Washington Post* and the *Economist* run editorials on Canadian defense policy in the same week,[1] it is clear that Ottawa is planning something truly extraordinary. This unprecedented transatlantic interest began with the announcement in last year's White Paper on defense[2] that Canada would acquire ten to twelve nuclear-powered attack submarines (SSNs). Not since the nuclear weapons controversy of the early 1960s has a defense issue attracted so much attention at home and abroad, and for good reason. Although the SSNs are to be used in an anti-submarine warfare (ASW) capacity consistent with the long-standing ASW emphasis on the Canadian Navy, the program has raised major questions concerning cost, technological feasibility and nuclear proliferation.[3] The proposal to acquire SSNs has also prompted much open discussion about the strategic and political fundamentals of Canadian defense policy.

This chapter examines the SSN decision from the standpoint of strategy and politics. What threats to Canada and the West are they supposed to counter and where? What is the relationship between the SSNs and Arctic sovereignty? To what extent would their acquisition complement or clash with recent trends in U.S. maritime strategy?

I will look at the SSN program in the context of Canada-U.S. relations and in the wider NATO (North Atlantic Treaty Organization) framework. Does the program signal a shift in Canadian policy toward the Alliance and how could this be related to the emergence of a new transatlantic bargain between the United States and the European allies? Finally, will the "balanced fleet" of the Mulroney government balance at home? To a certain degree, foreign skepticism about the SSN program is being fed by political uncertainty and an apparent lack of widespread public support within Canada.

Maritime Command (MARCOM), which sank into strategic and political obscurity since the last White Paper, is finally making waves. It is not yet clear whether the proposal for SSNs will propel it forward or swamp it.

THE SEA-BASED THREATS TO CANADA

The proposal to equip MARCOM with SSNs highlights rather than alters the roles of Canada's navy in national and collective defense. Since the rearmament of the 1950s, Canadian naval forces have been geared primarily for ASW operations to support NATO and to defend North America. Given the relative weakness of the Soviet Navy for much of the Cold War period, protection of the allied sea lines of communication (SLOC) in the event of a war in Europe dominated the Navy's planning and posture. Naval forces were concentrated on the East coast where they were earmarked for NATO's Supreme Allied Commander, Atlantic (SACLANT). Canada was given specific responsibility for a wide area of the Northwest Atlantic (the CANLANT area) and the East coast commander (now the commander of MARCOM) was subordinate to SACLANT.

The overwhelmingly NATO/Atlantic orientation of the Navy has meshed well with Canada-U.S. bilateral maritime cooperation. Using ships, planes and submarines, as well as the American underwater sound surveillance system (SOSUS), the two countries continually monitor the seaward approaches to the continent, just as the air forces cooperate in air surveillance. In contrast to air defense, however, no single bilateral command structure was established. Since 1946, the Military Cooperation Committee (MCC) of the Permanent Joint Board on Defense (PJBD) has prepared maritime sub-plans to support the Canada-U.S. Basic Security Plan, but the extent of actual day-to-day naval coordination varies from coast to coast. In the East, bilateral maritime cooperation is largely subsumed under NATO's Atlantic Command, specifically the WESTLANT area. Given that there are no other allied naval forces operating in the Western Atlantic, Canada's MARCOM works closely with the U.S. Navy's 2nd Fleet. In the Pacific, Canada's forces (MARPAC) work with the U.S. 3rd Fleet, based at Pearl Harbor and have specific responsibility for a wide area extending off the Canadian coast over 1,000 nautical miles westward from Vancouver Island and north to Alaska. Strictly speaking, all North American maritime defense in the Pacific, as well as the Arctic, should fall under NATO since the continent is included in the Treaty area. In reality, the Alliance is not involved in the Pacific and there is very little cooperation with regard to the Arctic.

In the context of the East-West balance of power, the maritime defense of North America has long been a strategic backwater. Even the advent of Soviet ballistic missile submarines did not prompt the U.S. Navy (USN) to devote more to continental defense. As the range of Soviet sea-launched ballistic missiles (SLBMs) increased, their SSBNs did not have to approach North America to hit targets in the United States. Soviet SSBNs and SSNs were located in continental waters, but the numbers were not sufficient to cause the USN to shift from a primarily offensive posture to a defensive one.

One of the basic premises of the 1987 White Paper, and one of the key justifications for the SSN program, is that the maritime approaches to North America are going to become more important for the navies of both super-powers.[4] The increased strategic importance of Canadian waters requires a "balanced fleet." It will still be a primarily ASW fleet postured to contribute to collective defense at sea. However, it will be one with better balance in terms of where it can operate (all three oceans), and in its mix of ASW platforms. The SSNs are considered essential to achieving this balance.

The USSR's attack submarines will continue to be MARCOM's prime concern in all three oceans. In the case of the Atlantic and NATO, the Soviet SSN threat is still viewed as directed against allied SLOC. In a sense, this threat, which has existed since the Cold War, is a function not so much of Soviet maritime strategy, but of the Alliance's plans, especially those related to flexible response. In order to sustain conventional resistance beyond a period of a few days, NATO will require a massive sealift from the United States, despite significant progress in airlift and prepositioning.[5] Improvements in Soviet naval capabilities, such as the range of their air-, surface-, and submarine-launched anti-shipping cruise missiles, have heightened the threat to NATO at sea, making it likely that the Alliance will suffer heavy losses in a European reinforcement effort.

The increased threat to allied SLOC does not require a change in missions for Maritime Command. Indeed, it only confirms the importance of its continuing commitment to NATO ASW efforts. The addition of nuclear submarines to the forces Canada earmarks for SACLANT will improve MARCOM's ability to contribute to SLOC protection, especially given the range of Soviet anti-shipping missiles and possible under-ice transits by their SSNs through Canadian waters. The combination of the SSNs and the new Canadian Patrol Frigate (CPF), will also afford MARCOM a greater capability to contribute to allied ASW operations in the Eastern Atlantic and European coastal waters where the threat is expected to be greatest.

The rationale for the balanced ASW fleet goes beyond meeting what is essentially an unaltered threat in the Atlantic. Were Canada to continue to concentrate its Navy primarily in the Atlantic, it is unlikely that the government would have decided for the acquisition of nuclear-powered submarines. The Alliance needs more surface ships, as useful as the SSNs would be. In asking for an additional six CPFs in 1984, the Department of National Defence (DND) said that, "the shortfall of surface combatants has been the most crucial deficiency of NATO's maritime forces" and thus the Department had "assigned the highest priority" to getting additional frigates.[6] The White Paper gives the Navy those ships, but no more, opting for the SSNs instead. The financial as well as intra-alliance political cost of this decision can only be justified if continued threats are expected not only from the Atlantic, but especially from the Pacific and Arctic Oceans.

Soviet attack submarines regularly patrol off the North American coasts. The Soviet Navy does not place a high priority on tracking U.S. SSBNs. It has difficulty with strategic ASW because of the quietness and global dispersal of the American boats.[7] Nevertheless, Soviet SSNs do operate in North American waters. They will patrol near U.S. SSBN bases and attempt to trail the submarines as they leave port.[8] The USN and MARCOM try to keep track of Soviet SSNs approaching the continent just as the United States Air Force (USAF) and Air Command (AIRCOM) continually monitor for Soviet aircraft under NORAD.

As noted, Canada and the U.S. have been cooperating in meeting the submarine threat in the Atlantic since the Cold War. Cooperation has been less extensive in the Pacific, where Canada has had fewer forces. This is something the White Paper seeks to change in what it calls the "growing importance of the Asia-Pacific region." It is a region of "rapid change" with vast forces confronting each other, including a growing Soviet naval capability. Particular attention is drawn to the rise of Japan as a world economic power which has become Canada's second largest trading partner and a leading foreign investor.[9]

The growing economic importance of Japan, Korea and other countries in the Pacific is undeniable, and Canada should and will likely expand its trading and political relations in this region. This would be insufficient grounds for expanding MARCOM's forces on the West coast. For Canada, the flag does not follow trade. Its maritime forces do not exist to protect shipping, even in the Atlantic. The naval commitment to NATO arises because of the need to protect the SLOC for possible military sealifts. Canada has no similar commitments to the defense of Japan or any other countries on the Pacific rim. It can also be argued that in the event of a global war, it is extremely unlikely that Canada will continue to import automobiles and other manufactured goods from East Asia or continue to export lumber and pulp and paper. If the Soviet Navy poses a threat to transpacific trade, then Japan and not Canada should be doing more to contribute to the Western military posture.

The Soviet naval presence in the Pacific has increased over the last ten years and now numbers approximately ninety attack submarines, eighty-three surface combatants, two aircraft carriers, thirty-two ballistic missile submarines and 360 long-range naval aircraft.[10] A modern naval facility has been established at Cam Ranh Bay in Vietnam, affording more support for extended patrols and some freedom from the narrow straits leading to the Vladivostok base and the winter icing at Petropavlovsk.[11] The Pacific fleet is meant to counter not only the powerful U.S. forces in the region, including those based in the Philippines, but is also directed against China.

In the event of war, the Soviets' main concern in the Pacific, as in the Atlantic, would be to protect the homeland and their SSBN fleets from the USN. The American maritime strategy's forward defense and horizontal escalation plans call for immediate attacks upon the Soviet's Pacific forces. Soviet interest in engaging in a large-scale effort to cut the Pacific SLOC is unclear. As Michael MccGwire points out, in a world war the USSR would initially attempt to keep Japan neutral or at least to make it "refrain from active belligerence." A long, drawn-out anti-shipping campaign would not necessarily serve this objective. "However, if Soviet policies were to go disastrously wrong, and Japan should join the West as a fully committed belligerent, then the Soviets would surely resort to rapid, brutal and certain methods rather than the oblique approach of commerce war."[12] The USSR would not forego attacks on shipping, if only to tie down American forces that might otherwise move against Soviet territory and the navy. This could include attacks near the North American coast. The Soviets would want to prevent the U.S. from reinforcing Japan and/or Korea. At the same time, they "could find other ways of attacking crucial supplies shipped by sea besides an indiscriminate campaign against shipping."[13]

That the main action in a war would likely take place closer to Asia than North America does not undermine the case for an enhanced Canadian naval presence in the Pacific. Soviet forces could move further out, and even if they didn't, the USN will have to move west and would benefit from larger Canadian forces. Moreover, Soviet SSNs are increasing their patrols off the Canadian coast and in the area for which Canada is responsible under arrangements with the United States. Oil from Alaska moves through these waters. Also present in the area are Soviet intelligence-gathering vessels. More important is the Strait of Juan De Fuca which leads to the USN's SSBN base at Bangor. This heightened naval activity is complemented by a marked increase in the number of Soviet aircraft which have appeared over Alaska and the Pacific coasts and have been intercepted by USAF and AIRCOM fighters.[14]

The Soviet maritime threat here should not be exaggerated. However, as in the Atlantic, there is a requirement for continual surveillance. The problem is that Canada's West coast maritime force of eight surface ships with little sea-borne helicopter ASW capability, four *Auroras*, three short-range patrol aircraft, and no submarines is wholly inadequate even for the peacetime surveillance of Canadian territorial waters, let alone the vast ocean areas for which Canada is responsible. Given even marginal increases in Soviet capabilities, it can be expected that the U.S. will assume a more active role in this area. The USN has stepped-up its operations, as has the USAF. Even the U.S. Army is conducting more frequent exercises in Alaska, including the Aleutian Islands.[15]

It cannot be assumed that the United States will share all the information on its own and Soviet naval movements. As former Deputy MARCOM Commander, Rear-Admiral F. W. Crickard, told a Parliamentary Committee in 1985:

> It is noteworthy that Canada is the beneficiary of much more data from the American undersea monitoring system in the Atlantic than in the Pacific, where Canada does not currently share in the burden of underwater surveillance apart from periodic Aurora Maritime air patrols. The message is clear — participation in joint operations opens doors to intelligence that would otherwise be closed to Canada.[16]

In fact, while naval cooperation is close in the Atlantic, even there, the USN gives Canada information on the movement of its submarines only on a restricted basis. When not operating directly under SACLANT, the movement of the three Canadian submarines is coordinated with, but not controlled by a NATO-sponsored "water-management" regime. As with submarine operating authorities (SUBOPAUTH), MARCOM issues submarine movement messages (SUBNOTES) to its own submarines and sends a copy of each SUB-NOTE to the appropriate Submarine Movement Advisory Authority (SMAA). In the Western Atlantic, the SMAA is SACLANT's subordinate command COMSUBWESTLANT. It monitors movements of all submarines and informs SUBOPAUTHs of possible interference. COMSUBWESTLANT may ask for changes in national submarine movements.

While COMSUBWESTLANT is an allied command, its operational staff consists entirely of the officers of the U.S. COMSUBLANT, which is the principal American submarine command in the Atlantic. Canada will inform the U.S. through COMSUBWESTLANT of its submarine movements, but the USN need not reciprocate and without any Canadians on the COMSUB-WESTLANT staff, MARCOM would not know of such movements.[17] With only three older submarines, the need to share information fully has not been great in the Atlantic, or in the Pacific where not even the NATO arrangements apply. A Canadian SSN fleet, it is hoped, will elicit a more equal exchange of information with the USN by providing a larger contribution to the maritime defense of the continent.

The requirement for additional surveillance in all three oceans is also justified on the grounds of the emergence of a new sea-based strategic nuclear threat — the sea-launched cruise missile (SLCM). Because it sees its primary mission as sea denial in the face of superior Western naval forces, the Soviet Navy has long placed special emphasis on anti-shipping missiles, both nuclear and conventionally armed, capable of being fired from surface ships, long-range maritime aircraft, and submarines. Until the 1970s, the USN did not develop similar weapons, but during that decade the United States moved ahead with a long-range SLCM, the *Tomahawk*, capable of anti-shipping strikes but primarily to be used for land attack. The *Tomahawk* has a range of 2,000 kilometres (km) and can carry either a conventional or nuclear warhead. The wide deployment of this SLCM on the USN's surface ships and SSNs has increased the number of naval platforms capable of striking the Soviet Union or Eastern Europe. Whether prompted by the U.S. or by its past success in sea-based missiles, the Soviet Union is now believed to have developed its own version of the *Tomahawk*, the *SS-NX-21* and is working on an improved SLCM, the *SS-NX-24*. While the *SS-NX-21* can be fired from the standard torpedo tubes of a number of Soviet attack submarines, the *SS-NX-24* will need a new or reconfigured submarine such as the *Yankee* SSBN.[18]

Thus far, deployment of the *SS-NX-21* has been slower than predicted. Moreover, there is no consensus that when deployed, Soviet long-range SLCMs will be primarily targeted on North America. They would be more effective in a European theater role where they would allow the Soviets to out-flank British and NATO air defenses and reduce the need for long-range ground interdiction aircraft.[19] Given the existing Soviet ballistic missile threat against North America, SLCMs would not greatly increase Soviet interconti-nental strategic strike capabilities. There is, however, concern that SLCMs, like the bomber-carried Air-Launched Cruise Missiles (ALCM) will give the Soviets the opportunity for "precusor" and "decapitation" strikes against "soft" targets in North America such as communications facilities, surveil-lance systems, and naval and air bases. The SLCM threat is also a factor in the American Air Defense Initiative research program.[20] Coupled with these efforts has been heightened concern about Soviet SSNs patrolling off North America. Because there are so many potential targets close to the U.S. East and West coasts, even the existing shorter-range Soviet SLCMs are considered a threat.[21]

It is expected that should the Soviets move ahead deployment of their *SS-NX-21s* and *-24s*, some will be targeted on Canadian installations such as air bases or radar facilities.[22] Perhaps more important is the fact that with their increased ranges, these weapons can be launched against targets in the U.S. from Canadian waters or waters for which Canada is responsible. At the very least, the SSNs might attempt transit through these waters.

While transit and firing from the Canadian Arctic would be difficult, there are certain routes and points that might be attractive to the Soviets that would bring their SLCMs within range of targets in the United States. The Canadian government acknowledges that it has yet to find a Soviet SSN in the Arctic (although given the state of its capabilities, it could not know if they were there). Ottawa argues that such a threat could develop: "that the Soviets have the weapons, the launch platforms and the capability to make Arctic deployments is sufficient cause for concern."[23] Overall, a new SLCM threat would again increase U.S. concern about Canada's submarine surveillance capabilities and provide an additional rationale for balancing the Canadian ASW forces with SSNs of their own and placing more of them in the Pacific and Arctic.

In the Pacific and Atlantic, the greater speed, area coverage and staying power of SSNs would allow Canada to maintain more effective and more continual surveillance further out to sea, i.e., at the range of Soviet SLCMs. In the Arctic, SSNs would add a heretofore non-existent capability. Nuclear submarines would have the same impact at sea that the modernization of NORAD's radars and the northern deployment of CF-18 fighters are expected to have on the Soviet bomber/ALCM threat: they will enhance deterrence and stability by improving surveillance of the approaches to the continent.

The acquisition of nuclear-powered submarines has been criticized because it indicates a lack of Canadian support for arms control solutions to the SLCM threat.[24] The SALT II agreement carried a protocol on SLCMs in which the two superpowers agreed to a two-year ban on deployment of SLCMs with ranges in excess of 600 km. When the protocol expired on 31 December 1981, the Reagan administration moved ahead vigorously with its SLCM program and now plans a force of over 2,600 SLCMs with an unknown number being nuclear-armed. In the current round of strategic arms-control negotiations, the Soviets have again raised the SLCM issue, calling for limits on the number of conventional and nuclear-armed, long-range SLCMs (600 of the former and 400 of the latter) and restrictions on which platforms could carry them.[25]

Limitations on the number of SLCMs would ease Canadian concerns and therefore Ottawa may well encourage the United States to include such limitations in any comprehensive strategic arms-control agreement. However, in light of the wide deployment of these weapons among the USN's forces and continued Soviet development, it is unlikely that this new weapon will be totally eliminated. Thus, an SLCM threat in the future is almost certain. Moreover, since Soviet SLCMs are expected to be placed on existing SSNs and reconfigured *Yankee* SSBNs, the continued patrolling off North America by these submarines would require additional Canadian surveillance regardless of any arms-control arrangements covering SLCMs. Even if agreements could be reached on prohibiting SSN patrols near the coasts of both superpowers, verification of compliance would require essentially the same type of surveillance MARCOM now undertakes in the Atlantic and would like to perform in the Pacific and the Arctic. For sovereignty reasons, it would be preferable if Canada could verify compliance in its own waters.

THE ARCTIC SSNs AND U.S. MARITIME STRATEGY

The maritime emphasis of the White Paper comes at a time when the "maritime strategy" of the United States Navy continues to generate considerable controversy and even unease.[26] Among the many criticisms directed against the White Paper, especially the nuclear-propelled submarines, is that Canada will be drawn into the maritime strategy, particularly in the Arctic.[27] As noted earlier, the naval forces proposed by the government are partially viewed as being necessary in order for Canada to fully participate in the defense of North America, notably in Arctic waters, in order to prevent unilateral American efforts there. However, it is not clear that the naval policies of the White Paper will either draw Canada into U.S. naval strategy in a manner different than it has been involved in the past, or that enhanced Canadian capabilities will inevitably elicit greater cooperation between MARCOM and the USN in the Arctic.

In assessing the possible impact of trends in U.S. maritime strategy on Canadian defense policy, it is important to recall that the Canadian Navy has been closely involved with American naval strategy since 1945. Indeed, the entire postwar Canadian maritime posture makes no sense except in the context of collective defense. This includes both nuclear and conventional defense. Given the widespread dispersal of nuclear weapons among U.S. naval forces, it has become almost impossible to distinguish between nuclear and non-nuclear maritime forces. To the extent that Canada's maritime forces cooperate with those of the U.S., for example, by joining carrier task forces, they are linked to the American sea-based nuclear posture. Canada is similarly linked by helping to monitor the approaches to the American SSBN bases, thereby contributing to the credibility of the sea-based strategic nuclear deterrent.

The maritime strategy developed by the USN is basically a variation, although a significant one, on the role of maritime forces in U.S. strategy since World War II. That role has been "transoceanic," directed toward the support of American allies and interests throughout the world, rather than the immediate security of the United States against rival maritime forces.[28] As such, the overall maritime strategy of the U.S. has been coalition oriented, especially with regard to NATO, and forward in that naval forces were to support land and air forces ashore and engage the Soviet Navy close to the Eurasian landmass. The USN also acquired a role in the American strategic nuclear posture, initially with carrier-based aircraft and later with SSBNs. The bulk of the USN's capabilities were directed toward securing use of the seas for reinforcement and resupply and for the projection of conventional force ashore.

For most of the 1950s and the 1960s, the United States and its allies did not face a serious challenge from Soviet maritime forces. By the mid-seventies, Soviet forces at sea had improved markedly and NATO was no longer assured of being able to secure immediate use of the sea in the event of a land war in

Europe. The Soviets also acquired a sea-based intercontinental nuclear strike capability of their own. Nevertheless, the USN remains the superior force and indeed its maritime strategy is based upon the exploitation of that superiority.

As elaborated in public in 1986, by the then Chief of Naval Operations, Admiral James D. Watkins, the maritime strategy is a broad concept for the conduct of global war — a war in which it is assumed Europe will still be the prime Soviet target. The goal of the strategy is to "use maritime forces in combination with the efforts of our sister services and the forces of our allies to bring about war termination on favorable terms."[29] One way to do this would be to deny the Soviets the luxury of concentrating all their forces against Western Europe by horizontally escalating the conflict to include the engagement of Soviet forces and those of their allies throughout the world.

Not only will a global forward maritime counter-offensive present the Soviets with a wider war, it will serve to meet NATO's maritime needs, in particular, the requirement to secure the Atlantic SLOC. In order to secure the SLOC, NATO maritime strategy has envisioned a combination of barrier ASW, chiefly along the Greenland-Iceland-United Kingdom (GIUK) gap as well as open-ocean escort of reinforcement and resupply shipping. With the growing power of the Soviet fleet, its attack submarines and its naval air forces, the Alliance has also been planning a more forward SLOC protection posture. Such a posture would be necessary for the defense of Norway which lies beyond the GIUK gap. The USN's maritime strategy goes further. It calls for defending the SLOC by putting direct pressure on the USSR in its home waters. As one U.S. admiral told a Congressional committee in 1984:

> In the absence of forward area pressure by our submarines, they (the Soviets) could concentrate major forces against supply lines we need for NATO reinforcement and against other naval forces. In short, they can pose many of the same problems for us that we do for them — problems that can be countered effectively by state-of-the-art submarines operating in their backyard.[30]

The forward operations of American SSNs are intended not only to tie-up Soviet attack submarines, but to threaten Soviet SSBNs in their northern bastions. Unlike the USN's ballistic missile submarines, Soviet SSBNs do not generally patrol in the open oceans. Most of them stay close to port or patrol in the central Arctic or in the shallow marginal seas above the USSR's wide northern continental shelf. Some may also deploy closer to the Canadian Arctic archipelago.[31] In the event of war, it is expected that the Soviets would collect their SSBNs in the North and extend their Arctic Ocean Theatre of Military Operations (OTVD) roughly 1,500 nautical miles out from the North Pole. They would attempt to deny entry to enemy forces to the Arctic bastions as well as the Barents Sea and Sea of Okhotsk, from which SLBMs can reach targets in the United States.[32]

In seeking to enter these bastions, the maritime strategy has several objectives. The first is one of damage limitation in the event of a strategic nuclear war. This is not particularly new since U.S. ASW efforts have never been exclusively directed against attack submarines.[33] The maritime strategy places special emphasis upon counter-SSBN operations as a kind of undersea equivalent of the counter-force capabilities being developed in the Intercontinental Ballistic Missile (ICBM) and bomber legs of the American strategic nuclear triad.

Strategic ASW is expected to be effective during a conventional war. In this context, a second objective would be to provide additional horizontal escalation, threatening the USSR close to home in order to compensate for possible U.S. and NATO losses elsewhere. This is connected with a third objective. Knowing that the Soviets put enormous resources into defending their SSBNs, horizontal escalation of the war at sea into SSBN bastions would help to tie-down Soviet naval forces, making them unavailable to attack NATO sea lines.[34]

The fourth, and most controversial, objective of the counter-SSBN operations during a conventional war would be to threaten and perhaps destroy these submarines as a means of applying nuclear leverage over the USSR. The USN argues that by degrading the Soviet's strategic nuclear reserves, the USSR, which places great weight upon the nuclear correlation of forces, will be less disposed to escalate to the nuclear level, and more disposed to terminate hostilities on conditions favorable to the U.S. and its allies.[35] The development of counter-SSBN capabilities is justified by the need to strengthen deterrence and stability, and is consistent with recent trends in overall American nuclear strategy. As Tom Stefanick observes in his recent work on strategic ASW:

> US nuclear policy is partly driven by the view that if Soviet leaders perceive ALL* their strategic nuclear forces to be theoretically vulnerable, then they will not be willing to risk any confrontation with the United States for fear that the escalation from such a conflict will lead to a level of warfighting in which they believe themselves to be inferior. Thus, the sum of the attrition threat from a conventional war — plus the threat from a disarming strike against land-based weapons — is becoming an explicit part of the US foreign policy of deterring direct Soviet interference with the United States.[36]

*Emphasis in original.

The maritime strategy is not without its critics in the United States, especially among the other services. Objections have been raised on grounds of strategic soundness, arms control and stability concerns and feasibility. As the plan of a single service, the maritime strategy cannot be equated with overall U.S. strategy and there is no certainty, should a crisis or war arise, that the USN would be directed to conduct the entire scope of operations envisioned in the strategy. In addition, the six-hundred ship Navy, upon which the strategy was based, experienced cut-backs in 1987 under the new U.S. Secretary of Defense, Frank Carlucci (leading to the resignation of the Secretary of the Navy in early 1988).

Nevertheless, it is unlikely that either forward defense or efforts to improve American Arctic capabilities will be abandoned, regardless of doubts and difficulties concerning the strategic ASW plans of the USN. The forward ASW approach appears to be part of a new master anti-submarine warfare strategy.[37] In this strategy the Arctic figures highly and the USN has been upgrading its *Los Angeles* class SSNs for under-ice operations. It is also developing a new class, the *Seawolf*, with an even greater under-ice capability as well as twice the weapons load of the *Los Angeles* SSN, including SLCMs.[38] The Defense Advanced Research Projects Agency (DARPA) is engaged in an Arctic Surveillance Program, attempting to develop "specialized surveillance techniques for ice-covered regions, beginning with a through-the-ice acoustic sensor" called Ice Pick, to be launched from the air.[39] As new weapons and under-ice technologies are developed, it can be expected that the USN will want to test its capabilities and thus peacetime probing of the USSR's Arctic regions will become part of its routine operations.

Up to a certain point, the maritime emphasis and naval acquisitions of the 1987 White Paper mesh well with trends in U.S. maritime strategy. This is not, however, because Canada subscribes to these trends and will be posturing its forces to complement them. Rather, it is because under the White Paper proposals, MARCOM will be undertaking the same kinds of roles that it has for nearly forty years — ASW in support of NATO and for North American defense, with the latter becoming more important. If, in the event of war the USN moves forward, it will as is now the case under NATO plans be looking to Canada to supply convoy escort forces. The United States may well also benefit by enhanced Canadian capabilities to monitor the Atlantic and Pacific approaches to North America. Although the USN would prefer Canada to concentrate on air and surface ASW forces, the balancing of Canada's fleet with SSNs will improve the allied position at sea in rear areas. If needed, Canada will also have the forces and capabilities to move forward with the USN and other NATO navies.

Critics of the submarine decision have charged that their potential role in the Arctic will draw Canada into the USN's maritime strategy. It is evident though, that the surface ships and long-range maritime patrol aircraft, as well as the conventionally powered submarines, which these critics propose as an alternative, are equally compatible with the USN's maritime strategy. It is difficult, however, to see how this potential linkage can be foreclosed unless Canada were to abandon monitoring its coasts, stop contributing to SACLANT, and allow the U.S. to provide for the entire maritime defense of the continent.

It is in the Arctic that Canadian interests could clash with U.S. maritime strategy in two ways. The first relates to the status of the Northwest Passage. In drawing straight baselines around the archipelago in 1985, Canada reaffirmed its position that the passage is internal Canadian waters. The United States disputes this, primarily because of the precedent it would set. If other states with straits that went through archipelagoes adopted a similar position, it might hamper the global movement of U.S. naval forces. In January 1988, Ottawa and Washington signed an agreement whereby the U.S. is now obligated to seek Canadian consent for the transit of its icebreakers through waters claimed by Canada as internal. Neither government abandoned its position on the legal status of the Northwest Passage though and the dispute may have to go to international arbitration. Nevertheless, a repeat of the *Polar Sea* incident is unlikely.

The dispute over the status of the Northwest Passage could be resolved if the U.S. accepted Canada's claim that being ice-covered most of the year, it is a special case. Therefore, recognition of it as internal waters would not change the status of other straits around the world. Moreover, the Soviets have declared the Northeast Passage internal waters for security reasons and it might well enhance North American security and bilateral maritime cooperation if Washington agreed to treat the Northwest Passage the same.[40]

It is still uncertain though, how much and what kind of cooperation both countries want in the Arctic. This doubt points to a second way in which Canadian and American interests may clash in the region. It is more complex and will be unaffected by the recent agreement on icebreakers or even a settlement of differing claims regarding the Northwest Passage. The USN's prime interest in the Arctic concerns its counter-SSBN operations; to increase the vulnerability of the Soviet fleet in its bastions. Soviet SSBNs are unlikely to enter the Canadian Arctic archipelago. Given the range of their SLBMs, there is no operational advantage for them to do so. Moreover, the size of their latest SSBNs, the *Delta* IVs and especially the *Typhoons*, would make transit through this region extremely difficult. If the Canadian Arctic is to figure at all in the USN's strategic ASW plans, it would be as a transit route into the Soviet Arctic bastions by attack submarines. The Canadian archipelago is not, however, the best avenue into the Soviet Arctic; its shallow waters and narrow channels make navigation difficult and lend themselves to being blocked by Soviet ASW forces.[41] Better access can be achieved by going around Norway.

The situation could change. George Lindsey has pointed out that the Soviets might view their defended Arctic bastions as becoming untenable because of advances in U.S. technology. They might decide to disperse their SLBMs, putting fewer missiles on more SSBNs and scattering them more widely, including closer to the Canadian Arctic. For its part, the USN might find that Soviet ASW defenses astride easier routes into the bastions will make the Canadian routes attractive as a means to "outflank" these defenses.[42] Such activity would not be precluded by the recent agreement on the Northwest Passage.

Given the highly secretive nature of the USN's submarine movements — a secrecy which can extend to allies as well as other branches of the U.S. military — it is unlikely that the United States Navy would welcome the presence of Canadian SSNs in the Arctic. Since two submarines cannot occupy the same space at the same time, the USN will have to supply Canada with information on its movements, which MARCOM would be in a position to verify on its own. The USN's freedom for unilateral activity in the region would be curtailed.

This indeed appears to be one of Ottawa's key objectives in acquiring a fleet of SSNs. To be sure, the SSN will greatly enhance ASW capabilities in the Atlantic and Pacific and will be useful in monitoring any Soviet movements in the Arctic as well. However, it is only in the Arctic that Canada currently lacks any credible sub-surface surveillance capability whatsoever, in waters it claims as sovereign. It is mainly there that MARCOM relies almost entirely upon information supplied by the USN under NATO and bilateral arrangements.

Despite the reluctance of submariners in the USN to share information on the Arctic movements of its SSNs, expanded bilateral cooperation in the region, assuming Canada acquires its own nuclear submarines, would seem to be in the U.S. national interest. The USN has global commitments. On a day-to-day basis, strategic ASW is not a high priority, and there are relatively few SSNs moving in the area, even fewer in Canadian waters. Informing Canada of such movements would hardly constitute a blow to the U.S. maritime posture. Moreover, such cooperation would require no new special bilateral arrangements with Canada. Either the NATO arrangements in the Atlantic, or the existing bilateral cooperation, would simply be extended and expanded to cover the Arctic. Coupled with American recognition of Canadian claims regarding the Northwest Passage, the United States would be assured of more solid Canadian support for collective defense in the region.

Ironically, it may be Canada rather than the United States that would have difficulties with more cooperative defense arrangements in the Arctic, if those arrangements allowed the peacetime transit of American SSNs through the Canadian waters into the Soviet Arctic. Having secured legal and military agreements that respect Canadian sovereignty, Ottawa would be unlikely to deny the USN permission for such transits. Moreover, if as noted, U.S. pressure on Soviet SSBN bastions from other directions becomes too great, the Soviets may seek to hide more of their fleet closer to the Canadian archipelago, making it even more attractive to the United States. The greater the American activity in the region, the more likely that Soviet SSNs will also enter the Canadian Arctic to monitor in peacetime, and in war, to stop USN attack submarines threatening their SSBNs.[43] Therefore, to the extent that a greater

Canadian Arctic capability and new arrangements with the USN do not preclude use of the region for counter-SSBN operations, it could result in an increase in activities by both superpowers, to the detriment of Canadian as well as American security.

Becoming a silent partner in the strategic ASW aspects of the maritime strategy would also be at odds with the approach Canada has taken to arms control and strategic stability. Ottawa has not taken a specific position on strategic ASW. Generally, Canada favors deep cuts in strategic nuclear arms while recognizing that nuclear deterrence will remain the basis for Western (and Canadian) defense for some time. Ottawa does not, however, favor warfighting approaches to deterrence based upon counter-force weapons and strategies, as these tend to undermine stability.[44] On these grounds, Canada should oppose the strategic ASW plans of the USN because their purpose is to place at bay the Soviet's assured second strike capability in peacetime and to systematically destroy it during a conventional war.

Yet, these arms control concerns must also be balanced against the reality that a Canadian decision to stay out of the Arctic with its own SSNs (which the USN would prefer) is unlikely to persuade Washington to abandon either strategic-ASW or the possible use of the Canadian Arctic by American SSNs. Even if an agreement were reached, wherein the U.S. recognized the Northwest Passage as internal waters, Canadian SSNs would still be needed in order for MARCOM to play a full role in Arctic defense as a means of fully exercising Canadian sovereignty.[45]

Changes in the maritime strategies and postures of both superpowers are likely to increase the importance of Canadian waters in the event of war, but more importantly, in the continuing peacetime naval competition. These changes are not dramatic and will not radically alter the role of seapower in the Soviet and American nuclear and conventional balance of power. They are significant for Canada mainly because they highlight the country's inadequate maritime capabilities; the result of a lack of spending in the 1970s, and a primarily NATO-orientation in naval forces since 1949. With the SSNs, the government has proposed the kind of balanced ASW forces it says Canada needs to contribute more to collective defense at sea in all three oceans, thus fostering both security and sovereignty.

Even if nuclear-powered submarines would meet Canadian interests better than a combination of conventionally powered submarines (SSK) and more frigates, are they the best weapons in the larger East-West strategic context? This is an important question, but it is one that can be asked about any weapons system an ally chooses to acquire. In the case of the Canadian SSN program, as with the whole panoply of nuclear and conventional weapons that constitute the Western strategic posture, no definitive answer can be given. The nuclear age has presented Canada with an unprecedented strategic environment, including the role of naval forces. The simple fact is that nobody, not the admirals or the political leaders and certainly not the academics, can say with any certainty what mixture and levels of weapons will assure security. Deterrence, after all, is ultimately based upon calculations about what would happen if deterrence fails. It seeks to influence Soviet behavior and decisions to undertake, or refrain from undertaking, certain actions under certain circumstances that can never be precisely defined. The NATO allies posture their forces according to hypothetical battles on land, in the air and at sea, which they hope to never fight by showing the Soviets that they are ready to fight them.

The Canadian SSN program has been criticized because it emphasizes North American defense rather than the protection of NATO SLOC. Yet, what is a more likely conflict scenario: one that involves a protracted conventional war in Europe with massive transatlantic convoys, or one in which the Soviets will use SLCMs in conjunction with other strategic weapons against North American targets? It is the case, that the Soviet long-range SLCM capability is limited and that their SSNs have not been identified in the Canadian Arctic. Even if the Soviet Union has only 100 SLCMs, some targets in North America would be vulnerable, and Arctic firing points could be used. Canada can no more ignore the present and potential threat from Soviet SSNs in its waters than the European allies can ignore the same threat in theirs. Moreover, the NATO convoy role only becomes crucial in the event of war, while the surveillance of the ocean approaches to North America is a day-to-day strategic necessity.

With the SSNs, Canada would indeed be acquiring weapons better suited to its own particular national interests. Yet the Alliance's two principal naval powers, the U.S. and the U.K., have both invested billions in their own preferred weapons; the British with the *Trident* SSBN and the Americans with the carrier battle-groups. Are these weapons any better for NATO than Canadian SSNs? It can be argued that the British SLBMs exist not to protect the U.S. or other European allies but, like the French nuclear weapons, to serve as a national deterrent force. As for the USN's carriers, their vulnerability to missile attack requires that they be surrounded by an array of ships. How many more surface escorts would be available for NATO convoy duty if these two navies had put greater efforts into SLOC protection?

Nor does arms control offer a clearly attainable and preferable alternative to Canada or its allies. It is unlikely that all SLCMs will be removed under a major strategic arms reduction agreement between the United States and the Soviet Union. Even if they were, attack submarines will not be removed from the superpowers' navies and these constitute the major threat facing Canada in North America and with regard to NATO. In one sense, major cuts in strategic systems would increase the importance of Canadian SSNs. If the number of SSBNs were reduced, but not the number of SSNs, then SSBNs would be more vulnerable to strategic-ASW. This could have the effect of increasing U.S. use of the Arctic as an avenue into Soviet SSBN bastions. It might also mean greater protection for American SSBNs in North American waters. In both cases, the need for Canadian SSNs would also be increased. A major reduction in nuclear weapons, without a reduction in conventional forces in Europe, will place more emphasis upon conventional deterrence, which in turn will mean a continuing importance for Canadian ASW forces.

In sum, Canada's SSN program makes as much strategic sense as most other elements of the Western military posture, and in some instances, a lot more.

THE TRANSATLANTIC POLITICS OF CANADIAN SSNs

In the final analysis, what is considered strategically sound within NATO is what is politically possible. This is the basis for the Alliance's flexible response strategy which Leon Sigal has aptly described as, "less a strategy than an agreement not to disagree over strategy."[46] In the always "troubled Alliance," problems with an individual member's defense policy tend to be highly political and in certain instances, somewhat theatrical. The allied reaction to Canada's SSN proposals has been no exception.

It is an understatement to say that had Canada's allies written the 1987 White Paper on defense, the one thing they would not have proposed for MAR-COM was nuclear attack submarines. John Moore, Editor of *Jane's Fighting Ships*, summed up foreign reaction by describing Canada's SSN plans as "startling."[47] The *Economist* characterizes them as an "Arctic antic," designed mainly for the protection of Canada's sovereignty from U.S. challenges appealing "to the anti-American plasma that flows through many Canadian veins." Canada should do "something useful" with its "extra defence cents, such as putting an armoured division or two into West Germany."[48] The *Washington Post* also saw the Canadian SSNs as mainly sovereignty weapons to be used for missions of its own choosing, not necessarily those of its allies.[49] In Washington and Brussels, there has been a marked coolness to Canada's decision to give its Navy an enhanced ASW capability.[50]

In the United States, several lawmakers have questioned whether the U.S. should approve the transfer of American technology if Canada decides to buy the British *Trafalgar* class SSN. It is being argued that because Canada has never built a submarine, let alone an SSN, it lacks the capability to build them. Questions have been raised about safety, one former Reagan administration official suggesting that Canada will try to cut costs, compromise safety and raise doubts about the SSN programs of the U.S. and Britain. Finally, it is contended that Canada simply cannot afford an SSN fleet.[51]

While some of these concerns are valid, the interest by U.S. lawmakers and some defense analysts suggests a deeper reason for this American opposition to the Canadian SSN program. The U.S. Navy's submariners simply do not want anyone, even an ally as close as Canada, operating under the polar ice. This would, as Canada indeed hopes, compel the USN to abandon its more or less unilateral approach to security in the Arctic. From the U.S. Navy's standpoint, the SSNs are primarily sovereignty weapons directed against it and not the Soviets. The Royal Navy, which enjoys a close relationship with the USN because of its SSNs, may share the American view out of concern that a Canadian SSN fleet would give Canada an entrance into this exclusive club. (This of course, is off-set by the British desire to sell Canada the means to buy in.)

Outside the USN, there is little enthusiasm for the Canadian SSN program. At their April 1988 summit meeting, President Reagan agreed to ask Congress to allow the transfer of *Trafalgar* technology. However, the Administration adopted a reserved approach, waiting to see if Ottawa will go ahead and how the outcome of the federal election would affect the SSN decision. There are several reasons why other Departments may not argue strongly against the Navy if the issue comes before Congress.

First, there is doubt that Canada will be able to pay for an SSN fleet given that it has had difficulty simply keeping MARCOM afloat. Ottawa estimates that the total cost of the program will be about $8 billion in 1986-87 dollars over twenty-seven years. Given the American experience, Washington expects costs to rise dramatically. Second, in terms of NATO requirement, surface ships are more important and the Canadian SSN program has already meant the cancellation of a third batch of new patrol frigates. Third, if Canada does indeed spend all that is necessary to build and sustain an SSN fleet, it may well have to reduce other military expenditures, in particular on land and air forces dedicated to NATO's central front. This American concern is shared by the European allies and is linked to the last, and perhaps most fundamental reason why the U.S. has misgivings not only about the SSNs, but also about the whole White Paper.

The maritime and North American defense emphasis of the policy is being interpreted as a partial turning away from NATO and Europe. "The problem for Canada," writes Charles Doran of the Johns Hopkins Center of Canadian Studies, "is that security begins as it does for the U.S. on the Elbe and not on the St. Lawrence." The continentalist emphasis of the White Paper will be seen in Europe "as the first step toward greater North American isolation. Sovereignty and security are not identical," Doran warns. Canada's search for the former could undermine the latter and lead to "fragmentation of the Alliance."[52]

Canada, of course, does not need to be reminded that its security is intimately tied to that of Europe. Since 1949, its defense policy has been overwhelmingly NATO-oriented. Under the White Paper's proposals, Ottawa will continue to spend nearly 10 percent of the defense budget just to maintain ground and air units in Germany. Many billions more will be required to equip the new armored division that will be dedicated to the central front. The maritime forces will also continue to support SACLANT, including the twelve new frigates, which will help meet NATO's current shortfall in surface forces available for SLOC protection. Most importantly, the impetus for increasing naval capabilities in North American waters does not arise because of specific Canadian national interests in having a greater maritime presence there. Canada does not expect to enforce its legal sovereignty claims by force of arms, or to adopt a neutralist position at sea. The naval posture set forth in the White Paper is a response to what Ottawa views as trends in the international security environment. It is the maritime strategies of its close ally, the United States, and their common adversary, the Soviet Union, that compel Canada to devote more resources to its posture at sea.

Still, American concerns are valid. In view of Canada's poor showing in defense spending in the past, the SSN program, if carried out in full, may well draw resources away from other forces, in particular the land forces dedicated to NATO Europe. Washington might accept a general re-orientation of Canadian defense policy, if indeed it maintained Canada's commitment to collective defense overall. The United States would benefit from an enhanced Canadian capability in North American waters. However, the United States must consider the wider Western Alliance context. Accepting a greater role for Canada in the maritime defense of the continent, one that complements the existing close links in air defense, could well have an impact upon the transatlantic ties of both Canada and the United States.

The American-European transatlantic bargain appears though, to be on the threshold of evolutionary yet profound change prompted by concerns on both sides of the ocean. From the U.S. perspective, there is the growing view that while an alliance with the West European democracies is essential to U.S. security, the United States can no longer sustain its present financial, military and political role in NATO given its global and domestic economic situation. In his recent work, *Beyond American Hegemony*, David Calleo has observed: "In a more plural world, the United States remains the world's most powerful country, but it is no longer an Atlas able to carry the global system on its shoulders...the fundamental challenge to American foreign policy has become what to do about this decline of American power in relation to the rest of the world."[53] Under present conditions, the European allies are "militarily underdeveloped" while the United States is militarily "overextended," a situation that bodes ill for the security of both. Calleo argues that the Europeans should assume more of the burden of deterrence in their region. The United States will remain engaged in collective defense, but under new arrangements that would enhance the political and military role of the allies. In this way NATO, unviable in its present form, would survive.

The Europeans are concerned about American disenchantment with NATO and the potential for a new round of U.S. isolationism and/or unilateralism based upon the view that the Alliance actually "weakens" the United States.[54] At the same time, in the wake of the INF Treaty, they may well seek a more identifiably European approach to security in Europe and relations with the Warsaw Pact.

There appears to be no immediate prospect that large numbers of U.S. forces will be withdrawn from Europe or that the essential elements of the American security guarantee will be altered. There is serious thinking within NATO about reformulating the transatlantic bargain in order to keep the Alliance together and the U.S. in Europe. On 18 May 1988, the North Atlantic Assembly's Committee on NATO in the 1990s released its report. It concluded that:

> A fundamental change has occurred in the U.S.-European relationship, reflecting the gradual, relative increase in the economic strength and the political potential of the West European members of the Alliance. Because of this change, the West European Allies should in the future share more effectively the political, economic and military responsibilities of Western defence and Alliance leadership. This need to adjust U.S. and European responsibilities in the Alliance should be confirmed in a new transatlantic bargain between the United States, Canada, and the European members of the Alliance.[55]

Among the recommendations of the Committee to promote a more efficient use of allied resources was one that called for more task specialization. The smaller allies in particular should "take on special tasks well suited to their geographic location and national resources as part of a tasking strategy organized on a European level and compatible with NATO planning requirements."[56]

The North Atlantic Council will move ahead with a long-term study of the future of the Alliance as suggested by the North Atlantic Assembly's report. It would be reasonable and necessary that in recasting the transatlantic bargain, Canada's role in NATO be examined as well as that of the United States and that the suggestion for greater task specialization be applied to Canada's contribution. Given resources and geographic location, the case can be made that the best contribution Canada can make to NATO security is at sea and in North America. From this standpoint, the SSN program should be welcomed in Europe. If carried through in its entirety, it will certainly provide the Alliance with a more appropriate and effective force than an armored division stationed in Germany.[57]

This is not to discount the political implications of putting Canadian resources into forces used outside the crucial central front. However, whether or not the SSN program has a negative impact upon Canada's relations with NATO will depend upon allied reaction. If the program is interpreted as a turning away from the Alliance, then the impact could well be negative. If Canada is pressured into canceling the SSNs, then the long-term consequence for

Ottawa's position in NATO is likely to be even more detrimental. If the SSNs are seen as an effort by Canada to meet its European, North American and national security interests within a framework of collective defense, the program can serve to strengthen transatlantic ties even as the character of the ties changes.

Allied fears and opposition to the Canadian SSN program may well vanish should it become clear that the program will proceed as planned. The Americans and Europeans will have no choice if they wish to maintain Canada within the Alliance. A Canadian decision to proceed will probably earn Ottawa more respect than one to drop the SSNs. Indeed, given the political capital already invested, cancellation would only confirm what Canada's allies have long suspected: when it comes to national security and sovereignty, Canada can be counted to talk and then balk at paying the bill.

THE SSNs AND DOMESTIC POLITICS: BALANCING THE FLEET AT HOME

Defense issues seldom figure highly in Canadian domestic politics and the merits or shortcomings of weapons systems for the Armed Forces are rarely a matter of public debate. In this sense, the nuclear submarine acquisition proposal is somewhat unique. Although the 1988 Federal election was fought on the Free Trade Agreement, defense issues, especially the SSN program, have been hotly debated in Canada since the release of the White Paper and the controversy will no doubt heat up as the Mulroney government moves to implement its defense agenda during its second term.

It is likely that the skepticism of Canada's allies about the SSNs is bolstered by electoral uncertainty and an apparent lack of strong domestic support for the program. The Liberal and New Democratic parties both vigorously oppose the SSN program, and have criticized the entire White Paper.[58] In the highly partisan setting of Canadian politics and in the bitter parliamentary environment that has characterized the Mulroney years, it is hardly surprising that the opposition parties have not supported the submarine program. Indeed they have singled out the SSNs as especially ill-suited to Canadian needs, and as indicative of all that is wrong with the White Paper and the Mulroney government's defense policy. The vehemence of the NDP and Liberal criticism of the SSNs may also account for the lack of strong public support for the submarines. In the case of the opposition parties, and in the case of public opinion, however, the SSN controversy seems to be masking a growing consensus on defense policy in Canada, at least in terms of what kinds of weapons the country needs and where it should deploy them.

The Liberals and especially the New Democrats have had a "field-day" with the opening pages of the White Paper with its strong endorsement of collective western defense and sinister characterization of the Soviet Union. In its April 1988 policy statement, the NDP said Canadian defense policy has to be based upon the "common security" of the East and West. The Party held to its plans to take Canada out of NATO and to renegotiate the arrangements for North American air defense. For their part, the Liberals would retain membership in NATO and NORAD, but like the NDP, say they would do more to achieve security through arms control, especially in the Arctic and with regard to air- and sea-launched cruise missiles. As with the Conservatives, the opposition parties stress the importance of sovereignty, but the approach is somewhat different than that put forth by Beatty in order to justify the SSNs. Whereas the White Paper stressed that Canadian sovereignty is best protected by contributing to collective defense at sea, particularly in North American waters, the opposition tends to stress the more national, non-military aspects of sovereignty protection.

Lost amid the charges of Cold War mongering and naive neutralism is the fact that among the three parties there is substantial agreement that the rebuilding of the Navy should be the top defense priority. The NDP and the Liberals both support the notion of a three-ocean fleet with more surface ships, *Auroras*, fixed sensors under the ice, and conventionally powered submarines. The consensus extends beyond maritime forces. The NDP and the Liberals would retain and augment air defense forces as well as ground forces stationed in Canada. While calling for more support for disarmament and détente, both opposition parties would spend more on defense than is currently being spent. This position appears to be in line with the public mood in Canada.

As in Europe, the Canadian public has become more concerned about the dangers of nuclear war in recent years and sees the arms race, rather than the Soviet Union, as the greatest threat to world peace. Canadians do not regard the two superpowers as morally equal and still favor being allied with the U.S. in NATO and NORAD.[59] But there is less confidence that the United States really wants arms control and a growing view that American policies can be as dangerous to world peace as those of the Soviet Union. While there continues to be a strong belief in the essential principles of nuclear deterrence, a recent poll conducted by the Canadian Institute for International Peace and Security indicated that 71 percent of Canadians believed that augmenting Western military strength was not the way to preserve the peace. There is widespread support for arms control and nearly 60 percent of the sample wanted Canada to become a nuclear weapons-free zone.[60] Yet the same poll also found that:

> Canadian enthusiasm for nuclear arms control is not, in fact, an antipathy toward armed defence in general. Nor does it simply or even necessarily spill over into the conventional area...Canadians support a maintained or stronger conventional defence effort. Asked simply whether Canadian defence forces ought to be larger, about the present size, or smaller, a strong majority, almost two thirds (63%), want

them to be larger. One third prefer them to be maintained at their present size. Only a small majority (5%) support reductions in Canadian forces.[61]

Nearly half the polling sample, 49 percent, favored the continued deployment of Canadian forces in Europe, consistent with widespread public support for NATO itself. At the same time, 63 percent would like to see the Europeans do more for their own defense.

Support for the SSNs has not been as strong as for general increases in defense spending. Some polls show it only as high as 47 percent,[62] while others as low as 32 percent, with less than 10 percent of the sample strongly in favor.[63] When, however, the question is posed in such a way that the SSNs are linked to the protection of Canada's Arctic sovereignty, support appears to markedly increase. Yet one government poll, which found 42 percent support for submarines to patrol the Arctic, did not mention nuclear submarines.[64]

Critics of the SSN program argue that the lack of public backing will undermine the consensus that exists within the country for the rebuilding of the forces, especially the Navy.[65] While a valid concern, it can also be argued that these critics are engaging in self-fulfilling prophecy. There is little wonder that public support is low, at odds with the general support for defense spending, given that the SSN program has been singled out as a radical departure from past defense acquisitions, too costly and too dangerous for Canada to undertake as well as being of little use for either sovereignty or security.

There are a number of reasons why the nuclear submarines have been so successfully singled out in this way. As noted, the SSN program has been characterized as indicative of the Mulroney government's anachronistic, misguided and slavishly pro-Reagan defense policy. It is surprising that while the White Paper has been interpreted outside Canada as quite a nationalistic, pro-sovereignty document, much of the criticism of it and the SSNs suggests a surrender of Canadian independence to a largely American-inspired global arms race.

Of course, Canada needs a Navy, a better Navy than the one it has, but another reason for the lack of support for the SSNs is that the cost of the program is usually juxtaposed against the cost of a conventional submarine fleet of four to six submarines, not against the fleet mix which the SSNs are to replace — that is, the conventional submarines and another six frigates and their ASW helicopters. Current estimates for the alternative fleet mix exceed the estimated cost of the SSN program.[66]

Even if the cost of the SSNs were less than the alternative fleet, there would still be strong opposition. Canada's SSNs will perform the same kind of ASW roles its surface ships, aircraft and conventional submarines do, only better. Critics associate the SSNs with the superpowers and the French and the British fleets. These countries, it is argued, have offensive, war-fighting navies, while the Canadian Navy, like the rest of its armed forces is postured only for defensive tasks. The notion that Canada would acquire a sophisticated weapon of war is being presented as somehow un-Canadian. That the new frigate, the *Aurora* aircraft, the CF-18 interceptor and proposed new main battle tanks are also sophisticated weapons of war is conveniently overlooked by critics of the SSN decision and, as a consequence, lost to the public.

Linked to this view is the most important reason why critics have been able to single out the SSNs amid a force posture they, by and large, support; the word "nuclear" is in the name. Even if the public is clear that they will not carry nuclear weapons, the very notion that Canada would deploy a weapon that uses nuclear technology flies in the face of the national self-perception of the country as staunchly non-nuclear. This image, carefully cultivated by previous governments, exists despite the fact that Canadian defense policy is based upon nuclear deterrence, and that both NATO and NORAD are fundamentally nuclear weapons-based collective defense organizations. It is significant that Canada has decided not to deploy nuclear weapons of its own within its forces. This is supportive of the Nonproliferation Treaty (NPT). However, the public would have trouble with nuclear-powered submarines even if the government received the blessing of the International Atomic Energy Agency for its safeguard plans. The only way it appears the government can overcome public opposition is to stress the more nationalistic sovereignty aspects of the SSNs. When it does so, however, it runs into more problems at home and abroad. Within Canada, critics charge that the SSNs are expensive flags to wave in the face of the United States government. If the Americans are the real target of the SSNs, what is all this talk about the need to contribute to collective defense? If the government should try and win the sovereignty debate by stressing how Canadian SSNs will compel the USN to respect Canadian claims in the Arctic, it will create problems with allies who already suspect that Canada's "Arctic antic" is directed against the Americans and not the Soviets. It is a classic two-audience problem for a government that has had more than its share of difficulty being taken seriously by either.

CONCLUSION

The Canadian proposal to acquire nuclear-powered attack submarines makes sense for Canada and for its allies. Yet the program is indeed extraordinary. This is so, not because the SSNs will radically change the roles of the Canadian Navy, but because the government appears prepared to proceed with the program in the face of weak domestic support and serious allied concerns. If nothing else, the Mulroney government should be given credit for a measure of political courage. The far safer course, one that would have made barely a ripple, would have been to vaguely promise conventional submarines and more frigates. Instead, it was decided to make a big splash. The danger is that if the waves of opposition become too high at home and abroad, not only will the SSNs be sunk, but the Navy itself could go down, perhaps for the last time.

Notes

This chapter draws heavily upon material drafted by the author for a study on Canada-U.S. defense relations funded by the Twentieth Century Fund. See, Joel J. Sokolsky, *Defending Canada* (New York: Priority Press, forthcoming).

[1] "Submarines for Canada," *Washington Post*, 1 May 1988, C6; "Arctic Antic," *Economist*, 7 May 1988, 14.

[2] Canada, Department of National Defence, *Challenge and Commitment: A Defence Policy for Canada* (Ottawa: Minister of Supply and Services, 1987). (Hereafter, White Paper).

[3] On these issues, see the chapters by S. Mathwin Davis and David G. Haglund in this volume.

[4] White Paper, 50-51. See also, The Honourable Perrin Beatty, Minister of National Defence, "Tabling of the Defence White Paper in the House of Commons," 5 June 1987, 5-6. (Hereafter, Tabling Address).

[5] United Kingdom, Secretary of State for Defence, *Statement on Estimates 1981* (London: Her Majesty's Stationery Office, 1981), 25. In the absence of further pre-positioning, sealift compares favorably with airlift as a means of reinforcement in terms of time needed. See, United States, Congress, *CBO, U.S. Airlift Forces: Enhancement Alternatives for National and Non-Nato Contingencies* (Washington, D.C.: CBO, 1979), 49; William P. Mako, *U.S. Ground Forces and the Defense of Central Europe* (Washington, D.C.: The Brookings Institution, 1982), 68; William Kaufman, "The Defense Budget," in Joseph A. Pechman, ed., *Setting National Priorities: The 1982 Budget* (Washington, D.C.: The Brookings Institution, 1981), 173.

[6] Canada, Senate, Special Committee on National Defence, *Proceedings*, 8A:6 (17 April, 1984).

[7] Tom Stefanick, *Strategic Antisubmarine Warfare and Naval Strategy* (Lexington, MA: Lexington Books, 1987), 2.

[8] Milo Vego, "Soviet Anti-Submarine Doctrine," *Journal of the Royal United Services Institute* 128 (June 1983), 48.

[9] White Paper, 6.

[10] These figures are an average and composite of statistics from: *Jane's Fighting Ships 1987-88* (London: Jane's Publishing Co., 1987), 541; Ibid., 1979-1980, 500; United States, Department of Defense, *Soviet Military Power* (Washington, D.C.: 1986), 13. On the strategic situation in the Pacific and U.S. naval policy see: John Lehman, "Successful Naval Strategy in the Pacific: How Are We Achieving It," Colin Gray, "Maritime Strategy and the Pacific: The Implications for NATO," Richard H. Solomon, "The Pacific Basin Dilemmas and Choices for American Security," *Naval War College Review* (NWCR), 40 (Winter 1987). On the situation in Southeast Asia, see, Alvin H. Bernstein, "The Soviets in Cam Ranh Bay," *National Interest* (Spring 1986); Richard K. Betts, "Southeast Asia and U.S. Global Strategy: Continuing Interest and Shifting Priorities," *ORBIS* 29 (Summer 1985).

[11]Bernard E. Trainor, "Russians in Vietnam: U.S. Sees a Threat," *New York Times*, 1 March 1987, 18.

[12]Michael MccGwire, *Military Objectives in Soviet Foreign Policy* (Washington, D.C.: The Brookings Institution, 1987), 180.

[13]Ibid.

[14]Brigadier General P. J. Tagart, "Canada's Blind Spot," *United States Naval Institute Proceedings* (USNIP) 113 (March 1987), 148. On Soviet and American Activity near Alaska, see Robert Matas' series of articles in the *Globe and Mail*, "U.S.-Soviets Raise Stakes in Vast Northern Area," 25 March 1988, A1, A11; "Nothing Quiet on the Western Front," 29 March 1988, D1, D8; "Pacific Trade Called Hostage to Weak Canadian Presence," "Subs Need to Guarantee Sovereignty, Admiral Says," 28 March, 1988, A3. On Canadian Pacific interests, see Frank Langdon and Douglas Ross, "Towards a Canadian Maritime Strategy in the North Pacific," *International Journal* 52 (Autumn 1987), 848-89.

[15]White Paper, 30; see also, Matas, "Nothing Quiet on the Western Front."

[16]Canada, House of Commons, Standing Committee on External Affairs and National Defence, *Proceedings*, 50:40 (28 November 1985).

[17]I am indebted to Prof. J. Jockel for clarifying the relationship between COMSUBLANT and NATO's COMSUBWESTLANT.

[18]Jorge Cruca, *Development of Sea-Launched Cruise Missiles in the Soviet Union: An Analysis and Extensive Lexicon* (Ottawa: DND, 1987), v. On the American SLCM, see, Charles A. Sorrels, *U.S. Cruise Missile Programs: Development, Deployment and Implications for Arms Control* (New York: McGraw-Hill, 1983).

[19]MccGwire, *Military Objectives in Soviet Foreign Policy*, 501-2.

[20]See, John D. Morrocco, "Push for Early SDI Deployment Could Spur Air Defense Initiative," *Aviation Week and Space Technology* (2 February 1987), 18.

[21]Much of the American urban industrial and military target system is vulnerable to Soviet SLCMs with ranges under 500 km. See, Harold Brown and Lynn Davis, "Nuclear Arms Control: Where Do We Stand?" *Survival* 26 (July/August 1984), 152.

[22]Cruca, *Development of Sea-Launched Cruise Missiles in the Soviet Union*.

[23]Peter T. Haydon, *The Strategic Importance of the Arctic: Understanding the Military Issues*, Strategic Issues Paper no.1/87 (Ottawa: DND, March 1987), 12-13.

[24]Tariq Rauf and Dan Hayward, "Nuclear Powered Attack Submarines: Does Canada Really Need Them?", *Arms Control Communiqué* 36 (Ottawa: Canadian Centre for Arms Control and Disarmament, 15 May 1987), 2; see also, Ronald G. Purver, *Arms Control Options in the Arctic*, Issue Brief no. 7 (Ottawa: Canadian Centre for Arms Control and Disarmament, 1987), 19.

[25]Michael R. Gordon, "Soviets Said to Harden Stand On Missiles," *New York Times*, 14 February 1988, 3.

[26]For the flavor of this controversy see, John J. Mearsheimer, "A Strategic Misstep: The Maritime Strategy and Deterrence in Europe" and Linton F. Brooks, "Naval Power and National Security: The Case for the Maritime Strategy," *International Security* 11 (Fall 1986); Norman Friedman, *The U.S. Maritime Strategy* (London: Jane's, 1988).

[27]See, for example, Tariq Rauf and Dan Hayward, "Nuclear-Powered Attack Submarines."

[28]This shift from a "Mahanian" fleet-against-fleet orientation toward the exercise of force and influence ashore was identified by Samuel P. Huntington in the early 1950s; see his essay, "National Policy and the Transoceanic Navy," *USNIP* 80, (May 1954).

[29]Admiral James D. Watkins, USN, Chief of Naval Operations, "The Maritime Strategy," *USNIP*, Supplement on the Maritime Strategy (January 1986), 4. Also contained in this supplement are statements by the Commandant of the U.S. Marine Corps and the then Secretary of the Navy and major proponent of the maritime strategy, John F. Lehman.

[30]Text of the statement by Admiral Kinnard R. McKee, USN, Director, Naval Nuclear Propulsion Program, before the Subcommittees on Research and Development and Seapower and Strategic and Critical Minerals of the United States House of Representatives Armed Services Committee, 6 February 1984, 9.

[31]Stefanick, *Strategic Antisubmarine Warfare*, 41.

[32]MccGwire, *Military Objectives In Soviet Foreign Policy*, 146.

[33]Hamlin Caldwell, "The Empty Silo-Strategic ASW," *NWCR* 34 (September/October 1981).

[34]Stefanick, *Strategic Antisubmarine Warfare*, 2-3.

[35]Watkins, "The Maritime Strategy," 14; see also, David B. Rivkin, Jr., "No Bastion for the Bear," *USNIP* 110 (April 1984).

[36]Stefanick, *Strategic Antisubmarine Warfare*, 4.

[37]Richard Halloran, "A Silent Battle Surfaces," *New York Times*, 19 March 1987, 17.

[38]See the testimony of Vice-Admiral Nils R. Thunman, USN, Deputy Chief of Naval Operations for Surface Warfare, United States, Congress, House Committee on Armed Services, Subcommittee on Seapower and Strategic and Critical Minerals, *The 600-Ship Navy and the Maritime Strategy* (Washington, D.C.: GPO, 1985), 139, 145; see also, Stefanick, *Strategic Antisubmarine Warfare*, 64; Oran Young, "The Age of the Arctic," *Foreign Policy* 61 (Winter 1985-86); Richard Halloran, "Navy Frontier: Submarines Rendezvous at the North Pole," *New York Times*, 16 December 1986, 15.

[39]Stefanick, *Strategic Antisubmarine Warfare*, 45.

[40]On the legal aspects of the dispute over Canadian Arctic sovereignty, see, Aldo E. Chircop and Susan J. Rolston, eds. *Canadian Arctic Sovereignty: Are Canadian and U.S. Interests Contradictory or Complementary, Proceedings of the 1986 Ronald St. John MacDonald Symposium*, Occasional Publication, no. 1 (Halifax, N.S.: International Insights Society, 1987); Thomas Pullen, "What Price Canadian Sovereignty?" *USNIP* 113 (September 1987); see also, Robert E. Osgood, "United States Security Interests in Ocean Law," *Ocean Development and International Law Journal* 2 (Spring 1974).

[41]MccGwire, *Military Objectives in Soviet Foreign Policy*, 147; see also, Haydon, *The Strategic Importance of the Arctic*; Edward B. Atkeson, "Fighting Subs Under the Ice," *USNIP* 113 (September 1987); Charles C. Petersen, "Soviet Military Objectives in the Arctic Theater," *NCWR* 40 (Autumn 1987); Capt. T. M. LeMarchand, RN, "Under Ice Operations," *NWCR* 38 (May-June 1985).

[42]As quoted in F. W. Crickard, "Nuclear-Fueled Submarines: The Strategic Rationale," *Canadian Defence Quarterly* (CDQ) 17 (Winter 1987/88), 23; see also, Purver, *Arms Control Options*, 19.

[43]Ibid., 18.

⁴⁴The Department of External Affairs has stated that Canada supports the "threefold objectives of the Geneva (arms control) negotiations, namely to reinforce strategic stability, to limit the growth and later reduce the size of nuclear arsenals and to prevent an arms race in space and end the one on earth." Canada, Department of External Affairs, *Canada's International Relations* (Ottawa, December 1988), 13; see also, Fen O. Hampson, "Arms Control and East-West Relations," Brian Tomlin and Maureen Molot, eds., *Canada Among Nations 1986: Talking Trade* (Toronto: Lorimer, 1987).

⁴⁵For an analysis along these lines see, F. W. Crickard, "An Anti-Submarine Warfare Capability in the Arctic a National Requirement," *CDQ* 16 (Spring 1987).

⁴⁶Leon V. Sigal, *Nuclear Forces in Europe: Enduring Dilemmas, Present Prospects* (Washington, D.C.: The Brookings Institution, 1984), 14.

⁴⁷*Jane's Fighting Ships*, 1987-88, 119.

⁴⁸"Arctic Antic," *Economist*, 119.

⁴⁹"Submarines for Canada," *Washington Post*, C6.

⁵⁰For views on the U.S. reaction, see, David Leyton-Brown, "Washington Views the White Paper," *International Perspectives* (IP) (July/August 1987); Joseph T. Jockel, "Canada's New Military Plans," *IP* (September/October 1987); see also, Joel J. Sokolsky, "Our Nuclear-Sub Policy Must Be Sold to Allies," *Financial Post*, 25 May 1987, 44.

⁵¹See an op-ed article by U.S. Congressman Charles E. Bennett, Chairman of the Seapower Subcommittee of the U.S. House of Representatives Armed Services Committee, "Tough Questions Rise to the Surface," *Globe and Mail*, 30 October 1987, A7. Similar objections were raised by Senators John Warner (former Secretary of the Navy) and Jim Exon, both members of the Armed Services Committee. See, Norma Greenway, "U.S. to Querry Any Transfer of Sub Secrets," *Globe and Mail* (26 March 1988), A1, A2. See also, Frank Gaffney, former U.S. Defense official, "Could Canada's Subs Torpedo NATO Navies?" *Globe and Mail*, 12 April 1988, A7.

⁵²Charles F. Doran, "Sovereignty Does Not Equal Security," *Peace & Security* 2 (Autumn 1987), 9. Congressman Bennett also raises the question of sovereignty and the Northwest passage, linking them to the submarines acquisition, "Tough Questions Rise to the Surface," A7.

⁵³David P. Calleo, *Beyond American Hegemony: The Future of the Western Alliance* (New York: Basic Books, 1987), 216.

⁵⁴See, for example, Melvyn Krauss, *How NATO Weakens the West* (New York: Simon and Schuster, 1986).

⁵⁵*NATO in the 1990s*, Special Report of the North Atlantic Assembly, 18 May 1988, 11.

⁵⁶Ibid., 23.

⁵⁷On the issue of whether Canada should remain on the central front at all, see, Joseph T. Jockel and Joel J. Sokolsky, *Canada and Collective Security: Odd Man Out*, Washington Papers, no. 121 (New York: Praeger, 1986); Ambassador (to NATO) Gordon S. Smith, "Canada on the Rhine: First Line of Defence," *CDQ* 17 (Special, February 1988), 15-20.

⁵⁸See, *Canada's Stake in Common Security*, Report by the International Affairs Committee of the New Democratic Party, (April 1988). For the Liberal position, see, "Building the Canadian Nation: Sovereignty and Security in the 1990s," a speech delivered by

the Right Honourable John N. Turner to Canada Conference III, Vancouver, 7 February 1988.

[59]P.H. Chapin, "The Canadian Public and Foreign Policy," *International Perspectives* (January/February 1986), 14-15.

[60]Don Munton, *Peace and Security in the 1980s: The View of Canadians*, Working Paper (Ottawa: The Canadian Institute for International Peace and Security, 1988), 23, 31.

[61]Ibid., 32.

[62]"The Re-birth of the Navy," *Macleans* 101, 30 May 1988, 9.

[63]"32% Want Subs, Poll Says," *Globe and Mail*, 26 May 1988, A5.

[64]"Beatty Says Public Backs Sub Plan," *The Ottawa Citizen*, 27 May 1988, A 11.

[65]Canada, House of Commons, Standing Committee on National Defence, *Minutes of Proceedings and Evidence*, 38: 26, 10 May 1988. (Testimony by John Lamb).

[66]Briefing by Department of National Defence, 8 June 1988.

Notes on Contributors

John Anderson is a former Assistant Deputy Minister (Policy) in the Canadian Department of National Defence, and is currently a Faculty Associate of the Queen's University Centre for International Relations.

Hans-Jochen Annuss, the Defense Attaché in Canada of the Federal Republic of Germany, is a Lieutenant Colonel in the Bundeswehr who was a Visiting Defence Fellow at the Queen's Centre for International Relations during the 1987/88 academic year.

Douglas L. Bland is a Lieutenant Colonel in the Canadian Forces who is currently on staff at the National Defence College of Canada, in Kingston. He is also a Graduate Fellow of the Queen's Centre for International Relations and a Ph.D. candidate in the Department of Political Studies.

Boris Castel, a Professor in the Queen's Department of Physics, is a Faculty Associate of the Centre for International Relations.

Christopher Conliffe is a Lieutenant Colonel in the Canadian Forces who is currently with the Directorate of Professional Education and Development at National Defence Headquarters, Ottawa. He was a Visiting Defence Fellow at the Queen's Centre for International Relations during the 1987/88 academic year.

S. Mathwin Davis, a Faculty Associate of the Queen's Centre for International Relations and an Adjunct Professor in the School of Public Administration, is a former Commandant of the National Defence College of Canada and a Rear Admiral (Ret.) in the Royal Canadian Navy.

Roger Epp is a Graduate Fellow of the Queen's Centre for International Relations and a Ph.D. candidate in the Department of Political Studies.

David G. Haglund is the Director of the Queen's Centre for International Relations and an Associate Professor in the Department of Political Studies.

Bruce A. Harris, a Colonel in the U.S. Army who is currently with the Deputy Chief of Staff for Operations and Plans, U.S. Department of Defense, was a Visiting Defence Fellow of the Queen's Centre for International Relations during the 1987/88 academic year.

Joel J. Sokolsky, a Faculty Associate of the Queen's Centre for International Relations, is an Associate Professor in the Department of Political and Economic Science, Royal Military College of Canada, in Kingston.

Charles M. Tutwiler, a Lieutenant Colonel in the U.S. Air Force who is currently flying B-52s with the Strategic Air Command, was a Visiting Defence Fellow of the Queen's Centre for International Relations during the 1987/88 academic year.

John Young is a Ph.D. candidate in the Queen's Department of Political Studies and a former Graduate Fellow of the Centre for International Relations who is now teaching in the Department of Strategic Studies of the Collège militaire royal, in St.-Jean, Québec.

Index